RECREATIONAL
CRAFTS:
PROGRAMMING AND
INSTRUCTIONAL TECHNIQUES

McGRAW-HILL SERIES IN HEALTH EDUCATION,
PHYSICAL EDUCATION, AND RECREATION

DEOBOLD B. VAN DALEN, *Consulting Editor*

ÅSTRAND AND RODAHL   Textbook of Work Physiology
FLORIO AND STAFFORD   Safety Education
JENSEN AND SCHULTZ   Applied Kinesiology
JERNIGAN AND VENDIEN   Playtime: A World Recreation Handbook
KNAPP AND LEONARD   Teaching Physical Education in Secondary
Schools: A Textbook on Instructional Methods
KRAUS   Recreation Leader's Handbook
METHENY   Body Dynamics
METHENY   Movement and Meaning
SHIVERS AND CALDER   Recreational Crafts: Programming and Instructional Techniques
SINGER   Coaching, Athletics, and Psychology

RECREATIONAL CRAFTS:

PROGRAMMING AND INSTRUCTIONAL TECHNIQUES

JAY S. SHIVERS

CLARENCE R. CALDER
University of Connecticut

McGRAW-HILL BOOK COMPANY

New York St. Louis San Francisco Düsseldorf
Johannesburg Kuala Lumpur London Mexico
Montreal New Delhi Panama Paris São Paulo
Singapore Sydney Tokyo Toronto

Library of Congress Cataloging in Publication Data

Shivers, Jay Sanford, date
    Recreational crafts.

    (McGraw-Hill series in health education,
physical education, and recreation)
    Bibliography: p.
    1.   Handicraft—Study and teaching.   I.   Calder,
Clarence R., joint author.   II.   Title.
TT168.S53   745.5'07   73-18437
ISBN 0-07-056980-0

RECREATIONAL CRAFTS
Programming and Instructional Techniques

4567890 VHVH 7987

This book was set in Univers.
The editors were Richard R. Wright and David Dunham;
the designer was Nicholas Krenitsky;
the production supervisor was Leroy A. Young.
Illustrations by Judy Harrington.
Von Hoffmann Press, Inc., was printer and binder.

CONTENTS

Complex Cutout Designs Paper Crafts Projects Paper Flowers Crepe Paper Flowers Paper Mosaic Torn Paper Pictures A Two-dimensional Picture from Paper Strips Colored Tissue Paper Painting Corrugated Cardboard Origami Paper People Foil Sculpture Papier-mâché Basic Materials Basic Techniques Mixing Procedures Finishing Papier-mâché Cardboard-Newspaper Jewelry

Sculpturing Soap Carving Styrofoam Zonalite, Plaster, and Sand Sculpture Carved Plaster Bas-relief Wax Sculpture Wire Sculpture Toothpick Sculpture Wood Scrap Sculpture Mobiles Casting Sand Casting Rubber Molds Spoon Molds Moldless Casting Mosaics

Glossary of Terms Clay Types of Clay Mixing Clay Wedging Storing Clay Modeling Making a Plan Pinch Method Coil Method Strip Method Sculpturing a Form Slab Method Convex and Concave Draping Slip Mold Construction One-piece Mold Two-piece Mold Slip Casting Throwing on the Potter's Wheel Drying Finished Objects Welding with Slip Repairing Defects Firing Procedure Glazes Kilns Techniques for Decorating Clay Objects Substitute for Clay Sawdust Clay Salt-Cornstarch Clay Salt-Flour Clay Cornstarch-Baking Soda Clay Uncooked Substitute Clays

PART III CRAFT FORMS AND INSTRUCTIONAL METHODS

Types of Craft Leathers Tooling and Carving Leathers Lining Leathers Miscellaneous Leathers Making a Leather Project Planning the Project Placing the Templates on the Skin Cutting the Leather Planning a Design Tracing the Design on a Leather Surface Tooling Leather Outline Tooling Flat Modeling Embossing Stippling Stamping Carving Leather Edging Tools Cementing Leather Punches and Chisels Lacing Techniques Hand Sewing Snaps and Fasteners Dyeing and Finishing Leathers Finishing Edges Protective Finishes

Basic Woodworking Tools Measuring and Layout Tools Hand Saws Jigsaw Hand Plane Shaping with Chisel, Gouge,

Carving Tools, and Knives   Files, Rasps, and Forming Tools
Drilling and Boring Holes   Hand Screws   Claw Hammer   Basic
Materials   Wood Screws   Nails   Wood Glue   Sandpaper
Finishing   Common Joints and Their Uses   Making Picture
Frames   Planning the Frame   Making the Molding   Cutting
the Miter Joints   Assembling the Joint   Wood Turning
Faceplate Turning   Spindle or Between-center Turning

Tooling or Embossing   Modeling Tool   Planning a Design
Procedure   Hammering   Beating into a Form   Raising a Shape
over a Sandbag   Beating over a Stake   Raising a Shape over a
Recess   Stamping   Chasing   Etching Copper, Bronze, and
Brass   Etching Aluminum   Enameling   Equipment and
Materials   Cleaning the Metal   Applying the Enamel   Alter-
native Techniques for Applying Enamel   Special Effects
Firing the Kiln   Cleaning and Polishing the Enameled Piece
Attaching Findings to Jewelry

Weaving   Simple Looms   Cardboard Loom   Indian Weaving
Loom   Cannister Loom   Circle Loom   A Weaving Project
Wrap Weaving   Card Weaving   Spool Weaving   Solid-
core Weaving   Paper Weaving   Bead Weaving   Inkle Loom
Weaving   Simple Tapestry Weaving   Basketry as Weav-
ing   Sewing   Stitches   Quilting   Appliqué   Hooking

Easy Projects   Spore Prints   Fungi Etchings   Fungi Ornaments   Pump Drills   Natural Baskets   Corn Husk Sandals
Candlemaking   Woodcrafts   Whittling   Bird Feeders   Hanging Flower Baskets   Log Stools   Knotting, Hitches, and Lashing   Knots   Hitches   Lashing   Flytying   Macrame
Project Construction   Basic Knots   Making a Wall Hanging
Netting   Making a Hammock   Braiding   Weaving with Natural Materials   Mat Weaving   Chair Caning

Puppets   Paper Bag Puppets   Stick Puppets   Styrofoam Pup-
pets   Cereal Box Puppets   Sock Puppets   Pinch Puppets
Substitute Clay and Papier-mâché Puppets   Finger Puppets
Paper Tube Puppets   Marionettes   Spool Marionettes   Balsa
Wood Marionettes   Wooden Marionettes   Paper Bag Mario-
nettes   Flip-Flop People and Animals   Puppet and Marionette
Stages   Cardboard Carton Stage   Frame Construction Stage

PREFACE

Although many books are available dealing with every conceivable craft, in terms of how to do it, there has been no single all-inclusive text for crafts instructors, recreational supervisors, teachers, or laymen offering nearly every form of craft together with the operational aspects of programming. This text, *Recreational Crafts: Programming and Instructional Techniques,* should satisfy the need for a one-volume omnibus of crafts methodology. It treats the myriad forms of crafts in realistic categories; provides clear directions for the instruction of crafts in almost any setting; details the specific tools, materials, and equipment necessary; indicates sources of supply and instructional aids; and explains the development of a comprehensive crafts program for use in schools, youth-serving agencies, camps, recreational service agencies, and the like.

This text will prove useful for instructors in (1) institutional recreational programs, (2) public recreational service departments, (3) elementary, middle, and secondary schools. In addition, it will be practical for use as a basic text, and certainly as a resource, for instructors at the junior and senior college level who teach recreational arts and crafts courses to students who plan careers in the field of recreational service, elementary education, industrial arts, or child development.

The book is conveniently divided into three parts. Part One deals with the nature and meaning of crafts in the instructional or recreational setting, whether formal or informal. Great emphasis is laid upon the development of a comprehensive crafts program. There is concern for the techniques involved in organizing instructional and resource activities, scheduling, arranging activities around themes, and making appropriate gradations for age-group characteristics and interests. Part One explains the rationale behind the open-school concept and develops a comprehensive arts and crafts program for the elementary and middle school.

Part Two deals with graphic and manipulative arts and instructional methods. In this section, there is emphasis upon art as a process and product and the experiences involved. Paper as an arts and crafts form is detailed, as well as print making and bookbinding. The manipulative arts are developed in the section dealing with sculpture, casting, mosaics, and ceramics.

Part Three is concerned with all forms of conventional and non-conventional crafts possibilities. In this major segment of the text, crafts are ramified into substance and material crafts, i.e., those crafts which use leather, wood, metal, fiber, natural materials, and recycled or junk materials, and what has been termed theater crafts. The latter treats the designing and crafting of puppets and marionettes and provides the stage setting and background stage effects for actual performances. Dioramas and peep shows are also included to round out this section. Perhaps the most interesting and significant chapter deals with materials which can be obtained from almost any junk pile or trash heap. It contains invaluable suggestions and directions for crafting perfectly good and usable materials so that they have an artistic life. In this day of ecological imbalance produced somewhat by an overabundant supply of supposed junk, there is a wealth of material that can be reclaimed and made into attractive, creative, and satisfying crafts projects.

The text contains arts and crafts activities for every age and talent. It is graded in such a way that readers may learn about and perform crafts activities ranging from simple to highly complex. In short, it is a book that will be useful to the novice and the adept, to those who function as supervisors or teachers, and to those who wish to become specialists or at least persons operating in recreationally oriented agencies. Of special interest is the flexibility which the text accentuates. It shows how crafts activities may be organized, but also permits alternative planning in the event that commercial materials, tools, or other equipment are not available. The section dealing with commonplace adaptations for crafts experiences and that concerned with scavenging for materials should be extremely helpful where inexpensive materials are needed.

The final section of the text deals exclusively with sources of supply and bibliographical information which is of current interest and has been compiled from personal exposure to the sources and reference works. The appendixes are arranged to inform the reader of commercial sources of supply for almost any arts and crafts media. Furthermore, audio-visual materials and their sources of supply have been listed. Such media are always beneficial in reinforcing teaching methods.

Throughout the text, specific requirements for tools and materials have been supplied. Many directions are included which give instructions on how to manufacture such items. This will prove useful to those who do not wish to spend a great deal on crafts programs. The text contains more than 200 illustrations which enable the reader to visualize the precise steps to be taken in the creation of some arts or crafts project.

A well planned arts and crafts program can provide the individual with some of the most creative and personally satisfying experiences into which he can immerse himself to achieve enjoyment and a sense of well-being. Being able to manipulate inanimate objects and produce an effect that is satisfying to the individual, as well as to others, should not be overlooked in contemplating the value of crafts for schools and community. The authors are personally dedicated to the premise that the growth and development of people can be greatly enhanced by exposure to the creative, innovative, and reproductive handling of a wide variety of materials. The enhancement of human life and the satisfaction of human need are the basis on which this book was written.

Jay S. Shivers
Clarence R. Calder

RECREATIONAL CRAFTS:

PROGRAMMING AND INSTRUCTIONAL TECHNIQUES

PART I

PLANNING AND DEVELOPING A COMPREHENSIVE ARTS AND CRAFTS PROGRAM

MEANING IN ARTS AND CRAFTS 1

People everywhere require some medium for self-expression and satisfaction. A nearly universal outlet for self-projection is through the manipulation of graphic or plastic forms. Whether by simple whittling, intricate scrimshaw, sand drawing, utensil decoration, clay modeling, stone carving, candlemaking, tie dying or countless other creative or reproductive outpourings of aesthetic or utilitarian production, people enjoy arts and crafts. Every culture in every era of human development has produced a wide variety of arts and crafts materials. In fact, it is by such artifacts that man has come to know about his history and development.

NATURE, SCOPE, AND INTERPRETATION

To understand the place of aesthetic experience in the history of man, one must be made familiar with the aesthetic. The nature of such experiences has, as the outline of cultural development suggests, been a part of mankind's struggle for survival. Crafts, by their very nature, incorporate aesthetic features and therefore art. Any comprehensive definition of crafts would number among its components certain distinguishing facets.

Sense

The object of aesthetic production and satisfaction is finite and material. Material entities are the definite concerns of arts and crafts. They require

3

the function of all the senses in the most valid use of physical components. The graphic and plastic arts and crafts are based upon sight, touch, smell, taste, and auditory responses. Through the use of various pigments, solids, textures, and fragrant substances which appeal to the receptors, aesthetic experience incorporates the entire range of sense perception. Because of this stimulation, which all the senses may share, arts and crafts provide a variety of experiences calling for qualities and combinations of many kinds. Aesthetic activity is broadly based and contributes to enjoyable responses of human sensitivity. The knowledge that arts and crafts are grounded in sense experience implies that one of the major responsibilities of any arts and crafts program is to promote and improve sense perception.

Particularization
The object of aesthetic experience is specific or personal. Aesthetics deals with particular things, unique and individual. Particularization can be ramified in several ways. Initially, it means that the significance of an object does not require dependency or relationship to any other item. The aesthetic object is autonomous. It requires no other reason for being, nor does it encourage comparison with other entities. Thus, particularization gives meaning to the aesthetic object for itself in terms of its singular properties. There is no need to contrast or seek relationships. The aesthetic object contains all those properties which attract the eye of the beholder— it stands for and by itself.

Unity
The idea of fulfillment or completeness underlies all aesthetic experience. The artist or artisan makes things as unified wholes. There is a feeling of integrity and unification which is perceived as indivisibility.

Value
The aesthetic experience is additionally characterized as one of inherent value. The aesthetic object is satisfying to the individual for its own sake and not because it introduces other values. The immediate enjoyment of some entity is not dependent upon some other object or experience. However, this does not invalidate the idea that aesthetic objects are useless; they may have great utilitarian value. In fact, the arts or crafts item, which is intrinsically valuable, may have immense practical value. However, the significance here is related to the quality of aesthetic experience itself. Appreciation is a foremost effect on the beholder. There is a desire to continue to see and enjoy the presence of the beautiful object. There is no other reason for contemplating except the attraction which the beautiful exerts upon the observer.

Creativity
The consideration of beauty and its enjoyment is not passive in nature. The aesthetic experience may be looked upon as active engagement of either a creative or a reproductive type. Art is essentially an act of

producing something. This is apparent insofar as the artist is concerned, whose function is to put materials together in some way that is satisfying to him and, perhaps, to others. This constructive act is the validation of the creative force of human intelligence. But it is also logical to understand that appreciation of the aesthetic is active participation and is probably creative as well. One who rises to the lure of the aesthetic object must assume some of the same experience of the artist who develops beautiful things. The observer may find meanings and values which were never conceived by the artist, but this cannot deny the act of creation. To the extent that the person appreciates what he sees, for whatever reasons or satisfactions he has, the element of creativity is present. Imagination through contemplation motivated by whatever is beautiful to the eye of the beholder is certainly an effort of active involvement. Thus, there is a creative element in aesthetic experience performed by the artist or derived by the observer.

Utility

A line has always been drawn between pure art and practical art. To the former, or fine arts, the seven classical forms have been attached. Thus, music, dance, drama, painting, sculpture, poetry, and architecture have been looked upon as having aesthetic value only. In the class of practical arts have been such activities as carpentry, sewing, weaving, cookery, clothing design, metalwork, and handicrafts. It is quite impossible and impractical to define what lies in the realm of fine and utilitarian arts. There is a soft interaction between all the arts and crafts. What has intrinsic value may also be practical. Surely pottery making may be both practical and fine—as are architecture, lapidary work, modeling, cabinetmaking, and many other arts and crafts.

The separation between utilitarian and pure art is an artificial concept that finds favor with those who regard aesthetic experience as having nothing to do with life and beauty as belonging to those who worship it. The removal of such a sharp line of distinction would be proposed by those who feel that art is both a development and improvement of life. Those who profess this view conceive of all human activity as having an aesthetic range, that life as a whole is creativity of the highest order—a work of art, and that every effort should be impregnated with beauty.

Any understanding of art in life will be reflected in the manner in which aesthetic experiences are undertaken on a routine basis. If the feeling persists that art is an integral facet of life, the sense of beauty will be a significant feature throughout the educational, vocational, and social phases of human interaction. To the extent that the sense of beauty may be learned and appreciated in all its varied ramifications, it can do much toward enhancing daily existence by the sharper impression of notable forms in all their infinite distinctions.

Interpretation

Crafts represent a particular mode of expression and are a vehicle for the inherently human desire to manipulate, fabricate, or experience the satisfaction of creativity. Indeed, the production of crafted objects may be likened to the process of communication where there is an attempt to transmit (or transform) ideas into concrete or synthesized entities.

Art may be defined as any individualized demonstration of a graphic or plastic nature expressing some symbol or concept. Fundamentally, it is a self-expressive process through visual factors arranged to satisfy the needs of the person who develops them. It is a procedure of technique and design for the conveyance of attitudes, ideas, or personalized feelings in visual form.

Crafts are essentially represented by the utilization of material for decorative, useful, or manipulative purposes from a variety of substances. Although the two aesthetic forms may be distinguished, it is probably safe to assert that to the extent that both require some motor manipulation they are coincidental. Crafts are as much art as art is crafts. The creative process of inherent value to those who seek satisfaction and enjoyment from shaping, molding, arranging, and modifying materials may be represented by fine or utilitarian crafts. It will be difficult, if not impossible, to state that a finely crafted piece of wrought iron scroll work is not sculpture or art or that the welded metal sculpture is not really craft.

From the recreationist or teacher viewpoint, the communicative process of crafts through art and art through crafts can be interpreted as a unified area with many ramifications for those individuals and groups who seek self-expression and happiness through this medium. It is a broadly ranging category of activities limited only by the ideas of people and the incorporation of substances employed.

INTEGRATION WITH OTHER RECREATIONAL ACTIVITIES
Although the crafts category may be thought of as a specific experience which can fulfill certain expectations of those who participate, it may nevertheless be part of a greater series of program activities if there is an attempt to relate or carry over the values, means, and effects of crafts into well-conceived, but completely different, areas. Thus, crafts may have accessory or complementary values for other activity forms which can only be enhanced by the medium of crafts. In other instances, crafts may be the irreducible factor which completes or synthesizes an activity idea. The integration of many activity forms with crafts may be necessary if the participant is to receive the greatest degree of satisfaction and enjoyment possible because the noncraft activity would be incomplete without its resolution or to stimulate interests which can attract and correlate many aesthetic, physical, performing, or social skills as a result of integration.

A well-thought-out program will consider and benefit from all the opportunities of correlation: coordination of instruction and utilization of arts and crafts to enhance social occasions, history, holidays, hobbies, athletics, games, dramatics, dance, communication, vocations, conservation of natural resources, music, themes around and toward which an entire recreational program may advance. In school programs as well relationships exist in the curriculum between arts and crafts and other subject matter areas. The integration of arts and crafts and handwriting, history, science, mathematics, chemistry, geography, physical education, music, literature, agriculture, and social studies are examples. A combination of every phase of the program will improve each activity so treated and therefore the final result. Activities programmed in this way contribute to the quality of the various facets of the experience and hence to the ultimate effect.

Program Development
Integration occurs when cooperative efforts are made to assure that blended experiences heighten participant satisfaction. The final test of integration occurs, not in terms of how many different categories of recreational activity are combined, but rather in how smoothly and naturally two or more programmed experiences enhance the participatory quality and effect satisfaction, enjoyment, and appreciation.

Crafts and Art   Art, being what it is, may be an aesthetic experience; but this is not always valid. When the attempt is crude or without redeeming features, the work may still have an aesthetic appeal to the performer, but probably does not exist for the observer. Nevertheless, certain art activities can be up-graded through the addition of crafts experiences. Thus, the outcomes of, let us say, finger painting may be enhanced by pasting the results around some receptacle, such as a carrying case, vase, wool holder, and toy box.

Crafts and Nature   The manufacture of simple utilities from natural materials has always appeared to delight participants. Building cooking or warming fires of various sorts and developing cooking equipment from logs, branches, or stone combine crafts and nature. Making spoons from whittled wood is both a creative and a practical experience. Acorns may be whittled out, carved, colored, and strung together to produce some handsome and decorative ornaments. The construction of shelters from canvas, tree boughs, and logs to form teepees, adirondack cabins, lean-tos, or reflectors requires knowledge of crafts and materials found in nature. The fabrication of water vehicles for travel in the wilderness may consist of crafting birchbark canoes or hollow log or dugout surface skimmers. Pirogue-type craft as well as reed boats require a high degree of artisanship, but they have a place within a crafts program that seeks to dovetail with the typical offerings of most recreational programs. The development of insect traps, nets, and other collecting devices for the collection, classification, and display of entomological specimens as well as small forms of wildlife requires craft techniques which can be learned and used without resort to sophisticated tools, materials, or shops. Woodcraft, naturecraft, and campcraft can be applied to natural objects and materials, thereby turning raw objects into useful and, in many instances, beautiful items which tend to enhance those activities conducted in the out-of-doors.

Crafts and Camping   The whole question of survival in harsh terrains and environment may come down to the individual's ability to fabricate the appropriate items from raw materials at hand. Emergency ladders from bits of twine or rope and branches may call upon the skill of lashing, braiding, or knot tying. The development of fishing lures from bits of feathers, bent pins, or sharpened and notched pieces of wood may enable the individual to obtain food. Weaving of reeds, grass, or rafialike materials may provide shelter, containers for food and water, or protection from the sun or rain. The utilization of knots, slings, and hitches with fabricated rope or cord from leather, tendrils, vines, or other fibers at hand could be utilized to tie on and carry packs, hold down a tent against wind or rain, suspend utensils over a cooking fire, cache food hanging from a high tree branch, or trap game. In the organized camp setting, crafts serve to enhance Indian lore experiences. The development of Indian artifacts such as bows and arrows, feathered headdresses, beaded belts and pouches, woven blankets, council fires, wigwams, and so forth lend enchantment to the stories and games that can be coordinated with such activities. Of course, camping itself, whether on the trail or in a residential environment, lends itself to all forms of handicrafts. The potential listing of objects and items that may become an integral part of such an operation is almost infinite.

Crafts and Dramatics   Dramatics can be performed without any props, but most, if not all, dramatic presentations can be made more stimulating— to both actors and audience—attractive, and atmospherically correct with appropriately designed, constructed and colored scenery. Crafts play a basic role in the creation of a sympathetic environment in which the dramatic arts occur. Painted flats, masks, lighting, and even the make-up which actors wear may be considered as crafts. In fact, the construction of a stage, the acoustics, the special effects, and the interplay of light, sound, and color arranged to produce pleasing results enhance the content of the presentation. The essence of puppetry, marionettes, costuming, circuses, carnivals, tableaux, variety shows, and revues lies in crafts. The entire idea of drama is intimately connected with imagery, fantasy, or graphic representations of the real world to stimulate and make the observer believe he is actually watching a slice of life. In almost all instances, these effects are best achieved by stage or cinema crafts of a high order. The technical proficiency of many craftsmen in producing the desired effects has become commonly accepted, but this does not negate their high art.

Crafts and Music   Music is, or can be, an aesthetic experience. Great virtuosi may dazzle thousands when they play or sing in concert. Yet even music may benefit from certain crafts effects programmed for heightened audience or performer appreciation. Opera, operetta, and musical comedy are three aspects of the performing musical art that are enthusiastically promoted by crafts of various kinds. To the same extent that dramatics receives additional encouragement, these musical expressions may also profit by the intrinsic relation of crafts to performance. Costuming plays no little role in the production of oratorios, formal choirs, barbershop quartet singing, or the particular effect an individual performer may wish to achieve. The adoption of costumes requires crafts. How often have audiences watching a live or televised performance of some popular singer, piano player, or ensemble been moved to greater appreciation in consequence of the costuming and stage effects which have been developed. Lights, colors, sounds, clothing, stage, design and placement of objects to focus attention are all craft entities.

Crafts and Dance   The dance in its many varieties is both a formal and/ or unstructured series of gestures, bodily motions, contortions, kicks, and stamps dealing with the universal and fundamental need for movement. It is, like other performing arts, a process of symbolic communication, expressing many attitudes as well as satisfying emotional and physical sensations. Whether performed as a social, interpretive, folk, square, round, modern, tap, ethnic, or ballet, dance may be enhanced by crafts. In certain dances costuming plays a significant role in creating the precise effect which the performer desires. In classical ballet, for example, the costume is of a traditional type (as is the dance itself), and specific costumes are expected. Again, stage design, lighting, make-up, arrangement, and scenery are utilized to enoble an existing aesthetic experience.

Crafts and Social Activities   Parties, club meetings, banquets, picnics, outings—whenever two or more people come together for some occasion to enjoy one another's company—there is a social experience. To the extent that any social activity may be enhanced through the addition of color, decoration, materials that have been made for the day, or those deft personal touches that tell everybody a personal attempt has been made to please, crafts come through. Gift wrapping, formal table setting and center-piece design, handcrafted napkins, napkin rings, special wooden or metal containers, and the utensils themselves are indicative of crafts-manship. Candlemaking, picture arrangement, furniture refinishing, dress designing, knitting, sewing, weaving, hooking, braiding, crocheting, whittling, carving, or sculpting materials that have practical or decorative use find expression at social activities. In some instances, crafts activities have been the single reason for social occasions. Quilting bees, sheep shearings, barn raisings, bandage folding, knitting and sewing circles—all carry intense social significance and developed around the need for cooperative effort or competitive stimulation in completing some voluntarily undertaken task, or simply to help out some less furtunate fellow. Wherever and whenever people have come together to construct some tangible item, there crafts have flourished.

Crafts and Motor Skills   Motor skills really deal with all the sports, games, and contests—individual, dual, and team—which involve gross or fine muscular efforts requiring strength, skill, endurance, coordination, flexibility, poise, speed, and willingness to train. Such activities do not need crafts of any type to enhance the image or stimulate attention, but all can benefit from associated efforts to do so. When there is the need to exhibit or display talent of a motor skill nature, there is great likelihood that aesthetic touches will promote enjoyment and satisfaction on the part of participants and observers. Depending upon the type of activity, costuming may have a role to play, and lighting will become important, particularly if the play occurs in the evening hours. Certain activities cannot really be made spectacular unless crafts activities are coordinated with the performance. Thus, not only do water pageants require lighting, make-up, costuming, and choreographic and acoustic effects, such presentations may also require the construction of special props, backdrops, or other scenery in the same way as do dramatics or musical productions. Gymnastic exhibitions, children's games, many individual sports, and certainly team games are suitably enhanced by uniforms, accessories, decorations, and such. One need only remember the panoply of Olympic Games to have a better understanding of how such athletic contests may be promoted by pomp and circumstance to which crafts contribute. That these effects are contributed by flags, lights, flares, costumes, pictorial representations, and carefully constructed mazes or barriers as in the steeplechase event or equestrian performances makes little difference. It is the practical realization of integration of crafts with all, or almost all, other recreational experiences and many other subjects within the school curriculum that becomes important. Crafts have intrinsic value and extrinsic value. The ability of crafts techniques and procedures to enhance recreational and educational experiences should be realized in the well-balanced and comprehensive program.

CREATIVITY AND SELF-EXPRESSION
Creativity
Man learns through his senses. Interaction between man and his environment occurs at the receptor level. The ability to utilize the five senses offers the medium by which environmental interaction can be accommodated. The development of perceptual sensitivity often provides concomitant learning. Through a variety of aesthetic experiences components of creativity may be learned, assimilated, and translated into formed manifestations.

Sensitivity may be the most striking aspect in the creative process. This necessarily means sensitivity to attitudes, emotions, problems, and the daily course of human events. The medium of the senses creates awareness of substance, condition, or any materials that have probable potential. All people have some sensitivity. We are susceptible to various textures—softness, hardness, smoothness, roughness. We recognize the outcome of color mixtures even as the combinations are stirred into being. We experience appreciation of materials through manipulation, whether the substance under consideration is clay, papier-mâché, polished wood, stone, or metal.

Originality or the quality of innovativeness is thought to be part of creativeness. The ability to define new dimensions, to make novel responses to cliche situations, to make new rules, or to determine one's way where there are no rules or guides to follow requires inventiveness of a high order. The aesthetic experience should emphasize uniqueness and stress the desirability of striking out individually. Responses thus generated should be permitted wide latitude. Experimentation with new materials can lead to discovered effects.

A facet of originality is the capacity to modify. To be able to organize ideas in new ways or to shift the uses and functions of objects so that they appear in changed form is obviously a quality that makes use of the known for purposes that might not have been perceived before. This can be fundamental in an aesthetic experience. The transformation of light bulbs into castanets or puppet heads, the creation of earrings, brooches, or medalions from lumps of hardened plaster of Paris, give new purpose and meaning to prosaic material. The whole process of reorganization by changing components of a unit to make another design or the modification of elements in a composition to produce an entirely different use or form is the basis for creativity.

Self-Expression

The term self-expression is exhibited through some medium or mode and should not be thought of only insofar as general content is concerned. As great a degree of self-expression is evinced in the scribblings of a child as can be observed in higher art forms if the effort proceeds from a unique or original intent and the latter is merely some reproduction or base imitation. Thus, primitive or crude expressions of self may be directly related to emotional states, at least in the child. Art forms of quite technical perfection may not be a true representation of the artist's emotional state. They are but empty promises incapable of revealing the nature of the individual, but rather masking that person's needs for expression behind some stereotype or facade.

Self-expression occurs in those satisfying activities which permit the individual to give full and personal vent to his feelings. It is, in a sense, the idea of that participant actually giving a part of himself, his personality, to the creation of some object. That this can occur in any recreational activity, more particularly in the performing arts, is certain. But to the extent that interested individuals take the time and make the effort to shape some substance or design an object with the intent of forever placing the stamp of their personality or emotional needs upon it, it is self-expression. The results of this effort need not be perfect. It is sufficient that the individual has permitted his vision of an ideal or real objective to be consumated.

The ability of any person to identify himself with the work that he does probably assists in the process of communicating ideas, attitudes, or traits. The characteristic mark of ego will inevitably appear in the finished product. An item given that extra hand-rubbed sheen, a few more coats of lacquer, the precise cut to fit one piece of wood to another, the careful overlay of one piece of leather on another, the exquisitely wrought metal filigree, or the polishing and grinding of a mirrored surface prior to mounting for telescopic viewing to all speak volumes for modes of self-expression.

The achievement of fulfillment or satisfaction in fabricating a material good where there was none before gives rise to an inner harmony which all people require. Too often, people run the course of their lives in conformity to the customs and codes of their times. They are restricted to narrow ways and never attain the deep satisfaction of breaking out of a precast mold. Through aesthetic experience, more specifically in one of the many crafts forms, any individual may begin to express his anxiety, hostility, ambiguity, security, or love or any combination of these emotions. Shaping, changing, manipulating a variety of substances to conform to one's desire can contribute to a freedom of expression that is typically denied the individual who functions in a conformity-producing society. How the person views himself and the world about him will undoubtedly influence the medium he chooses, his technical proficiency in organization or arrangement, his innovative ability, his perception and sense of value and design, and the complete manner or half-hearted attempt by which he rises or falls in his efforts to achieve.

Self-expression means recognition of self and awareness of those emotions, concepts, and attitudes which represent us to others. When an individual finally undertakes the task of trying to tell the world about himself through a plastic or graphic medium, a much-needed outlet will be furnished. Here is a way to communicate. Crafts are the means whereby we can substitute symbols for the inexpressible and transmit ideas of our deepest desires or highest ideals. Self-expression may not always depict what is best in man. It may also vent the negative forces and darker side of human behavior. But even here self-expression is not restrained nor contravened. What the individual is will become evident. Evidence of personality disintegration may be as readily discernible as is the motivation of those who are filled with a genuine affection for humanity. No one has a monopoly on personal identity with his work through crafts. In every human being who has the intelligence and sensory appreciation lies the talent—either latent or overt—to reorganize material or use substances that can benefit him by exposing, in a sublimated way, whatever lies buried behind the veneer of arbitrarily imposed behavioral strictures. For a little while, the individual may be able to get out of himself, disregard the anxieties of his existence, and play at being what he would really like to be. Self-expression through crafts may provide the catharsis that everybody needs to retain inner balance and harmony with an enervating environment. Here we are free to create and enjoy.

Expression by aesthetic experience, particularly through crafts, has been a significant source of satisfaction to individuals since man devised the first tool. It is obvious that the need for this form of self-realization is more important than ever before. Involvement in crafts offers at least one outlet in a world of mass production and piecemeal contributions.

Experiences and opportunities to experiment, innovate, explore, and dramatize inculcate feelings that stimulate further undertakings, deepen enjoyment, and hone heretofore hidden talents or skills. Additionally, the desire to facilitate the process of communication through crafts brings the satisfaction and personal achievement. "I made, invented, painted, molded, changed, or produced that!" carries with it the recognition of personal competence and immense satisfaction of accomplishment. Nor does such accomplishment have to be perfect. It is sufficient if the participant, the doer, feels that his needs have been met.

Human dignity has long been expressed through craftsmanship. The special skills which repose in certain individuals may have brought them world acclaim, but in each of us there is a residual capacity to perform, given the right key to unlock the skill. Recreationists and educators must find the key and motivate people to express themselves through the joy of performance. In the final analysis, it is not so much the object formed that is significant, but the effect of the effort on the performer.

It is also well to understand that there exists a broad range of skills, knowledge, appreciation, and desire. Every degree of personal experience, talent, and aptitude can be represented in any community. For that reason it is probably best to interpret the crafts experience as a process in communication. With this concept as a guide, all those connected with the crafts enterprise may justify the outcomes of their diverse attempts as personal strivings in the fulfillment of self-expression, self-identification, and commitment to some goal.

ANALYSIS OF COLOR, DESIGN, AND CRAFTSMANSHIP
Color
The subject of color is appropriate to a discussion of arts and crafts. However, it is not the intent of this presentation to probe the technical intricacies of color theory. Rather, a simple discussion of color principles is offered here. There are three characteristics of color which anybody who desires an understanding of its use should know. Of these the properties of hue, value, and intensity are the elements which distinguish color.

Hue   Hue is the name by which a color is known. It indicates the class or group to which the color belongs. There are the primary colors of red, yellow, and blue; the secondary colors which occur when any two primaries are combined in equal amounts to produce orange, green, and purple; and the intermediate colors which are produced when any two primaries are mixed in unequal amounts. From this latter combination are produced an infinite number of hues.

Hues may be classified in two groupings—warm and cool. The warm category contains red, orange, and yellow hues, while the cool colors are made up of blue, green, and violet or purple. Intermediate colors which contain a mixture of the warm and cool colors are classified according to the predominating hues which are produced.

Value   Value is the second element of color. Value is explained in terms of the direction which the color takes toward white or black, that is, the degree of change from normal or pure state to either lightness or darkness. Purple has the darkest quality of all colors, while yellow has the lightest. Color which tends to be lighter than normal is said to be a tint. Thus, tints of any color are obtained by adding white pigment. Color which tends to be darker than normal is said to be shade. Thus, shades of any color are obtained by adding black pigment to the normal value.

Intensity   Intensity is the third element of color. Intensity deals with the brightness or dullness of a color and should not be confused with value. Dull colors have grey overtones, while pure colors are considered to be intense. A pure color may be dulled by adding a complementary color to neutralize it. (Complementary colors are colors which are directly opposite in hue; thus, the complement of red is green, and the complement of blue is orange.) The quantity of complementary color added will determine whether a completely neutral color is produced. If almost equal amounts of complementary colors are mixed, the resulting product will be gray. To the extent that warm colors predominate, the result will be warm. If cool color predominates, the neutralized color will have cool tones.

Color Schemes   Color schemes are combinations of hues or the use of value. The single, or monochromatic, color scheme consists of one hue in various values. The values must be differentiated rather sharply or the pattern created becomes rather bland and uninteresting. The adjacent color scheme combines hues which are related insofar as tint or shading is concerned. Value is an important factor in this scheme, as is the concept that adjacent hues share a common hue; for example, red and red-orange have red as a common color. The complementary color scheme uses opposite hues to form its combinations. Mixes of color schemes where a combination of complementary and adjacent hues are brought to play may also be found satisfying. Variations of these patterns tend to create interest. In complementary schemes, a wide range of values and intensities may assist in producing favorable results by neutralizing one or both hues.

Finally, the equalized scheme may be created. Here the composition consists of three equidistant hues. Thus the primary colors belong to this class. Although difficult to utilize, the equalized color scheme may be quite pleasing if one of the hues is grayed.

The possibility of creating color harmonies without reference to color schemes lies with the sensitivity of individuals. The freer the use of color, the more personalized is the product. Such effects should be assiduously cultivated because they enrich the experience of the participant.

Use of Color   While it may be said that art imitates nature, it is also true that nature is not the only possibility whereby color schemes may be obtained. Color suggestions abound in nature, but culturally produced artifacts may assist in enlivening color propensities. Many examples of outstanding crafts are the products of artisans and artists from throughout the world. Fabrics, both printed and embroidered, and ceramics having a variety of glazes offer additional stimulation and inspiration.

The proportion of color utilized is important in any work. A well-developed color plan maintains a logical correlation between color areas and hues. The color areas should be so proportioned that color dominance is permitted. The color covering the greatest space usually conveys the overall impression provided by the design. Of course, there can be subordinate colors which depend upon the character of the design. These should be proportionally represented.

In any color plan the allocation of color areas must show balance. Intensity and value invariably outweigh size in determining color balance. Thus, a spot of intense color can be used to balance a large neutrally colored area. The necessity to maintain good color balance is required if the structural quality of the object, which the design enhances, is to be preserved.

Color stress is concerned with the concept of attraction. Consideration for size, form, placement, and hue tends to determine the focal point of attention in a design. Color is extremely important because it tends to call attention to itself and therefore to the significant feature of the design. Color gradations, in value and intensity, develop a rhythm which leads the eye from one part of the design to others. Such rhythm can be of a compelling nature or may promote disturbance and distraction.

Design

The modification of materials to conform to some prearranged plan may represent design. Any item or scheme having a commitment to a predetermined end for some specific purpose is design. Essentially, design is the artisan's conception of how a piece of material will be utilized and in what way or ways its form will be shaped or reorganized to fit the plan of the maker. The outcome of such planning effort may be good or bad, depending upon the inherent value of the original design as developed by the artisan and the ability of the craftsman to carry out the intent of the design. There are two phases of design which may be analyzed for simple explanation, i.e., structural and decorative.

Structural Design   Structural design is primarily concerned with the form of an object. Shape permits one item to differ from another and represents the distinguishing feature of identity. This fundamental quality is significant in evaluating good or poor design. Incorporated in structural design are color, texture, and the material out of which the object is made. Use determines form. The function of the article will indicate of what material it will be made, suggest the shaping or molding process, and influence the color and texture desired. Every material has inherent qualities that make it appropriate for certain uses and unfit for others. These properties may be manipulated in such ways as to effect distinctive results. The development of an item requires careful planning if it is to function in the most effective and efficient way possible.

The structure of an object conforms closely to function, and the proportional relationships of its parts should be satisfying to the eye. It is unlikely that aesthetic enjoyment will be reached at the expense of functional disuse. The more an object approaches the function for which it was originally designed, the more harmonious are the components and the greater is the beauty of expression.

To the extent that objects are enhanced by color or that materials utilized in fabrication have colors, consideration should be made for this important property. Depending on the function of the object, color may provide the necessary ingredient to complete the item. When certain materials are utilized, the role of color can become as important to the item as its primary function. In clothing design, for example, color in relation to structure determines use.

Decorative Design   The second aspect of design is decorative in nature. This means that an object may be treated in some way that is not required insofar as the function or use of that object is concerned, but that enhances its fundamental structure or form. Structural design essentially governs use of an object; however, decorative design should be concerned with total support and relationship to structure. Both design objectives should be to enrich, complement, and support the complete object.

The application of decorative design can never be one of supplanting. Decorative design, if adroitly conceived, may be so harmonious that it will appear an intrinsic part of the item. However, decorative design should never interfere with the function of the object to which it is applied. Decoration, like color, focuses attention on the object and attempts to stimulate interest in, appreciation for, and enhancement of the article. Decorative design should not seek to hide flaws in the structural design. In modern life we are too often witness to this attempt at deception. Close inspection or use soon enough reveals the faults and errors which a glossy or decorative surface tends to obscure from the nondiscerning eye. In the same manner, excellent structural design should not be weighed down or debased by ostentatious surface design. Simplicity and harmony are advantageously employed in all aspects of design.

Design may be thought of as,

> . . . the arrangement in a work of art; it establishes the proportion of parts to the whole and to each other, disposes them in relation to each other, and creates a pattern. Design has rhythm or movement, and balance or equilibrium. Rhythm may be obtained by alteration, by graduation, by transition, and by progression or growth. Balance may be of unity with variety, either symmetrical or free, or of principality or subordination. The satisfactory application of the principles of design results in harmony.[1]

Craftsmanship
The ability to utilize tools in the shaping, treatment, or manipulation of substances and materials to produce something of functional and/or

[1]Leon L. Winslow, *The Integrated School Art Program* (N.Y.: McGraw-Hill Book Company, Inc., 1939), p. 353.

aesthetic value is craftsmanship. Among nature's evolutionary gifts to man was the appositional thumb to fingers. In consequence man could manipulate things, which in turn led to the use of things to work on other things. Man's clever hands and growing brain permitted an exquisite coordination to form. The ability to grasp large or small objects and utilize them to create innovative designs by which materials are given form and substance is the essence of craftsmanship.

Another aspect of craftsmanship is the desire or ambition to complete a unit of work having the mark of one's own efforts forever stamped on the fabricated object. Perhaps craftsmanship should also be called pride of workmanship. It is the delight of making the best effort possible by exerting whatever talent or ability innately held on the article crafted. It means the time taken for design, the energy expended in carrying out the design with quality, and the satisfaction derived only when form and function, together with such surface or decorative design as is necessary, are brought to fruition.

Poor craftsmanship abounds everywhere. There seems little left of the pride of work which formerly marked the efforts of craftsmen in many trades. Perhaps the factor of machine-made goods precludes such individual ambition, but there are still many productive trades in which craftsmanship could manifest itself. The ideal of pride in the work being done has apparently been forsaken. Time, now, is looked upon as money. There is no intent to offer satisfaction or guarantee a job well done. Yet, there are those who do provide the last ounce of devoted work because they look upon their handiwork as a piece of themselves, carrying their reputation. Some people are concerned with reputation, and their work shows the unmistakable signs of pride.

Today, craftsmanship is more avocationally oriented than vocational. It is within the hobby activity, the recreational program, or the directed-learning environment that individuals tend to exhibit craftsmanship. The hobbyist, particularly, infuses a part of himself into his crafts activities. For him, crafts have become a lifelong interest. He is not only learning by doing, but perhaps he has matured and attained excellence in the work of his own hands. The hobbyist glories in whatever he makes. He has freely chosen this form of self-expression and sets to work with a willingness to spend whatever time, care, and attention to detail such activity requires. Crafts which become hobbies involve meticulousness, classification, patience, and absolute absorption by the artisan. This almost fanaticism and loving attention paid to performance and product has nearly passed out of existence. But those who spend the time and carry their devotion to full flower are repaid handsomely in terms of personal satisfaction, and sometimes, the mark of excellence.

SATISFYING INDIVIDUAL NEEDS

Crafts permit the individual the occasion to experience fulfillment. Crafts offer the opportunity to personally identify oneself with an idea, carry it through every stage of development, and finally realize utter satisfaction as the finishing touches are added. The completeness of the project adds a dimension to the life of the craftsman that seems to be disappearing from common life today—integrity and unity. A soundly developed program in crafts brings the individual in direct confrontation with a variety of problems, not the least of which is conflicting desires. Within the confines of the crafts room the individual can apply himself, or more importantly, his ideas to a medium. By using design, tools, and knowledge he can subject any material to his will and create a new arrangement, new combinations, new proportions, unique outcomes.

It is in consequence of handling tools and materials that the inventiveness of the human mind shows tangible form. Experimentation with possible avenues of productivity indicates individual potential and self-development. It is the total commitment which creative experience demands that allows the individual to realize what he can do. What follows offers unending enjoyment, exploration of various materials, creation of designs, and upon completion a sense of release and deep satisfaction.

Participation in arts and crafts is rewarding in personal growth and satisfaction in all stages and levels of life. It has special significance in our present society because there are times when most everyone seeks to capture the joys of meditation and solitude in order to shut out pressures and excitement and to slacken the pace of present day living. Evidence of this urge to find a retreat is manifested in the nation-wide sale and use of home workshop equipment. This trend indicates carry-over values of arts and crafts into the quiet of the home, and provides endless opportunities for enriched family living.[2]

Attention to the way people live indicates that those who are mentally healthy attain satisfactions in the conduct of their lives. Certain needs must be satisfied if the normal person is to achieve a happy and effective life. There are specific basic human needs that temper the human condition and are presumed to be the stimulation behind the organism's activity. Fundamentally, satisfactions have origin in psychological and physiological needs which tend to motivate conduct.

Those who recognize the importance and character of needs can more intelligently select those courses of action which will lead to a fulfillment of needs. Such individuals can avoid experiences which do not coincide with the successful pursuit of satisfaction. This is not a hedonistically oriented plan, but the opportunity to explore possible avenues that tend to offer a more harmonious life style.

All individuals differ insofar as latent or overt skills, knowledge, talent, or desire is concerned. Each person probably wants to achieve in some way. A vague feeling persists in us all that creates a drive to reduce tension. Tensions produced by the urge to activity and achievement are alleviated by participating in suitable behavior which leads to actual accomplishment.

Unaccustomed experiences are worthwhile in satisfying the desire for achievement, but even more satisfying is the effective performance of some task. The human organism requires some purposeful activity in

[2]The Athletic Institute, *The Recreation Program* (Chicago: The Institute, 1965), p. 17.

order to live a well-balanced life; some objective or work to complete affords the satisfaction of the need to effect accomplishment. Crafts activities, providing an almost infinite variety of choices, new experiences, media, and purpose, can offer opportunities that end in genuine fulfillment.

The basis for program achievement in arts and crafts lies in its ability to satisfy individual needs. Scrupulous attention must be paid to individual wants and needs. Accentuation of opportunities for individual participation should be held as a paramount goal. Because of individual differences, personal satisfaction may be derived in a remarkable number of ways. Group encounters will not always satisfy a person's desire for activity. There will be people in every community who either cannot or do not want to participate in socializing experiences; they prefer solitary avenues where they may express themselves alone. Some individuals especially seek out crafts as an outlet for solitary activity. Recreational and educational programs should promote frequent opportunities for individualized learning, skill development, and achievement. Being alone may very well be utilized as a means for self-development.

. . . if we really want to recapture the essence of experiences, if we want to restore color to our faded personalities and vitality to our languid minds, then we must learn to do things, to think things, to become someone, alone. For in order to gain from the world of experience and of people what the world has to offer us, we must frequently withdraw from it to find new experiences within ourselves.[3]

Value of Group Experiences
Conversely, arts and crafts activities provide the basis for group experiences, which people also require for a balanced existence. A variety of classes for beginners, intermediately skilled persons, and advanced or expert artisans may be programmed to meet the diverse and special needs of those who desire the companionship of peers in attaining satisfying results of successfully completed projects. Recognition of individual achievement within the group may be an important means for motivating participants to continue with their efforts, to try harder, or to progress to another level of efficiency. While the best interests of the group are emphasized, the progress and promotion of individuals within the group are kept uppermost. As with all recreational situations, it is the individual for whom the total program is developed. The individual is the measure of the program's success. To the extent that all individuals within the group or aggregate situation are well served and satisfied by their respective endeavors, the entire program succeeds.

Arts and crafts provide program material through which individuals can obtain a rich experience in self-realization; secure confidence in decision making; become knowledgeable about color, design, harmony, and materials; and perceive the significance of both fine and practical arts in the lives of people past and present. Participation can be initiated on an individual basis, since each person is involved with his own materials and

[3]Mary Ellen Chase, "Time to Oneself," *The Yale Review,* vol. 30 (Autumn, 1940), p. 132.

is working on something with his own hands. However, many crafts activities are undertaken within a class or group setting, thereby offering an invitation for the timid to enter into group life. Although each participant is occupied with his own project, there is still opportunity to ask questions, compare styles, enjoy the companionship of others behaving in similar ways, receive inspiration from the efforts of others, and maintain close contact without surrendering individuality. Members of any crafts group must share work space, materials, tools, and the attention of the instructor. Cooperation is fostered and individuals are enabled to perform with peers. As skills develop, gradually there may also develop a concomitant feeling of integration with others. This is particularly helpful in extreme heterogeneous situations. Arts and crafts offer opportunities for individual satisfaction and for combining people into groups under conditions where intense feelings and tensions can be resolved. The individual can achieve status and recognition in consequence of performing in activities that are personally satisfying to him. At the same time there might also be a simultaneous build-up of contact and mutual confidence that goes into the development of group feeling.

Many persons, adults in particular, seek and find immensely satisfying hobbies or avocational interests through their experiences in arts and crafts. The crafts instructor may have no motive beyond offering opportunities to create and enjoy through aesthetic media, but he recognizes talent and interest. In many instances the crafts instructor can serve as an important guidance or counseling resource in directing students toward further preparation. There is little question but that exercise of skill is one of the ways by which individuals can attain optimum satisfaction and adjustment throughout life. Arts and crafts activities have the propensity to foster such growth and accomplishment.

FACTORS IN PLANNING RECREATIONAL ACTIVITIES 2

The development of any recreational program requires attention to various factors whose presence or absence determines the quality of performance, comprehensiveness of purpose, and ability to satisfy students. The program is the only reason for the establishment of an agency whose charge is the delivery of recreational services. In this, the program is analogous to the school curriculum. Through the program different activities are coordinated, applied, built upon, and integrated into an achievable and enjoyable experience. The program permits the advanced scheduling of whatever activities are desired, either by interest designation or to motivate interest. It also brings together competent leadership (instruction or guidance), in a setting that elicits performance, with the materials and equipment necessary for the proper learning or participation within the activity. All this is cemented by the correct appeal for public support through directed public relations or educational releases in whatever media are used. The basic components of any program, therefore, are leadership, materials, equipment, space, and students, all combined at a time and place conducive to active participation.

Participation in crafts activities has provided meaningful experiences for countless persons, of almost any age, during their free time as well as for those for whom instruction in arts and crafts is a directed learning experience during their school or adult education years. Among the values derived from work with crafts are the material satisfactions which occur from actually completing a design or putting the finishing touches to a long-worked-on project. Expertness does not always have to be a part of the inner satisfaction received by the individual participating. Satisfaction may just as easily accrue to one who is motivated by wanting to present his labor to someone else. The child may spend hours sanding, grinding, polishing, or shellacking a finish on a wooden or plastic product that may not be perfectly smooth or even well constructed. The motivation to produce a definitive shape or a recognizable object for presentation to another may be as rewarding to the novice as is the finished design of a master craftsman. There are certain satisfactions about which one cannot quibble or describe, but which are, nonetheless present.

Working with the hands has been found to bring healing to mental, emotional, and physical aberrations. It relieves tension. It soothes and restores. Creating an original design or producing a piece of work well done brings satisfaction in accomplishment, in personal endeavor and success. Planning a project and bringing it to satisfactory completion develops initiative, self-reliance, and orderly thinking. It brings one a feeling of individual personal worth and respect extremely valuable in personality development and satisfying living.[1]

CONDITIONS INFLUENCING THE DEVELOPMENT OF COMPREHENSIVE CRAFT ACTIVITIES

Whatever the agency involved, whether school, voluntary, or public recreational service department, the program is everything. It is the program, meaning the total offering of services, for which the agency was created. Participation within the program has value for the individual, the agency, and the community at large. Although schools have distinct advantage, insofar as attendance is concerned, they are presently feeling the pinch of criticism and disenchantment. School bond issues are repeatedly turned down, and vociferous critics are demanding the abolishing of compulsory education.[2] Other critics desire alternative choices for children of school age. Whatever the philosophy of those who feel that schools are no longer providing relevant curricula, or that schools should be more permissive, or that teachers must be made accountable for the learning of their students, the schools may be defended on the basis of curriculum. The curriculum contains the subject matter which students require. Within the curriculum there should be a place for a crafts program. To win supporters, to fill the relevant place it has always had in society, the curriculum of the school must be pertinent, cognizant of current problems, attractive and interesting.

What is true of the schools is of even greater necessity for voluntary and public recreational service agencies. There is no legal requirement to attend such agencies. They are, by their very nature, of the discretionary type. People participate or attend recreational service department offerings because they want to, not because they have to. If the program of

[1] H. Dan Corbin, *Recreation Leadership,* 3rd ed. (Englewood Cliffs, N.J.: Prentice-Hall, Inc., 1970), p. 158.
[2] Ivan Illich, "The Alternative to Schooling," *Saturday Review* (June 19, 1971), pp. 44-48, 59-60.

activities is of a kind and variety that draws interest and attention it will be successful. Successful recreational activities attract high attendance, increase public support of the agency in question, and fulfill a useful role in the warp and woof of the community's social fabric. How are successful programs planned and developed?

There are a number of factors operating concomitantly which must be recognized and accounted for if the program is to render those services for which the agency was created. In this instance the factors are the aims of the organization, leadership, conditioning circumstances, local customs, participant planning, diversity of activities, students to be served, and coordination. Program development in any recreational agency is never simple. Bringing interested potential students together with competent leadership at a time and place suitable and accessible for the greatest stimulation possible, with adequate materials and equipment all smoothly organized to prevent friction and disaffection from arising is an intricate process. To the extent that crafts instructors can coordinate all integral features, overcome irritating irrelevancies, and match the student to a group, class, or activity that will meet his particular recreational needs, the ultimate success of the program will be determined. Program is the end all and be all of the agency. The program which attains maximum capacity satisfies the goals and achieves the centrality of purpose for which the agency stands.

Aims of the Program

What is the primary objective which the program seeks to reach? Essentially this may be answered with the overriding statement of recreational service to all the people during their respective hours of leisure insofar as recreational agencies are concerned. For the school curriculum it is exposure of students to learning experiences that will enable them to participate in the world around them. The program must therefore contain the widest possible range of activities, both active and passive, which have the capacity to attract interest, appreciation, and participation. To perform this task requires a knowledge of the community. This means an analysis of the people in terms of age, sex, ethnic, racial, religious, social, economic, political, educational, and interest categories. From such data the levels of skill, interest, need, previous experience, capacity to perform, and willingness to underwrite a diverse program will be ascertained.

Since the only activity in question for this volume is crafts, major emphasis must be placed on the way that crafts can meet the fundamental program questions of planning and development. Can crafts actually provide the variety of experiences necessary to meet the demands and needs of a diverse public? Are there contained within its potential projects the range of forms, levels, and attractions which would allow nearly everybody to find something of value for themselves? The answers to these questions are central to the chief thrust of the text. Crafts experiences are so widely different that in this one aspect of possible recreational activity people may find a specific item, subject, or interest that will meet whatever need or desire they have.

Since crafts may be performed in solitary or group situations, they contribute to the function of social intercourse. Because crafts promote aesthetic interest and appreciation, they contribute to the function of cultural enhancement. Because they permit media and technique exploration, they contribute to the function of personal innovation and creativity. Because participants can find self-expression and self-development through them, crafts contribute to the function of individual satisfaction and therefore enjoyment. Finally, crafts may be integrated with all other categories of the recreational or school program and by so doing enhance the contributions of each while multiplying their benefit to the participants as well as the agency involved.

Availability

Crafts activities are conducted at whatever outlets the community has and under widely differing circumstances. Simple crafts may be offered on playgrounds or at centers operated by the public department of recreational service. The school system may offer every grade level, from elementary to postgraduate, in course work developed as an intrinsic part of the school curriculum. Thus arts and crafts may be found from kindergarten all the way through to adult education classes in the high school. Voluntary agency offerings may include simple to complex crafts for hobbyists, artisans, avocationists, workers in specific trades or others. These crafts activities will be located in Y's, Boys' Clubs, Boy and Girl Scout troop unit pavilions, church basements, or Grange halls. Wherever there are people who constitute the potential students of the agency, there crafts activities will be found. It is a most ubiquitous recreational and educational experience.

The fact that crafts serve equally well as a recreational medium for young children and older adults, for the healthy as well as the ill, for the typical as well as the atypical, for those who are institutionalized as well as for those who are free indicates the surprising attraction that crafts have for all kinds of people. Crafts are both an intellectual and a manual enterprise permitting the most fanciful flights of imagination as well as the routine reproduction of ready-made objects or the simplified construction of models. Crafts accommodate the talented, the near talented, and those who want to participate, but who have no talent at all.

Publicity

No crafts program can achieve full participation unless there is a well-thought-out public relations procedure which can inform the general public about the times, places, costs (if any), materials, media, and so forth. People must know about an activity before they can participate. More importantly, the educational campaign must have an appeal that whets the appetite. The entire promotional preparation should be such that people are drawn to the activity as much out of curiosity as by previously satisfying experiences. Responsible leadership is required to see that every ethical advantage is taken of the diverse means for disseminating information about the program. Care must be taken to assure rapid and accurate information. The use of local mass media, displays in food markets, banks, movie houses, and other popular places in the community should be used. Flyers, newsletters, posters, bulletin boards in strategic locations—all should be exploited if the widest dissemination of information in the most attractive way possible is to be developed.

Age-group classifications must be carefully fixed so that potential participants may make the best use of their leisure. Readily accessible and available facilities should be provided so that there is little in the way of extra travel to discourage some individual from participation. In the promotion of a crafts program the schedule should clearly reflect the needs, interests, skills, and attitudes of the students. Routine and special events should be mixed to maintain the activity's attractiveness. Innovational presentations, displays, recognition of individuals for excellence should be encouraged. Crafts activities should become a staple in the total community recreational program and in the school curriculum. In this way there will be continual growth and development of individual interests, and each program may thereby be mutually beneficial to the other. Where the formal instructional aspect of one leaves off, the recreational endeavor of the other may carry over.

Dependability of the program to do what it purports to do will be a significant factor in developing participation. When a crafts activity is scheduled to begin at a certain time and place, it should absolutely start on time and in that location. Many parents may, in fact, send their children to a recreational crafts activity when they feel that they can depend upon the routine operation of the activity to begin and stop at specific times. This factor may also eventuate in the parent becoming a student when crafts projects are made available to adults in the community.

Local Expectations

Conditions which govern the attitudes of people may be a reflection of local history, custom, or mores. Shifts in employment may alter the makeup of a neighborhood or community so that previous plans have to be modified to accommodate an entirely new set of needs, interests, or circumstances. Political manipulation may freeze supporting funds with the consequent curtailment of planned crafts activities. Economic, political, religious, ethnic, or any changing social situations may require strenuous efforts on the part of community agencies to change schedules, initiate new activities, omit certain productions, or operate in different locations under vastly speculative conditions. Employment, housing, and transportation may force rapid development or accelerating abandonment of proposed crafts activities. Where there are great expectations for certain kinds of crafts activities in the local community, such experiences must be prepared. Starting from such a familiar base permits crafts instructors to proceed at a rate commensurate with the individual's ability and desire to learn. Working from the known to unknown quantities and qualities, the individual is introduced to new and unfamiliar items, media, and combinations that should do much to stimulate his ideas and enthusiasm. Local expectations may only require that some crafts activity be made available, but the adroit recreationist will build upon this conditioning factor in planning his crafts activity.

Participant Planning

Perhaps one of the more significant aspects of program planning is the role which the layman takes in advising and assisting the development of the program. When citizens can be involved with the various considerations and problems that accrue as a program is being fleshed out, they are more appreciative and supportive of the end product. Even greater import should be given to the factor of ego-identification which results from participant planning. The individual who is intimately connected and concerned with the development of a program will also be concerned about its success. When an individual has taken the time and made the effort to contribute something of a positive nature and has shared the exigencies of program planning, he is much more likely to work energetically for the ultimate success of the activity than if he had not assumed some personal responsibility for such representation.

Participant planning can be encouraged through the use of neighborhood recreational advisory councils, district committees, arts and crafts interest groups, state, county, and local art councils, and other such legally established or purely advisory laymen's groups which can more completely represent the average citizen's interests and goals. Citizens may be enlisted to assist in community surveys, to determine the precise population make-up of the community, to make population samples, and to serve on a variety of boards, commissions, councils, or committees all devised to permit a wider representation of the people to be served. The necessity of offering people a chance to participate in the intricacies of program development and administration should not be minimized. Perhaps in no other way do the people come to accept responsibility and share the emotional involvement of doing something to help themselves and their fellow men. Through this method the citizen is going to see that his efforts are successful by encouraging participation, requiring cooperation, seeking coordination, and widely supplying information about the program.

Instructional Personnel and Leadership

There seems little doubt that the success of any recreational program is directly attributable to the quality, competency, and adequacy of personnel involved with leadership. No program can operate successfully without leadership. It is the key factor and determines, as no other single element can, the probability of program success. As Butler has indicated:

Employment of a leadership staff with sound recreation education and practical experiences assures a well-rounded program; the specialized skills and interests of individual workers make it possible to offer a wide diversity of activities. The fact that competent leaders discover the capacities and skills of people in the community and enlist them for volunteer service further emphasizes the significance of leadership as a factor in program planning.[3]

Among the aspects of leadership which are crucial to the operation of successful crafts activities are those dealing with personal understanding and capability. Recognition of individual differences, insight into the needs of those who take part in the activity, and a philosophy that supports the ideal of service to all are essential for crafts program leadership.

Technical competence   Of necessity, the crafts instructor must possess specialized skill, knowledge, and a broad background of crafts experiences. Special preparation is required because of the multiplicity of media, possibilities of design, and different technical skills encountered in arts and crafts. The professional preparation of the crafts instructor will probably be formalized as he or she receives exposure to aims, ideals, practices, and philosophy within a professional preparatory course in an institution of higher education. However, even before the crafts instructor goes to college, there are the informal recreational experiences in arts and crafts which may assist enormously in the production of a skilled craftsman. Self-directed activities and hobbies may also prove of importance in the development of a competent crafts instructor.

Understanding of People   Although technical competence is one important factor in the make-up of a crafts instructor, it is by no means the only attribute which must be possessed. The crafts leader has to go far beyond craftsmanship. He must have the ability to communicate with his students. He should be as capable of listening as he is of telling, of reception as of transmission. All this is confirmed in being able to teach others. The crafts instructor starts his teaching at the level of understanding which his students have attained and by slow and easy steps brings them to a more effective level of participation. He does this by carefully noting the clues which each person offers. This means that the instructor is sensitive to the spoken and unspoken needs of his students. His understanding of their behavior, attitudes, and expressions of satisfaction or deficiency enables him to facilitate their learning. The ability to empathize with his students often helps the instructor to resolve problems or make explanations that can clarify sometimes opaque situations. This sensitivity to people permits the instructor to discern benefits from the efforts of each of those whom he serves and by so doing he can direct the attention of the student toward a recognition of desirable progress or outcomes. On those occasions when students do not detect improvement in their work, the instructor, with his more knowledgeable command of media and technique, may be able to pinpoint those areas of progress to further motivate the students. It is the instructor's responsibility to

[3] George D. Butler, *Introduction to Community Recreation,* 4th ed. (N.Y.: McGraw-Hill Book Company, 1967), p. 272.

provide instruction, guidance, and stimulation to students so that continued effort is made which will eventuate in satisfaction and enjoyment.

The crafts instructor should be concerned with differentiating between simple and complex crafts, with determining whether an individual is capable of handling particular activities, and with facilitating the efforts of students by anticipating design or construction problems before they become pronounced. Additionally, however, the instructor is aware of and has a concern for the individual's need for recognition and achieving success. He should infuse his teaching groups with his own enthusiasm for the activity and realize that whatever accrues to students through crafts endeavors will be valuable despite any imperfection noted in the completed crafts project. Surely he will strive to teach those techniques that will enable the student to fashion crafts objects that are satisfying to him. More importantly he will initiate the process by which the individual may broaden his own horizons, foster creativity, and arouse the desire for self-improvement. By assisting with the aquisition of skills and stimulating positive attitudes toward crafts activities, the crafts instructor increases the probability of satisfaction and enjoyment which derives from such participation.

Specialists Adequacy of craft leadership within a community-operated program is a question of the number of competent personnel needed and available. The type of crafts program to be administered is basically dependent upon how many specialists can be employed. If the community centralizes its crafts activities, it may require fewer specialist personnel to carry out the instructional and guidance function of the program. Of course, this will necessarily restrict the number of potential students because fewer persons will be able to be accommodated at any one time in a single facility. In a decentralized program where crafts activities are provided at neighborhood centers, playgrounds, and through mobile units bringing the crafts activities to where the people are, rather than having people congregate to participate, many more crafts instructors will be required. Any combination of the two plans is indicative of the philosophy of the operating department or system. If the primary objective is to provide the widest possible range of services, it follows that the combination approach will be followed. The recruitment, selection, and employment of professionals and specialists and the utilization of volunteers to supplement and complement such employed personnel will be reflected in agency understanding of its own function. To do the job there must be a sufficient number of crafts instructors.

Leadership may be seen as a combination of special skills and a basic ability to work with and through people. It is concerned with learned abilities to function in instructional and inspirational ways. It may be observed that:

The professional person has the responsibility to help individuals to develop the skill to work out their own decisions and function as participants in the group rather than as isolates. In accord with this concept, the recreationist performs in ways which will lend support to individuals so that they may gain confidence in their own strength and the respect of others while carrying the obligations which group living thrusts upon them.[4]

Volunteers and Part-time personnel   Voluntary leadership may be recruited from the general population of any community, but intensive and practical in-service education must be made available so that the purposes of the agency are promoted by those who assume some of the teaching responsibility. This means time set aside for the development of volunteer and staff personnel. It can require lectures, workshops, demonstrations, staff conferences, and other methods by which working personnel may be' brought to the most effective and efficient state of readiness in serving the needs of people.

Depending upon the range and scope of the crafts program, there may be desired recreationists who have specialized in crafts, school teachers who may be hired after their responsibility to the school system is fulfilled, and commercial specialists who are employed for short-term or seasonal work. Where local recreational centers and playgrounds are staffed with permanent personnel, it may be possible to program a complete crafts program ranging from elementary to advanced levels. These activities may be supplemented by traveling crafts instructors who circulate through the system's program centers. By scheduling the traveling crafts instructor one or more times each week at a given center or playground, specific crafts activities may be instructed and greater skill achieved by students.

When the financial resources of the agency permit, mobile crafts units may be called upon to make the rounds of neighborhoods which are not served by any recreational structure. These mobile units are completely outfitted crafts shops and are capable of providing guidance and instruction for all skill levels. Such units systematically make scheduled stops after public information has been disseminated. In conjunction with other municipal departments, a city block may be closed to traffic while the mobile crafts unit becomes the focus of neighborhood attention. To the extent that diverse crafts activities are thereby carried to citizens in this manner, specialist personnel may have to be added. Where the mobile unit operates out of a district or community recreational center or school, crafts instructors already employed by the department may be utilized to attract and serve many more people who might otherwise never come to the structure or building. It is even possible to utilize the traveling crafts instructors as the mobile unit force. By adroit scheduling on the part of the central administrative office, such traveling crafts instructors in mobile units may make rounds of neighborhoods unserved by recreational structures during those hours when they are not otherwise engaged in instructing crafts at the centers.

However it is performed and maintained, the crafts program of any school system or municipality will be only as good as the quality of

[4]Jay S. Shivers, *Leadership in Recreational Service* (New York: The Macmillan Company, 1963), p. 173.

its leadership. Each crafts group that undertakes instruction in any aspect of crafts must have competent leadership personnel assigned to it. If sufficient numbers of professional personnel cannot be employed, skilled volunteers should be used to supplement the work force. To the extent that some groups require little in the way of directed instruction, or are essentially self-directing adults, volunteers may be recruited to assist such groups. Crafts instructors are basic to program survival, and they must be recompensed in a manner that will lead to the most satisfactory results for all concerned.

Financial Support

The amount of funds made available for the support of any municipal or school program determines the scope or limitation of that program. On financial support hinges almost every aspect of program planning. No program is possible unless funds are appropriated for all the elements required in operating the activities. Funding determines the quality and number of crafts instructors. It permits or restricts the use of areas, facilities, and structures which can accommodate a wide-ranging and diverse program. The very pieces of equipment and supplies without which no program gets very far are dependent upon fiscal response. The budget will eventually determine whether all skill levels can be accommodated, how long the craft sessions will be, whether they can be conducted in public places, whether custodial and maintenance functions can be assured, if there will be service to the homebound, ill, or handicapped, and the type and variety of activities which can be programmed. The richness and variety of activities and when, where, and how such activities will be offered are all predicated on monetary support. A well-conceived budget affording generous support can do much to enhance and make vital any crafts program. Without adequate financial support little can be done and very nearly total negation of program aims is likely.

While it is true that there are many low-cost crafts activities, the funds necessary for leadership, facilities, and so forth should not be stinted. The community will benefit immeasurably from the fiscal support given to maintain and operate the crafts program in an effective manner. The benefits to people in terms of appreciation, skill development, and personal satisfaction far outweigh the monetary allotment necessary. Professional leaders may be able to cut down on the expenditures necessary for materials and equipment, they may be able to utilize make-shift spaces, and they will surely be able to recruit volunteers to assist in the program, but there is no substitute for high-quality personnel. This is where a major proportion of the money must go.

Space and Facilities

Some crafts activities may occur on vacant lots, in parks, in playgrounds, on the beach, in camps, in vacant lofts, in offices, or in church social halls. Where communities have realized the need and heeded the demand for the support of crafts activities, special facilities have been constructed.

These arts and crafts centers are devoted to the operation of activities throughout the year. Such centers may contain fully equipped rooms designed to offer a variety of crafts activities of certain types. Thus, there are rooms set aside for woodworking, ceramics, sculpturing, automotive crafts, electrical crafts, metalwork, art studios, photography, or leather crafts only. These areas designed for one type of craft make possible the development of a highly specialized program concerned with individuals who may begin as novices and, in time, emerge as specialist master craftsmen. Specialized facilities feature the capability of maintaining a wide variety of supplies and equipment which can be utilized for every type and level of craft. Additionally, they serve as focal points of specialized interest and intent. Centralized facilities enable the scheduling of crafts activities throughout the year and may be programmed to offer the widest possible range of crafts. Centers may be opened and accessible to the public from early morning until late at night every day throughout the year. The public's demand for such activity may be more easily met on this basis. Many skill levels, various crafts opportunities, and entire courses may be programmed simultaneously since there is no competition for space by other recreational activities beyond crafts.

Typically, however, crafts activities must share space in a general recreational center with all other recreational activities which can be programmed indoors. More often than not, a crafts room will be provided in the center. Such a room can be well equipped for sophisticated crafts experiences or, as is usually the case, be capable of accommodating very simple and basic crafts activities. Where there is a general crafts room, many different crafts activities may be scheduled, but the probability of directed learning is limited when many different crafts are being performed at various skill levels. Of course, such activities may be more formally organized so that even when diverse crafts are programmed, those participants with the same skill levels may be arranged in groups or courses.

It is not unusual to find that no special crafts area is reserved and that crafts activities must compete for space in whatever nooks and crannies are available. When no special rooms are planned, little may be expected insofar as complex crafts or crafts which require machine tools or permanent equipment. Crafts that require nothing in the way of permanent equipment may do well, although there is a need for storage space. Leather work, sewing, knitting, finger painting, model making, and other handicrafts may be carried on in almost any space available. However, activities which need fixed or large tools, benches, and other nonportable equipment must be either neglected or handicapped for space.

The utilization of schools as public recreational centers has opened up excellent facilities for citizens. Usually centrally situated and serving local neighborhoods, districts, or communities, the school has specialized rooms which are designed as shops of various kinds; home economics laboratories, art rooms, industrial and vocational arts and crafts rooms— all may be utilized. Any classroom may be opened and used for simple crafts activities. The specialized shops, when available, permit the school to become crafts centers and also to perform as general recreational centers. When schools are employed within the public recreational service system, it may be feasible to hire the teachers who normally operate the shops, art, crafts, and home economics laboratories, thus reducing possible friction and disruption when crafts activities are conducted after school hours.

ORGANIZATIONAL METHODS

The single purpose of organization for the conduct of a crafts program is to coordinate all the elements necessary for the operation in the smoothest possible way so that discord is minimized and personal satisfaction and enjoyment are optimized. Organization really combines the individual segments into a carefully woven pattern so that each component delivers maximum efficiency and effectiveness in the program. Organization is, therefore, concerned with present levels and conduct of activities wherever they operate; the degree of sophistication or lack of experience on the part of the potential students; available spaces and facilities; demographic factors which indicate the type of community and the people who make up its citizenry. Examination is made to determine the availability of leadership personnel who will staff the program and the personal resources of the community insofar as potential volunteer leadership is concerned. Of extreme concern will be the willingness of the community to financially support a crafts program.

The scope of preparation, methods of organization, and techniques used in the operation of a comprehensive crafts program play a significant part in the planning of activities. Community interest in arts and crafts experience is growing, and this popularity is reflected in the diversity of activities, the need for special and general facilities, the availability of supplies, equipment, and leadership resources. Crafts activities can be performed in the basement of one's home, but more frequently there is a demand for qualified instruction and assistance in learning how crafts activities can become available. The fact that many people of all ages, degrees of experience, levels of skill, and appreciation call for the establishment of crafts activities indicates the need for organization.

Informal organization occurs when crafts activities are based on one-a-day simple functions which may be performed by transients or during the course of a single morning or afternoon. When the crafts project can be completed in a short period, the group participating may consist of both regular students and those who may attend on an irregular basis. Since there is little carry-over from one session to the next, they miss nothing and are content to perform as the mood moves them. There is no stimulus which holds their attention and arouses enough interest to overcome inertia or apathy. When, however, the crafts activity requires attendance on a relatively prolonged basis, especially where the processes and techniques of crafts are taught along with the objective of a finished project, individuals are motivated toward regular attendance. If sufficient interest is aroused, a group may be formed and specified times and places arranged, together with leadership and material resources. Thus, prolonged interest and numbers of participants require organization. Informal activities require almost no organization, but wherever there are instructional classes, logical procedures must be instigated. This is organization.

Flexibility of Organization   To assure a rational approach to the development of a sound program of arts and crafts, the program organization should be flexible to permit inclusion of those who feel more comfortable in an informal program and those who, because of interest and desire, willingly attend classes and sessions and learn through the more formally conducted experiences. Allowances must be made for population changes as various groups and individuals move into or out of the community. New interests, whether fads or ones that assume the classical proportions of durability, must be considered. Where quality performance is one of the objectives of the activity, formal organization should be initiated. Such organization is conducive to routine scheduling of activities where those with the interest will attend and develop higher skill levels and greater appreciation for the work involved.

Degree of Organization   The degree of organization varies with the numbers of participants, its major intent, the diversity of experiences which will be engaged in, the sophistication of the membership, previous experiences, and attitudes. In many communities the establishment of a comprehensive crafts program will require a high standard of organization. Organization becomes significant when the objectives of the program extend beyond the immediate participants and embrace the entire community. The program not only is a teaching medium for those directly involved with learning techniques and performing crafts projects, but attempts to involve all the citizens in the community directly or indirectly. Thus, classes and sessions must be organized, and city-wide demonstrations, displays, and exhibitions should also be included in order to acquaint the public with the potential of the program. Since the range of the program can be increased through the recruitment of volunteers, the deployment of lay leaders, hobbyists, and interested persons who speak for and to the public can be immeasurably valuable in reaching those who might otherwise not be reached.

In those communities where participation in crafts programs has reached proportions that embrace many who seek the enjoyment of advanced crafts, there is a necessity for specialized as well as general facilities. Communities should be able to provide widespread opportunities for engagement in vastly different crafts experiences. The organization of the crafts program becomes a significant and complicated function. It must provide for the varying ages and skills of the students, offer opportunity for those who desire to take part informally, and satisfy the needs of those who want to participate on a more formal basis. There must be assurance to all that space and facilities will be available for use not only in local or neighborhood facilities, but in district, community, and city-wide specialty centers which attempt to promote the most highly skilled form of crafts-manship.

Organization under circumstances of widespread popularity or where the program is just being established requires technical proficiency and the ability to stimulate participation. In the former instance, community surveys must be undertaken to determine the degree of probable involvement so that schedules can be arranged which will avoid conflict among diverse groups, classes, and individuals who intend to participate. This means the discovery of all potential work space for crafts, the development of good public relations procedures to inform the public about the program, establishment of sound budgeting means for the support of the program, and the employment of professional crafts instructors in combination with willing lay leaders. In the latter instance, organization is required if only to arrange for the distribution of crafts activities at the various recreational centers so that people who casually drop in may take part if they so desire. By offering a cafeteria of crafts activities at many locations throughout the community in concert with a massive public education program dealing with the values of crafts to individual satisfaction and enjoyment, demand may be aroused. The development of interest in the crafts program is at least as important and complex as is the scheduling of space, instructors, and supplies after demand has been indicated.

The intricacies of programming are bound up in the conditioning factors of organization. The pulling together of many disparate elements so that coordinated effort results in meeting the needs of the people in any community necessitates innovative ideas, sensitivity to people, and intelligence in delivering the kinds of services on which people thrive. The process of involving people in ways that can enrich their lives must be facilitated; such facilitation is a major task of organization.

POTENTIAL PARTICIPANTS

From any point of view crafts may be looked upon as a comprehensive series of manipulative activities finding expression within varied personality types and age groups. There are crafts activities to meet the broad and varied needs of people regardless of age, experience, skill, or talent. From the tyro to master, crafts activities are so numerous and reflect such variety of subject matter and treatment that few people will not find something of interest to them. That there exists a broad range of qualifications, insofar as degree of skill, sophistication of technique, personal expression, media experiences, and materials used, cannot be denied. However, to the extent that crafts are looked upon as a communications process rather than a product or material-oriented outcome, the personal satisfactions derived should be the basis of the program.

Within a community recreational service program, the crafts aspect of the program contains as many potential experiences as there are media and individuals to work on them. It is the quality of experience, rather than the quantity of production or numbers of people involved, that should become the criterion on which the program develops. After all, the enhancement of cultural values within the community as a result of participation in a comprehensive crafts program may be advanced as much through the pedestrian efforts of novices and those who lack the talent to innovate as from those whose technique and strivings transcend typical mundane manifestations. The crafts program cannot afford to rehash time-worn activities or remain static in its outlook. There must be a continual analysis of what is being offered along with new ideas, new techniques, and an increasing challenge to those who seek their leisure outlets through crafts. The individual remains the dominant factor in any crafts program, and a widening scope of play must be provided so that individual expression is permitted.

Typically, communities require expert appraisal to determine the interest and need for a crafts program at the local level. Our society has been so conditioned that, from the earliest years, individuals are expected to participate in physical activities. If these are not forthcoming, there will always be a private group who can advance the interest of athletics. Sports and game enthusiasts make up a determined interest group in every community and their demands are not long unheeded by local authorities. Interest in crafts activity, however, is neither as clearcut nor as conditioned as is participation in sports. It has been only in recent years that the performing arts, of which crafts is one, has come to receive broad attention. This has been due in part to what some people call "the cultural explosion," the manifestation of which is seen in the organization of community orchestras, theater groups, art shows, etc. Whether or not this holds promise and will be strengthened in the future or is simply another fad trend by parties who have influence with supporting authorities at state, federal, and local levels of government remains to be seen. Currently, cultural opportunities through the various performing arts are being promoted. Exploitation of this fact should be taken by those educational and recreational service specialists who can take this opportunity to whip up enthusiasm and generate mass participation in such activities.

There is in every community a reservoir of people who have a determined interest in crafts activities and others whose interest lies dormant. It is squarely up to educators and recreationists to arouse latent and long-sleeping interests if crafts are to assume their rightful place as a popular expression of individual need. Recreationists and educators alike have the responsibility for guiding and initiating crafts activities throughout the community. They may stimulate participation by simply announcing opportunities for participation, through the development of instructional classes in various crafts forms, and by inserting crafts experiences in organized recreational activities on playgrounds, community centers, schools, camps, or wherever people gather to take part in expected public services.

Participation in crafts is rewarding at any stage of life. It has a peculiar import because it can be performed either in groups or in the solitude of one's own home. Evidence of the desire to seek the satisfaction of retreat from the hectic pressures of modern life is reflected in the millions of homes where basement hobby shops have been installed. Home workshop equipment, do-it-yourself kits, artist's supplies, and the staggering quantity of crafts materials sold each year stand as unquestioned testimony to the popularity of crafts participation. Crafts provide the participant with more than the simple process of production. Surely there is great and genuine satisfaction in the statement, "I made it myself," but there is an additional objective beyond the materialistic one of plastic manifestation. There is the enriching value of developing an appreciation for and a recognition of beauty in design, execution, and accomplishment. Perhaps appreciation for craftsmanship and the knowledge of what it takes to produce a well-wrought object may, in the long run, more favorably capture the imagination of potential participants and stimulate them to try their hands.

The scope of participation in a community recreational crafts program should reflect the variety and flexibility of human experiences involved. Stress should be laid on similarities and differences of age, sex, skill, previous experience, interests, traditions, mental or physical limitations, and the degree to which the crafts instructor can elicit participation through instructional or other public relations devices.

A comprehensive recreational program of crafts activities must recognize several important points: (1) any community is made up of diverse groups of people whose special needs and interests must be incorporated into the would-be comprehensive program; (2) in program planning there are a variety of events and conditions which have application to the different groups and individuals who become the potential students. Both of these operating facts are significant from the standpoint of program building. Among the groups which make up the community are school-age groups, out-of-school youth, young adults, adults, and older adults. These, in turn, may be further classified by whatever affiliation they prefer, for example, interest groups, ethnic groups, racial groups, religious groups, fraternal or social groups, business and professional groups, service groups, and ill, homebound, or handicapped groups. Although each of these groups may require specialized attention, it must not be forgotten that, taken together, they constitute the entire community. It may be necessary to have specialized or adapted activities to meet the distinct limitations of certain of these groups, but crafts instructors must recognize that these groups are not separated from community life and must, by their very nature, be considered an integral part of the total community constituency. As the needs of these groups and individuals are met through consistency and through consideration, the fulfillment of a comprehensive and varied program of crafts activities will occur. The delivery of these services is a responsibility which devolves upon community authorities and which consists of opportunities being made available to potential participants.

Elementary School Children   Throughout the elementary school and any recreational service agency, crafts may be looked upon as an intrinsic part of the school curriculum or community program. Because some encounters with crafts are involved in nearly every form of human activity, the subject assists the child to learn about the world in which he lives and enjoys. Insofar as the elementary school is concerned, there is no aspect of curriculum which cannot be taken up or around which the subject of crafts may not be inspired. The elementary school teacher should not experience any difficulty in relating crafts to almost any other curriculum matter. As the child advances from the kindergarten to the sixth grade, there should be a constant exposure to such matters as color, harmony, design, and fabrication. All these crafts facets should be a part of creative activity drawing upon the life of the child and the things and interests which surround him.

The crafts activities organized by recreational service agencies will offer maximum exposure to experiences that provide opportunities for the child to develop aesthetic appreciation. Through the informal methods of discussion, slide shows, puppet theater, dioramas, and displays of fine craftsmanship, the child is encouraged to begin making things for himself. Simple successes may then lead to more complex and varied crafts forms. Though less formal in content and conduct than is the classroom crafts activity, there is, nevertheless, still the need for competent instructional technique at a pace and level which will motivate the child to attend and participate. Unlike the school situation, the primary emphasis of any recreational crafts program is on the satisfaction and enjoyment one receives from participation. There is no legal requirement to attend such recreational sessions; rather, any compulsion which the child feels will probably be wholly self-instigated.

Middle School Children   A sustaining program of instructional crafts is continued in the middle schools. This includes grades five through eight. In such a system where crafts are offered as an integrated function of the curriculum, the course is designed to enable boys and girls to become aware of and appreciate aesthetic objects and experiences. Whether prompted by curricular assignments that take them to public displays of crafts, industrial products, art shows, or other exhibits where craftsmen demonstrate their skill or stimulated by participation in recreational agency crafts activities, middle school children are particularly sensitive. It is at this time that whatever artistic or creative talent the child has will probably be manifested. School teachers should pay particular attention to those children who display an artistic bent because they should be encouraged to continue with special preparation. Middle school children are the delight of crafts instructors, for it is at this age level that the child for whom crafts are an abiding interest will begin to seek greater involvement in the media and technique of crafts production. The child, although still in the experimental stage, is beginning to find himself in terms of the material or substances that appear to evoke the greatest degree of interest. The child who is drawn to crafts activities has a healthy desire to make things, to see how they tick, to disassemble as well as to construct. The desire to know should be promoted and enhanced by proper guidance and instruction through offerings of the recreational service agency found in the local community.

Senior High School Children   Any crafts program that is taught in the senior high school will probably revolve around shop work. Typically, crafts activities are of the industrial, manufacturing, marine, or agricultural types. For those who enroll in such courses the guidance and instruction received often permit a fuller enjoyment of leisure. Additionally, the crafts course may open opportunities for later vocational employment. Printing, woodworking, mechanical engineering, automotive, and other skills provide the initial preparation for potential trades as well as for lifetime leisure activities.

Out-of-School Youth   For those who drop out of school, for whatever reason, and for those who no longer attend school, but have not yet found employment in the job market, public recreational service activities, of which crafts are but one aspect, may be the opportunity needed to gain needed skills for work and leisure. Recreational service departments can provide crafts activities that are modeled after the shop courses of schools without the emphasis on attendance and grades or other restricting mechanisms. Those who drop out of schools seem to have an aversion to the formal and regimented atmosphere which pervades the school environment. Recreational service agencies, on the other hand, operating on a wholly permissive basis and founded primarily upon the interests, wants, and inclinations of program participants do not present a condition of threat. For this reason there appears to be the likelihood that out-of-school youth might take advantage of the learning situation offered by such recreational agencies and utilize the opportunity to further enhance their vocational status or simply to make their leisure enjoyable.

The possibility of learning a valuable trade through participation in a recreational crafts activity is one that should not be overlooked by recreationists, educators, or civil authorities. There is as much to be learned in recreational experiences as can be obtained from the more formal preparations of school classrooms. The voluntary aspect of recreational crafts participation may actually serve as the instrument by which the youth will fulfill his potential. Self-expression, motivation, and urge to perform will reflect the individual's inner strivings. In the recreational situation the individual can be himself as in no other place or way. What the individual actually does in his leisure may be the best indication of what and who he is. In the recreational context the individual no longer has to conform or compete to live up to an image with which others have burdened him. Free to perform at his own pace and in media or designs of his own choosing, he may find the right combination of learned skills and materials to discover his own place in life.

Adults   All adults, whether young or old, within the labor force or out of it, may be categorized insofar as legal maturity is concerned. Needs may differ from individual to individual, but taken as a group, the adult population participates in crafts activities as an outgrowth of previous experiences or because of some intense stimulation of recent origin. Crafts for adults run the gamut of all crafts activities, ranging from the most simple handicraft to complicated industrial and/or commercial forms. Young adults who participate in crafts activities are as likely to be continuing interests that were begun in school as they are to undertake something vastly new and different from what they have done before. Adults are given to involvement with crafts experiences that have become deep and abiding interests with them. For some a type of crafts specialization occurs that forms the basis for a lifetime hobby.

Young adults, however, often try new and unfamiliar projects either as a way of learning new aesthetic appreciations or for the more practical reasons of desiring to learn the methods necessary to repair minor electrical, wood, metal, or automotive devices. For some adults the outcome of a crafts project is ornamental, with practical overtones, for example, a bookcase or server. For others the joy of home repair is often enough to motivate crafts or shop participation.

Adult education courses provided under the auspices of local school systems may sometimes offer a wide-ranging variety of crafts projects which can lure the reluctant adult from his television set and into the classroom for several hours of learning every Wednesday evening. Crafts for the adult have a scope and content the listing of which would fill several volumes. It must suffice here to state that the adult population of any community will be an important segment of the students to be served by either the school system or the recreational service agency.

Homebound, Ill, or Handicapped   Many communities have a large, and as yet still unserved, portion of the population confined at home or in treatment or custodial institutions as convalescents, as permanent residents, or for short-term rehabilitation. Individuals such as these usually cannot participate in the average community-operated recreational program. Unless there are specific voluntary agencies dedicated to the provision of recreational services to the homebound, ill, and handicapped, such people never receive the benefit derived from recreational participation. They are ill-served who only lie in bed or sit at home and wait. Crafts instructors have the responsibility for offering recreational opportunities to the atypical or confined person. They must lead the way in giving those who cannot attend community schools and centers a way of leading more satisfying lives through recreational activity. Community-based crafts instructors should know who the homebound person is through population analysis of the community. Once the crafts instructor determines the number of persons who fall within the atypical category, he has a better chance of being able to offer pertinent recreational opportunity.

Among the many recreational activities that can be adapted to meet the needs of the physically or mentally limited is crafts experience. Crafts may be modified to meet whatever limitation the individual sustains and still offer the satisfactions which one gains through participation. Whether the individual is totally bedridden, has no arms or hands, is confined to wheelchair, or needs to resort to canes or crutches, he may still find intense satisfaction and enjoyment through a variety of crafts experiences that are open and arranged for him.

Working at the individual's level of comprehension or physical capability, the crafts instructor may, by patience and understanding, build confidence in the student and eventually gain the psychic reward of seeing another individual flourish as achievement and satisfaction are attained. Crafts are an important instrument by which recreational values can be received. Homebound, ill, or handicapped people should not be deprived of such recreational experiences, when, with a little effort and modification, the activity can be brought to the place where the individual resides or is confined. The necessary effort will be more than compensated by the ethical and moral considerations involved in the undertaking.

PROGRAM MAKING

All the factors which have been described are concerned with the development of activities which are designed to provide learning and enjoyment for those who participate. How the disparate elements are brought together and fused into the opportunities in which people may find fulfillment is the process called program making. The general forces which influence where, how, with whom, for how much, and when activities take place are bound up in why people want to participate and how they are acquainted with the offerings.

Planning for Experienced Adults   Insofar as community recreational service programming is concerned with the specific activity of crafts, there are always several probabilities from which to work. One is that a segment of the population to be served has had previous experience with crafts and wishes to continue to learn new techniques or to undertake a particular project. This means that there are people in the community who have the desire to participate in crafts activities and require only the opportunity, in terms of facility, instruction, and materials in order to satisfy themselves. This group needs no selling job. They know what they want. All that the recreational service department must do is provide the place, the leadership, and, perhaps, the materials. Even the latter is not really necessary, for such people, especially those who have a certain project or object which they wish to complete, may possess materials. They come to the crafts activity for a variety of reasons. They may seek guidance or desire information on techniques for handling the material on which they want to work. Others come only for the space or facility which they may use. Some arrive because they feel that only in such a facility or shop may they bang, saw, or use foul-smelling finishes, paints, or varnishes without fear of being condemned. Still others do not have the tools or equipment that may be vital for work on some project. Thus, a portion of the population becomes the core of any crafts program, and almost any crafts opportunity that is provided to the public will have some takers.

Planning for Inexperienced Adults   Another segment of the population consists of people who would probably like to participate but may never have had any previous experience in crafts. While this seems little likely, there are people whose only exposure has been in elementary school or at a camp which they once attended. In too many instances these prior experiences may have been disastrous. Boredom, discipline, projects of little interest, or personal inability may have contributed to a dislike for crafts. This is particularly valid for part of the adult population. Such people think of themselves as being inept, or they can remember only the disenchantment, smells, and noise with which they associate all crafts. This group needs a great deal of selling, and even under ideal circumstances their disaffection is such that they may never be motivated to make a further attempt. Nevertheless, the crafts instructor must constantly tempt this group and tax his ingenuity to the utmost for innovative and thought-provoking propaganda which may eventually stimulate a reluctant few to try once again.

Planning for Children Children's groups are probably the easiest to interest in a community recreational crafts program. Children are delighted with new things. They want to try tools, equipment, and various media, specifically that which they can manipulate with their own hands. Children have to be actively discouraged before they will give up on crafts activities. Of course, there are unfortunate situations where unthinking counselors, teachers, or crafts instructors do more to discourage than encourage. These individuals are more concerned with correct procedures, discipline, and neatness than they are with what the child is actually learning. It would have been better for all concerned had such persons never attempted to guide children in crafts. They cause more harm to psyche, frustrate attempts at creativity, and stifle every thought and magic moment when real learning could occur. Instead of building a foundation for a whole lifetime of active association with crafts, they systematically destroy the child's desire to participate. It's all well meaning of course, for the good of the child, to teach correct work habits, precise uniform requirements, all the prohibitions, while stamping out any thought of fun and satisfaction. Surely, there is a place for neatness, good procedure, and step-by-step technical development, but not at the expense of killing whatever animated the child in the first place. Despite all the poorly prepared and motivated individuals who are charged with the responsibility for operating crafts activities, whether in school or community recreational agency, children continue to come back because most crafts activities are absolutely fun.

For those children who, at an early age, are exposed to a competent crafts person who instigates exploration and feels that it is more significant to attract learners than to repel them, crafts activity is a great magnet. All that is necessary is the organization of the activity at a time and place most appropriate for all concerned. The children simply have to be informed when and where; they will bring their own enthusiasm and desire to learn.

Planning for Youth Secondary school youth are a mixture of elementary school children and adult individuals in terms of attitudes, likes, and dislikes. They have been exposed to some arts and crafts activities and have, for whatever reasons, drawn conclusions about the experiences. Not everybody is attracted to crafts. One presupposes some talent, gift, or manipulable skill ready to be inspired by a crafts supervisor, but this is not the case. There are those who can never be delighted by crafts. They simply do not have the interest and never intend to participate. They cannot be reached.

Only dire exigencies will promote any semblence of petulant participation from them. They will have to be marooned on some isolated island without entertainment, without sport and game facilities, and without reading materials. Then, and only then, will they barely participate in crafts.

Just as many of this age group are enthusiastic about crafts. They willingly participate whenever opportunity is afforded. Sometimes, crafts specialization is required. This may come to mean automobile repair and/ or maintenance, but it is a crafts activity and that is important. Boys and girls may find pleasure in any of the countless items which can be developed in any number of media. Crafts clubs, courses, hobby groups, prevocational interest groups—all or any of these may be the means through which active participation in crafts may flourish. Again as with other age groups where there is unflagging interest, all that is necessary is an announcement of time, place, leadership, and other pertinent information. The course will fill because it is available.

Planning for the Majority   Finally, there is an indeterminate group, which contains the greater part of the population. Here will be found individuals whose interests range from profound to nil. Here will be people who have not thought about any other recreational activity, except passive entertainment, for years. Here, too, will be those who are constantly seeking new experiences, exploring long-dormant ideas, or encountering new ways in which stimulating efforts may be observed or performed. For this vast potential clientele the department must bend its untiring endeavor to activate the passive and encourage creative participation. Here the innovative talents of public relations expression will be called upon. It is to this population that the department must aim its central propaganda effort. These people must be attractively solicited before they commit themselves to involvement.

For the most part, people are terribly apathetic about doing anything that requires them to leave their residences. Most craft activities can be done in one's home or apartment, but for those projects which need larger space, equipment, and materials than are provided in the average home, the single most productive area will be at the local recreational center or school building. People must, of necessity, come to these recreational or school centers if they really want to participate. To get them to forego the simple pleasure of television watching may require efforts that go beyond what the typically dedicated recreationist may have to expend. However, if the information is worded cleverly enough, arouses curiosity to the point of desire, and provides sufficient stimulation, it can bring the pleasure seeker to the activity and expose him to whatever mind-grabbing experiences may be offered.

Arousing Interest   Because almost every community contains a number of people who have an interest in some aspect of crafts, the development of an activity designed to satisfy the needs of these people is relatively simple. The need exists, and the agency has the responsibility of providing the opportunity to participate. This really means that a variety of crafts offerings may be made at whatever locations are most convenient to the potential students and participation will ensue. But what of those who are not so inclined to come out for crafts? Other means must be found to persuade them of the value which they will find in participation. Here the utilization of volunteers, laymen's groups, advisory councils, and committees is very important. If nothing succeeds like success, then those who have had wonderful experiences within the crafts activity should be prevailed upon to pass along the good word to their friends, neighbors, and acquaintances. Word-of-mouth communication can be a most effective stimulus to others for joining in.

The Hobbyist as Publicist   Hobbyists are prime examples of how laymen can be utilized to augment the meager public agency staff in perpetuating the enjoyment of any activity. The hobbyist is already convinced that crafts are the answer to most of society's problems. It is for this reason that he has chosen crafts as his life's avocational interest. The hobbyist is somewhat of a fanatic, at least about his hobby. The more people to whom he can speak about his hobby, the happier he is. Thus, two good ends may be served by enlisting the aid of the hobbyist to speak to others about his consuming interest, perhaps to act as a resource person to groups, to exhibit his talents, or to display his craftsmanship at public meetings. This serves a basic public relations function. The hobbyist is made happy because he can talk about his favorite activity, the agency has turned up a promoter of the joys of crafts, and many people may become interested in crafts as a result of being exposed to the enthusiasm of the hobbyist.

The public recreational agency will find that there are diverse ways by which people can be made aware of crafts and their potential meaning, whether active participation or only aesthetic appreciation is concerned. If the substance of the message is repeated in a variety of ways, many people may be induced to take part in activities that can be of lasting satisfaction and pleasure.

TIME FACTORS

Crafts opportunities and their development are subjected to the vagaries of financial support, available facilities, leadership, and other administrative considerations. Even such mundane factors as transportation to and from the crafts activity and the precise timing of courses, classes, or special events can inhibit or promote active engagement. Timing is an essential ingredient in the planning of activities. It may either afford opportunity to participate and generate enjoyment or actually prevent people from attending.

The time factor in program making is important for several reasons. First, there is the element of currency and relevancy. This includes the timeliness of activity which is strengthened through association with current events, topics, attitudes, and situations of a cultural, social, economic, political, or religious nature, or other conditioning forces. The calendar has a special meaning for crafts activities which are adopted to encourage or otherwise be concerned with themes around which design ideas or entire projects may be worked. Holidays, seasonal changes, traditions of the community or neighborhood, fads, or other motive forces can be utilized to maximum benefit in creating crafts interest and exploiting the appropriateness or timely approach in selecting items and projects.

Time of Day   Consideration must also be taken for the most suitable time of day to schedule the various crafts classes and coordinate activities. As Shivers has indicated:

Time is the basic on which the recreational program operates. Leisure is the free time which people have to participate in recreational experiences. The work of the recreational service department finds its rationale for establishment in the leisure which people have to spend. At almost any time during each day of any week there will be those in the community who have free time. One of the elemental procedures necessary, if the public agency is to serve its constituents well, is to determine who has leisure and when. On this foundation the program structure will be built.[5]

Activities for the youngest children must take into account the time when they are free to participate. Thus, preschool children may be involved during the mornings, and elementary school children may be involved in the afternoons after school closes but before the evening meal. Other school-age youth must be scheduled when such activities do not interfere with schoolwork or homework. Out-of-school youth may be accommodated at almost any time they prefer to participate, particularly if they have the maturity, ability, and knowledge to engage in self-directed experiences. Where sufficient numbers of this group are collected, more directed crafts opportunities may be offered, if acceptable to those who make up the group. For adults the best times may come during the evening hours. For those who are employed in positions where odd-hour shifts occur special accommodations may have to be arranged so that those who are interested may participate freely. Older adults may have a great deal of leisure, especially those who are retired and find themselves with much time on their hands. Separate crafts facilities may have to be given over to the older adult population, for their hours of use may very well coincide with those of young children, school-age children, and some adults. To the extent that a given crafts facility can accommodate all who wish to participate without crowding, there is only the necessity to schedule various classes, groups, and individual students so that conflicts are avoided. Where, however, the crafts facility is physically unable to accommodate more than a few groups simultaneously, scheduling becomes more complex.

Time becomes important in planning the program because it deals with all persons who live within the community as well as those who are just passing through. One requirement is that an analysis of potential students

[5] Jay S. Shivers, *Principles and Practices of Recreational Service* (New York: The Macmillan Company, 1967), p. 375.

must be made to determine at what times such individuals and/or groups are free to participate. Planning the crafts program, whether at a centralized location or in various facilities situated throughout the community, will be based upon time factors.

Length of Classes   Duration of activities is also important in terms of student needs. The more mature and responsible the individual, the more probable it is that longer sessions will be necessary for work upon time-consuming projects. Children, on the other hand, have shorter attention spans and become restless even if they maintain an interest in the activity. Shorter craft sessions more frequently operated may be the best response to the needs of young children. The time factor continues to play an important role for any age level insofar as frequency, length of period, time of day, timeliness or association, and seasonal specialities are concerned. Whether the activity is prepared for morning, afternoon, or evening sessions, it must be organized to maintain interest, stimulate repeated attendance, and be of a duration commensurate with the requirement of those who participate.

Punctuality   Punctuality is another time factor that must be consistent. The public expects, and rightly so, that when activities are announced for a specific time, they will occur at that time, be completed on time, and not deviate from the schedule. It is a poor public relations practice to frustrate people by making them wait. Not only is it discourteous, but it may lead to outright disaffection with the activity and, perhaps, with the department providing the opportunity. No public department can afford to alienate its would-be supporters. Parents expect children who attend crafts sessions to be enrolled and participating in a group. They will not act favorably to a service that permits their children to wait around the door of the center or playground on the street because personnel have not yet arrived. Similarly, parents expect children to appear promptly at the conclusion of a session. Time schedules should be adhered to. Perhaps parents have made certain plans which include picking up their offspring at a specified time. If children are involved beyond a reasonable length of time, plans go awry. This does not lead to good feelings on the adult's part. Routines are important, and the starting and stopping times must be maintained. Whatever time must be taken for clearing, cleaning, and other maintenance functions should be decided upon so that there are no last-minute problems which may cause an overlapping of periods, thereby stealing time from another group's activity.

SCHEDULING

Scheduling is really concerned with coordinating time periods with students, leadership, and space. The schedule is the visible result of planning, development, public relations, and personnel assignment along with suitable space and appropriate materials and equipment. It is dovetailing the various elements into a harmonious pattern of the right place, people, time, and interests, coincidental with sufficient notice.

Schedules also permit flexibility of arrangements so that emergencies may be treated with alternate plans. Should there be forced changes, substitute plans should be put into action to prevent loss of time or participant interest.

In scheduling crafts activities, time may be considered in daily, weekly, monthly, or other periods, depending on the nature of the program. Thus, there may be scheduled individual crafts sessions which occur at a given hour one or more times per week in which different activities are performed each time without continuity or carry-over. On the other hand, there may be a specific course with a set length of from four to ten weeks, meeting once or more often each week. In such a situation the class is designed to teach students about some selected techniques, to provide directed learning, or to offer the opportunity for continuous work upon a project. In some instances, the class may combine all these attributes. Clearly, the goals of the class must be considered in planning the schedule.

Hourly Schedule The program day may be apportioned into half-hourly, hourly, and multiple-hour segments. This will depend upon the sophistication of the students. When young children are scheduled, it may be beneficial to offer forty-five-minute periods of which thirty minutes are given over to crafts activities and fifteen minutes are devoted to setting up and cleaning up. Such a time segment may more nearly meet the requirements of children who may be expected to become restless when activities are prolonged. As children mature, their attention span increases and they may be able to participate for longer periods. Where the crafts program day is segmented into hourly periods, there will be the necessity of providing enough time between sessions so that the crafts shop or facility can be restored to an appropriate and clean condition in time to accommodate the next group. For this reason, it is unwise to schedule a class or group for each hour of the day. Where crafts are in great demand, it is probably well to schedule session starting times to take into account the time lapse needed to replace tools and materials, and to give leadership personnel at least ten minutes to recuperate from the previous group. A single crafts instructor may be able to work with from four to six groups daily, depending upon when the instructor is scheduled to begin and the types, or level of attainment, of the groups in question. Table 2-1 indicates a typical hourly schedule during one full program day.

Depending upon the size of the facility and the number of professional personnel available to work with individuals and groups, a recreational crafts center may be scheduled in the same manner as is the curriculum of a school.

If crafts activities are extremely popular, the sample daily hourly schedule would require not less than two working shifts to satisfy the need indicated by many different age groups, experience groups, or self-directing groups. Since the work day might require uneven distribution of working hours between personnel on the day shift and those on the afternoon and evening shift, there could be compensatory make-up hours on Saturday and perhaps Sunday if the call for

HOUR	CLASS TYPE	FUNCTION	AGE GROUP
9:00 A.M.	Elementary	Instruction	Preschool
9:30 A.M.		Clean up	
9:45 A.M.		Set up	
10:00 A.M.	Elementary	Instruction	Preschool
10:30 A.M.		Clean up	
10:45 A.M.		Set up	
10:50 A.M.		Break	
11:00 A.M.	Elementary or other level	Instruction	Older adult or maternal
12:00 A.M.		Clean up	
12:15 P.M.		Set up	
12:30 P.M.		Lunch	
1:30 P.M.	Elementary or other level	Instruction	Older adult or other age group
2:30 P.M.		Clean up	
2:45 P.M.		Set up	
2:50 P.M.		Break	
3:00 P.M.	Intermediate	Instruction	Elementary or youth
4:00 P.M.		Clean up	
4:15 P.M.		Set up	
4:20 P.M.		Break	
4:30 P.M.	Intermediate	Instruction	Elementary or youth
5:30 P.M.		Clean up	
5:45 P.M.		Set up	
6:00 P.M.		Dinner	
7:00 P.M.	Intermediate	Instruction	Youth
8:00 P.M.		Clean up	
8:15 P.M.		Set up	
8:20 P.M.		Break	
8:30 P.M.	Advanced	Instruction	Adult or youth
10:30 P.M.		Clean up	
10:45 P.M.		Close up	
11:00 P.M.		Lock up	

Table 2-1   HOURLY PERIODS OF DAILY PROGRAM

crafts activities is extreme. It is possible that groups can be scheduled to meet one or more times each week. Younger children's groups may meet daily or every other day. Upper elementary children may meet two or three times per week. Adult groups may meet only once each week, although certain groups can meet daily when scheduled for sessions of less than two hours. There are innumerable variations to such scheduling. Among the factors influencing the number of times and/or the duration of a crafts session may be maturity, interest, skill, and need of the students; the availability of the facility to accommodate the group; the leadership available; and the demand made upon personnel and facility by other groups.

Daily Schedule   Schedules should be well publicized in advance and listed on a daily basis so that people of the community will know when and where activities which interest them are presented. A daily schedule arranged by class and time segments is most helpful to all concerned. The daily schedule is designed to meet the needs of the various groups which the local agency serves in terms of functions, space, activity, and time. There is little likelihood that the various neighborhoods which make up the entire community will be homogeneous. Some neighborhoods will have similar compositions insofar as age, racial, religious, economic, ethnic, or other categorizing aspects are concerned. For the most part, however, the people in different neighborhoods are quite heterogeneous. Particularly is this true in large metropolitan areas. To the extent that public recreational service or other recreational agencies have facilities situated in any given neighborhood or neighborhoods, the staffing will reflect differences in personnel skills, experience, and talent. Two neighborhood recreational centers may be staffed by the same number of personnel, but the capabilities for service may differ insofar as personal interest, skill, or experience. Even where the program content is the same, individual variations may produce a marked difference in presentation and format. In any event, each daily program for each recreational facility will show major or minor differences. These differences will reflect the population to be served, personnel employed, space available, financial considerations, and other administrative elements. Even with such differences as a heterogeneous population contains, the crafts instructor should be aware of population needs and composition so that the schedule will be practical and benefit all who wish to participate. It is fruitless to schedule activities for a certain age group at a time when it is either inopportune or absolutely improbable that these people will come to the activity. For example, preschool children are generally ready for activity between 9:00 A.M. and 11:00 A.M. They may also have activity during the early afternoon.

Sometime before noon, older adults may appear at the facility. If the facility is organized to accommodate such individuals, as are so-called adult centers, these people may spend the entire day at the center and eat their lunch there if some cafeteria facility is made available. While this is not likely at the routine recreational or school center, the older adult may find that a good part of his day is spent at the center.

Out-of-school youth tend to frequent recreational places in the early afternoon. Having nowhere else to go, they may become interested in a crafts activity out of sheer desperation and stay to find satisfaction and enjoyment from such participation. After school lets out for the day, usually after 3:00 P.M. in most places, elementary school children begin to frequent the center. The younger of these school children will be able to participate until supper time. The older children may return after supper. Senior high school students start to drift into the center from 7:00 P.M., and if they find an interest in crafts at that time, can be counted on to remain until closing. Young adults who are interested in crafts will probably make their appearance on a routine basis at least once each week. The young adult who participates in a crafts session does so in terms of specified time segments. Thus, he arrives at the time when the activity is scheduled to begin, say at 8:30 P.M. and remains until the session is concluded. If the community requires that the recreational center be opened on Saturdays and Sundays, elementary school children will arrive earlier than during the week and stay later. Rarely will there be a shift in hours of use by adolescents or older adults. Their routines are fairly fixed by social pressures or other conditioning factors. Of course, transients may come to a recreational center at almost any time. Every schedule should contain reserved time and space to accommodate those who can shift for themselves in self-directed activities. Some space or area can be set aside so that those who want only the use of such space or the use of tools or equipment may participate on an individual basis, not on a specified time basis. Scheduling should provide for flexibility for the widest possible community use.

Weekly Schedule   A weekly schedule permits the planner of a crafts program to arrange for the recurrent and teaching activities which normally make up a course or series. A course consists of an instructional class at any level, from beginner to advanced skill, which meets on a regular basis for a fixed period. Depending upon the degree of skill attained, rapidity of progress, personnel available, and other conditioning influences, a course may meet for from four to ten weeks. Thus, there is offered a sense of continuity and a feeling of achievement as the individual moves from one approach to another and from one skill level to another. The weekly schedule provides participants a choice in selecting particular activities prior to the time of their commencement and furnishes them with precise dates for start and termination of classes; it guarantees that at specific times and places a particular crafts experience is offered. Weekly schedules facilitate the development of a yearly program of themes, events, central or culminating exhibitions, and other focusing activities.

Multiple-Weekly Schedule   When schedules are arranged in weekly series, there is opportunity to develop a continuous crafts program that takes care of all levels of skill, sophistication, and experience. There is also the opportunity to accommodate courses to meet the needs of many, rather than a few, people. Crafts classes, as an example, may be organized on a ten-week basis. Thus, five different groups may be instructed during five consecutive ten-week sessions per year. Depending upon the groups in question, it may be preferable to operate concurrent courses and sessions, i.e., running for four- or five-week sessions throughout the year while the ten-week sessions also operate. Such programming allows the person who desires a class to be informed of the commencement and stopping times, while the irregular student or even the transient may find a suitable crafts session into which he may fit.

The multiple-weekly schedules permit the formulation of obviously graded or progressive sequences in which students may gain increasing skills at the level on which they start. By operating a variety of skill-level crafts classes, it would be theoretically possible for an individual to take part in a beginning or elementary course and through constant participation, with appropriate class changes, finish a forty-week cycle in the advanced section of the crafts program. While this indicates extreme devotion to crafts participation, it could be done. Since each crafts course is designed to teach techniques as well as aesthetic appreciation, it is much more likely that individuals would remain at the initial level and practice their accomplishments before seeking to advance.

The termination of each course cycle might be highlighted with a display or exhibition of projects and crafts items fabricated during the course. The culminating event could be associated with any number of themes, current happenings, traditions, historic events, or situations of opportune moment. Additionally, there would be opportunity to combine a variety of other recreational categories together with crafts so that each might enhance the other for the more complete satisfaction and enjoyment by students and spectators.

Seasonal Schedule   As the seasons change, many opportunities are offered to the competent crafts instructor to program appropriate events in order to reach as many people as possible. Seasonal programming follows not only the annual modifications in temperature and climatic conditions, but also traditional activities so dear to the hearts of people. The four seasons offer a colorful natural resource upon which the construction of a varied, interesting, and comprehensive crafts activity may be based. As the seasons run their course, multiple themes and special events may be instituted. Seasonal scheduling permits planning of activities not less than three months in advance. It may be reasonably assumed that where the public department of recreational service is firmly established, yearly program planning of recreational activities at the neighborhood, district, community, and city-wide basis becomes routine.

The development of the seasonal program is not merely the extension of daily, weekly, and multiple-weekly schedules, but operates to ensure that special projects and events may be inserted into the program to bring variety. Perhaps such events require long and arduous planning. The seasonal schedule allows sufficient time for preparation to achieve the objective of the activity. For some activities many weeks or even months may be assigned to planning all the myriad details that accrue in the development of a culminating display, exhibit, demonstration, or combination of the foregoing.

Seasonal programming accounts for the nature and scope of the crafts activity or activities under consideration, determines the community elements which tend to exert pressure for or against participation, the timeliness of the activities, the duration of the activity, the time required to accomplish the aim of the activity, and the competency of the leadership staff to encourage interest and promote participation. Seasonal changes may permit greater incentive for moving indoors or going outdoors. Seasonal variations also determine numbers of students and, perhaps, the age levels of students. For example, it is likely that more children and secondary school youth will participate in a crafts activity during early summer than in the later part. Many families take their annual vacations in the month of August, thereby cutting attendance of children. Conversely, it may be that activities scheduled for older adults and out-of-school youth may be more profitably undertaken during the times when children desert the playgrounds and recreational centers. Such shifts of attendance may be noted throughout the year, and schedules should be adapted to handle these variations of population interest and attendance.

People have leisure at all times of the year. The public recreational service department must be attuned to the needs and interests of people and be ready to provide opportunities for crafts participation, among other activities, when people do have leisure. Public agencies cannot exercise their options for total community recreational responsibility by meeting the leisure needs of people on a part-time or half-way basis. To live up to the mandate of responsibility required of them, public recreational service departments must provide opportunities each day, every day, throughout the year, subject only to the limitations of budget and the numbers of competent personnel necessary to carry out the functions of the program. Since there are always some people with leisure during any given day, the department must provide the wherewithal to ensure adequate provision of recreational services, in this instance crafts. Recreational activity has come to be a significant employment of the free time of people in the United States, and the public department is under obligation to schedule activities and develop a program for people, it really has no other function. All efforts, all ideas, all techniques are directly concerned with the establishment, development, and scheduling of the program.

GRADATION
OF ACTIVITIES

The arts and crafts fortuitously may be classified by a variety of methods. Because crafts lend themselves to instructional purposes, the program of activities can be subdivided into grades for easier administration and the comfort of participants. Crafts, by their very nature, should be exciting and stimulating to the individual, whether tyro or expert. Yet, many crafts activities fall far short of maintaining the interest of students after they have reached a specific level of skill or experience. The chief cause of loss of interest is a lack of progress beyond a particular point of achievement. Progress is best sustained as those who take part are facilitated in developing proficiency at a higher level of skill than that which they possessed when first they started.

Gradation of crafts experiences requires more than one level of opportunity for participation. By this is meant that each skill to be learned can be offered at almost any stage of the student's development as a craftsman. It should not matter that the individual is the merest novice, a highly competent designer, or someone who falls within the middle range of these designations. Gradation offers opportunities for continued enjoyment and satisfaction in crafts.

Gradation also permits differentiation by age group, interest, and media. There are projects formulated which assist the individual's familiarization with materials, equipment, aesthetic appreciation, form, and function. Whatever the age, skill, or interest of the group in question, there will be crafts appropriate to meet individual needs or group requirements. As with other fields, maturity and experience permit wider latitude and greater discretion in selection of crafts. As the student becomes more capable in handling the various crafts possibilities, wider potentials are provided or suggested. While age alone is not the single most important criterion for deciding the type of crafts activities which will be programmed, it does play an important part in the overall development of the crafts program.

With maturity, in terms of understanding and competence or ability to handle design, media, and tools, the craftsman will move on to ever more intricate and complex craft forms and/or media. This latter development remains at the discretion of the individual. Some people begin to specialize in one medium or form; others become disenchanted and desire novel experiences. When basic skills have been acquired, the individual is much freer to make value judgments and select crafts activities that characterize his personality, need, or self-expression. Of course, a point will or may be attained where the individual essentially becomes a master craftsman or artist and no longer requires or wants instruction. It is to this end that all crafts programs are oriented. Most will never achieve the ultimate objective, but those who continue to participate will receive the subjective satisfactions that accrue in such activities and will have been enabled to function in ways that tend to enhance their lives. The pleasure derived from working with one's hands, from manipulating plastic or visual objects, from creating, and thereby communicating in a process that is at least as old as man, carries with it the seeds for a life-long interest.

At the youngest age levels simplified and easily understood crafts projects are introduced. Crafts may assume such unhampered and recognizable forms that they may also be adapted for those whose intellectual capacity is greatly limited. If some crafts activities are intensely complex aesthetic forms which appeal to few, there are, at the other end of the scale, crafts experiences which can appeal to those who may not be able to grasp elementary concepts. Crafts are so broad in scope and appeal that they may easily be adapted to meet the peculiar needs of nearly every individual or group. Even at the earliest age-group level there will be those who evidence precocity or unusual talent. Such individuals should not be retarded and deprived of more advanced techniques because of their age. Rather, they should be encouraged by participation in groups where advanced skills are the centralized focus, despite the age differential which may be encountered.

Graded instructional courses can do much to maintain participation and interest and advance the cause of recreational crafts from earliest childhood through old age. Gradation prevents stagnation and routinization of activities to the point of dullness because it allows for expansion of horizons and ever-increasing ability. The graded method of programming facilitates modification of experiences to satisfy mental, physical, social, maturational, and experiential limitations, or previous restrictions. Gradation should be a required process in the development of any program because it encourages the acquisition of skills, interests, and appreciation that will have carry-over value for those people who participate.

AGE-GROUP CHARACTERISTICS

The physical growth pattern of the individual throughout his life span is important if some understanding is to be gained insofar as the extent or limitations to which individuals may participate in crafts. We are interested in not only physiological, but psychological and social development as well. Interest in human growth and development provides the crafts instructor with guides that assist in any instructional or recreational program. Age-group characteristics help to indicate the individuality, apparent proclivities, and maturity of the person involved. Such characteristics suggest differences in the ability to manipulate tools, media, and concepts at various ages. By awareness of the most pronounced growth differences likely to occur at each age level, the crafts instructor is capable of determining whether, for example, a particular crafts experience is appropriate for those exhibiting large or fine muscle dexterity. Particularly with children and youth can this knowledge add to the value to be received by the potential student. Crafts instructors should understand and recognize individual differences. On that basis they will best be able to recommend and/or guide activities for maximum advantage to the student.

Although age-group characteristics are offered on the following pages, they should in no way be thought to include all possibilities. Individuals are unique, if only for the differences in genetic construction, compounded by an overlay of environmental conditions. Thus, it must be understood that despite the attempt at specificity at particular age levels, each individual's development and growth vary greatly from anybody else's. Nevertheless, there are certain general tendencies which are referred to here.

Each person develops and matures at his own rate of speed. There will be no startling changes observed within the individual as he passes from one age group to the next. Slight variations will be noticeable, but there will be no radical breaks with previous behavior or character. This pattern is usually observed in the same individual throughout the life process. Unless there is some cause, such as trauma, excessive pressure, or personal catastrophe, the individual maintains personality continuity throughout his life.

In the use of age levels an attempt has been made to show the probable general tendencies of a hypothetical average person. Those factors which condition and influence individual character develop during the first twelve years of life—and are reinforced thereafter. Whatever salient marks are noted in the make-up of any individual have occurred over many years. They simply do not arise overnight.

The Four-Year-Old

Typically, the child at four is articulate and loves to use words whose sounds are enjoyable, rather than because he understands the meanings of the words. He is active physically, verbally, and socially. His large muscles are under control or almost so. This child enjoys a whole host of imaginative games, whether with playmates or by himself. Generally, the child enjoys repetitive activity, is adventuresome, and is not restrained by fear of injury or the ridicule of peers. Heightened emotionality is common among four-year-olds. Children of this age often feel that they can do more than their parents will permit them to do and rebel against restrictions. Overestimating their own capacity to perform, they may become fatigued, irritable, and susceptible to emotional tensions. Contradictory behavior is also observed at this age. With equal ease the four-year-old may be tractible and acquiescent or belligerent and obstinate.

Almost all physical activity which requires large-muscle effort will be enjoyed by the four-year-old. Large objects which can be manipulated are often favorites. Thus blocks, clay work, finger painting, sand play, and construction activities are very popular. The make-believe activities of children develop from life experiences. Construction experiences which demand the making of items or objects are essentially those which he sees in his daily life.

The Five-Year-Old
On the average, the five-year-old appears to be more calm than does the four-year-old. The child at five miniatures the adult world. He prefers those things with which he is familiar and therefore comfortable. His long-used toys, other possessions, and friends are what he likes best. He tends to resent the unknown, untried, or exploratory activities to which he is introduced. His dramatic play focuses on his everyday world, rather than on the fantasy which intrigued the four-year-old. He is at home with the familiar and rebels against intrusions which seem to attempt to change the known or to substitute unfamiliar situations. The five-year-old has developed a social sense as well as the beginnings of a sense of humor. He has matured to a point where he seems to be at rest in preparation for a momentous developmental thrust.

At age five, the child has relatively well-developed large-muscle control. His balance is better, and he shows a marked inclination for rhythmics. His greatly improved finger dexterity and arm and leg coordination show up in such daily efforts as buttoning clothes, playing with small objects, even sewing. The five-year-old is at a developmental stage where crafts activities can be more complex, insofar as manipulative experiences are concerned. The favorites of five-year-olds consist of plastic materials, housekeeping materials, action toys, beads, and clay. By age five the child is drawing with form and meaning. The five-year-old differentiates parts in his drawings, which are clearly recognizable for what the child indicates they are.

Since the child at this age is excited by his ability to represent what is meaningful to him, any art experience should provide the opportunity for developing mastery of the material itself. Since the process of creating is of greater significance than the final product, an art material should be selected that meets the need of the age group for which it was planned. Constantly introducing or changing art materials may actually stand in the way of a child's mastering the material enough to express his own feelings, his own reactions to his sensory processes and his own intellectual concepts of his environment.[1]

In addition to play acting, the young child spends much of his free time in making things. Given the opportunity, the five-year-old is happy to play in mud, sand, water, and with blocks, beads, clay, crayons, and paints. He enjoys drawing with crayon and is not at all hesitant about using scissors, paper, or paste. All these materials enable the child to construct items which abound in his everyday environment. He is a creature of the moment and is invariably concerned with what is happening to him and around him in the present.

The Six-Year-Old

By age six, a child should be in complete control of all the activities required for clothing, feeding, and cleaning himself. Rarely will he need assistance in performing these tasks, although there is a marked tendency to perform them in ways which leave much to be desired. The six-year-old washes himself perfunctorily, puts on clothes without particular thought as to how they look or hang, and occasionally spills or dribbles food while at the table. Gradually, however, such routine activities become accepted and with steady practice are at last perfected. Now that he has entered the elementary grades, he will learn to write, form numbers, paint, draw, model, and manipulate tools for creative and constructive purposes.

Making things just for the pleasure of making them, with little or no thought as to the use of such constructs, is a popular form of recreational activity among six-year-olds. Construction with wood and tools seems to be popular with young males, while females seek out such constructions as sewing, drawing, clay modeling, jewelry making, and painting. Arts, crafts, and the materials associated with these activities are found to be satisfying to the child in whatever situation he finds himself. Thus, the schoolroom or the playground, camp, or other recreational setting may offer the opportunities for this kind of participation.

Socially, the six-year-old exhibits patterns of behavior that are extreme. He displays emotions ranging from love to hate, joy to sorrow, fear to daring almost simultaneously. He enjoys all opportunities to take part in games; he will not be a spectator for long. Friendships of lasting association are formed at this time. The child is building a foundation for adjusting to his social environment. His emotional outcries are essentially experiments and explorations to determine what, if anything, can be accomplished. Social contact is a daily need, and he seeks out others for play. In most activities he throws caution to the winds and will attempt the most appalling stunts. Nevertheless, he still craves some solitude.

The six-year-old demands action. He has developed physiologically to the point where large muscles are under control and fine-muscle coordination is beginning to assert itself. Most six-year-olds have comparatively

[1]Victor Lowenfeld and W. L. Brittain, *Creative and Mental Growth,* 4th ed. (New York: The Macmillan Company, 1964), pp. 127-128.

good manual dexterity and hand-and-foot coordination. The average six is an old hand at using scissors and coloring within the lines of his picture book; he enjoys manipulating plastic materials and building things. High energy output is characteristic of this age, and it is not unusual for the child to exhaust himself unless stopped from doing so.

Good supervision is necessary for the child of six. Limitations must be imposed to prevent undue frustration from participation in activities which are well beyond the capacity of the child to perform. This is an age where the child's ego can be bruised by criticism and yet with competent guidance and counseling the child may be subtly led into areas which are more amenable to his developing skills and talents.

The Seven-Year-Old

Generally, the seven-year-old has reached the same plateau as did the five-year-old. There appears to be a harvesting of strength for a similar growth spurt. Where the six-year-old acted on impulse and never looked beyond the immediate results of his actions, the seven-year-old calmly appraises each situation before acting. He recognizes other people as having certain rights and feelings as he does. He is now more concerned with rules and regulations than formerly, and his free-time games are heavily laden with ritualistic activities that follow intricate procedure. While he indulges in large motor activity, he has become better coordinated and is in greater command of fine motor skills.

Drawing, painting, and clay modeling, in which young children frequently participate and which satisfies them to a remarkable degree, become somewhat less popular with the seven-year-old. This is not to say that the child loses interest in such activities; far from it. Rather the cause may be found in the child's own recognition of his inability to keep up with his peers. In effect, the social awareness and sensitivity of the child to criticism from peers or adults may stifle participation in creative activities. Poor performance in comparison with others leads to frustration or withdrawal. Only where the child shows precocity or unusual talent will creativity continue. Except when the child exhibits the gift of exceptional craftsmanship or prodigality, originality soon disappears.[2]

The child of seven retains his interest in arts and crafts and responds favorably to suggestions that do not carry overtones of rebuke or correction. He is eager to learn and still finds the plasticity of clay and the use of crayon and paint fascinating. In fact, at this stage of development the three-dimensional quality of clay permits exploration and involvement with the known as well as with fantasy shapes. While the child may linger over familiar forms which fill his daily world, he is learning about material manipulation and what can be done with some stretching of the imagination.

The Eight-Year-Old

The child of eight is growing rapidly both mentally and physically. This growth is shown in his socialization with peers and his attempts to accommodate himself to the expectations of adults. His motor capability is vastly superior to that of the seven-year-old. He has excellent control over large

[2]Cappe, J., "Les Manifestations artistiques chez l'enfant," *Nouvelle Revue Pédagogique*, vol. 3 (1947), pp. 89-93.

motor movements, and his coordination and fine-muscle command make for fluid and graceful actions. He enjoys almost any physical activity with which he is familiar and exhibits the testing and exploratory ambitions that were first observed in the six-year-old. Although he likes to show off, he is also adept at team games and cooperates well with others.

Eight is the age where fine-muscle skills begin to show. The ease and dexterity with which he uses implements indicate the probability of future appreciation. The child of eight has become more group- than ego-oriented and sees himself as part of a larger society in which he is no longer the center of the universe. He looks beyond the here-and-now conceptions of the seven-year-old and attempts to plan and save for the future. Collecting becomes a very important activity at this time. Almost anything may be collected, but in most instances only a few special kinds of items are collected. However, a wide variety of objects within the special categories he has chosen make his collection all the more satisfying.[3] Because collections become important at about this age period, it is often consistent with both school and recreational program objectives for crafts activities to be focused on the development of crafts which are collection-oriented. Thus, for example, specimens may be collected and mounted as both an outdoor educational and a crafts activity. Woodcraft and woodworking experiences may be directed toward making containers for whatever the child collects.

More significantly, the eight-year-old requires leadership and competent supervision. He still cannot make accurate judgments about himself, his capabilities, or things within his environmental sphere. Many accidents occur at this age because of the child's inability to take the precautions necessary for avoiding hazards. Professional instruction should be available and operating when children of any age are learning to work with tools and materials. Even more important to the health and welfare of the child is that good guidance be a part of the school or recreational situation since the mature judgment of the adult is substituted for the hit-and-miss pattern of the young child. With his increased span of attention and social awareness, he participates in a greater variety of social games and those activities where cooperation and group effort are manifested. Crafts activities which require not only individual, but group or team participation as well, are well received and enjoyed.

The Nine-Year-Old

If anything characterizes the nine-year-old, it is his desire for increased social group activity. The early childhood stage has now been passed, and the individual begins to assume the social outlooks of future adulthood. This is a time for increased fine-muscle coordination and development. Activity is the hallmark, and there are no lengths to which the youngster will not go to test and explore his physical capacity to endure. Eye-hand coordination becomes more pronounced as skill and practice occupy a greater proportion of the child's free time. Most of his recreational activity is with members of his own sex, but under certain conditions he will socialize

[3] Durost, W. N., "Children's Collecting Activity Related to Social Factors," *Teachers College Contribution to Education*, no. 537 (1932).

with girls. In many respects he reflects a miniature image of the adult world. Ever active, he is a sparkplug bursting with energy and ready for anything.

Because of better coordination and almost complete command of finger movement, more intricate crafts skills can be introduced to the child at this age. Both boys and girls are quite adept at manipulation of tools and small objects. It is not unusual at this time for children to be interested and active in drawing, painting, and clay modeling with emphasis upon complicated details. Craft construction may take the form of fabricating flying models of airplanes or other automotive forms. Woodworking with tools appeals to boys, while girls prefer jewelry making, needlework, and painting.

The Child from Ten to Twelve

Children between the ages of ten and twelve have begun to turn to their peers for a wide variety of activities. This is the age of club or gang membership. This is still a time for secret societies, devotion until death, and a staking out of the group's domain. Of course, this is also a time for divided loyalties, hurt feelings, and the temporary withdrawal from the group which is smoothed over and reconciled overnight.

Generally, children of this age group have achieved good neuromuscular development. Much of their physical activity calls for agility, strength, competitiveness, skill, and regulation. The rules are almost as important as the game, and a great deal of time is spent discussing whether or not a rule was broken during the course of the game. Almost any competitive activity requiring a high degree of skill in which rules are a constant source of reference will be of interest to this age group.[4]

There will be "late bloomers" among this group, some that have not yet attained the fine neuromuscular coordination that is normally accepted for this age. However, most children will be able to compete favorably with their peers, and fierce competition results in interminable practice sessions to develop the degree of skill which the child feels is necessary.

The attention span of children in this category has increased to the extent where he is content to watch without desiring to participate. He has developed an appreciation for the efforts of others and now remarks knowledgeably about the skills involved in performance or silently observes performances as an entertaining medium. Span of attention also permits greater involvement with complicated activities requiring care and attention to design, detail, and cooperation. Group projects often develop, with each member contributing to the whole. Because they offer opportunities for the gradual development of social group interaction and mutual concern, crafts activities have proved to be outstanding organizational forms for initiating close cooperation with others so that mutually beneficial outcomes are realized.

Summary of the Child from Four to Twelve

As the child's social awareness broadens with his entrance into school, new items of significance start to impinge upon his personal development. His entire visualization of himself must undergo frequent revision. Having seen himself totally through the eyes of his parents during his

[4]John P: Zubek and P. A. Solberg, *Human Development* (New York: McGraw-Hill Book Company, 1954), p. 345.

first few years of life, it is understandable that he will view himself with their prejudice. As he enters school, he comes under the scrutiny of those who are not automatically biased in his favor. He must now be concerned with attitudes and analyses of his teachers, classmates, and other acquaintances. The attitude of his parents toward him will undergo modifications, and this will also serve to demolish the structure upon which his earlier self-concept was founded. As he grows older, the child's personality assumes a more settled pattern, exhibiting less flexibility than formerly. Whatever personality traits characterized the individual will not be changed whether such traits contribute to peer and group acceptance or not.

As the child continues to spend more time with his peers, he increasingly recognizes the fact that specific personality traits are admired and others are rejected by the peer group. Social opinion thus plays an important role in influencing the older child's personality. The child attempts to adapt his personality to suit the pattern which is admired in hopes of gaining the recognition and status which he desires. Children's ideas of acceptable personality traits change with age, and this is reflected in a hardening pattern of individuality. Whatever else he is or does to conform to the social pressures of his environment, the child is an individual with certain needs, attitudes, and ambitions already crystallized by his first twelve years.

The Thirteen- to Sixteen-Year-Old
New interests develop throughout the adolescent years in consequence of the enormous changes made during the process of maturation. The onset of puberty with physical and hormonal modification and development and a heightened sense of status within social groups establishes emotional tensions. Adolescent interests may be looked upon as an attempt to throw off the previously held role of child and assume more adult activities. Thus, personal interests are likely to center upon their rapidly changing physique and accompanying bodily modifications. There will be greater appreciation for the individual's appearance as there is increasing acceptance of social amenities between the sexes and between the adolescent and adults. At the same time, there is increasingly a desire for autonomy as the independence which first appeared during the closing stages of childhood now manifests itself strongly.

Recreational interests also undergo changes during adolescence. While a great deal of energy is still expended in competitive physical activities, there appears to be more selectivity toward activities. Young adolescent males show a marked inclination for shop crafts, while females show an interest in sewing, knitting, and cooking. Both boys and girls enjoy art activities, insofar as drawing and painting are concerned, but tend to be reticent about such productions.

Sexual interests are awakened during this postpubertal period. However, despite the need for recognition by the opposite sex, young adolescent boys and girls are rather timid when this desire is fulfilled. There still seems to be an attempt to reduce such shyness by group activities, but in the main most youngsters use the group situation to hide self-consciousness. It is only during the close of early adolescence that pairing off becomes characteristic.

The changes that are seen in personality patterns result, at least in part, from social pressures that are brought to bear on the individual. There are specific personality traits for both sexes which receive acceptance or rejection. In his need to gain recognition by the social group of which he is a part, the adolescent attempts to develop personality traits that will establish him within the group. Undoubtedly, most of the factors which influence personality development during the years of childhood will be the same for the adolescent. The significant difference, however, comes in terms of the stress placed upon particular behaviors. As the individual matures, it is found that childhood patterns which once were of dominant influence tend to diminish in adolescence while formerly apparently unimportant factors assume important positions of influence.[5]

The Seventeen- to Twenty-Year-Old

The years between seventeen and twenty are years of change. Adjustments must be made to an increasing adult role in society. The problems which seemed insurmountable to the early adolescent are now easily resolved. Perhaps the essential problem revolves around social adjustment. Physical growth that began with a spurt at the onset of puberty slows down dramatically during late adolescence. Whatever increases there are in height or weight become barely noticeable. Thus, integration of functions is enabled to be accomplished more swiftly, surely, and with a coordination that finally rids that individual of the awkwardness displayed during early adolescence.

During late adolescence selectivity of activities and acquaintances is even more pronounced than before. There will be fewer friends who may be termed intimate, while a broadened circle of social acquaintances is usual. The individual begins to assert himself insofar as personal recognition is desired. He sees himself as having a distinct contribution to make in his group as a personality, and his efforts attempt to reveal himself as distinctive from everybody else. Independence from adult authority is a particular issue, and every opportunity to rebel will be exploited.

Late adolescence is the age when the complete range of socially acceptable behavioral patterns for both sexes is imposed. Thus, there is a marked difference in behavior between boys and girls. Males begin to take an interest in personal health, vocational choices, civic activities, learning, and recreational experiences. Girls reveal greater interest in personal attractiveness, social adjustment, and life style. The desire for independence comes to a peak during late adolescence.

The recreational interests of the late adolescent appear to be even more restricted than previously. More time is spent on fewer activities. There is a gradual decline in participation in strenuous physical activity

[5] H. R. Stolz and L. M. Stolz, "Adolescent Problems Related to Somatic Variations," *43rd Yearbook National Society for the Study of Education* (1944), pp. 80-99.

and greater inclination to be passive spectators. Unless the individual excels in a particular sport or game form and there is peer pressure or other opportunity to participate, there is less likelihood of increased physical activity. Social activities, intellectual activities, and some hobby forms appeal to adolescents. Those who participate in hobbies tend to seek construction experience. Reading also becomes an extremely pleasurable form of activity. A whole range of entertainments opens for late adolescents as they have more money and greater discretion in the expenditure of money on activities which they find enjoyable. Attendance at dances, concerts, movies, theatre, and the like are popular.

Adulthood

What occurs to interests as the individual progresses through the varied opportunities provided by school and leisure to the stressful adjustments which the adult assumes? The need to earn a living invariably forces a diminishing of recreational activity. There is a consequent narrowing of interests, although younger adults have a more varied series of recreational experiences than do older adults.[6] Almost all participation in strenuous physical activity shows decline, while nonfiction reading and attendance at spectator performances appear to increase with age.

Up to a particular point, participation in hobbies seems to increase with age. Apparently hobbies offer an intense satisfaction, challenge, and enrichment lacking in other forms of recreational experience. Hobbies are thus likely to offer opportunities for satisfying basic needs when other forms of involvement are no longer open or accessible. Of great interest to the programmer is the increase in interest of crafts activities which occur throughout the life span, but are quite noticeable as spurts of interest after age fifty and again after age sixty-five. Among the crafts most defined are those which are useful or serve a practical purpose. Thus, automotive or mechanical repairing and tinkering, electric wiring, gardening, woodworking, sewing, cooking, bookbinding, and furniture remodeling are among the crafts forms frequently mentioned in studies which survey the recreational outlets of adults.[7]

Interests are largely determined by social influences, cultural expectations, opportunities available, and the physical capacity and mental ability of individuals. Moreover, they mirror desire, needs, and drives, representing fundamental outlets of satisfaction, either directly or vicariously. Striking differences exist among the interest patterns of individuals, each with his own special and unique model of personal-environmental relationships. The relative stability of interest patterns over the years is evident. While change is rapid in the years from childhood to adolescence, certain general orientations may be noted as having been established by age nine or earlier. By late adolescence interests have become crystalized to the extent that they are measurable for guidance purposes.

The fundamental relationship between broad and varied activities and good personal adjustment throughout the life span is well researched

[6] G. H. Johnson, "General Backgrounds and Activities of Teachers," *School and Society*, vol. 77 (1953), pp. 129 - 132
[7] J. T. Landis, "Hobbies and Happiness in Old Age," *Recreation*, vol. 35 (1942), p. 607.

and substantiated. Recreational activities of all kinds offer enriched living potential and amply demonstrate the need to cultivate constructive and purposeful experiences of this nature. The child is a product of his nature and nurture. He must have wise parental guidance so that the development of satisfying interests will emerge with development and permit the individual to invest his time creatively, pleasurably, and ethically. The intelligent adult should attempt to develop a life style offering the depth, range, and intensity that will fulfill personal satisfactions and a sense of achievement despite the exigencies and ills of life. In this way basic needs can be satisfied. The entire problem of good personal adjustment to life in relation to individual interests and capabilities has become of such significance that governmental agencies have properly been appointed to assist such adjustment and take responsibility for providing the opportunities for growth and learning. As leisure becomes increasingly prevalent, more people will be afforded ample opportunity to participate in recreational experiences of various types. Among these, crafts may be an appropriate avenue for finding individual achievement, enjoyment, acceptable social activity, creativity, constructive outlets, and the resources for satisfaction of a basic human need.

MOTIVATION FOR PARTICIPATION

The drives of human behavior also motivate recreational engagement. They are the human needs, wants, desires, and emotions. Both children and adults are activated by some impelling desire or compelling force. They are motivated through a complex behavioral pattern by a conscious or innate striving until the objective is attained and the urge is satisfied. Some behavioral patterns are of short duration; others are prolonged and may be of a lifetime's duration. Creative activities motivate behavior by stimulating the senses. As Mearns has written:

All our adult ways of interacting one with another, in short, call on the creative spirit, and our life is artistic or dull in proportion to our creative gifts. But adults are in the main wingless; convention, tribal taboos, mechanistic living; long years of schooling, something has stilled the spirit within or walled it securely. It is to children we must go to see the creative spirit at its best, and only to those children who are in some measure uncoerced. . . . This then is the torrential force that comes unbidden out of the mysterious recesses of personality and fashions things out of wood, color, fabric, clay, and words. . . . Children seem to be driven by an inner necessity of putting forth something; that it shall turn out to be beautiful is not their concern; their impulse at its best is to place something in the outside world that is already (or almost ready) in their inside world of perceiving, thinking, feeling; they measure their success or failure by the final resemblance of the thing done to the thing imagined. And in their best moments they seem to know exactly what to do; the muscles ripple in perfect harmony to the right touch, line, blow; in painting the brush is swung fearlessly and surely, in pottery the punches and patches are thumbed without hesitation. In this regard they are in tune again with the professional artist. Experience has loosened his fears, his trusts, his instinct for level, balance, and swift adjustings of the medium and his materials to satisfy those flashing demands from within.[8]

Readiness to Learn The readiness to learn is an equally important source of behavioral motivation. When the need to know is such that it stimulates activity on the part of the learner, it may be said that such learning will not be frustrated until the need is satisfied. A specific maturation in development is reached. Energy outputs attain higher levels. Focus of attention is sharpened. Curiosity is released, and the individual pursues his desire with a single-minded purpose until he succeeds in mastering the idea, skill, or information. When learning is self-activated, the individual is interested in what he is doing and attempts, by whatever means are at his disposal, to undertake those experiences which will provide optimum enjoyment from achievement.

Attitudes Attitudes and interests are heavily weighted with strivings and affective factors that appear to hide cognitive elements to a certain extent. Attitudes are developed and modified by home influences and peer and social pressure groups. Favorable attitudes do much to motivate behavior. Appropriate incentives may activate behavioral patterns which can develop healthy and favorable attitudes toward specific activities. Incentives are those extrapersonal elements that spur the individual on and arouse a latent or previously nonexistent desire to perform. Incentives that appeal to the ego or self-interest are most often effective. The utilization of incentives should always be under ethical control of the crafts instructor so that behavior is channeled to those behaviors which are socially acceptable and constructive for the individual or the community as a whole. Incentives may be impersonal or personal. With very few exceptions, impersonal incentives should never be used. They are of a tangible and invariably of a meaningless form. Personal incentives, on the other hand, are those inner satisfactions received from a job well done, a sense of achievement, self-expression, approval, recognition, and a feeling of enjoyment or fulfillment when the goal is attained. The most appropriate incentives are those which serve to stimulate these feelings which in turn tend to motivate reinforcing and consistent behavior.

Knowledge of Progress Perhaps of singular importance is the individual's own knowledge of his progress which tends to stimulate and extend the behavioral pattern. An individual's knowledge of his own achievement may serve to motivate him toward further goals. This technique is well within the command of instructors to the extent that obvious indicators, such as completed projects, skill with media and tools, appreciation of aesthetics, and understanding of design, utility, and decoration, form a part of the verifiable elements involved. Subjectively the individual knows when he has made progress in terms of preset estimates or expectations.

[8] H. Mearns, "The Creative Spirit and Its Significance for Education," in G. Hartman and A. Schumaker (eds.), *Creative Expression* (Eau Claire, Wis.: E. M. Hale and Co., 1932), pp. 13-17.

An individual can see whether or not he is performing correctly by virtue of the designs, objects, or understandings produced. The individual undergoing some aspect of growth and development as a craftsman is aware of particular achievements as they occur. For that person the process often becomes the significant factor rather than the technique involved in solving a problem or finishing an item. The satisfaction derived from knowing that one is capable of performance is sometimes more rewarding to the individual than any performance can be.

Tangible evidence of mastery comes about when the methods of work become smoother and well coordinated. Shaping and molding materials to a desired size, design, or consistency also afford satisfaction. The well-planned program will permit opportunities for growth and exploration by offering the participant a chance to continue. The entire concept of gradation is formulated on the proposition that people will be motivated to activity if and when they are confident of their ability to achieve. They also know that they may remain in the same activity until they feel that their skill is such as to enable them to take on the next set of opportunities that promote mastery. Surely, the crafts instructor must recognize the means whereby people of differing abilities, backgrounds, and levels of skill may be motivated to perform. One of the techniques which can be used positively to encourage participation and stimulate or renew interest is the concomitantly programmed graded levels of crafts activities which tend to supply the individual with the support or status that one seeks in such participation.

Personal Interests   Psychological studies have indicated that there are general tendencies toward which people of various ages, socioeconomic, educational, vocational, cultural, and other groupings veer insofar as personal interests are concerned. For this reason, program planning may be based upon certain interests which people are presumed to have. However, programming is never imposed upon the group to be served. There is more to programming than the superimposition of a crafts instructor's ideas upon those who are looked upon as potential students. Essentially, the inventory of general interests which are assumed to be a part of every individual's make-up is utilized as a point of departure for the initiation of activities. To the extent that such interests are actually present and capable of attracting participation when established within a program, the crafts instructor can provide clear and present opportunities to stimulate interest.

Because of his special knowledge of the age-group characteristics, growth, and developmental needs of individuals, the crafts instructor can assume that certain interests are present and that at a particular age level individuals have attained a physical, social, or intellectual ability to participate in specific activity forms. In some instances, individuals will express without equivocation their desire to perform or engage in activities. By trying out the suggestions of those who express interest, there is great likelihood that the crafts instructor will better be able to serve his students. Where individuals express interest but perform in a perfunctory manner, exhibit boredom, or where attendance is sporadic, the crafts instructor can conclude that the expressed interest may have been something less, could have been used to gain attention, or could have implied a desire for experiences of a similar type, but not necessarily the kind which were suggested.

As in many situations, the expression of interest in a given activity may merely cover the individual's real desire for social acceptance, for broadened experiences within the community, to seek mastery of a skill and thereby gain ego-satisfaction, or show a desire to be innovative and independent. The crafts instructor who understands the clues which people offer in their attempts to adjust to or cope with their respective environments may be better equipped to assist those who come to him in finding the means of satisfying felt needs through meaningful and valuable experiences.

Stimulating Interest   There are a variety of ways in which the crafts instructor can stimulate interest and motivate performance. He may bring to the class samples of crafts at the level which the group should be able to perform. He may introduce students to a highly skilled craftsman whose special technique may fascinate and attract their interest. He may arrange for the group to see exhibits and demonstrations or through visitation expose the group to activities which can arouse curiosity and/or a desire to try a project. Members of the group may be the very reservoir of talent which the instructor needs to stir excitement and create demands for activity. Some students are bound to have abilities which give them satisfaction and pleasure as they perform. These individuals may be the active stimulant which, by personal enthusiasm, can create attention and tempt others to try that particular interest. Nothing stimulates a group as much as a hobbyist. While students may not be prepared to adopt or even try to engage in the hobby immediately, they often can be introduced and exposed to the potential of the activity where before there was no basis on which to judge. When people see others apparently having an enjoyable time doing some activity, their curiosity may be awakened as to why the activity should elicit such a response. The instructor must recognize curiosity as a first step in motivating individuals.

Building Confidence   Some people are hesitant about joining a group or class because they feel less capable of performing well. Nobody wants to be made uncomfortable by having to participate in activities where knowledge or skill is the single distinguishing criterion. All people feel more comfortable in situations and activities which are familiar. The crafts instructor must assure novices that they will not have to compete to participate. Further, each student should understand that all the others, with the exception of the instructor, are learners, too. To build confidence and help the individual who wants to participate, but hesitates because of inability or lack of skill, the crafts instructor will schedule practice sessions for those who consider such assistance necessary. To prevent any individual embarrassment at having to attend tutorials, the instructor may very well introduce a plan of practice so that everyone can improve.

Depending upon the maturity, education, previous experience, and other such factors which students display, the crafts instructor can adjust his presentation. If the group is mature and has had previous experience with the activity, there is little reason why intricate or complicated crafts activities cannot be offered. When the group is immature or has had little or no experience, it is better for the instructor to simplify the processes involved, take the group step by step through the methods of activity, and attempt to lead and guide students by example. Crafts should be analyzed by the instructor so that their components may be treated separately. A very difficult project may be effectively broken down into comparatively simple phases, enabling the student to perform in a satisfying manner. Initially, exposure to crafts activities should be such that the student can easily complete the project within the single session. As the individual's interest is continuously aroused, more prolonged crafts projects may be attempted. The desire to finish a project, especially if it involves an endearing item, will draw the student over and over again. In this way, he is led progressively to more skilled levels of performance, better technical proficiency, and a deeper understanding and appreciation for the medium and the processes which transform the object to a desired shape, size, or design.

Continuing Progress   As the individual begins to gain command of appropriate tools and materials and tastes success in manipulating plastic objects, he may start to experience a desire to broaden his newly found knowledge and skill. The program should be designed for just this purpose. People must be permitted to work intensely as well as inclusively. This permits the development of latent talent, enhances self-expression, and gives range and scope to ideas which were formerly limited. The scheduling of learning or activity sessions should be such as to promote a feeling of progress and achievement within the performer. The individual should have some objective in view. But the attainment of the objective must not be permitted to conclude interest in continuing on with the activity. By enabling the student to progress from beginner to expert over a given period of time, the crafts instructor can add immeasurably to innate satisfactions and enjoyment received from an interest that will carry over for a lifetime. There is a crafts activity for people of every age group, skill level, level of appreciation, and physical or mental limitation. Crafts represent a series of varied activities and experiences which by their own distinctive design, color, shape, size, or material consistency have the capacity to focus attention and stimulate effort. The energy expended in such experiences is negligible in comparison with the self-fulfillment, confidence, and happiness received by those who desire this participation.

EXPERIENCE, TALENT, AND SKILL

Any community crafts program must provide for the discovery of potential talent and the development of latent or obvious skills and must offer experiences to those with previous exposure to specific training. When such a program is formulated, it may then serve the greatest number of people by offering the widest possible opportunities and choices for participation. In order for a crafts program to reach a maximum number of people and afford the widest range of opportunities, there should be provision made for every skill, talent, or education which people have. Provision should also be made for those without any previous experience or specific skill or whose talent is a negligible quality.

Relating Activities to Experience
Successful planning for recreational or educational crafts activities concerns the selection or modification of experiences to the level of skill immediately held by those who desire to participate. Initiating a crafts group of inexperienced persons to methods, materials, and tools beyond their ability to appreciate or perform only leads to frustration. In like manner, an introduction of fundamentals to experienced craftsmen can lead to boredom and a disinclination to take part. Just as people are likely to become discouraged when they undertake activities which prove too difficult for them and in which there is little probability of success the opposite situation among the highly skilled conduces to ennui.

Crafts activities must be offered which elicit varying degrees of skill so that everyone who is interested may find a level at which he can involve himself successfully. As individuals develop greater skill, gradation permits them to seek out and join groups engaging in the activity at a more advanced stage. By no means should the crafts instructor attempt to plan activities to meet the needs of a single group to the exclusion of everybody else. This can in no way lead to the comprehensive program designed to account for all those who might possibly be interested in a crafts activity. Such practice will definitely hinder the impact of the all-inclusive crafts program within the community at large. While age-group classification may be a necessity in the schoolroom situation, where the teacher is dealing with a restricted age range, there is no need to foster the same thinking in the wider community beyond the school curriculum.

Development of Skills
Skill development is required if the individual is to attain command of materials and the necessary control of tools which require manipulation so that expression is possible. For this reason some instructional process must be offered or undertaken if the individual, whether child or adult, is to grow into a skilled performer. Instruction, then, is not designed to teach creativity, but rather its purpose is to foster the possibility of future creativity on the part of the student. Instruction prepares the individual by developing the particular and special skills that can find outlet in creative work. Through direct experiences with materials, fundamental understandings of design, color, tools, and discussion of aesthetic values, individuals are assisted in recognizing beauty.

Aesthetic objectives cannot be realized by directed learning experiences unless the individual's creative behavior is to be aesthetically rehabilitated so that his artistic taste and skill will improve. It is the responsibility of the instructor to assist the individual, child or adult, in realizing where suitability lies in the use of materials. Further the instructor can help the individual to achieve his idea creatively, thereby obtaining aesthetic satisfaction through the manipulation of media. A basic tenet for such directed learning is that the instructor offers assistance at the current level of intellectual and physical ability to perform.

Nature of Talent

Crafts certainly furnish a desirable outlet for individual self-expression and self-realization for those who participate. They are a valuable means of recreational activity for those who have learned to appreciate their potential. For the novice, practice of a crafts activity often leads not merely to personal satisfaction, but on occasion to skills beyond the dreams of those who first undertook it by chance or choice. Although little is known about what constitutes talent in the various art forms, there is a tendency on the part of instructors to indicate their ability to recognize talent. Sometimes what appears to be talent is nothing more or less than a superficial facility. This may cause the instructor to spend an inordinate amount of time with the individual who shows such facility to the detriment of the rest of the group. Facility comes about because of exposure, practice, or maturity. It may be cultivated, as with any other skill, but it should not be confused with talent.

Talent is a natural ability or power which confers on the individual a special or superior ability to perform. In some instances of genius, it may spring full blown upon a ready world, needing but a few refinements to reveal it in its glory.[9] In other cases, talent implies a natural endowment for a particular pursuit which must be developed by hard study and prolonged practice before the performer is ready to reveal himself. Unlike a gift, talent must be cultivated in order to attain the full scope and range of ability. The gifted are already capable without having to resort to practice.

Talent may be latent or overt. Where it is revealed, as in actual performance or product produced by the individual, the instructor should encourage its development by every ethical means possible. For in this way the individual may be brought to the realization of self-expression that can be truly phenomenal. No less is this true for hidden talent. The individual who participates because of interest or stimulation and finds, to his delight, that he has an unexpected facility which enables him to innovate or at least reproduce well-designed objects should be judiciously guided along the paths of craftsmanship until, by repetition and constant exposure, a highly skilled performer develops. Between these two positions, the individual with latent talent may never perfect it unless there is some opportunity to have it exposed. The crafts instructor should enter the situation with the assumption that everybody has some talent, regardless of degree, and that it should be enhanced for the pleasure and self-realization it may bring to the possessor. Of course, the instructor may be inaccurate in his assessment. Perhaps the individual has talent, but not in the crafts. Something may still be taught to the individual without talent,

[9]Frederic V. Grunfeld, ". . . the most gifted human being that has ever been born," *Horizon,* vol. 13, no. 4 (Autumn, 1971), pp. 97-103.

if only of appreciation for the skill, the process, or the product involved. However, when the instructor can discover talent for crafts, he should do whatever he can to stimulate and promote practice until the individual has the confidence and skill level to continue on his own.

For the diverse levels of skills found in individuals, whatever reasons they have for engaging in crafts, there must be an organized structure through which experience, skill, or talent may receive optimum appreciation. Levels of performance attained, simple intent or interest, desire to learn something new—all require an environment which protects the inept while it promotes the advanced. Such structure may well be the graded series of crafts activities based upon the leadership available, financial support provided, community interest shown, and facility accessibility to accommodate the program.

CLASSIFICATION FOR LEARNING AND PERFORMANCE
Age Groups

Activities may be organized around age groups, ability to learn, or current performance. Age differences have been defined and characterized elsewhere, but the obvious reason for segregation by age group is the distinct physical and mental capacity of the individuals involved. Simple physical coordination required for the manipulation of certain tools may be absent or undeveloped in children, while adolescents and adults have already mastered the fine-muscle qualities vital for control of tools and intricate movements. Attention span is another factor that would preclude the mixing of the very young with older individuals. Young children do not have the span of concentration required for prolonged activities. For this reason the matter at hand, whether of subject, object, or requiring explanation, may be too difficult for the child to grasp. The material and the crafts process should be geared to the level at which the individual functions. Precocious children, sophisticated in understanding and manipulatory powers beyond their chronologic age, are rare. There might be some justification for permitting a young child with superior performance levels to enter a group of older persons if there were no other way in which the child could be served. However, the age variation might prove so uncomfortable, to both the child and the older persons, that any benefit would be lost. It might be better, certainly more expedient, to retain the child with his age-group peers, but provide more sophisticated and specialized instruction on an individual basis.

Skill Levels

Age-group categorization may be one method by which performers can be classified for instruction purposes, but age alone is not the single determinant. Within the age group there will be varying levels of skill, experience, and ability to perform. Thus, there may very well be the organization of at least three, and perhaps four, basic crafts groupings to account for variations in personal skill and experience. Together with age groupings, this can constitute a large number of crafts classes.

The practicality of any one agency, be it a school system, public recreational service department, or other public or private agency, having the personnel capacity to accommodate the diverse age and skill or experience levels is questionable. At best, for example, the school system will certainly be able to accommodate the children who make up its student body, for this is the way that the school is organized. However, extracurricular crafts activities may prove more difficult of organization if many children of different age ranges wish to participate. After school programs would have to be arranged much like regular school classes. This difficulty is not insoluble as the school treats high school youth. There, age differences become less a matter of physical coordination, but more of a social problem. It could only be presumed that those youth who were interested in crafts activities would subordinate their desire for "fooling around" to their crafts interest and not disrupt the interest group with rambunctious or immature behavior.

When the school also provides adult education programs during the late afternoon or evening hours, the social mixture and problems of juvenile behavior would be omitted. Here, the criteria for classification and separation, if such were necessary, might be based almost exclusively on level of skill and experience. Some older adolescents, young adults, and older adults might conceivably be grouped together without undue strain on any student with the central interest of crafts performance at a particular level being the central focus of attention. In such instances, there would hardly be any suggestion of personal embarrassment or social discomfort insofar as age differential were concerned.

It is only when there is an extreme difference in the ages of would-be students that activity disruption, personal discomfort, or socially embarrassing situations might occur. It is primarily for this reason that age groupings are suggested for classification.

Grouping Problems

A far greater difficulty is perceived for the public recreational service agency. Its primary function is to provide recreational opportunities to all the people within its constituency, regardless of age. Now the recreational service department could organize crafts classes much like the school system. While the school system may have the necessary teaching personnel to offer differentiated crafts classes by age and skill level, the public department of recreational service rarely has sufficient numbers of crafts specialists, or even volunteers, so that it can schedule the necessary crafts activities. Under these circumstances, the recreational service department does what it can with the limited personnel at its disposal. This may mean that many people who might want to participate in crafts are not provided with the opportunities for engagement.

The department of recreational service might have every intention of fulfilling its mission and responsibility, but restricted funds, lack of competent personnel, or other limiting factors might preclude that effort. This is not to say that no public recreational service department can satisfy the crafts needs and interests of its constituency. There are several public departments which have extensive crafts programs, catering to every imaginable skill level and age group. Unfortunately, such departments are in a distinct minority. If public recreational service departments had the funds, they could certainly assume a greater share of their own responsibility for supplying recreational opportunities, in the form of crafts, to the citizens residing in the community. Those departments which perform an outstanding job, at least in the area of crafts activity provision, do so by employing crafts specialists who organize, teach, and disseminate information about crafts opportunities and satisfactions. Such specialists not only instruct students on a face-to-face basis but are also utilized to upgrade technical competencies of other employees of the agency so that a wider range of coverage can be given to the community. Furthermore, many laymen are enlisted in the campaign to supply qualified instructional personnel to groups of people who express the desire to engage in crafts. This may be performed on a neighborhood, district, community, or city-wide basis.

Finally, classification is essentially brought about by the level of skill or capacity to perform which the individual has attained. For this reason, crafts activities may be broken down into three or four categories, for example, beginner, intermediate, advanced, and expert. Except for gifted children, there seems little likelihood of the necessity for such classification among young children. It is more probable that they will be tyros requiring fundamental introduction to and basic instruction in learning to appreciate crafts forms, materials, simple tools, and so forth. It is only as the individual matures and is continually encouraged to engage in arts and crafts activities that skills begin to appear. It may even be feasible to work out some interior arrangement whereby each category is further ramified. Thus, individuals of an intermediate class could be looked upon as beginning, intermediate, or advanced within the range of crafts skills, ability to manipulate tools, conception of design, appreciation of aesthetics, and other criteria which would constitute the type of crafts and the elements involved with that category. Such distinctions might result from age differentials, previous experiences, maturation rates, and other measurable factors.

Depending upon the adequacy of instructional personnel, the numbers of people interested and engaged in crafts, and the space or facilities available to accommodate them, the crafts program could be capable of supporting interested people. By scheduling crafts activities during the leisure available to potential students, the crafts program would be operating from early morning until late at night—possibly 365 days per year. Any restrictions of service would be in the form of financial support, spaces to be used, and the influence which money has on all the factors constituting a successful crafts program.

When all these elements are examined—age, skill, interest, and experience—it is probable that classification of individuals within the crafts program may be achieved without difficulty. The greatest drawback comes from extraneous aspects, not from a disinclination on the part of the general public to participate. Such requirements as money, personnel, materials, equipment, and facilities (although the latter is not vital) may either vitiate the promotion of crafts performance or vitalize it. Little hardship is involved in determining whether an individual should be in one crafts class as opposed to another, although there may be some social implications influencing real choices. The individual usually recognizes his own abilities and limitations. There may be a few who overestimate themselves, but even these have a tendency to sort themselves out after a brief bout with frustration.

The chief factors with which the crafts instructor may have to deal are interest and ambition. Perhaps the prospective student has an overwhelming desire to participate in a facet of the program for which he is ill-prepared. Through judicious counseling that individual may be guided to a more acceptable skill level for him. The promise, however, is explicit. To the extent that the individual's ambition equals his learning ability and performance level, he will progress to whatever goals he is capable of reaching. This is really the crucial need for gradation in crafts or any other recreational activity. There is the personal and satisfying reward of the end in view—master craftsmanship. This lure or stimulation impels the individual on to further his control of media and skill with ideas and objects. The student may justifiably look forward to a lifetime of pleasurable experiences which enhance his realization of self as he becomes involved within the crafts process.

FROM NOVICE TO SKILLED PERFORMER

Although children appear to be naturally curious and seem to want to explore the world about them, not every child can or wants to manipulate materials. Those who claim that artistic capability is inherent in every child are simply perpetuating a popular myth. There are many children who will explore their environment and express themselves through adapted arts and crafts activities. However, it is fruitless to assume that the craving to know the world around them is a sign of latent artistic attribution. More probably, when the child is conditioned from an early age to seek expression through aesthetic devices, he will grow to enjoy such expression. This early pleasurable experience can, indeed, lead to later development of artistic tendencies and creativity.

Most people come into contact with crafts forms at an early age. They learn to handle and manipulate a variety of toys, some of which may be suggestive of real tools or actually tools scaled down to child size. In this way does the child typically come to associate crafts with the pleasurable sensation of hammering, sawing, constructing, etc. If this interest is cultivated, the individual may find a significant outlet for satisfying expressions and realizing a method of personal fulfillment. Kraus has written that

Arts and crafts activities fill the important need of all human beings to explore their own resources, to manipulate the environment, and to create something that is beautiful, personally expressive, decorative, or useful. While every individual certainly does not have the capacity to become an artist in the sense of becoming a highly professional and technically skilled creator of outstanding art products, he certainly can make a personal expression that is valid for himself and can uncover heretofore untapped talents and abilities. In addition, he can and should begin to develop his own aesthetic judgment, and heighten his own interest in the arts and his sensitivity to them—an important component of the fully rounded individual in our culture.[10]

Every instructor who specializes in crafts activities should have a thorough understanding of the psychological, physical, intellectual, social, and cultural stages which individuals pass through as they mature from early childhood to old age. In this way crafts instructors are more likely to better enable the individual to move from initial and simple efforts to those of great complexity and lasting value. Thus, a crafts program may be implemented in any community by starting with young children and introducing an activity consisting of inexpensive and simple crafts. For the most part these will be standard experiences of paper craft, clay modeling, block printing, mobiles, stenciling, finger painting, beadwork, needlework, and many others that have stood the test of time for popularity. Such activities can be offered easily without recourse to specialized facilities or great financial outlay.

Simple Craft Needs

Almost any practical space will accommodate the simplified crafts. Indoor areas, whether in a classroom, a corner of the auditorium, or a spacious closet, will serve. Such areas must, of course, permit illumination, floor space, and sink with water tap. Tables are really not necessary for simple crafts, although they may make for a more comfortable working arrangement. Outdoor areas require the availability of water, work tables, and a storage cart for easy handling of materials.

As successful outcomes and enjoyment lead to the growth and development of individuals in the crafts process, greater desire to learn more about crafts will be generated. As the individuals mature and gain appreciation for media and tools, additional groups will have to be formed. All such groups will be ongoing enterprises with individuals passing from one classification to the next in a logical growth pattern based upon developing skills, ability to perform, and maturity. There may be initiated at least four beginning crafts classifications, each encompassing a specific age group. While crafts experiences for the very young might be concerned with basic understanding of color, tool designation, media, and easy-to-perform activities, the crafts experiences for older children, adolescents, young adults, and adults would be reflective of their capacities to perform and would have to consider any previous experience with crafts.

Of greater likelihood and practicality, the products of instructional classes in arts and crafts will require a more sophisticated facility in which the developing or proved skills can be performed with optimum satisfac-

[10]Richard Kraus, *Recreation Today: Program Planning and Leadership* (New York: Appleton-Century-Crofts, 1966), p. 215.

tion. As individuals gain skill, more possibilities are opened to them in terms of intricate and technical projects, and there is increasing need for particular kinds of tools and/or machinery and a wider range of crafts experiences where advanced activities can be implemented. Skills calling for effort in the plastic and graphic arts and crafts, initially through uncomplicated forms, may become the foundation upon which ambition and desire to fabricate intensify. Thus, from the simple experiences, more complex crafts forms are attempted. As the individual grows surer in his tool manipulation, more appreciative of physical dimensions, proportion, and texture, and finally creative in his own right, the crafts process will be pronounced successful. Progressing from the simple to the complex crafts activities can serve as the skein of continuity which permits fulfillment of certain human needs.

Once preliminary explorations have been made by the student and some learning has been achieved, the enjoyment of handicrafts and immersion within the crafts process may lead to undreamed-of levels of skill, personal perception, and an activity that can enhance individual existence throughout life. To be sure, there must be present the necessary space, tools, equipment, and materials for such progression to occur. One cannot expect to attain high skill levels by discussion. Practice is required. Only when the facilities for practice are available does realization of potential become apparent.

Opportunity for All
To the extent that crafts may be performed throughout the year, both indoors and outside and appeal to all age groups and both sexes and beginners and experts alike, it is imperative that an ongoing program of wide-ranging crafts opportunities be organized to provide the environment for those who wish to participate. Additionally, the concept of graded activities should be initiated so that personal growth and achievement can be stimulated at every level of performance. The democratically oriented recreational program is based on the premise of voluntary activity. It is not likely that autocratic imposition of ideas for crafts will attract very many participants. For the fact that recreational participation is within the purview of the individual who is so inclined, the attendance at activities is an effective measurement of how well the activity is meeting the needs of potential students. Any attempt to dictate to potential students will probably be rebuffed—as indicated by attendance figures.

Nevertheless, almost every novice, of whatever age, is willing to learn from those who are more experienced and skilled. That is why students come to the activity in the first place. They want a sampling of the kinds of experiences they can expect. They also want to know how they will be treated as individuals and the degree of pleasantness which is associated with the activity. For these reasons, the instructor organizing a crafts program must consider the ideas of those who want to participate. Sometimes there is a tendency on the part of the expert to assume that nobody else has valid ideas. There might be some validity in such a concept, but it is hardly conducive to the promotion of activities where people want to socialize, exchange thoughts, and also learn skills. When dealing with people, the expert should listen respectfully to ideas that are generated. It may be necessary to point out difficulties to be encountered if particular avenues are followed, but that is one of the functions of the instructor—to give counsel and guidance where necessary. The instructor may have to inject his own ideas into the group situation, but such instrumentation should be done by indirection and suggestion, never by fiat.

As with all recreational activities, the less rigidity and the more spontaneity, the better for all concerned. Naturally, this will call for a highly skilled crafts instructor. Such a person will have to depend on ingenuity, resourcefulness, and a flexibility of mind that elicits admiration and response from students. It should not be supposed that such individuals are easy to employ. The highly skilled individual may not have the flexibility to adequately guide group efforts. Fortunately, a solution lies quickly to hand.

Without doubt, there are people residing in every community who have specific skills which can be utilized in a crafts program. Some people have spent a lifetime perfecting some skill—be it cookery, etching, glassblowing, or electric wiring, to cite but a few. The resourceful recreationist may not, himself, have the necessary skills or talent to instruct or guide crafts activities, but he must have information about those who do or can. This is a part of his job. It is his responsibility to compile information on people residing in the community who might, at some time, want to volunteer their services in some way. There are always people who when called upon to perform or demonstrate their skills, are eager and happy to do so. There are just as many who are resentful. The recreationist must be able to call upon the right people at the right time if the crafts program is to meet the diverse needs of the public and function successfully.

A very balanced and well-supported crafts program can be developed and kept operational by employing part-time and seasonal workers, by encouraging volunteers to come forward and organizing crafts activities around them, or by hiring many single-skilled instructors on a part-time basis instead of full-time employees. Particularly will volunteers enable the base of the program to be sufficiently broadened so that many more people of all ages and with all levels of skill can be served. The adroit crafts instructor should seize every opportunity offered to discover what people are interested in or are willing to learn. Of even greater meaning is the instructor's willingness to experiment with new ideas, activities, and groups. He must dare to travel in previously uncharted areas, perhaps making errors, but affording a wealth of satisfying and creative activities that can attract students. Such efforts are not always crowned with immediate success, but the venture provides opportunities where none existed before. This may be the single most important contribution that the crafts instructor makes.

In summing up the need for gradation in the crafts program, it might be well to include a statement of the Athletic Institute implying the innate progression which occurs in the comprehensive recreational program.

A well rounded recreational program includes arts and crafts. Every community, regardless of size, should and can organize a beneficial arts and crafts program using existing resources. Once started under good leadership, a simple program will expand through its own enthusiasm. It must be realized, however, that sound and permanent progress requires time and patience.[11]

Process- and Product-centered Activity

The development of the individual from novice to expert encounters several problems whether approached from the community or school point of view. Any instructional course, specifically those which engage beginners, will have to determine the purposes for which the activity was originally established. It is the repeated question of project- or process-oriented activity, compounded by difficulties concerning procedures and techniques. Generally, elementary or beginning crafts activities, whether in school or community, should probably concentrate on the communicative process rather than on solid outcomes. By this is meant quality of workmanship rather than quantity of output. Certainly there will be an expectation, on the part of the performer, to fabricate some material item in consequence of his efforts. However, the perfection of the finished product, at least initially, is not important. The chief focus should be on the various activities that can be clarified within the overall structure of the plan being presented.

Process permits the interplay of converging forces whereby the would-be performer is both influenced and influences the instructional environment, media, tools, and ideas. It is, in fact, a means of communication between the individual and the rest of the world. It is one method by which the individual may express himself personally without threat of recrimination or intimidation. If he succeeds, satisfaction results. If he fails, there might still be satisfaction in terms of the aesthetic statement or design even if no one appreciates it. The difficulty encountered in formally organized crafts classes is that the instructor may attempt to impose his own artistic view on the learner. Technique should develop naturally as the beginning crafts worker applies himself to the materials and achieves a sense of understanding. Technique is the personal signature of the individual and grows out of an inner need to communicate.

Schools should no more restrict the teaching of crafts to a few constantly reiterated procedures than they should concentrate on results. There are so many new materials to be studied that children may experiment almost endlessly with media that did not even exist ten years ago. The fallacy of the project-centered program comes to light when the student is forced to conform to preconceived patterns, preset periods, and syllabi that preclude all spontaneity. The individual then rarely receives

[11] The Athletic Institute, *The Recreation Program* (Chicago: The Institute, 1964), p. 42.

the time and attention required to become competent with the tools and materials introduced in the activity. The emphasis is placed on end products, not on how well the individual understands or senses relationships to media and design. Under such conditions there is little likelihood that the individual will develop a desire to continue with crafts activities. Imagination is scrupulously stifled, and this has a tendency to thwart what otherwise might have grown into lifelong pleasure.

Properly prepared for the activity, the student can be creative. He will be interested in what he does and how he does it. When the crafts activity necessitates the use of imagination, the student will make every attempt to enhance his skill with tools and materials. He will thrive on the attempt to develop a personal signature. It is not unusual to see an individual flourish in a climate of permissiveness. Some individuals become so capable of artistic judgment that their appreciation for form, function, texture, color, and the parts of objects, for example, curves, swirls, and planes, provides intense personal satisfaction. The individual whose interest has been awakened by crafts discovers harmony and logic in constructive activity, finds enjoyment in shapes, and develops an intense feeling of unity for the project on which he expends effort.

It is requisite that the crafts program strike a balance to provide recreational opportunities for all concerned. It may do this by offering simple, easy-to-finish projects, utilizing a great many materials in diverse ways. Additionally, it deepens understanding by providing sufficient time for skill development in fundamental crafts experiences. This method pursues standard activities, such as work with clay, woodwork, needlework, drawing, and printing. The student can achieve a level of skill that should permit him to execute crafts concepts without undue emphasis on having to learn how to use the tool. Instruction in tool use and how materials can be used should permit the widest latitude for creative development because design conceptualization will be the focus of attention, rather than how the tool is to be used. Perhaps Mattil has written the most practical statement:

Although there is a case for depth approaches to crafts teaching, the schools would err if crafts were limited to just a few processes. The school is one of the main instruments for the development of children's potentiality, and it is up to the school to provide the conditions that foster such development. One of the main conditions is opportunity, where materials and facilities are present to try out one's potential. Such a program allows for the opportunity to try one's ability in a variety of activities and to repeat with regularity those activities of special interest to the individual. Another condition is the presence of a mature and sensitive adult, who guides, suggests, evaluates, and encourages the child.[12]

Of course, as the individual grows older and becomes more adept at tool and media manipulation, there will be a greater desire to concen-

[12] Edward L. Mattil, *Meaning in Crafts*, 2d ed. (Englewood Cliffs, N.J.: Prentice-Hall, Inc., 1965), p. 3.

trate on the product of the crafts process. This seems to be a natural outgrowth of the individual's desire to make permanent his original idea. It is a concept which is derived from the communicative process. With maturity there comes a greater need to project oneself through some object. For the mature craftsman the process is still absorbing, but now the result or product takes uppermost place. The craftsman wants to produce some tangible item which can show the world his skill, artistry, and imagination in crystallized form. It must be recognized, however, that mere quantity of production is not very satisfying. To the immature, how much and how fast means more than quality and aesthetic judgment. If the craftsman concentrates on a particular end in view, it is with the objective of offering an item that shows mastery of medium and equipment. Satisfaction for the artisan is derived from producing a personal statement in material form stamped with the undeniable signature of expertness. All this is possible through the rising progression of the graded crafts program.

4 CRAFT IMPLICATIONS FOR THE ELEMENTARY AND MIDDLE SCHOOL

The learning-by-doing process has been in use for years. It is still one of the most effective methods for teaching difficult concepts quickly. Emotion-arousing activities may provide the child with sufficient stimulus to provoke interest and develop self-confidence in a learning experience. Children learn faster and retain more information when they can perform functions or act out situations. Arts and crafts experiences offer unique opportunities for such learning to occur.

Having the right materials, and equipment and enough of them to support a given activity is particularly important. An exciting and challenging range of available materials can do much to inspire the desire to learn. As enthusiasm grows for the learning activity, the child reaps the benefit. Skills are commanded, ideas flourish, enjoyment ensues, and learning takes place.

For the very young child, just reaching kindergarten, arts and crafts may serve as media by which a variety of manual and visual skills are developed. Such skills invariably prove useful when the pupil enters elementary school. Crafts and their processes supply the curiosity-arousing and exciting experiences of creative expression. The production of crafts experiences is less important than the process undergone by the child. Self-expression, spontaneity, and personal creativity are outcomes that can only be beneficial in the educational life of the pupil.

The kindergarten program should be concerned not only with line, crayon, and paints, but with manipulative materials which can best be termed crafts. Thus, pasting, cutting, clay modeling, puppet making, papier-mâché, and other crafts activities can be utilized to ignite the learning process of a child.

THE CHILD-CENTERED OR OPEN-EDUCATION PROCESS

Many elementary schools are experimenting with an open educational concept of learning.[1] The child-centered program concentrates upon small groups or individual learners rather than upon the class as a whole. One significant feature of the child-centered approach is the obvious enjoyment of activities with which the children involved perform. In open education reasonable classroom engagement covers a wide range of activities. Pupils participate in manipulative experiences dealing with sand, clay, water, wood, metal, and other materials. There are abstract and symbolic activities where books, numbers, maps, and problem cards are available. Children are given the option of selecting from a wide array of experiences—anything that interests them—whether in the classroom or outside of it. This apparently frivolous use of class time for such activities may seem misspent by the casual observer, but to the children concerned the results have been dramatic. Greater interest, involvement, and enjoyment are noted. Subject matter is retained better, and more intense study of abstract and symbolic concepts and work-oriented and physical activites are performed.

Patterns of learning occur as a consequence of spontaneous involvement in a specific learning experience. Thus, a child engaged in a solitary experiment who succeeds may desire to share his enthusiasm and success with his peers. The effect extends the child's learning while others are exposed to the concept raised by the experiment. Since free association and partnerships are promoted, one learning experience invariably sets up a reaction which leads to others.

Open education is not anarchical. There are limitations, but these have to do with the prevention of destruction of tools or materials or interference with the freedom of others to learn. A minimum series of restrictions seems to provide the necessary security for children to understand that there is authority not dictatorship. Learning seems to flourish in such situations.

The children's enjoyment of schooling is not a central aim of open education, but there is a distinct correlation between enjoyment and learning. Minimizing performance differences, offering meaningful choices, encouraging problem solving, fostering cooperation and collaboration, promoting feelings of mutual trust and confidence, and establishing stability without authoritarian overtones contribute to a learning environment where learning becomes enjoyable.[2]

Aims

The aims and objectives of open education, as reflected by a crafts program, are to help children become less rigid and more flexible in their thinking and

[1]Vincent R. Rogers, "Primary Education in England: An Interview with John Coe." *Phi Delta Kappan* (May, 1971), p. 536.
[2]Roland S. Barth, "Open Education: Assumptions about Learning and Knowledge," *Educational Philosophy and Theory*, vol. 1, no. 2 (Oxford: Pergamon Press, 1969).

dealing with others. Flexibility in attempting to resolve problem situations is also a consequence of this type of education. The child should be able to react to his experiences in the most beneficial way possible without the hindrances of previous bias. Crafts should assist the child to achieve spontaneity, involvement, and skill.

More importantly, there is a cross-fertilization of ideas as teachers cut across disciplinary lines in dealing with any study that may develop in the classroom. All subjects may be used to focus attention on a particular problem or subject. By offering a wide variety of crafts opportunities in context with other studies of the curriculum, a greater appreciation may be generated, on the pupil's part, as his curiosity is awakened. The teacher's role then becomes one of stimulation and individual counseling or assistance rather than having the class dominated by a central teacher preparation.[3] Concentration of effort on the child's needs while presenting attractive and interesting possible crafts choices can do much to enhance the speed of learning and retention of what is learned.

During the highpoint of "progressive" education in the 1930s, a famous cartoon showed a young pupil asking the teacher pathetically: "Do we have to do what we want again today?" Such humor may be on the rebound, for much of progressive education has been revived by the current movement toward open education. As well-known educators begin to reexamine the school systems throughout the country, they are finding an all-too-frequent rigidity in instruction which appears to stifle, not release, curiosity and desire to learn on the pupil's part.[4] With this revelation there also comes the danger of fad. In hundreds of tiny private, so-called free schools and in public schools, the lesson plan and the rows of desks have given way to a new style and decor. Children are encouraged to roam from one project to another, theoretically following their native curiosities and learning at their own special rate. Such situations can deteriorate into chaos unless the teachers systematically adopt the new methods and apply them consistently.

Open education derives from understanding of learning patterns that are traceable to Montessori and Dewey. Contemporary psychologists like Jean Piaget confirm these insights that the most intense form of learning is the child's learning through play and the experiences which he searches out for himself.[5] A structure is operating, but it demands the time and talent of expert teachers wholly committed to the concept that curiosity and learning are best stimulated by free expression rather than by restricted and static techniques which do not permit exploration beyond the preconceived lesson plan. Still, children have to be guided and cannot be allowed to drift aimlessly at different rates. For this reason, there must be some evaluative method whereby comparisons are made. This interaction may best be developed through discussion groups where all experiences are made available through informal social exchange.

[3] Marilyn Hapgood, "The Open Classroom: Protect It from Its Friends," *Saturday Review* (Sept. 18, 1971), p. 66.
[4] Phi Delta Kappan, "Carl Rogers Joins Ranks of Radical Critics of the Public Schools," *PDK*, p. 294.
[5] Herbert Ginsberg and Sylvia Opper, *Piaget's Theory of Intellectual Development* (Englewood Cliffs, N.J.: Prentice-Hall, Inc., 1969), pp. 230-231.

Implications for Learning

For Lowenfeld, art and its related experiences had the twofold function of serving as an outlet for self-expression and was a means for self-adjustment in the elementary classroom situation. As always, he declared that it was the process rather than the product which was significant in learning. Furthermore, he wrote that "in creative activity subject matter is based upon the subjective experience of man and environment according to the various age levels."[6] A basic learning concept is that children need to manipulate things in order for learning to occur. A second significant principle, formulated by Piaget, is that children's cognitive structures differ. This really means that group instruction is almost impossible and that children should probably be free to undertake individual work at activities of their own choosing. From this, it is a relatively easy step to acknowledging the need for establishing teaching methods which rely on the foundation of a progressive approach to teaching and learning.

If arts and crafts forms could successfully be installed within the curriculum of the elementary school, children could become familiar with the materials of crafts and through their manipulation could assert self-expression as well as proceed at their own pace. Thus, there is an implicit association between crafts activities and adaptation to the environment around them.[7] The chief objective of an education where children are stimulated through exposure to experiences in crafts is the development of sensitive, imaginative, innovative, and artistically literate persons who may develop aesthetically, emotionally, and intellectually by active participation or studied appreciation in artistic enterprises, of which crafts is a major part.[8]

Role of the Instructor

The function of any instructor in the development of the individual through school procedures or during leisure will necessarily include four aspects. The initial role is that of libertarian wherein there is a democratic environment which encourages untrammeled inquiry. This atmosphere occurs when the instructor believes that each child has the unquestioned right to explore and seek the answers to what curiosity about subjects or materials urges him to investigate. Thus, the classroom or playground environment permits the learner to analyze his ideas and evaluate them. The schoolroom or the recreational center, properly equipped with instructional tools and materials, is at least as important to learning as are ideas.

Instructional personnel are resources for the learner. Children should not be expected to initiate or create the concepts that will be employed by them in arranging, exploring, and interpreting their environment. It is less important that each child originate the ideas used in the process of inquiry than it is for the instructor to be able to stimulate the learning experiences of every child.

The process of coordination plays a vital part in bringing together the

[6] Victor Lowenfeld, "The Meaning of Creative Activity in Elementary Education," in George Pappas (ed.), *Concepts in Art Education* (New York: The Macmillan Company, 1970), pp. 53-61.
[7] Vincent R. Rogers, *The English Primary School* (New York: The Macmillan Company, 1970), p. 74.
[8] Irving Kaufman, *Art and Education in Contemporary Culture* (New York: The Macmillan Company, 1966), p. 33.

diverse ideas, plans, and activities suggested and used by learners. The instructor must also encourage and motivate the child in his efforts. As previously indicated, there should be no attempt to arrogate the role of final authority to the instructor. The child can also profit by making mistakes, specifically when the mistakes are recognized and corrected by the child. It is unnecessary for the instructor to prevent any errors on the child's part by anticipating them or supplying the right answer even before a request for assistance is made. There is no harm in permitting the child to work a puzzle through to its conclusion, knowing that the attempted solution is wrong. If adequately guided, the child will attempt to examine his response and determine why it did not succeed. More learning may be gained by this approach than by dismissing the child's wrong efforts, showing a correct method, but refraining from going through a sequence of experiences which may illustrate how and why particular steps are important if a valid solution is to be reached. Naturally, no instructor will allow frustration to develop if the child becomes hopelessly mired with a plan that has no answer. Thus the instructor ensures the smooth operation of the activity by supervisory expertise and organization and coordination of materials and experiences.

In the last analysis the instructor assumes the role of evaluator. To do this, there must be effective plans which guide children's activities. The instructor has the responsibility for diagnosing "the learning problems and decide on their possible solutions. The teacher needs to decide what is to be taught, how it should be presented, and how the learner should be evaluated."[9] This means that the structure of the learning environment cannot be completely spontaneous, haphazard, or unrestricted. There is a plan, and the instructor must be able to arrange the classroom and the materials and extend the child's curiosity into systematic knowledge. If learning is conceived as modified behavior in terms of directed learning sequences, the instructor has the responsibility for assessing the child insofar as the behavior changes are contained in the aims of instruction.

Basic Learning Principles

Among the basic learning principles which should provide guidance to those who attempt to teach, the following should be kept uppermost:

1   Desirable behavior in terms of attainment of objectives should receive reinforcement. Thus, a conditioned pattern of response is built up when appropriate learning or achievement of ends is effected. Verbal reward is the typical method used for reinforcing successful behavior. However, personal satisfaction, self-expression, and the pleasure of mastery of new skills or technical capability to perform probably contains a greater degree of sustenance for the individual because it is through personal effort that results are gained.

2   Signals that arouse the drive toward achievement of goals will certainly enhance the probability of attainment. The instructor is prepared to emit those signals which should elicit positive response from the

[9]Clarence R. Calder, Jr., and Eleanor M. Anton, *Techniques and Activities to Stimulate Verbal Learning* (New York: The Macmillan Company, 1970), p. 19.

child. However, not all children are sensitive to or capable of receiving these suggestions for action. Anxiety can be applied to stimulate activity and its reduction will serve to reinforce behavior. Too much anxiety can prohibit learning. When the child is placed in a position of jeopardy or such stress that anxiety about the situation replaces all other thoughts, learning is effectively blocked. Frustration leading to anxiety about performance restricts learning ability. An enriched atmosphere of learning may combat excessive fears and promote learning as the child responds to the signals of instruction. This form of motivation commends itself to the crafts instructional experiences described in the text and may be utilized effectively in the school, on the playground, or in the recreational center.

3   Transfer of training is a fundamental concept in all learning. Where activities require the same principles for solution, even though the problems are different, there is great likelihood that the principles will be applied. There is a great deal to commend the concept that self-discovery offers greater opportunity for total involvement and real understanding of a given situation. When the individual has a chance to work out a problem for himself, as opposed to being told what to do, there is every indication that the former process becomes more deeply ingrained and permits a degree of insight that might otherwise not be a part of the learner's behavior. The opportunity afforded learning through crafts will do much to inspire the involvement necessary for self-discovery to occur.

4   Activity which is consistent with the current level of achievement on the part of the learner will probably be assimilated. Intellectual comprehension, motor coordination, and span of attention are all significant factors in determining the capacity of a child to learn. A variety of methods may be tried so that the individual is enabled to achieve success with the least frustration and the maximum degree of satisfaction. This may be accomplished when the individual is facilitated by self-selection of activities and materials. This may be one of the innovative methods by which learning can be supported and encouraged.

5   If a child has been exposed to a variety of skills over a period of time, he may be inclined to imitate such activities, especially when they appear to be interesting, pleasurable, stimulating, or exciting. Imitation is a learned experience. Within a crafts situation there are countless opportunities for imitative learning to take place. Working with tools, manipulating materials, observation of skilled performance, and copying of movement to perfect skills are integral parts of any crafts program. The classroom teacher should take every opportunity to promote this type of learning, and provision for practice should be optimized.

6   There is much to recommend the principle that individuals learn more effectively if they perform activities in response to problems posed. The individual who must work out a solution when confronted with a given situation is more likely to learn by such experiences than if he simply observes others making correct responses or attempting to solve

problems. Vicarious experience certainly is a valuable method by which learning occurs. However, the most certain process is learning by doing. The carry-over value of this principle may have its most spectacular benefit in the elementary school classroom or on the playground. What can be more conducive to learning than the actual manipulation of objects and materials guided by the individual's desire to explore and the development of some design in view? Crafts activities can be one of the outstanding avenues to employ in developing a well-rounded individual, in associating a series of apparently unrelated studies to the crafts process, and in assisting the child to assimilate new skills by actually participating in aesthetic experiences of a crafts nature.

Individualized Instruction

The instructor has a mandatory responsibility to deal with each child as an individual. Each child, then, cannot receive the exact same educational exposure as every other child. There is, therefore, a requirement for learning experiences that allow for the uniqueness of each individual. These learning situations should be organized with the objective of providing an educational program in which the child's learning capability is enhanced by utilizing whatever potential he has. A learning experience should be made available to accommodate the individual in terms of the method by which he best comprehends. In this way individuality may flourish and optimum learning will occur. Working with real objects and participating in specific projects that combine abstraction with visual and concrete materials may do much to facilitate learning, and incidentally be personally satisfying and enjoyable.

The program suggested here would provide optimized individual instruction by involving children with activities that are enjoyable. Many children are bored in school situations because they cannot visualize the connection between schoolwork and the "real world." If much of schoolwork could be offered in a situation which permits a child unlimited freedom of inquiry, movement, and pleasurable activity and enables self-expression through many media, there might be greater likelihood of learning. Thus, many facets of the curriculum could be combined or singled out for attention in innovative ways that are stimulating and which tend to extend the child's desire to know more and more about the subject.

The following concepts and observations about an enriched learning environment may be better understood in the context of a crafts program in the elementary and middle school.

CRAFTS IN THE ELEMENTARY SCHOOL

Crafts should be an integral part of the elementary curriculum because they are a medium through which opportunities for self-expression are derived, thereby assisting the child to learn more effectively. Crafts may very well prove to be an ameliorating experience which can bring positive social development while broadening cultural and educational perspectives. Crafts, as a subject, may foster awareness of design which might later be useful for the enrichment of individuals' daily lives in terms of where they live, how they dress, their environment, and the decorations or ornaments which they employ. Moreover, crafts activities uncover latent talent or encourage aesthetic ability which will prove valuable to anyone in whatever future work he ventures. The crafts program contributes liberally to the intellectual and aesthetic development of the child.

The crafts program not only has the objective of encouraging meaning through substances, it also assists the pupil to be more effective in the form in which he expresses himself. As he proceeds through the elementary grades, the pupil obtains constant instruction in color, materials, design, and representation, all of which are employed in innovative handicrafts. Nearly every teaching subject contains some crafts aspect which can be capitalized upon and through which the child is assisted to improve his learning. Thus, intellectual pursuits are encouraged.

Selection of Activities

The selection of work to be performed during any specified period should be based on several conditions. Among these are pupil choice, personal interest, ability to perform, and those factors incorporating proper technique. The unit itself should be something that interests the class. Such interest will manifest itself through the selection process. Perhaps the essential aspect is interest. Unless the child has an interest in what is going on, little can be accomplished in the way of instruction or learning. Interest is the chief stimulator for learning. The components of the unit should be encompassed by the children's capacity to perform yet difficult enough to require their total effort in carrying the project to a satisfactory conclusion. The unit should offer opportunities for both personal and group development. It should also provide exercise for initial direction, planning, participation, and appraisal; and it should establish the foundation of appropriate work habits, inclinations, skills, and tastes. The work unit should have pertinency for other subjects which might develop into units in those subjects.

On the other hand, a unit of instruction in crafts may stem from work in almost any other subject of the curriculum, for example, music or geography. A school assembly, let us say, developed during the music period, might be capable of contributing to music, but also to crafts and other curriculum subjects as well.

The opportunity should be included on the grounds of its reflecting a well-rounded body of knowledge in which enlightenment, as well as activity, can have a significant role. Information which is included should be closely correlated to that of other curriculum subjects. The quantity of information presented in the crafts unit should be adequate to fulfill the demands of the activities.

The activities which make up the program should encourage individual acquisition of technical skill and problem solving in addition to personal activation, exploration, and innovative expression. Such activities must also be capable of presenting cooperative behavior and social effort. Activities with which children cannot have direct contact probably should be emphasized occasionally because of the consequent values which accrue insofar as vicarious experiences are concerned. Nearly all the activities should concur with information dealt with in the program, and the crafts projects should be developed insofar as is necessary.

Topics for Crafts

The curriculum which is presently being operated in countless elementary schools makes reasonable a wide array of topics around which teaching models may be effectively deployed. A recommended listing of subjects from which a choice may be made in relation to student interests and skill, and to the position in the curriculum where the subjects appear, should be thoroughly understood by the instructor prior to actual performance in the classroom.

The instructor should have definitely conceived, from the beginning, the connection to be established in the curriculum between crafts and other subject fields. Arithmetic, geography, physical education, music, English, and social studies must be related to crafts; or these subjects should be taught in terms of visual, concrete, or symbolic materials expressed through crafts.

Any listing of topics appropriate for elementary school crafts could incorporate the following:

1 Crafts and ethnic groups
2 Crafts in trade and commerce
3 Crafts in history
4 Crafts on the frontiers
5 Crafts for recreational activities
6 Crafts for exploration
7 Crafts for survival
8 Crafts in relation to thematic subjects
9 Crafts and arithmetic
10 Crafts for the performing arts

Of course, these are only suggested topics, for there are many possible themes which may be undertaken in relation to subjects of the curriculum.

Interpretive Material

The instructor should obtain representative samples and produce relevant illustrations suitable for the understanding of children on such crafts procedures as handling plaster of Paris, clay modeling, finger painting, weaving, woodwork, lettering, pottery making, and so forth. Simple illustrations depicting each step of the procedure become extremely helpful as well as affording experience for innovative explorations. Overhead projectors, opaque projectors, and other audio-visual aids are significant teaching instruments, for they offer vicarious contact vital to creative expression in crafts. Audio-visual materials not only provide clarification of the crafts process, but also supply an interesting focal point for some crafts objectives which might otherwise be boring in the abstract.

For most effective results, audio-visual aids should be carefully chosen for their content and be at the level which will appeal to the intelligence and interest of the pupils in question. The more difficult the material, the more likely the need for visuals. Any illustrations utilized should be of a quality that can easily depict the information to be learned, thereby crystalyzing the instruction.

If slides are to be shown, they should be arranged in proper sequence so that the lesson unfolds systematically. Discussion about the presentation may be made during the presentation or immediately after its completion. It would appear logical, however, for discussion to occur while the illustration could be viewed so that any pertinent question might be answered or technical elements be pointed out.

The Preparation of the Classroom

In developing the factors for a learning experience, a balance should be struck between practice and information. Equality should also be maintained between the general and specific facets of knowledge and of guided and innovative practice. Although general knowledge is nontechnical, general information should be closely correlated to the crafts expressions on which the subject is focused. Specific information is concerned with the method and aesthetic factors. Guided experience is not innovational, but is, rather provided to bring out whatever talent or ability the pupil has for expressing innovational concepts. Innovational experience is not guided, but solely within the province of the pupil. The development of an environment suitable for elementary school grades is offered in Table 4-1.

Methods

The development of an atmosphere conducive to learning crafts must be the instructor's responsibility. This means appropriate arrangement of all physical facilities and properties in addition to the stimulation of pupils to a point where they are highly motivated to learn. All previous exposure to a crafts project may have come about by vicarious and direct experiences. Reading about the subject, field trips to museums, stores, factories, audio-visual presentations, music appreciation, and other such exhibits or displays are suitable for reference. Every session can have a short period of explanation to activate the class.

Class discussion should include the types of materials and equipment that will be utilized to execute the project. Attention should be given to the technique to be used, the size, form, and finish of projects, material, or media, and planning and design formulation.

Whatever crafts activities are performed by students in accord with learning, they must be the result of purposive planning. While the session continues, the instructor should be offering suitable assistance and guidance. Pupils should be encouraged to perform at the highest technical and aesthetic levels possible. The entire class should obtain a great deal of information from this portion of the program.

As the crafts projects develop, the pupils should be assembled periodically for appraisals of the work in progress. Such activity can be used to discuss any problems encountered and to resolve technical difficulties. The

INFORMATION		PRACTICE	
General	Specific	Guided	Innovative
Readings dealing with children's toys	Supplies and materials used for making toys	Graphics Scrap book	Paper bag puppet Puppet or marionette
Toy manufacturers	Assembly line production showing specialized jobs, e.g., painting, shaping, designing	Puppet heads and faces Preparation of materials	Plan for a puppet; Toys made from paper bag; Toys made from tongue depressors; Models
Accoutrements	Selection of toys Toy design Toy coloring Protective finishes	Audio-visual materials	
Music for toys	Utilization of tools and equipment	Dramatization of stories with music	Creative drama and improvisation with pupils playing self-creating roles
Types of toys		Trip to toy store	
Why toys are used by children		Trip to factory where toys are manufactured	Puppet theater
Popular toys			

Table 4-1 CRAFTS PROGRAM FOR ELEMENTARY GRADE
Topic: Toys of the World

most effective time for such discussion will occur toward the end of the class period. As the projects reach their respective finishing stages, time should also be set aside for consideration of individual achievements.

Learning Experiences
Planning for crafts should consist of the definite activities which the teacher expects to undertake during each and every period for the life of the project. While plans need not be written, it may prove to be advantageous for teachers to have some preparation developed so that the child's curiosity can be continuously activated. This will permit the kind of attention necessary so that significant technical factors will not be lost. The child's spontaneity can be enhanced only when the instructor is fully prepared with alternative plans. An instructor who has developed several possibilities to stimulate learning should be able to prepare materials without any difficulty.

Sequential possibilities for the development of a crafts program at the elementary grade level are offered to illustrate appropriate planning. Outlines such as these may be developed to satisfy the requirements of crafts classes at almost any elementary school level.

Indian Crafts
For an Elementary School Grade
Developmental Sequence

1 Introduction
   Topic 1   American Indians of the plains, the desert, and the mountains; various characteristic crafts

2 Design
   Topic 2   Consideration of specific projects and their respective plans
   Topic 3   Design formulation and planning, including material selection
   Topic 4   Review information concerning procedures and processes
   Topic 5   Ornamentation
   Topic 6   Color

3 Performance and manipulation
   Topic 7   Execution of design in medium selected
   Topic 8   Performance of appropriate tasks in treatment of project
   Topic 9   Completion of project

4 Evaluation
   Topic 10   Appraisal and critique of projects

The detailed construction and ramification of the sequential outlines are offered for the better comprehension of instructors who must adapt materials to meet the needs of specific grades.

I. Introduction
Topic 1   American Indians of the plains, the desert, and the mountains; various characteristic crafts
Other curriculum work which relates to the subject:

History or social studies: American history dealing with relations between colonial settlers and coastal Indians. The westward migration of pioneers and Indian wars. Exploration of the frontier and Indian exploitation. Wars, treaties, political, social, and economic relations.

Geography: Continental United States and Indian migrations. Development of settlements along trading routes. Land and water travel. Terrain features of the East and West.

English: Recognition of words, spelling, and reading. Design, color, hue, decoration, artifact.

Arithmetic: Numbers involved in Indian crafts.

Assembly: Oral reports on the habits, lives, and culture of American Indians.

Physical education: Survival experiences, games, and sports of Indians.

Audio-visual aids: Frederick Remington's pictures and bronzes. American Museum of Natural History slides, Encyclopedia Britannica film series on Indians. Exhibition of Indian arts and crafts.

Indian products: weapons, pottery, rugs (weaving), utensils, picture writing, clothes, ornaments, housing, parfleche, toys, carving, boats, leather work.

Pupils are reminded that in American history they have read and learned about the first real Americans who came over the land bridges from Asia into what is now North America. The various settlements were scattered in all parts of America. Pupils are asked to name some of the tribes and give their locations. The following questions may be asked: What are some of the crafts for which the Navaho are best known? The Oglala Sioux, Seminole? What are some of the typical crafts which Indians use for survival? How do they differ from the crafts made by colonials? What are the general characteristics of Indian crafts? If we were Indian craftsmen what could we make?

1 Pottery
2 Rugs
3 Copper crafts
4 Toys
5 Beadwork
6 Woodwork
7 Art

What materials will we require? (Information should be written on blackboard.)

1 For pottery: clay, work boards, modeling tools, wet cloths
2 For toys: cardboard, wood blocks, construction paper, glue, paper bags
3 For beadwork: various colored beads, string, lace, or thread
4 For art: poster paint, brushes, paper, pans

The pupils should be asked which group they would like to work in. Although movement from group to group is permissible, aimless drifting should be discouraged as children can be frustrated in their efforts by others who obstruct the work. The various groups should then be segregated about the classroom. Pupils should be instructed to fix their minds on the development of ideas which Indians might have in the performance of crafts. Thus the work group dealing with pottery might be oriented to water jars or other food-carrying utensils; the toy work group might receive suggestions for the construction of a model Indian village. The beadwork group could be asked to think of color schemes and various designs while the art group might develop ideas concerning a mural of village life. The session should be concluded with the idea that the pupils must decide what it is that they will do and that subsequent periods will be devoted to the initiation of their respective decisions.

II. Design

Topic 2   Consideration of specific project or projects and their respective plans

Form work groups

Pottery group assigned to area with sink

Toy group assigned to area with large work table

Beadwork group assigned to area with small work benches

Art group assigned to area with easels

The materials for work will be placed at individual places according to assignment:

Pottery group will require workable clay and modeling boards.

Toy group will require appropriate materials for construction.

Beadwork group will require suitable beads, threading materials, needles.

Art group will require paintbrushes, paper, shallow pans.

The instructor should then question the children in order to determine whether any have ever participated in such crafts. There might be preliminary experimentation on the pupil's part to get the feel of the materials, perhaps to manipulate clay or draw or paint with brushes. The instructor may show one of the groups some possibilities while the others are exploring with their materials. Let us say that the toy group works with the instructor. He should attempt to interest the children in the development of a crafts project, in this case the construction of a model Indian village. It might be feasible to procure a picture of an Indian village.

The class is called to attention after ten minutes of activity. Various children are called upon to tell what they did. Questions should then be asked to determine whether children who had never before handled some of the material had discovered anything about the material. Opportunity for raising some questions should be offered. All materials should then be collected from each group. One child from each group could act as the receiver.

The instructor should then attempt to explain crafts in terms of the plan which was followed during the previous class session. The discussion should then center on American Indians and lead to the development of projects on which the class will work. The instructor should remind the class about work methods. It might be well to begin with clay products. Examples should be shown of various bowls, dishes, and figures. Indicate the various methods which can be used to make utensils. It should be observed that clay products may be designed and decorated so that they will look like Indian wares.

During this period the instructor will determine who in the clay work group desires to work on which project. Provide information on the type of project for a later report by the pupil. Indicate how work procedures are organized. The class must understand that they do not work without a plan. Therefore each pupil will work out a design from which the project will be developed. Permit the students to think about and visualize the completed project. Ask what their initial thoughts were concerning the shape and size of the product. Each group should determine what the subject will be about. Permit groups to plan what each member of the group will do. When sufficient time has elapsed, ask the pupils if they think they know how to produce their projects. Rehearse the need for a design. To facilitate the process, distribute information about Indian life which can be the subject of construction or painting as well as for reports.

Show headbands, bracelets, or pictures of teepees. Call attention to one unit of the overall design. Show how the unit is repeated to form a whole. The single unit is the motif. The motif is the basic or simplified drawing of a more complex form. Show examples of motifs.

The design for the decoration of the project under consideration may be anything that the pupil desires. It may be a natural object or a series of lines, circles, squares, or other symbols. The clay group might plan a motif which is repeated around the rim or body of their bowls. The toy group may utilize a motif which appears on teepees or long houses. The bead group may select a motif that runs through the arm bracelet or headband. The art group may utilize figures to tell a story in their design. When the art work group decide on their design and are ready to paint, they will be most concerned with color. They should be asked to notice what colors were most used on the pictures which they saw. When they paint the mural, the colors for the figures should be similar to those which they observed in the paintings.

Topic 3 Design formulation and planning, including material selection

During our first class, pupils saw some Indian arts and crafts projects. The class listed some of the materials that would be required in order to produce works based upon Indian designs. At the last session, the class experimented with a variety of materials and discovered some properties which these materials have. The instructor should ask the class what they found out. Discuss materials and handling of tools. Review how projects are initiated through methods of work. Ask for any reports. Ask what methods could be utilized. Ask whether the methods of work are similar to those used by Indians in producing their products. Show how work procedures are similar and have examples prepared. Each group representative indicates to the class the project which his group will produce.

Art group will design a series of pictures that can be incorporated into a mural depicting Indian life and times and social and recreational activities.

Pottery group will produce jars, bowls, and masks through the processes of pressing, coil building, and modeling.

Beadwork group will design headbands, arm bands, bracelets, belts, and decorative beading for cartouche.

Toy group will produce a model Indian village.

The instructor then reviews the fundamental steps in the development of the various projects, i.e., design, color, shapes, sizes, decoration. Children from each group should be called upon to explain examples of each aspect from previous class sessions. The design of the various projects should be initiated at this point. Needed supplies and materials are available, and each child obtains what he needs for work. The instructor should select the group which requires the greatest assistance and work with it while other groups work independently.

At the close of the period each group should select a typical piece of work from the group to be shown by those who have worked on it. Analyze the work performed and tell why it is good, or report on group achievement. Determine whether any difficulties were experienced. At the close of the period have all materials returned to assigned cases.

Topic 4   Review information concerning procedures and processes

Topic 5   Ornamentation

The instructor will discuss the use of color in decorating and continue with the procedures of the previous session. All groups will continue their work in design. Each group member should indicate the names of the colors he will use to ornament his design.

Topic 6   Color

Review discussion concerning color. Have the art group explain what must be done with paint before it is applied to a mural. Show how colors may be lightened, darkened, complemented, or transformed.

III. Performance and Manipulation

Topic 7   Execution of design in medium selected

The materials should be accessible when the class enters. Allow five minutes for class organization. Ask the class to come to order. Determine whether any pupil needs special help. If no assistance is required, the class should begin its work. Determine how much should be accomplished during the period. After the class has been working for half the period, ask the children whether they have been working rapidly enough to complete their objectives. Just before the period ends, discuss the material needs with the pupils.

Topic 8   Performing appropriate tasks in treatment of project

All work groups should continue with their projects. Attention should be devoted to the art group and the progress of the mural. Are the designs developing according to plans? All pupils who are using colors in their work should have the appropriate selection with which to decorate and color. All pupils should be continuing work until they have completed their projects. All completed projects may be displayed on suitable shelves or hung in place.

Topic 9   Completion of project

The instructor opens the session by displaying all finished work. The final step in the crafts process is to decorate the design and complete all finishing that is required. Discuss how the Indians decorated their crafts. For those who are working on the model village, teepees and long houses can receive ornamentation depicting totems, pictograms, or other decorations in keeping with the Indian motif. The beadwork group will have automatically included decorations in the headbands, arm bands, and bracelets which they have designed. The clay group may ornament their bowls by painting appropriate decorations around the rim or the walls of the bowl. All work should be continued until projects have been completed, including the decoration.

IV. Evaluation

Topic 10   Appraisal and critique of projects

The instructor should review, with the class, the intent of the program. Begin with the objectives of the class to discover arts and crafts which have been produced by American Indians. The instructor should seek answers to the following questions: Have the various groups produced good likenesses of Indian arts and crafts? Is there now a better understanding of Indian culture? What has the class achieved in the way of design? Is there a better appreciation of color, crafts processes, and the use of tools? Selected items from each of the work groups should be displayed for all to see. Projects should then be discussed by the class to determine authenticity, realistic design, and appropriateness. The instructor should ask the class whether they feel that they are good Indian craftsmen and whether some improvement could be attained in the future.

The following questions are considered significant in the development of the program and in carrying out discussions:

Topic 1

1   How was the first session developed from other curriculum experiences?
2   How was interest in other curriculum subjects transferred to crafts?
3   How was history utilized to motivate crafts appreciation?
4   How were music and arithmetic used to demonstrate utility?
5   How could the instructor develop receptivity for the appreciation of Indian arts and crafts? How did the instructor present objects to be appreciated?
6   How were the groups organized? What basis was used for grouping?
7   Did there appear to be some pupil appreciation during the course of the program?

Topic 2

1   How was the class prepared to begin the second session?
2   Was it worthwhile for the pupils to explore various materials during the previous class period?

3   Where had the pupils found information which permitted them to start work following the orientation?
4   Of what value is the discussion period? What percentage of time should be given over to discussion?
5   What emphasis should be placed upon working in groups as opposed to providing individual assistance?
6   Was there noticeable improvement in the work habits of group members?
7   How was the class made to understand the part that design plays in the creation of crafts?
8   Did the pupils receive a good grasp of the concept of design? How was this apparent?
9   How was the class made aware of the significance of design?
10 Was sufficient time allowed for the accomplishment of creative work?
11 Was instructor guidance appropriate?

Topic 3

1   Why was a discussion period omitted from this session?
2   Who determined the amount of work to be performed during this period?

Topic 4

1   To what extent was the purpose of the class achieved in this period?
2   Did pupils gain considerable command of materials used?
3   Did students gain ease of expression as the period continued?
4   To what extent did the students engage in processes which made use of the following:
    a   Utilization of designs which were developed in class
    b   Participation as group members
    c   Expression of individual ideas
    d   Suitability of materials and projects
    e   Time saving
    f   Safe work habits

Topic 5

1   What was the value of making preliminary designs for the mural before working up full size?
2   How did the instructor obtain the class's attention when necessary?

Topic 6

1   How was this session different from the preceding ones?
2   How did the discussion period differ from the preceding session?
3   What was the instructor's role during the discussion?

Topic 7

1   How was this topic developed?
2   How did each group decide to complete its respective projects?

Topic 8

1   What method was utilized in developing a concept of decoration?
2   What part did color play in ornamentation?
3   What other methods might have been used as effectively?

Topic 9

1   Every crafts unit must include some information and expression. Were both factors included in this session? To what extent?

Topic 10

1   How was the class begun?
2   How was the assignment for the next session provided?
3   How did the session end?
4   Is a critique of the individual and group projects helpful for evaluation?
5   Was there an apparent pupil growth in understanding and appreciation of subject matter and experience?
6   Was the objective of the program accomplished?

THE MIDDLE SCHOOL CRAFTS PROGRAM

The development of the middle school, a relatively recent establishment, serves to ease the child's process from elementary to senior high school. Thus, a four-four-four plan has been arranged to accommodate the mid-childhood years. According to this organization, grades five through eight constitute the middle school.

In the middle school, individual and group effort of boys and girls may be more highly organized than was apparent at the elementary school level. Because of its specialized program, the middle school makes a strong appeal to the individual needs and differences of those who constitute its student body. The curriculum should be able to offer a great deal that can attract students at a period which is usually considered significant in physical and mental development.

Paramount among the benefits derived from the middle school organization is the ease with which transition is made between elementary and senior high school. The pupil is prepared to cope at precisely the time in his physiological and psychological growth when he is ready. There is no abrupt change and thrust into a social milieu which the child cannot handle. Included in the gains which the middle school organization contributes are that it affords pupils an enhanced educational opportunity, provides a larger field of exploration, offers better educational and career guidance, has the flexibility of curriculum that was lacking in former organizations, and encourages socialization while making the individual more responsible for his personal activities.

Pupils in the middle school should be afforded continuous opportunity to exploit their knowledge of arts and crafts in various school functions. The development of a school newspaper, wall murals, sculpture for halls or grounds, and the staging of dramatic performances and pageants—all may be promoted in extracurricular arts and crafts clubs.

Clubs may focus attention on any aspect of arts and crafts. All will be participating in meeting the interests delineated by curricular subjects, working in conjunction with other clubs representing extracurricular activities; or they will relate more pertinently with older-school experiences. In the latter, they will visit arts and crafts studios, manufacturing plants, crafts shops and speciality outlets where they may, at first hand, see craftsmen at work and the process of aesthetic production. In short, such clubs may lend themselves to enhancing the standard of taste within the school by interesting students in the varied media and projects through which crafts are utilized. These may be literary efforts, dramatic presentations, decorations, architecture, exhibitions, industrial arts, and numerous other ways in which crafts and all the arts occur in everyday life.

Objectives
The objectives of crafts instruction in the middle school, directed to the student, can be itemized as follows:

1 Some understanding of crafts is required in almost every field of endeavor. Crafts can assist the individual to live a more effective life.
2 The need for self-expression is fundamental. Crafts activity is one of the most satisfying means for providing a channel for creative imaginations and motivation.
3 All history reflects the craftsmanship which man has achieved. Crafts can provide a better understanding of historical epochs in human development.
4 Literary contributions to arts and crafts have been produced by some of the world's most gifted writers. Arts and crafts may assist the individual to a better appreciation of literature.
5 Crafts are enduring forms of human achievement. Pride taken in craftsmanship can stimulate the desire to attain mastery of some crafts forms.
6 Design is a significant factor in nearly every product and material that is fabricated. Crafts will help the individual in technical subjects.
7 Crafts can assist individuals to develop control over various materials or media.
8 The development of personal taste can be fostered by a better understanding of arts and crafts.
9 Crafts activities can help the individual to utilize leisure most effectively. Crafts are an outstanding form of recreational activity and can lead to satisfying and lifelong involvement.

Crafts Course Implementation

Crafts, in some of their many ramifications, should be offered as a course of study in all middle schools. There can be elements of creative crafts, which reflect the aesthetic aspects of art, as well as shop, industrial, and mechanical crafts.

Pupil experience can, if appropriately encouraged and directed, result in some worthwhile form of art expression. While a unit of work is proceeding the instructor should clarify to the class the different visual features of the unit which are vital if comprehension of it is to follow. Furthermore, such understanding will greatly influence the creative meaning emanating from it.

Such preparation can easily be offered through the preliminary display of illustrative means, such as supplies, materials, objects, and pictures. Included also might be dioramas, progressive procedure, slide presentations, and class discussion. Class visitation to museums, galleries, crafts shops, and localities where various objects may be seen and appreciated are also valuable. Independent excursions to resource places within the community and certainly to nearby areas should probably be encouraged. Such essential student experiences can, with competent instruction, develop into estimable existent expression. Instructors should offer a climate where the talent and interest of the child may be brought out.

In order to enable the formation of creative representation, the instructor may assist the students to review and discuss their varied experiences with emphasis on what for them is most compelling or of significant interest. These evidences of self-interest may then become points of departure from which crafts project themes can be derived. Insofar as a crafts project is concerned, the ultimate selection of medium and theme may be accorded to the student, even if it is not pertinent to the unit under consideration at the time.

The real performance of crafts work should be accomplished by the individual student, unless there is a call for assistance or guidance. Any discussion of aesthetic principles such as those relating to design, media, or texture should normally await the appraisal or critique session, which is typically scheduled just prior to the close of the period.

Choices of Instructional Units

The crafts instructor in the middle school should be aware of the peculiar objectives of the middle school and take into consideration these aims when choosing subjects for instructional units. The choice should usually be made on the basis of standards which have already been detailed for the elementary grades (see pages 86-89). In consequence of the differentiated program in the middle school the areas selected should correlate more directly to crafts interests. It is at this stage of learning that the crafts program can assume a role in accord with that which it possesses in daily life. Man's crafts activities are obvious in all industrial arts, sculpture, engineering and most technology, architecture, and the trades. For these reasons greater interest may be taken by pupils as direct relations between crafts activities and out-of-school life are made manifest.

The instructor should make a detailed inspection of the crafts field and

PLANNING AND
DEVELOPING A
COMPREHENSIVE
ARTS AND
CRAFTS PROGRAM

100

initiate a potential list of topics appropriate for incorporation in the program of study. This survey should be undertaken with the typical purposes of the middle school and of the students' interests and abilities in clear perspective. The instructor should also be cognizant of the relation between crafts and other subject-matter fields in the middle school organization, such as physical education and scientific, classical, industrial, commercial, technical, and historical studies. An array of subjects appropriate for middle school crafts units might, under different curriculum needs, incorporate such areas as the following, the specific grade level placement being designated by the particular school program.

Suggested Topics for Middle School Instructional Units

While there may be duplication, the collection of topics for units under general categories might help the instructor to be aware of the aims of the middle school. The range of proposed topics is neither exhaustive nor comprehensive, but serves only to offer possible guides and to present opportunities of choice.

Topic 1   Aesthetic activity

1   Social history through crafts
2   The spectrum of color
3   Sculpture as craft
4   Handicrafts
5   Utilitarian craft forms
6   Natural architecture
7   Mechanized crafts

Topic 2   Industrial activity

1   Industrial arts and crafts
2   Automotive crafts
3   Metal trades
4   Cabinetmaking
5   Glass blowing and glass sculpture
6   Electric wiring
7   Block printing
8   Leatherwork
9   Ceramics

Topic 3   Commercial activity

1   Lapidary
2   Copper enameling
3   Precious metal jewelry design and fabrication
4   Rug making
5   Sewing, weaving, braiding, batik
6   Furniture making
7   Pottery

Topic 4   Recreational activity

1   Stagecraft
2   Puppetry
3   Marionettes
4   Masks
5   Etching
6   Clay modeling
7   Wood carving
8   Plaster work

Performance of an Instructional Unit

The classroom and the students themselves are prepared for whatever activity has been selected. This includes the adaptation of required materials and equipment, as well as the appropriate mental attitude of students toward the experience. Previous exposure to crafts activity either through vicarious simulation or actual presence may be reiterated. Each lesson should afford a preview or short synopsis to assist the students to adapt to the new situation presented. The orientation is followed immediately by student planning. Incorporated in such planning endeavors will be the consideration of media and procedures important in executing the project. Discussion will center upon design, medium, size, shape, color, and finish. All such proposals, as well as any sketching or preliminary drawing of projects, fall within the purview of design. Design is the process by which the overall unit of the work is conceived. It is both an intellectual and manipulative procedure.

While the activities of the unit are taking place, the instructor should be prepared to offer verbal assistance as needed. The instructor's objective should be to stimulate the maximum effective performance of which the student is capable. During this stage of the unit's progress the class should obtain a great deal of information concerning specific themes, technique, and logical activity. The entire class should be brought together at various times to discuss problems, experiments which have been performed, and progress that has been made and to appraise whatever endeavors have been undertaken and the projects which may still be incomplete. The opportune time for such evaluation is typically toward the end of the class period. Time should also be set aside for the final evaluation and appreciation period at the conclusion of the whole unit.

Description of a Middle School Unit on Modeling and Maskmaking

The instructor should have readily available for use illustrative materials which will be helpful to students in relation to their work in crafts. Motion pictures and still pictures in the form of slides, prints, and photographs should be filed and accessible and used whenever possible. A display case of crafts projects and objects should be given prominent play and used to stimulate student ideas. Additionally, such products might also serve as models against which students may wish to gauge their own work.

Slides or motion pictures can be used to stimulate discussion of model-

PLANNING AND
DEVELOPING A
COMPREHENSIVE
ARTS AND
CRAFTS PROGRAM

102

ing and maskmaking throughout history. Attention can be focused upon the use of masks in religious rituals, festivals, theater, as decorations, and as symbolic representations of legendary characters or other customs. Consideration should be given to the media utilized for the production of masks, such as wood, papier-mâché, cloth, clay, metal, plastic, rubber, and fibers. Pertinent readings about the beginnings and development of early religions, theater, masques, disguises, social occasions, and other events of historic and contemporary significance should be performed. Inquiry into the use of masks throughout history and into modern times can be helpful.

Have students trace pictures of masks showing how aesthetic considerations have been incorporated. Show how various masks depict personality characteristics by vertical, horizontal, diagonal, or curved lines. Indicate that the maskmaker's function is to develop some specific characteristic or stereotype, to suggest some force, beauty, or design. Show how some masks, of a traditional type, are used to terrify or to indicate friendliness. Discuss the influence of certain societies on the form of mask produced: Mardi Gras, Bavarian Fasching, Japanese Kabuki, American Indian ceremonial, Greek drama, modern interior decoration.

Explain the use of clay in modeling in terms of understanding form from all aspects of view. Provide practical and explicit instruction in the use of hands, tools, and the processes of developing a particular base from which a mask can be developed. Explain the action of plaster of Paris in the production of masks which can be used for decorative purposes. Demonstrate how reference material may be collected and stored. Such material may be kept on file in the classroom for ready reference and potential suggestions for projects. Plan for the composition of various interest groups who will first model in clay and then separate for work in several media.

Make arrangements for the sketching of masks which may be displayed at local agencies, such as an art museum or gallery, commercial stores, theaters, or wherever collections are accessible and available. Some masks may be made available by loan to the school. Students should be encouraged to make portfolios for filing original drawings and other illustrative material. Students should be permitted to execute their own designs for masks. The class may be divided into interest groups according to the material that will be utilized in maskmaking, although all will originally be involved in the procedures of modeling. Instruct the students in the use and care of all materials and equipment. Complete masks. Apply whatever finish or design is required.

The middle school teacher who has worked out a logical sequence of activities for a program should be prepared for whatever spontaneous or innovational attempts the students make.

Modeling and Maskmaking
for a Middle School Grade
Developmental Sequence

1   Introduction
    Topic 1   What we know about the mask as a historical device
    Topic 2   What we know about the uses of modeling and maskmaking

2 Design
    Topic 3   Sketching and planning for the masks
    Topic 4   Modeling procedures and practices
    Topic 5   Transforming models into masks
    Topic 6   The styles of masks and materials used in making them

3 Performance and Manipulation
    Topic 7   Execution of design
    Topic 8   Performing appropriate tasks in treatment of project

4 Evaluation
    Topic 9   Appraisal and critique of projects

The detailed construction and ramification of the sequential outlines are offered for the better comprehension of instructors who must adapt materials to meet the needs of specific grade levels.

I. Introduction
Topic 1   What we know about the mask as a historical device
Other curriculum work which relates to the subject:

History or social studies: An intimate knowledge of the environment was fundamental to the survival of primitive peoples. The best hunters were those most familiar with the habits of those creatures which were stalked and killed for food, clothing, and utensils. Primitive men probably gathered around campfires to demonstrate their hunting skills. It is possible that these demonstrations, in which animal hides and skulls were used, developed into magical rituals, dances, and finally were totally simulated by masks. Masks would appear to be socially and culturally significant. Discuss the anthropological importance of masks.

Geography: Identify various peoples who utilize masks insofar as social, political, religious, or cultural activities are concerned. Discuss whether masks are of importance in contemporary societies. Locate contemporary societies that use masks and indicate why masks are in use.

English: Dramatizations of life functions were early recorded through masked dancers and pantomimists. An entire mythology has developed around the use of masks in heroic legends and epics. This might lead to the study of Greek and Roman mythology and literature as well as to the mythology of the North American Indians. Theater arts and drama may be an added supplement, as various explanations for the use of theatrical masks can be introduced.

Physical education: Masked animal dances of primitive man offer excellent opportunities for coeducational activity in dance. Rhythmics, poise, physical fitness, and appreciation of movement can be instilled.

Outdoor education: Nature observation and lore may be initiated as facts

PLANNING AND
DEVELOPING A
COMPREHENSIVE
ARTS AND
CRAFTS PROGRAM

104

about early hunters' transference of actual hunting and survival experiences into dance and mask forms are discussed.

Topic 2   What we know about the use of modeling and maskmaking

The making of masks should be performed in the easiest way possible so as to enable all those who wish to participate to take part. Initially, the cardboard cylinder mask affords the optimum result with a minimum of expended energy and skill. An almost infinite number of masks may be made from the cylinder by making use of one's imagination. Almost any figure, face, or symbol can be produced. In making the cardboard cylinder mask, a rectangular piece of cardboard is placed around the head to determine the necessary size of the cylinder. A symmetrical drawing of the desired figure is then made upon the flat cardboard and painted or otherwise decorated. The base of the cardboard is cut and shaped so that when the mask is arranged in cylinder form it will fit over the shoulders.

When a more advanced technique is required, modeling and plaster of Paris work can be used for making of masks. Essentially, with very few materials and little specialized knowledge a wide variety of objects, projects, and figures may be made from clay. The self-hardening clays are, with some talent, formed into whatever figure or symbol that comes to mind and may be utilized as a base for the making of masks.

Plasticine is still the easiest clay to utilize and is excellent for the practice where permanence is not necessary. For maskmaking and modeling it should serve admirably. Clay modeling requires little equipment. Even what is needed for work can be easily manufactured right in the classroom with a few orangewood sticks or whittled wooden tools. The work table should be of linoleum or covered with oilcloth. The base for building clay models should be of any stiff material. Other supplies will include a sponge for smoothing the clay, some wire for scraping excess clay off the figure, and a few metal cans in which to keep the clay.

Finally, at the end of the class session, the instructor should summarize the lesson, indicate the various properties observed in the clay or Plasticine used, comment upon the tools, and prepare the class for the next session.

II. Design
Topic 3   Sketching and planning for the masks

Paper, pencils, and other assorted materials are required so that ideas may be transformed into concrete sketches. The instructor should open the class by summarizing the work that has gone before. The class should be oriented to the problem of design from which models will later be developed. The instructor should emphasize the importance of perspective, proportion, and elaboration of details which may be difficult to model, Additionally the class may be reminded of out-of-school excursions which may have been taken to familiarize them with various cultures and the masks which served in their respective religions, legends, dramas, or literature. Reference to the slides, pictures, or other illustrations which have been presented should also be made.

The primary purpose of the class, at this point, is to set to work and sketch individual masks. The sketches will become bases for producing a finished project. During the remainder of the lesson all pupils are enjoined to make their sketches. The instructor should circulate freely among the children and provide whatever assistance is required.

In sketching, nearly everyone will concentrate on some kind of head, whether it be animal, human, or grotesque. Careful attention should be paid to the method in drawing a head. Students should begin by drawing in straight lines the general contour of the head. The direction of the neck should be drawn from its center, above the bony projection to the hollow at the junction of the collar bones. A line may then be drawn through the length of the face, splitting it in two. A line perpendicular to the center line should be drawn on a level with the bottom of the ears. Points should then be measured off on the vertical line for the position of nose, mouth, and chin. A line through these points will parallel the original line drawn from ear to ear. The edges of the forehead are roughed in with straight lines. Lines may then be drawn from each cheek bone at its widest part to the chin at the highest and widest part on the corresponding side. Features may then be drawn in.

Topic 4   Modeling procedures and practices (see Chapter 8)

Topic 5   Transforming models into masks
Materials: Clay, old newspapers, flour, water, basin, plaster of Paris, and other materials
During the last session students transformed original designs and sketches into Plasticine and self-hardening models. In this session, those who have not yet completed their models will have a chance to do so. Students will then begin to complete their projects by utilizing materials which can transform the models into masks for use and/or decoration. Those completing models may begin to work on papier-mâché forms with the instructor assisting with suggestions if requested.

Topic 6   The styles of masks and materials used in making them
Materials: Plaster of Paris, paint, newspapers, flour, water, and other supplies as needed
Some students have completed their modeling; others have gone on to work with papier-mâché. Those who have worked in self-hardening clay may apply whatever finishes their design suggests to them. Those who selected plaster of Paris as the material for decorative masks will undertake that assignment. The students work on completing their respective projects from the materials which they have previously selected. The instructor should provide suggestions and assistance as requested.

III. Performance and Manipulation
Topic 7   Execution of design
Work on all projects continues. It should be possible for every student to have transformed his sketches into three-dimensional shapes and worked within the medium of his choice so that a figure has developed. From this step it is but a small effort to turn the models into the desired

PLANNING AND
DEVELOPING A
COMPREHENSIVE
ARTS AND
CRAFTS PROGRAM

106

masks. Work should be kept up until all models have been completed. Work with papier-mâché and plaster of Paris should be finished during this lesson. During the rest of the period the instructor assists the pupils individually in their work.

Topic 8   Performing appropriate tasks in treatment of project
Materials required: Sandpaper, tempera paints, clear shellac, varnish
The instructor should tell students that they have made extremely good progress in designing, selecting media, and transforming their models into masks and decorations and that now they should try to finish their projects. This means finishing them to the texture required, painting, and applying whatever protective coverings are necessary.
The design sketches call for certain colors to be applied. Some students will be emphasizing contour lines and facial expressions. Others will be attempting to add abstract and/or stress lines to enhance or provide character to the masks whose models they have made. Those whose plaster casts require smoothing may utilize the fine sandpapers. Make sure that depressions or projections are smooth and that no chips, nicks, or scrapes are visible on the surface. For those who wish a roughened texture, scouring with a stiff wire brush is recommended.
Those who have worked with papier-mâché may apply a neutral base paint to hide the paper material from which the mask is made. Painting should be performed carefully so that the best possible effects can be gained. During the remainder of the class period all students work on their respective projects by applying whatever paints and finishing coats are needed. Clear lacquer, shellac, or varnish may be added after all painting has dried. The finishes, regardless of their clarity, will tend to darken whatever they are applied to. The finishes serve to protect the masks. It is at this time that the instructor may be called upon for suggestions or assistance.
At the termination of the class, the instructor informs the children that all masks will be exhibited and appraised during the next session.

IV. Evaluation

Topic 9   Appraisal and critique of projects
Objectives: To better understand the history and uses of masks and modeling; to discuss and evaluate projects
Students have now completed their designs and models and transformed them, via different media, into masks. Now it is proper to discuss the efforts which have gone into the production of these projects. With the instructor's help, the class should arrange the masks in terms of their historic, and religious, ethnic, dramatic, or modern use. The instructor should ask the following questions: What do you observe about the masks that depict religious ritual or legendary designs? What motif or central characteristic may be seen from symbolizing historic or dramatic use? How have emphases been made to produce what the artist wants the observer to see? What other materials could have been utilized to transform design sketches into masks? Which of these materials will be more durable for practical use in dramatizing action? Which of these materials

is most suitable for interior decoration? Why? Are the masks painted in a manner to show realism or fantasy? Can you indicate other media in which the craftsman can work to produce masks? A discussion concerning the use of wood, plastic, fiber, or rubber might ensue. Particularly well-done projects should receive praise, and the salient features that establish the form as an excellent representation should be pointed out. Other discussion should focus attention on the cross-curricular subjects that have influenced the entire lesson. There should probably be some attempt to display outstanding masks in a manner which can be seen by the entire school. Other pieces may be exhibited within the classroom itself. Students should be stimulated to critique their own, as well as other projects—and, more important, to be objective in their praise or criticism with logical reasons for each.

PLANNING AND
DEVELOPING A
COMPREHENSIVE
ARTS AND
CRAFTS PROGRAM

108

PART II

GRAPHIC AND MANIPULATIVE ART FORMS AND INSTRUCTIONAL METHODS

BASIC ART TECHNIQUES 5

The following pages describe in detail a number of techniques which are important to a recreational program in arts and crafts. The presentation should prove beneficial to those individuals who are unskilled in the basic arts and crafts processes of coloring, painting, sketching, and etching. Elementary teachers and recreational instructors generally understand children in terms of growth and development. They understand their characteristics and behavior, but too often have a limited knowledge and understanding of how children learn to work with paints, crayons, and other crafts media.

Any arts and crafts program should provide children with an opportunity to make a preliminary sketch, to make a deliberate and sensitive color choice, to develop contrasting patterns and detail, and most important to evaluate each stage of a technique. Too many programs are more concerned with the end product than with enriching the children's knowledge and understanding of the properties and characteristics of materials. Limits should not be placed upon the length of time children have to create with crayons, paints, sketching materials, or other arts and crafts media. They should be provided with the time to experiment and think about the various techniques. These techniques should also expand and enrich the child's world of color and relationships.

WATERCOLOR PAINTING

Watercolor painting is a very old art. Centuries ago the Chinese drew with a brush using light tints of color to brighten their designs and give them a sense of space and distance. Later Michelangelo, like so may Italian fresco painters, used these thin pastel shades of color, called washes, to create preliminary drawings on paper of his great wall paintings like those found in the Sistine Chapel in Rome. However, watercolors were not actually used to make finished paintings until the eighteenth century in England.

Fun with Watercolors

There are many techniques used in watercolors that when used creatively can assist the individual in painting an interesting and exciting picture. Experimenting with paintbrushes, paints, and paper can be fun. Playing with watercolor paints will usually result in the discovery of new techniques that can be utilized in the painting process. The following suggests some of the techniques and the materials needed for children, young adults, and adults to have fun painting. Try experimenting with these techniques. Can you think of other techniques and materials that can be used in painting with watercolors?

Materials

Very few materials are needed to begin a watercolor painting. A paintbrush, sponge, watercolor paints, paper, and plenty of water are the only materials that are required.

W atercolor paints are made from a pigment which is held together by a binder. The pigments for watercolor paints are obtained from rocks, soil, and plants ground into a very fine powder. The pigments are held together with a jellylike binder material called "gum arabic." Watercolors can be mixed and thinned with water.

Transparent watercolors are mixed with water and usually applied in washes or tints of color. The white paper shows through for highlights. There is also an opaque or nontransparent method for painting with watercolors called "gouache." This method requires mixing transparent watercolors with white.

Look at a watercolor painting. Can you see its transparency and freshness of color? Once an object is painted in watercolors, it is usually allowed to remain that color. If the object is repainted or overworked, the watercolors usually lose their freshness and transparent qualities and become "washed-out," looking like old faded clothes. Overworking also causes the fibers of the paper to lift.

Brushes   The first brush used for painting was probably a stick, mashed at one end into a clump of shredded fibers. Today's brushes are manufactured from animal hairs that have been carefully shaped so that they come to a delicate point or broad flat edge. Different kinds of animal hairs are used to make brushes; some are very stiff, like pig bristles, and some are very soft, like sable and mink. The soft, easily managed sable brushes are usually

GRAPHIC AND
MANIPULATIVE
ART FORMS AND
INSTRUCTIONAL
METHODS

112

used for watercolors. However, a stiffer bristle brush can be used to make some very intriguing stroke patterns.

Brushes are also manufactured in a variety of sizes and shapes. Pointed, flat, round, and dome-shaped brushes are all used to obtain different effects when painting with watercolors. The dome-shaped brush is known as a wash brush. Because of its bushy shape, it holds a great deal of liquid and can be used to make long, sweeping strokes without having to be refilled with paint. The pointed and round-tipped brushes are used to make lines, while the flat-sided brushes are excellent for short, broad strokes. Brushes also come in sizes from very large with long, fat handles to very thin—at times having no more than three hairs at the tip. Brushes are numbered from size 1 to size 12. The big fat brushes, sizes 6 through 12, are the most fun to paint with. The tiny brushes are good for detail, but tend to make a painting look more like a drawing. These brushes sometimes limit the individual from really working with the wonderfully splashy liquid of watercolor. When painting, it is important to experiment with the different sizes and shapes of brushes and not stick to an old favorite. The finished painting will have a much freer, enthusiastic look if different brushes are used.

"Puppy-dog Tails"   Many other materials and things make superior lines and strokes that can give a painting a texture that no one else has created. Use your imagination! Remember how the first brush was made. What if you tried using a stick mashed at one end? Match sticks, cotton-tipped swabs, frayed rope, unwound string, and slivers of wood can be dabbled, dragged and scribbled all over the surface to make spontaneous designs. Strips of cardboard, steel wool, and crumpled paper can also be used to paint a design with watercolors. What other "puppy-dog tails" can be used to make a line? Experiment with these crazy things and have fun, but remember that lines, shapes, and colors are the important ingredients of a finished painting. Watch what happens when these techniques are combined on the surface of a piece of paper. Ask these questions as the painting takes shape: Is the line smooth and solid? Is it dry and broken? What happens if a small amount of paint is used? What happens if too much paint is used?

Paper for Watercoloring   Take a piece of white drawing paper and a piece of writing paper. Run both pieces of paper between the index finger and thumb. Do you feel any differences in the texture of the papers? The surface of the writing paper is smoother and almost shiny, while the drawing paper is rougher and harder to pull between the finger and thumb. Most recreational and educational programs will probably use only drawing paper for painting activities because watercolor paper is so expensive. Individuals should be encouraged to experiment with different types of paper. Paints will react differently as they are applied to paper with a smooth or textured surface. Some watercolor papers are very bumpy, and others are smooth as writing paper. The weight (thickness) of the paper also varies from very thin paper like writing paper to the thickness of shirt cardboard.

The difference in texture and thickness is related to the watercolor technique used. Paint on some small pieces of paper using different amounts of water and pigment. Note how the paper curls and wrinkles. This curling and wrinkling occurs because the water and pigments soak into the paper and are not merely deposited on the surface. When the paint dries, the surface usually goes back to its original shape. A slight bumpiness may remain where the pigments are locked into and around the fibers of the paper. If a large quantity of water is used, a heavy-weight paper should be used to prevent or minimize the wrinkling. For small amounts of water, a thinner paper can be used. The weight of the paper alone will not prevent wrinkling. Securing the paper to the working surface correctly can cut down on curling and wrinkling. One of the following three methods can be used for this purpose.

1   Brush a 1-inch strip of library paste around the outside edge of the paper. Turn the paper over and attach it to the working surface. After the painting dries, a single-edged razor is used to cut around the border on the inside edge to free the painting. The glued piece of paper can be soaked off.

2   Sponge the working surface all over; then soak the paper thoroughly and while it is still dripping wet, lay it on the working surface. With a damp sponge, squeeze out the extra water from underneath the paper by firmly wiping the top surface of the paper. The sponge should be pushed from the center of the paper toward the edges. If the paper remains wet, it will not buckle.

3   Lay a piece of dry paper on the working surface. Tape around the four edges of the paper using one-inch masking tape. The surface can be dampened by running a wet sponge across the top.

Painting

Fill two large jars with water. One is to be used to mix the watercolors to make a wash. This water must be kept very clean in order to prevent dirty colors from getting onto the painting. The second jar of water is for rinsing the brush. It is important to keep the brushes very clean and change the water often. A palette or dish should be used to mix the paints if the watercolors are not in a paint box. Some watercolors come in tubes. The little cakes of color in the paint box are the same as the paint in a tube except that they have been dried. When painting with colors from a paint box, the cover can be used to mix the watercolors.

Mixing Colors

It is important to understand a few basic color principles before working with watercolor paints. There are two ways of mixing colors with watercolor paint. One is to mix the colors directly on the palette. A chart could be presented that describes the colors that can be mixed to make another color, but the best way to find out what happens when colors are mixed is to experi-

GRAPHIC AND
MANIPULATIVE
ART FORMS AND
INSTRUCTIONAL
METHODS

114

ment. By mixing different colors, one can see how many different colors can be created. An interesting record can be made by putting down on a piece of paper a little dab of each new color. Next to the new color, put the two or three colors used to mix it. This record can be used later as a guide for selecting colors. Remember, when mixing colors, that the amount of water used will determine the darkness of the color. The color will be dark when very little water is used, and it will be light when much water is used. The differences in the lightness of a color caused by adding another color are called "tonal differences." The different tints of color are called "tones."

A second method of making new colors with transparent watercolors is by using washes. Washes are tints of color that are applied in a simple stroke. Once the wash has dried, a second colored wash can be brushed partially over the first. Because the watercolors are transparent, it is possible to see part of the first wash. To the eye, these colors seem to mix to form a third color. Try this technique on a practice sheet.

If the second wash is applied before the first wash dries thoroughly, the method is called wet painting. When paint is put directly on top of a wet wash, one color blends into the other, creating a blurry line. This technique can be used to create a feeling of distance in a landscape painting, because distant objects do not have a definite line. The amount of blurring can be controlled by varying the amount of time that the first wash is allowed to dry before applying the second color.

If the first wash is allowed to dry completely before the second color is applied, the method is known as wet-on-dry painting. This technique is fine for building up shades of color with distinct lines.

In seascapes, colors can be blended by using the following technique. Paint the surface using long sweeping strokes and very little water. Before the paint dries, rinse the brush in clear water, and without any paint on the brush at all, make a stroke right along the edge between the sky and water. The colors should blend together.

FINGER PAINTING

Finger painting allows the individual to create beautiful and colorful paintings without knowing how to sketch or paint. It is a wonderful activity for children and adults and can be done anywhere. Finger painting is a good activity for releasing tension. Young children enjoy it because it provides them with an opportunity for large arm and finger movements.

It utilizes free, rhythmic motions of the closed fists, open hands, sides of the hands, lower arms, and knuckles. This technique lends itself to flowing designs rather than pictures. Pictures are usually rigid and do not bring out the characteristics of this medium. Good quality finger paint can be purchased, but finger paints can also be made from a few common household ingredients.

Procedures for Making Finger Paints

1   Mix dry starch with cold water until it is a smooth, thin paste. Place this mixture into the bottom of a large container and mix it with boiling

water. Stir the mixture so that no lumps form. Do not mix the boiling water slowly because this will permit lumps to form. A small handful of soap powder or liquid detergent will make it easier to wash the finger paints off anything. Powdered tempera paints can be added to the starch mixture to obtain the desired colors.

2   Mix 4 tablespoons of cornstarch to 1/2 cup of cold water until smooth. Add this mixture to 3 cups of hot water. Place the mixture in a double boiler and stir over a low heat until mixture thickens. Add food coloring or tempera to the mixture to obtain the desired colors.

The starch mixture can be used over long periods of time before it gets tacky. If the mixture gets too tacky, a little water can be added to the surface and the paint should spread freely again.

Painting

Before starting to finger paint, cover the working surface with newspaper. Take a piece of shelf or butcher paper and wet it thoroughly in a pan of water. Drain the excess water by shaking or drawing the paper against the side of a pan or sink. The piece of wet paper is then placed onto the working surface with the coated side up. Press the surface of the paper with the side of the hand to remove all the air bubbles from under the paper. When the surface is flat, put a teaspoon of paint in the center of the sheet and spread evenly with the palm of the hand over the entire surface. The surface is ready to paint.

Work with different parts of the hands and fingers to learn the effects that can be obtained. Delightful new forms and shadings can be created by using the elbows, knuckles, fingernails, wrist bone, palm, and heel of the palm. The effects can be changed by increasing or decreasing the amount of pressure used to form a shape. Add different colors to the design.

TEMPERA PAINTING

Young children love tempera paints because they lend themselves to bold designs. The various and complex possibilities of tempera painting can be explored by older children because of their ability to control the paint and brush. For example, they may explore with paint on moist, colored construction paper; utilize the dry-brush method to achieve texture; try the mixed-media technique of tempera and crayon; tempera and india ink; or tempera and yarn. Children should be encouraged to use their imagination to create a painting that utilizes the properties and characteristics of tempera paints. They should be offered the opportunity to paint on materials such as burlap, corrugated cardboard, or papier-mâché. Older children should mix a variety of tints, shades, or neutralized hues rather than always painting with the available colors.

Construction paper in assorted sizes and colors makes an excellent surface or background for tempera paints because the color of the paper can be utilized as part of the design. The colored background will also help to unify the composition. Children should try painting on other background

GRAPHIC AND
MANIPULATIVE
ART FORMS AND
INSTRUCTIONAL
METHODS

116

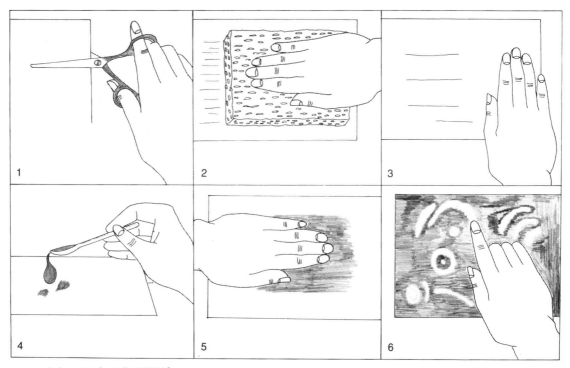

Figure 5-1 FINGER PAINTING

Materials: shelf paper, scissors, spoon, sponge, finger paint.

1. Cut the shelf paper to the desired size.
2. Wet the paper with a sponge.
3. Smooth the surface of the paper with your hand.
4. With a spoon, drop some paint on the surface.
5. With your hand, spread the paint over the surface.
6. Using different parts of your hand, form a design.

papers, for example, white drawing, cream manila, gray manila, bogus, oatmeal, chip board, corrugated board, wallpaper samples, brown wrapping, or classified sections of newspapers.

Sufficient time for the children to explore the various techniques that will enable them to develop a feeling for tempera paints must be scheduled. An individual cannot rush through a tempera paint project.

ACRYLIC PAINTING

Acrylic paints have many advantages over tempera and watercolors. They are water soluble and are versatile, ranging from watercolor to oil consistency. They also dry quickly. However, they are difficult to remove from a surface and are more expensive than watercolors or tempera paints. Special nylon brushes are manufactured for use with acrylic paints. These brushes have short stiff bristles and come in different widths.

Cover the working surface with newspaper and place all the material on it. Squeeze a little paint onto a palette (piece of Masonite). Decide on a picture or design to paint and use one of the following techniques:

Transparent Painting

Acrylic paints, when diluted with enough water, can be used in the same manner as watercolors. Colors can be made lighter by diluting the paint with water and allowing the white paper to show through. If white paint is used to make a color brighter, the color becomes opaque.

Opaque Painting

Mix the paint with a small amount of water until it has a creamy consistency. Using a variety of colors, apply the paint in short strokes. Layers of paint should be gradually added until there is a three-dimensional quality to the painting.

Scribble Painting

Mix the paint with water until it is creamy. With the paintbrush, quickly sketch the design or object in a scribbling manner. The effects are quite interesting.

Flat Two-dimensional Painting

Mix the paint with water until it is creamy. With a small brush or pencil, sketch a design or picture. Paint each form with one color. Note how flat each shape looks.

Cartoon Painting

Follow the instructions for flat two-dimensional painting but exaggerate the shapes. Use some black paint to outline the shapes.

After the painting is finished, be sure to wash the brush and palette carefully. Once acrylic paint hardens on the brush, it is very difficult to remove. Acrylic paints can be used to paint many wooden or plastic objects such as toys, jewelry, picture frames, or screen posters.

NOVELTY PAINTING TECHNIQUES
Sponge Painting

Sponge painting, like sponge printing, utilizes the textured surface of the sponge to obtain its effect. In sponge painting a rectanglar sponge is used to color drawn shapes that are assembled to form a design or picture. Draw a picture of a bottle, vase, or dish on a piece of white drawing paper. Dip a 1-inch rectangular sponge into a pan of tempera paint. Squeeze out any excess paint. Holding the sponge between the thumb and first two fingers, dab it against the surface of the drawing paper. The sponge is used to obtain a textured surface. Repeat the dipping and dabbing procedure until the total shape is completely colored. After the paint dries, cut the shape out with a pair of scissors. A second and third shape can be drawn and painted. These painted shapes are mounted onto a piece of colored construction paper. The shapes can be arranged to form an attractive still life.

Straw Painting

A soda straw can be used to blow a drop of paint into an interesting design or picture. This requires experimenting with the amount of water added to the

GRAPHIC AND
MANIPULATIVE
ART FORMS AND
INSTRUCTIONAL
METHODS

118

Figure 5-2 STRAW PAINTING

Materials: drawing paper, straw, paintbrush, paints.

1. Place a drop of paint on the paper.
2. Hold the bottom of the straw 1/4 inch from the drop of paint and blow into the straw.
3. Blow the drop around the paper.
4. Place another drop of paint on the paper.
5. Blow the drop around the paper.
6. Finished design.

paint to form the drop. Too little paint produces a drop that will not spread or run when air is blown on it.

With a paintbrush, place a drop of watercolor paint onto a piece of drawing paper. Hold a straw 1/4 inch away from the drop of paint and blow through the straw. The paint should start to run; keep blowing the paint around the paper until it disappears. Place another drop of paint on the surface. This time hold the straw directly over the drop and blow through the straw. The drop of paint should spread in several directions. Try adding different colors to the design or picture. Start over again on a clean piece of paper and make a complete composition. Children usually have fun giving their compositions names.

Squeeze Painting with a Flour Mixture

An empty plastic detergent bottle can be used to deposit a mixture of flour and water onto a piece of cardboard to form a raised surface. With a pencil, sketch a design or picture on a piece of cardboard. Mix some flour and water

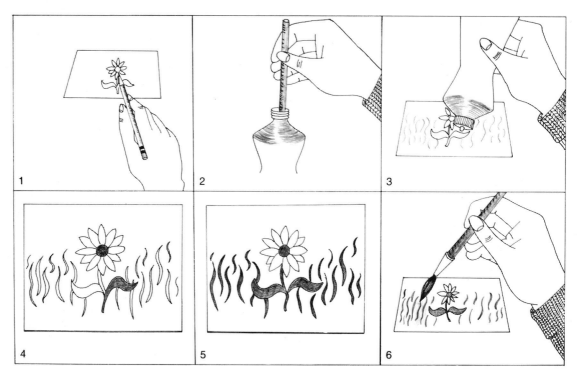

Figure 5-3 SQUEEZE PAINTING
Materials: pencil, paintbrush, stirring stick, paint, flour, empty detergent bottle, drawing paper.
1. Sketch a design on a piece of drawing paper.
2. Pour 1/2 cup of flour and 1/3 cup of water into the detergent bottle and stir until a thick paste is formed.
3. Squeeze the mixture onto the design.
4. Fill in whole areas and the outline of the design with the flour mixture.
5. Set aside to allow the flour mixture to dry.
6. Paint the raised areas.

into a thick paste in a detergent bottle. Tip the bottle upside down and squeeze the mixture onto a piece of cardboard through the small hole in the cap. The mixture can fill whole areas or follow the outline of the design. A combination of both of these techniques can be used to make the picture or design more interesting. Set the design and picture aside and allow to dry. After the mixture dries, paint the raised areas with either tempera or watercolors. The finished painting can be sprayed with a fixative to protect the surface.

Squeeze Painting with Tempera

In this activity an empty plastic detergent bottle is used to squeeze tempera paint onto a piece of paper held on an easel. The paint is squeezed onto the top edge of the paper and allowed to run down the surface to form a series of lines. The lines will be straight, curved, or latticelike. Different colors will

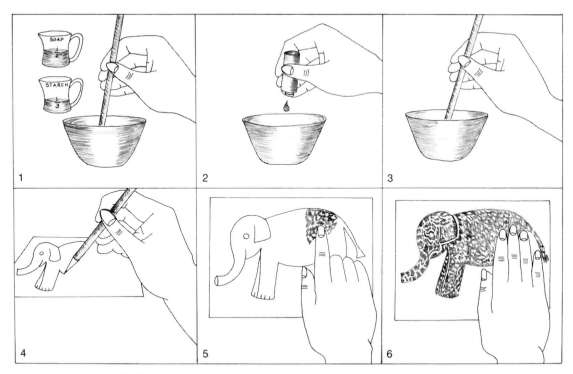

Figure 5-4   SOAPSUD PICTURES

Materials : mixing bowl, liquid starch, measuring cup, stirring stick, pencil, food coloring, soap powder, drawing paper.

1. Mix 1/2 cup of soap and 1/3 cup of starch together in a mixing bowl. With a stick, stir until the mixture looks creamy, like thick marshmallow.
2. Add food coloring to the soap-starch mixture.
3. Stir the soap powder, starch, and food coloring mixture. Additional food coloring can be added to obtain the desired color.
4. Sketch a design on a piece of drawing paper.
5. Apply the soap-starch mixture to the design.
6. Press the soap-starch mixture gently to form the desired effect.

add to the design. Squeeze different colors on a surface and experiment with the thickness of the tempera paint.

Take a piece of paper, place it on a flat surface, and squeeze a series of different colored drops around the edge. Pick up the paper with both hands and tip the surface in different directions so that the paint will run. The paints should form a number of spider web designs. Mix several colors together. Experiment by placing the paints in different positions.

Soapsud Pictures

A mixture of soap powder, starch, food coloring, and water can be used to paint a picture. Mix 1/2 cup of soap powder to 1/3 cup of starch. With a stick stir the liquid starch and soap powder until it looks creamy, like thick marshmallow. The mixture can be placed into plastic containers and food

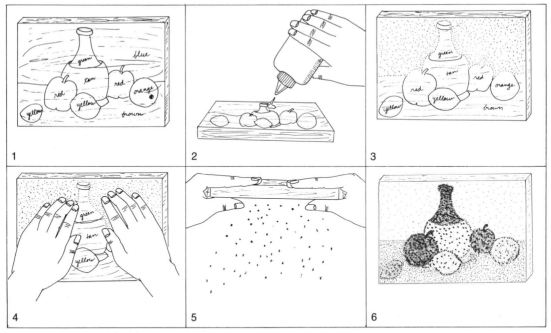

Figure 5-5   SAND PAINTING

Materials : plywood, containers of colored sand, pencil, shellac, paint brush, glue.

1. Sketch a design on plywood and label the areas for various colors.
2. Apply glue to the areas to be one color.
3. Pour sand of this color onto these areas.
4. Press the sand down firmly.
5. Turn the board over and shake off the excess sand.
6. Repeat procedure for each color.
7. Shellac the finished design.

coloring added to obtain the desired colors. Different shades and tints can be made by varying the amount of food coloring added to the mixture. Cover the working surface and place a piece of paper on it. Sketch a picture or design on the paper and apply the different colored mixtures to the desired areas with the fingers.

Sand Painting

Natural colored sands can be used to make beautiful sand paintings. If they are not available, white silica sand can be purchased from a sand and gravel dealer and tinted with different mortar colors. Sketch a design lightly on a piece of cardboard or wood. Cover those background areas that will not be covered by a sand coating with tempera, watercolors, or acrylic paints. Select one of the areas to cover with sand and coat it with a thin layer of shellac, varnish, or glue. A spoon or paper cone can be used to sprinkle the colored sand over the coated area. Allow the sand to sit for a few minutes and then pick up the cardboard or wood. Holding it in an upright position, tap lightly to remove the excess sand. Before using another color, gather up

GRAPHIC AND
MANIPULATIVE
ART FORMS AND
INSTRUCTIONAL
METHODS

122

the excess sand and put it back in the container. Repeat this process until all the desired areas are covered with sand.

A coarse black piece of emery cloth can be used as background material to obtain an interesting effect. The emery cloth is glued to a piece of stiff cardboard with contact cement. Care should be taken not to get any glue on the decorative surface. To dry, place the glued materials under a heavy weight for three or four hours. Draw a design on the mounted piece of emery cloth with chalk. White background areas can be painted with white acrylic paint to screen out the black background. The sand is applied to the surface in the same manner as for a cardboard or wooden base.

DRAWING TECHNIQUES

Learning to draw requires an understanding of certain fundamental principles. Artistic talent cannot be taught; however, the techniques needed to express feelings and ideas can be learned. These fundamental principles usually represent the difference between good pencil, charcoal, crayon, or ink drawings and poor ones. A good drawing usually gives the feeling of being three-dimensional and utilizes the concept of perspective. The following eight fundamental principles are important to consider when sketching and drawing.

1 Position.   Objects or parts of objects that are drawn near the bottom of the paper appear to be closer.
2 Size.   Objects or parts of objects that are nearer the observer will appear to be larger.
3 Surface lines or texture.   Surface lines help give an object a three-dimensional appearance.
4 Overlapping.   Overlapping is similar to position. The front object hides some of the lines of the rear object, thus creating an illusion of distance.
5 Shading.   Shading gives an object three-dimensional qualities because it suggests thickness.
6 Shadow.   A shadow shows the patch of darkness that is caused by the blocking of light by the object.
7 Density.   Objects nearer the viewer should be drawn darker and with more detail than those objects in the background.
8 Foreshortening.   The horizontal lines are drawn closer together than they normally would be, thus distorting the shape slightly and creating an appearance of distance.

It is impossible to draw anything in perspective without using one or more of these fundamental principles. Therefore, it is safe to say that any individual who understands these fundamental principles can draw, provided he can draw the outline shape.

Success in drawing depends on more than knowing the various drawing techniques. The important thing is not how much is known, but

Figure 5-6 CARTOON PEOPLE

Materials : paper (newsprint or drawing), crayons or felt pen.

1. Draw a large circle for a head and a smaller one for a nose.
2. Draw two dots for the eyes and a curved line for the mouth.
3. Add hair to the head.
4. Draw a triangle for the body of a girl and a circle for the body of a boy.
5. Draw a neck to connect the body to the head.
6. Add arms to the body.
7. Add legs and feet to the body.
8. Dress the cartoon character to look like a boy.
9. Dress the cartoon character to look like a girl.

what can be done with this information. A scientist may know all about aeronautics but not be able to fly a plane. The only way he can learn to fly is to practice flying. The only way to learn how to draw is by practicing the various drawing techniques.

Drawing Cartoons

Cartoons are drawn by combining straight lines, curved lines, and circles into the basic shape of a man, woman, animal, insect, or some unusual creation. The first step in drawing cartoons is to practice making straight lines, curved lines, and circles, or combinations of these lines. These lines are then combined into a basic body shape. A head, arms, legs, and other characteristics are added to the body by modifying the basic lines.

GRAPHIC AND
MANIPULATIVE
ART FORMS AND
INSTRUCTIONAL
METHODS

124

Figure 5-7   CARTOON ANIMALS
Materials: paper (newsprint or drawing), felt pen or crayon.
1.   Practice making loops and curved lines.
2.   Practice making basic body shapes.
3.   Combine these loops, curved lines, and basic body shapes into cartoon animals.
4.   Create a scene composed of cartoon animals.
5.   Combine these loops, curved lines, and basic body shapes to create another cartoon animal.
6.   Create another cartoon animal.

Drawing Stick Figures

An endless variety of stick figures, both animal and human, can be drawn by connecting circles and straight lines. The head and spine are drawn first in whatever attitude the situation calls for. Arms and legs are added to the body in the necessary position. The required characteristics or features are added to help the finished stick figure convey a message. For example, a skirt and long hair help distinguish female from male. Size, clothing, and hair style help distinguish the adult from the child. Stick figures create easily recognized stereotypes.

Object Drawing

A rectangular prism, square, triangle, cone, pyramid, or sphere can be used to simplify the drawing of familiar objects. The form in object drawing that is basic to all other shapes is the rectangular prism.

Figure 5-8 OBJECT DRAWING
Materials : paper (newsprint or drawing) and pencils (different shades : HB, 2B, 4B).
1. Use basic shapes to draw a picture.
2. Add texture and tone.

The first step in object drawing, through the use of the basic shapes, is to analyze the model. Determine what basic shapes or modification of those shapes can be used to draw the object. For example, in drawing a house, the base may be a rectangular prism, while the roof may be a triangular prism. These geometric relationships are common to innumerable objects. A candy box is a rectangular prism; a bowl, a hemisphere; a lamp shade, a truncated cone or pyramid. Even highly complex architectural structures can be resolved into comparatively simple geometric elements.

Contour Drawing

Set the object to be drawn in front of you and place a piece of drawing paper on the working surface. Focus your eyes on some point along the outer edge of the object to be drawn. Place the point of the pencil on the paper. In contour drawing, it is important to imagine that the pencil is touching the model instead of the paper. Concentrate on the model and without looking at the paper or pencil, start drawing the object. The eye moves slowly along the contour of the object as the pencil slowly moves along the paper. Imagine that the pencil is touching the contour of the object and that the object is

GRAPHIC AND
MANIPULATIVE
ART FORMS AND
INSTRUCTIONAL
METHODS

126

Figure 5-9   GESTURE AND CONTOUR DRAWING
Materials : paper (newsprint or drawing) and pencils (different shades : HB, 2B, 4B).
1.   Contour drawing of a still life.
2.   Gesture drawing of a still life.
3.   Contour drawing of a baseball player.
4.   Gesture drawing of a baseball player.

being traced. The key to success is the coordination that is developed between the pencil and eye. It is important not to move the eye ahead of the pencil. Consider and concentrate on the point being drawn and not the total contour of the object. This requires practice and patience. When first starting to draw using this technique, the artist should not worry about proportions because they will become correct with practice.

Contour drawing is not an outline of an object. An outline is a diagram or silhouette, flat and two-dimensional. It is the type of shape that is obtained by tracing one's own hand on a piece of paper. It is difficult to determine whether the drawing is of the front or back of the hand. Contour drawing has a three-dimensional quality because it shows thickness, length, and width of the form being drawn.

Gesture Drawing

In gesture drawing, an endless line is drawn rapidly and continuously from top to bottom, around and around, without taking the pencil off the paper.

Figure 5-10 PENCIL TECHNIQUES

Materials: paper (newsprint or drawing) and pencils (different grades: 2H, HB, B, 2B, and 4B).

Technique 1. Draw gray strokes first and then add blacks. Outline with tone areas located. Add darker grays. Add the blacks.

Technique 2. Draw dark areas first and then add grays.

Technique 3. Apply lights and darks as needed.

The end product may have the appearance of a scribble. Set the object to be drawn in front of you and place a piece of drawing paper on the working surface. Take a pencil and let it swing around the paper almost at will. The form the lines take is determined by the action that the individual feels in the model. Let the pencil roam, capturing the gesture of the model.

The difference between contour drawing and the gesture drawing is that the purpose of the latter is to capture what the model appears to be doing and not what it looks like or what it is. In contour drawing the essential thing is to touch the edge of the form, while in gesture drawing, it is important to capture the feeling of the object's movement. The finished drawing may be meaningless to the observer once the model has been removed. There may be nothing in the finished scribble to suggest the shape of the model. This is not important.

In gesture drawing, the edges of the form being drawn are not fol-

GRAPHIC AND
MANIPULATIVE
ART FORMS AND
INSTRUCTIONAL
METHODS

128

lowed. Instead, the pencil is allowed to roam, striking the edges of the form, but more often it will travel through the center of the form being drawn. Many times the pencil will travel outside of the figure and even off the paper to create the desired gesture. Remember, it is only the action, the gesture, that is being drawn and not a detailed illustration of the structure. A gesture drawing should be dynamic, not static. The finished gesture drawing has no precise edges, no exact shape, no jelled form, because the forms are changing.

Pencil Drawing

The first task in pencil drawing is to learn about the materials used in this medium. All pencils are graded by degree of hardness on one end and should be sharpened at the opposite end. The grades range from 6B (very soft and black) to 9H (extremely hard). For preliminary sketches, the HB is the most commonly used, while the B and 2B are usually used for all around purposes. The lead can be sharpened to a needle point or chisel point to obtain different effects.

Several types of paper can be obtained, and various effects may be achieved by using different grades of pencils. Apply even pressure or graded pressure as the strokes are drawn. Try cross-hatching, wavy or broken strokes, or accenting the ends of the lines to obtain different effects. The surface of the paper is very important to pencil sketching and it is important to learn the advantages and disadvantages of different surfaces before starting any sketch. A photographic effect can be obtained on a smooth surface, while the surface texture of rough paper will enhance a drawing of a stone wall.

Any one of the following three methods can be used to make a pencil sketch. The first method is to draw the object and shade in the tone areas with light lines. With an HB pencil add the gray areas to the drawing, leaving the dark areas until last. These areas can be shaded with a 2B or softer pencil. The advantage of this method is that the picture gradually develops and is always under control. The disadvantage is that light pencil strokes sometimes spoil the tooth of the paper, making it difficult to add a dark shade to an area.

The second method reverses the previous order by adding tone to a drawing. The blacks are the first areas shaded, followed by the middle grays and finally the light grays. This approach presents two problems: first, once the dark areas are finished, it is difficult to keep from smudging the surface; second, this approach does not allow for any experimentation. The individual is forced to decide at the start of the drawing which areas will be dark and which are to be light. This type of decision making is difficult for the beginner who might prefer to build his value more gradually.

The third method does not use any rules for arriving at a finished drawing with the desired light, gray, and dark tones. It is an experimental method in that once the basic sketch is made, the tones are randomly added to the various parts of the drawing to obtain the effect. Segments are shaded two or three times to obtain contrasts. Black is important to the finished drawing, and many individuals are afraid of dark tones. Without dark tones, the finished sketch will appear wishy-washy and have little character.

Charcoal Drawing

As a medium of artistic expression, charcoal has been popular for many years. It is especially fine for quick effects. Its softness and generous size make it ideal for filling large areas of tone quickly. Errors can be easily corrected by dusting the paper clean. Charcoal produces the most vivid blacks.

There are many kinds of grades of charcoal, and the price is usually a fair indication of quality. A few assorted sticks, soft and hard, are necessary to make a charcoal drawing. A number of imitation or synthetic charcoals in crayon or pencil form are available. These are more uniform and reliable than real charcoal, but are generally much more expensive.

Although charcoal can be used on many different types of paper, the best results are obtained by using the paper made for this purpose. It comes in tints, as well as white. Charcoal paper is also good for drawings produced entirely in chalk or crayon. For the beginner, the inexpensive grades are satisfactory. A chamois skin is excellent for dusting the surface clean, while a rubber eraser is ideal for lifting tone, and picking out highlights.

Because of the crumbly nature of charcoal, it is best to start drawing a large object. To lay out the subject, use a rather hard stick with a point. The piece of charcoal is sharpened by drawing the knife away from the point to prevent it from breaking. Sandpaper can also be used to sharpen the charcoal. Block in the proportions freely, with an arm and wrist motion. Mistakes can be dusted off with the chamois and new materials added.

There are two common methods of adding tone to the drawing. In the first, each area is covered with a hard piece of pointed charcoal and the tiny pits or depressions in the paper are allowed to show through the tone to give sparkle and vibration. If an area gets too dark, dust off the charcoal and start over or use the eraser to lighten the tone by gently rubbing the surface. Care should be taken to keep from smudging the charcoal surface.

In the second method, charcoal is applied in the same manner as in the first method and is then lightly rubbed with a finger or highlighted with an eraser. The eraser can be used to clean away some of the charcoal, allowing the white surface to show through. These white areas will represent highlights. The eraser should be cleaned by rubbing the edge on a piece of scrap paper after each highlight is made or the whole surface will be black, making it impossible to create the desired highlights.

These two methods can be combined in various ways. Areas can be smudged and then restored with a piece of pointed charcoal, producing a smooth, but vibrant texture. Another technique is to lightly rub the entire background and then erase the highlight areas. A sharp piece of charcoal can be used to touch up the surface. The success of charcoal drawing depends upon an understanding of the characteristics of charcoal and charcoal papers.

GRAPHIC AND
MANIPULATIVE
ART FORMS AND
INSTRUCTIONAL
METHODS

130

Figure 5-11   CHARCOAL TECHNIQUE

Materials: paper (newsprint, drawing, or charcoal), charcoal, eraser, chamois skin.

Technique 1.   Tiny pits or depressions in the paper are allowed to show through the tone to give sparkle and vibration.

Technique 2.   After applying charcoal, rub the surface with a finger and highlight with an eraser.

COLORED CRAYONS

Crayons are an inexpensive art media that can be used by very young children and adults for artistic expression. Crayons are usually misused because of incomplete understanding of their characteristics and properties. A crayon composition should have brilliant color, heavily applied to give it character. A light crayon drawing is uninteresting, flat, and dull. Crayons are superb media for small, compact drawings utilizing a combination of strong dark and light contrast to bring out the details. Colored crayons are not an easel material, nor are they appropriate or effective when used to cover large surfaces.

How to Use Crayons

Many objects, such as fruit, are not just one color. An apple, for example, may have red, orange, green, brown, and even blue in it. Why then do we color the apple one shade of red? The answer is probably related to visual literacy and the lack of understanding of what techniques can be used with colored crayons.

The most effective method for learning how to crayon is by use. The following technique can be employed to develop sensitivity to the properties and characteristics of colored crayons.

Try putting one color over another to make a different shade or to make a new color. As the colors are mixed, write the names of the colors used next to each sample.

Coloring Techniques

1   The greater the pressure on the crayon, the darker the color will appear.
2   Start with light tones and progress gradually to darker tones.
3   The lightness and darkness of a single line used to outline an object can express depth.
4   The appearance of distance can be obtained through light and dark tones.
5   Cross-hatching tends to flatten an object.
6   The direction of the strokes can be used to show depth.
7   Rough crayon marks can be smoothed with a knife to give the surface a pastel appearance.
8   Use colored crayons on different colored paper. The colored paper produces results similar to applying one color over another.

Flat Crayons

Short pieces of broken crayons can be flattened with a knife and used on their side to obtain some interesting effects. Place about 1 inch of newspaper under a sheet of paper. Hold the crayon on the flat side and, applying light pressure to one end, pull it across the paper. The line should be dark on one edge and fade to a light edge. This technique requires practice to obtain the desired line and effect.

Crayon-Eraser Stencil Designs

Oak tag, drawing paper, crayons, scissors, and an eraser can be used by children to make a stencil design. On a piece of oak tag, draw a variety of designs with a pencil. Then cut out each shape. Care should be taken not to damage either piece of material because both can be used to make the final design. Select a colored crayon, and color around the edge of either the negative or positive shape. The heavier the crayon is applied to the edge of the shape, the greater the variation of technique that can be used on the finished design. The shape should be placed on a piece of paper, crayon side up. The crayon is transferred to the drawing paper from the stencil by rubbing an eraser over the surface. The eraser strokes must be even and close together. Stencil designs can be used in a variety of combinations to obtain the desired effect.

GRAPHIC AND
MANIPULATIVE
ART FORMS AND
INSTRUCTIONAL
METHODS

132

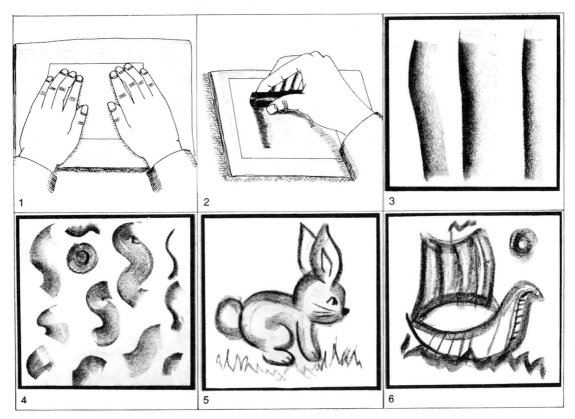

Figure 5-12 FLAT CRAYONS

Materials: paper (newsprint or drawing), newspapers, crayons.

1. Place a piece of drawing paper on a 1/2 inch layer of newspaper.
2. Hold the crayon flat and push it across the surface of the drawing paper, applying light pressure to one end.
3. Practice drawing straight lines.
4. Practice drawing curved lines.
5. Draw a picture using a combination of these simple strokes.
6. Draw a second picture using different strokes.

Crayon Etching

Crayon etching can be used by children to obtain some interesting effects with color. The technique requires a minimum amount of supplies: crayons, paper (oak tag, coated paper, shelf paper), etching tool (knife, nail, toothpick). The working area should be covered and a piece of paper placed on the surface. Color the surface of the paper completely with bright colors, distributed randomly. Rub the crayon-colored surface with a facial tissue. The entire surface is then coated with black crayon. When the surface has been thoroughly blackened, rub it with a facial tissue. It is ready for etching. The surface can be etched with a knife, nail, or other sharp object. The pointed tool is used to scratch through the blackened surface so that the bright colors underneath show. Simple lines can be scratched through the surface or large areas of black removed to modify the effect.

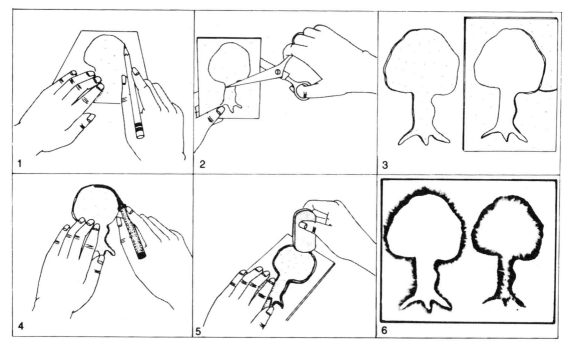

Figure 5-13 CRAYON-ERASER STENCIL DESIGN
Materials: oak tag, scissors, pencil, crayons, eraser, drawing paper.
1. Draw a shape on a piece of oak tag.
2. Cut out the design.
3. Care should be taken not to damage the negative or positive parts of the design.
4. Color around the edge of the negative or positive shape with a crayon.
5. With an eraser, rub the crayon from the stencil onto a sheet of drawing paper.
6. Finished negative and positive design.

This technique intrigues children because it removes some of the restrictions placed upon them when they use colored crayons alone. It also provides the individual with an unusual experience with color. If the children etch a leaf shape, it may turn out to be red, green, and yellow, rather than just green.

Crayon-Tempera or Ink Etching
The crayon-tempera or crayon-ink etching technique is similar to crayon etching in that the face surface is covered with bright colors. The bright colored surface is then covered with black tempera or ink. If tempera is used, soap must be applied to the paintbrush before painting over the waxed crayon surface. When the paint or ink dries, a pointed object can be used to scratch a design through the blackened surface.

Crayon Shadow Pictures
Colored crayons rubbed across a piece of paper that has been placed on top of a cut out shape will result in a picture that has a shadow effect. Draw

GRAPHIC AND
MANIPULATIVE
ART FORMS AND
INSTRUCTIONAL
METHODS

134

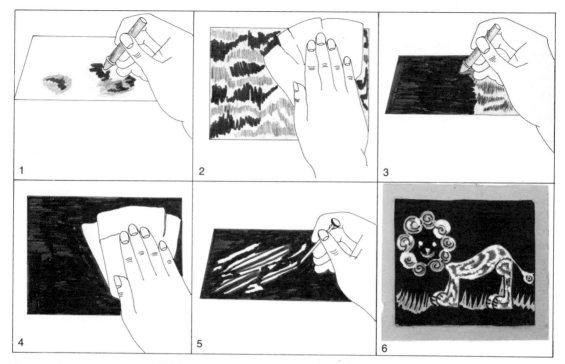

Figure 5-14   CRAYON ETCHING

Materials: crayons, facial tissue, nail, paper (coated).

1. Cover the surface of the paper with small patches of different crayon colors.
2. Rub the crayon-colored surface with a facial tissue.
3. Cover the entire surface with black crayon.
4. Rub the blackened surface with a facial tissue.
5. Scratch a design through the blackened surface with a nail.
6. Finished design.

some shapes on a piece of thin cardboard or oak tag and cut them out with a pair of scissors. Arrange the shapes into a satisfying design or picture on a sheet of newspaper. Place a piece of construction paper, newsprint, or drawing paper over the shapes. Care should be taken not to move the shapes. Rub the side of a small piece of crayon across the surface of the paper. The edges of the shapes beneath the paper should appear darker, giving the finished picture or design a shadow appearance.

Crayon Resist

A waxed crayon drawing or design can be enriched by applying black tempera or watercolors over the entire surface. In fact, this technique can be used to change the characteristics of a picture or design. Many children are amazed and thrilled to see the difference that occurs when the black paint is brushed across the colored crayon surface. Areas covered with a heavy coating of waxed crayon will resist the water-based paint, while those not colored will retain the paint.

The drawing or design can be planned so that large or small areas will be entirely free of crayon. Mix some black tempera paint with water or use watercolors to brush across the entire surface of the drawing. The black paint will fill in the areas that have not been covered and will be resisted by those areas covered by the crayon. Small amounts of black paint will be picked up between the strokes of crayons. These small patches of black add new dimensions.

Crayon Encaustics

This technique utilizes those small pieces of crayon that usually accumulate as children draw and color. The small pieces of crayon are placed in an old muffin tin. The various colors are separated. The muffin tin is heated and the wax crayons melted. While the wax is in liquid form, it can be applied to a surface with a paintbrush. A stiff-bristle brush is better than a hair brush for applying the wax to the painting because of its consistency. The wax cools and solidifies quickly when the container is removed from the heat source. Therefore, children must work very quickly with these materials.

A crayon encaustic drawing and design will result in a picture with vivid colors. It can be painted on almost any surface—plywood, hardboard or Masonite, cardboard, poster board, and wood. After the painting dries, one of the etching techniques can be used to obtain some surprising effects. Heat can be applied to the work for greater fusion of the colors.

An understanding of the properties and characteristics of material permits an individual to be more creative with the media. Understanding and sensitivity toward material can only be derived from use of the media.

Crayon Painting

Crayon painting uses heated crayons instead of brushes and paints. The crayons are only used on canvas, cloth, or Masonite. The surface to be painted can be held either horizontally or vertically. Plan a rough sketch of the design or picture that is to be painted. With a black crayon, lightly sketch the design or picture onto the canvas or Masonite surface. The sketch should be in outline form and not concerned with detail. Peel back the top edge of the paper on the crayons. As the crayons are used, the paper should be continuously peeled back. Place a candle into a holder of some type and light it. The tip of the crayon is placed over the heat for a few seconds. The crayon is then removed from the heat and dabbed onto the surface being painted. Simultaneously, it should be rubbed around, as when used to color a drawing. Because the crayon is soft, small lumps of colored wax will be deposited on the surface. The dabbing and rubbing process should be repeated until the entire painting is finished. A wide range of colors will make the painting more attractive. Colors can be mixed by putting different dabs on top of each other. As always, experimentation is of paramount importance.

DYEING TECHNIQUES
Batiking

This dyeing technique utilizes wax to cover areas of a design that is not to be dyed during the dipping operation. The wax can be removed and applied in

GRAPHIC AND
MANIPULATIVE
ART FORMS AND
INSTRUCTIONAL
METHODS

136

different areas, forming a new design. The material is dipped again, adding another color to the design for an interesting effect. Cover the working surface with newspaper. On a large piece of newsprint, lay out the design for the batik, using crayons. When the design is ready, tape a piece of muslin to a cardboard surface cut from an old container. Lay out the design on the piece of muslin. With a paintbrush, apply heated paraffin or beeswax to those areas of the design that are to remain free of the first dye color. When the desired areas are covered, the fabric is dipped into a bath of cold dye. If more than one color is used, the light colors should be used first. Allow the material to sit in the dye bath for a sufficient length of time (see package directions). Remove the fabric from the dye. The wax is removed by scrubbing the fabric in a bath of warm water. Apply a second coat of wax, covering parts of the dyed areas to form a new design. The fabric is dipped in a dye bath of another color for the required length of time. Remove the wax and hang the fabric up to dry. The fabric will be covered with a multicolored pattern. Additional colors can be added to the design by repeating the process with different colored dyes. A crackling effect can be obtained by twisting the waxed surface. Paraffin wax will crack, although beeswax will not. The wax will crack much easier if it is cold.

Crayon Batiking   Young children can use crayon wax to create attractive batiks. On a piece of newsprint, lay out the design. When the design is ready, tape a piece of muslin to a piece of cardboard from an old container. Fill each section of a muffin pan with small pieces of wax crayons, keeping the various colors separate. Place a cookie sheet over a heat source, with the muffin pan on top of it. Allow the crayons to melt slowly. Beeswax or paraffin can be added in equal parts to the crayons to increase the quantity of wax. Paint the wax directly on the fabric with a brush dipped in the melted wax.

When the painting is completed and the wax solidifies, some of the large areas can be broken or crumbled to create fine hair cracks through which the dye will seep to produce unusual effects. Mix the desired colored dye to cold water in a bucket according to the directions on the package. Place the piece of fabric in the dye and allow to sit for the sufficient length of time. Remove the fabric from the dye and hang from the edges on a clothesline to dry. When the fabric is dry, place it between layers of newspaper and press with a hot iron to melt out the wax. The newspaper must be changed frequently as it absorbs the wax from the fabric. The areas covered with colored crayon wax will produce a tinted surface. Although only a single dye was used, the finished batik will be multicolored and can be mounted and framed.

Dip Dyeing
In the dip-dyeing method, the design is produced by folding a piece of paper and then dipping it in different colored dyes. Cover the working surface with newspapers. Place a piece of 9 X 12 inch rice paper or paper towel on the working surface and fold the bottom edge up about 1 inch. Turn the paper over and fold the bottom edge up again about 1 inch. Continue turning the

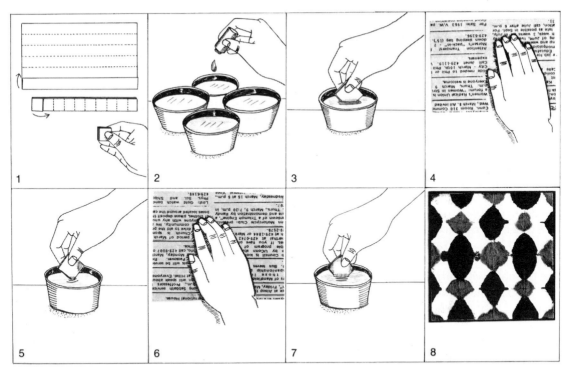

Figure 5-15   DIP DYEING

Materials: rice paper, food coloring or tempera paint, small containers, newspaper.

1. Fold a piece of rice paper as illustrated.
2. Add a few drops of different food colorings to each container.
3. Dip a corner of the folded paper into one of the colored solutions.
4. Blot the excess moisture with newspaper.
5. Dip another corner of the folded paper into a different colored solution.
6. Blot the excess moisture with newspaper.
7. Dip another corner of the folded paper into a different colored solution.
8. Finished dip-dyed design.

GRAPHIC AND
MANIPULATIVE
ART FORMS AND
INSTRUCTIONAL
METHODS

138

paper over, folding the bottom edge up until the top edge is reached. Hold the strip vertically and fold the bottom end up about 1 inch. Turn the paper over and fold it again. Continue folding the paper until the top edge is reached. Fill four small containers with water and add a few drops of a different color dye, food coloring, or tempera paint to each container of water. The lightness or darkness of the tone is controlled by the amount of color added to the water. The more coloring added, the darker the tone. Dip one corner of the folded paper into one of the colored solutions. Remove from the solution and blot with a piece of newspaper to remove any excess moisture. Turn the paper and dip a different corner into another color. Remove the paper from the solution and blot with a piece of newspaper to remove any excess moisture. Repeat the dipping process for the other two corners, using different colors for each corner. Unfold the paper and hang up to dry. A brush may also be used to apply the color. As the color is absorbed, it spreads and forms a design. The paper can be folded in different ways and dipped to create a more complex design. The size of the paper sheet dyed can vary with the requirements of the activity.

Tie Dyeing

In tie dyeing, fabric is dipped in a dye bath after having sections twisted and tied tightly with string or cord. Tightly tying the material prevents the dye from penetrating sections of the fabric, resulting in areas that retain the original color of the cloth. When the fabric is untied a two-color design will appear on the surface. The fabric can be retied and dyed with another color or different intensity of the same color. The fabric to be dyed should be free of all sizing. Sizing is removed by washing the fabric with soap and water.

The fabric can be tied in a number of different ways to obtain a wide variety of designs. If this is the first attempt at tie dyeing, it is advisable to practice on a piece of scrap material. A circle design is obtained by picking up the fabric from the middle and folding the material as evenly as possible into a strip. Tie string tightly around the material at different intervals. After dyeing, these tied areas will appear as circles the same color as the original fabric. Varied shapes are obtained by tying marbles, pebbles, or different shapes of hardwood in the fabric. The material can be rolled into a tube and tied with string to create a series of strips.

When the fabric is tied, it is ready to be dipped in the dye bath. Mix the dye according to the directions that come with the package. Dip the tied fabric into a container of warm water before dyeing. Remove from the warm water and wring out the excess water. Dip the tied fabric in the dye mixture and stir constantly with a stick for about three minutes. Remove the fabric from the dye and rinse in cold water. Do not leave the fabric in the dye too long or the color will penetrate the tied areas, destroying the design.

A second color is added, if desired, by removing the string and tying the fabric in new locations. The fabric is dipped into the new dye solution and rinsed out in cold water. The fabric is allowed to drip dry until damp and then pressed with a hot iron, which helps set the color.

FLOATING DESIGNS

Floating designs may be used to decorate the surface of a piece of paper. Single-color and multicolor designs may be created by using this technique. Children enjoy interpreting the patterns that are formed as the paint-turpentine mixture is swirled. Fill a wide, shallow pan with water. Into a small jar, pour a small quantity of turpentine and then add enough powder or oil paint to bring it to the required color strength. Pour a small amount of paint-turpentine mixture onto the surface of the water. With a stick, stir the water, causing the paint-turpentine mixture to form a series of interesting swirl designs. Pick up a piece of drawing paper and place it on top of the water and swirl the design. Carefully lift the paper from the water and place it on a piece of newspaper to dry. The piece of paper can also be dragged across the surface of the water to pick up the design. More than one color can be used at one time, creating a multicolored design. The second or third colors

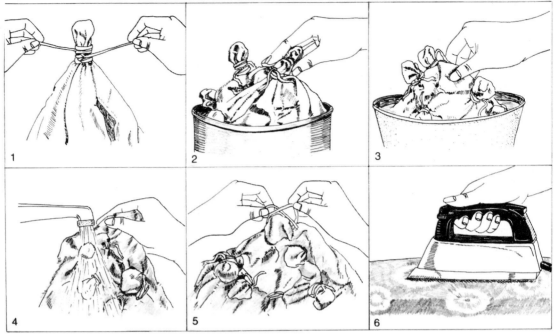

Figure 5-16 TIE DYEING

Materials: string, cloth, dye, large containers, water, stirring stick, iron.
1. Gather small bunches of material and tie them with string.
2. Place the tied fabric in a container of warm water. Remove fabric from the warm water and wring out the excess water.
3. Dip the tied fabric in the dye and stir for about three minutes.
4. Rinse the dyed fabric under cold water.
5. Remove the string and allow the fabric to drip dry until damp.
6. Iron the material with a warm iron.

are mixed in the same way as the first paint-turpentine mixture and then added to the water. The designs may be controlled or they may be spontaneous, depending on the desired effect. If oil paints are used, the water and paints should not be washed down the sink. After emptying the container, wipe the surface clean with soap or detergent and a cloth or paper towels.

DECOUPAGE

Decoupage is the art of decorating a surface using cutout paper pictures. The picture is transferred to the new surface with a special medium that picks up the printed design but not the paper backing. Printed pictures can be transferred to wood, glass, china, plastic, and metal. The transfer medium can be purchased at most paint stores or craft shops.

Select a picture and cut it out. Brush four coats of transfer medium onto the front surface of the picture. Coats one and three are brushed on the surface vertically, while coats two and four are brushed horizontally. Fifteen minutes should be allowed between each coat or until the film covering the surface is clear. The brush should be cleaned between each application. Allow the final coat to dry for at least two hours.

GRAPHIC AND
MANIPULATIVE
ART FORMS AND
INSTRUCTIONAL
METHODS

140

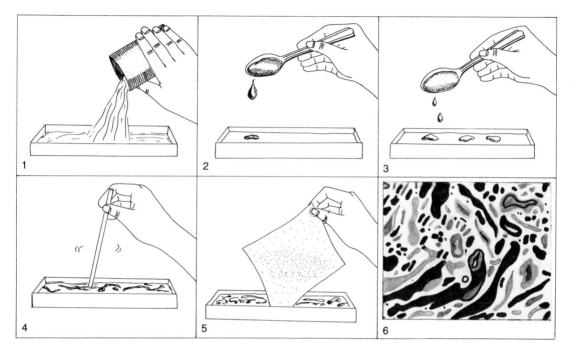

Figure 5-17 FLOATING DESIGNS

Materials: water, paper, turpentine, paint, large shallow pan, stirring stick, spoon.

1. Fill a wide shallow pan with water.
2. Add enough paint to a small quantity of turpentine to obtain the desired color. Drop a small amount of the paint-turpentine mixture onto the surface of the water.
3. Add a second or third color to the surface of the water if desired.
4. Stir the water, causing the paint-turpentine mixture to form a series of swirl designs.
5. Place a piece of paper on top of the swirl designs.
6. Finished swirl design.

Trim 1/16 inch from the edges of the picture with a razor blade or knife. Place the picture face down in soapy water and allow to soak for one hour. Remove from the soapy water and rinse the picture in clear water. After rinsing the picture, place it face down on a smooth, hard surface. Rub firmly over the surface with your fingers to peel the paper from the film. It may be necessary to add water or resoak the picture to remove all the paper. The picture will show through when all the paper is removed. Allow the surface to dry, and then apply a coat of transfer medium to the back of the picture. Also apply a coating of transfer medium to the surface on which the picture is going to be attached. The surface to which the picture is being transferred should be painted or stained before the picture is applied. Place the picture on the surface and use fingers to press the picture flat. Care should be taken to remove air bubbles and excess transfer medium. Allow the picture to dry until completely transparent. Apply decoupage finish with a brush, brushing in one direction with long flowing strokes. Remove any brush hairs from the surface. The finish should be allowed to dry one hour before a second coat is added. Repeat until the desired finish is obtained, and then clean the brush with thinner.

Many individuals ask the questions, "What is the right way to use paints?" and "What is the right way to use crayons?" The answers are that the good arts and crafts program should provide children with an opportunity to express themselves in their own unique manner. The program should provide an environment that encourages children to explore and create. Participants should also be afforded the chance to work with other materials that can be used to print, paint, or color a design or picture. Children will create their own techniques in using paints, crayons, and other art materials if provided with the opportunity to do so.

GRAPHIC AND
MANIPULATIVE
ART FORMS AND
INSTRUCTIONAL
METHODS

142

PRINT MAKING AND BOOKBINDING

Printing, silk-screen printing, etching, and bookbinding are all techniques that bring an added dimension to the creative process for children. Linoleum, cardboard, vegetable, stick, leaf, and sponge printing are common to most recreational and school crafts programs. However, silk-screen printing, etching, and bookbinding are usually neglected in the planning of activities for these programs. This chapter describes in detail these processes so that they may be included in the development of any crafts program. They do not require any more equipment or skill than linoleum printing.

The important point to remember in any of the print-making techniques is that they should be used to reproduce more than one copy from the original form. Too many crafts programs have children spending hours cutting a design to make a single print. Children should be encouraged to use a single design to create an overall design or to use a combination of designs to decorate a surface. Explore the different techniques presented in this chapter and see how they can be used to enrich any recreational or school crafts program.

PRINTING TECHNIQUES
Printing is the process of decorating a surface by stamping it with an inked design. Generally, the procedure is to ink a raised surface which bears the design to be printed. The inked design is then pressed against

the surface to be imprinted, transferring the design to it. Printing from a raised surface provides unlimited possibilities for any crafts program. Any textured surface, such as old floor tile or string wrapped around a tin can, can be used to print a design. The suggestions for materials presented in this section are only ideas to stimulate interest in printing from a raised surface. Many other materials can be used, and the only real limitation is one's imagination.

Linoleum Block Printing

Linoleum block printing is the most difficult of the printing techniques. Therefore, it would be advisable for a beginner to try a simple method of printing (vegetable, stick) before attempting it. The beginner should have the experience of cutting a design into some material which is soft and easy to cut. A potato or carrot will be most suitable for the beginner to learn the "hows and whys" of block printing. A gum eraser, a discarded bottle cork, or a Styrofoam meat container may be used to learn the techniques of block printing.

Cutting Tools   Linoleum-cutting tools are needed to carve the block print. These tools have replaceable blades, so that dull or broken blades are easily and quickly replaced. A set of cutters consisting of U-shaped and V-shaped gouges of different sizes, a flat chisel, and a cutting knife are the tools used to carve a linoleum block. The U-shaped gouges are used to scoop out large areas, while the V-shaped gouges are used to cut fine lines for detail. The chisel is used to smooth flat areas, and the knife is used to trim edges for clear, sharp lines. A few well-cared-for sets of linoleum-cutting tools will serve the needs of most recreational programs.

Preparation of copy   Selecting a design for the block print is the most important aspect of the printing technique. Block printing in most recreational and educational programs too often means copying designs from Christmas or birthday cards. Students in any crafts program should be encouraged to create a picture or design for their block print. The inspiration can come from a film, story, or field trip. It may be the result of a discussion on nature.

Draw the sketch or design on a piece of paper the size of the desired block. When the sketch is completed, it is ready for transferring to the block. Place a piece of carbon paper on top of the block with the carbon side down. Place the sketch on top of the carbon paper and tape it to the block with masking tape. Use a pencil to trace the sketch on the linoleum surface. Darken the carbon impression with a pencil so that all the details and outlines are clear and easy to follow. Words or letters should be in the negative on the block if they are to print in the positive.

Carving a Linoleum Block   The cutting is done on a bench hook made of a flat board that has a strip of wood fastened across each end, with one strip on the top and the other on the bottom surface. The bench hook is held against the edge of the table top by the bottom strip, while the top

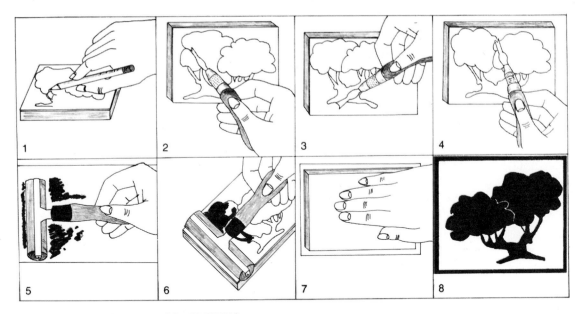

Figure 6-1 LINOLEUM BLOCK PRINTING
Materials: linoleum block, paper to be imprinted, printing ink, pencil, brayer, inking plate, linoleum cutter.

1. Draw the design on the block.
2. Cut around the outline with a V-shaped cutter.
3. Cut away large areas with a U-shaped cutter.
4. Finish details with the V-shaped cutter.
5. Roll out ink on the inking plate.
6. Apply ink to the design.
7. Press the inked design against the surface to be imprinted.
8. Set the printed design aside to dry.

strip provides an edge against which the block is held for cutting. This device protects the working surface and makes the cutting process easier and safer. The hand holding the block must be behind the cutting tool. This will reduce the chances of injury should the cutting tool slip.

Place the block on the bench hook. Select a cutter that is found to be most convenient for accomplishing the desired cut. Experimentation on a scrap piece of linoleum will enable the individual to determine the characteristics and advantages of each cutting tool. When using the cutters, always make a thin, shallow cut in the linoleum around the design. The small V-shaped tool works very well, and for this reason it is usually referred to as the "liner." After the outline of the design has been cut, take the large V-shaped gouge and make a deeper cut directly over the fine cut made with the liner. Be careful not to cut into the inked area.

Remove those linoleum surfaces which are not part of the inked areas of the design. The cuts should be deep enough toward the burlap backing so that just the design stands out in relief. The U-shaped gouge is used to make these long cuts from the edge of the design outward toward the edge of the piece of linoleum. These cuts should overlap so that no high areas or ridges remain. When cutting around the edge of the design, do not make the cuts perpendicular to the surface of the linoleum, but slope them gradually outward from the outline of the design. This sloped edge adds strength to the printing surface, and reduces the possibility of the edges breaking down during the printing operation.

Procedure for Printing   After the block is completely carved, it is ready for inking. Cover a working surface with old newspapers and prepare an inking slab. The inking slab can be a piece of Masonite, Formica, metal, or plastic, or even a cookie sheet on which a small amount of printing ink can be squeezed. Water-base ink can be used for most activities. However, oil-base inks should be used for printing on textiles or any other surfaces that may be exposed to water. Water-base inks can be cleaned with water, while oil-base inks require special solvents, such as paint thinner. Roll a brayer across the ink until it has a "tacky" sound and feel. Transfer the ink from the slab to the block with the brayer. Ink the block by rolling the brayer across it in both directions until the entire surface is evenly covered.

The inked block is ready for printing. Place the material to be imprinted on top of a 1-inch padded surface of newspaper. The padded surface will compensate for the fact that the surfaces may not be flat and even. Pick up the block and carefully place it onto the surface to be imprinted with the inked side down. Press it gently but firmly against the surface. The back surface of the block can be rubbed with the hand. If the ink has been applied correctly and the padded surface used, the printing of the block design should require only finger pressure for a good-quality print. Care should be taken not to smudge the ink when removing the block from the printed surface.

The print should be checked to see if additional cutting is desirable. If additional cuts are required, wipe the block clean with a paper towel or cloth and return it to the bench hook for further cutting. If no additional cutting is needed, the printing operation can be continued.

Colored inks can be used to make the block print more interesting and attractive. Another technique that adds to the quality of a print is the cutting procedure used. Instead of leaving large areas of solid or blank design, a texture technique can be used which will break up solid areas. This technique makes the print more appealing. Encouragement to explore with different types of printing should be made. Emphasis should not be placed on the finished product but rather on understanding the characteristics and properties of the materials used in the process. Children have intuitive feeling for design and need opportunity to foster this ability. They cannot succeed if forced to concentrate on finishing a block print without any provisions for experimentation with the materials and process.

Stick Printing

A wide variety of different shaped moldings can be purchased from the local lumber yard and used to print designs or pictures. Old broom handles also can be cut and used to print circles. Rectangular and square pieces of

GRAPHIC AND
MANIPULATIVE
ART FORMS AND
INSTRUCTIONAL
METHODS

146

pine can be used to print, or they can be shaped with a file and sandpaper to the desired form. The end of the stick should be sanded smooth before it is used as a printing surface.

Place the material (cloth or paper) on a padded surface. The padded surface compensates for the fact that neither surface is flat and true. Take a wide-mouth container and place about ½ inch of paint into it. Then place a sponge in the container. The combination of sponge and paint will replace the inking pad. Select the stick or sticks, remembering that the shape can be changed with a file, knife, or sandpaper. The shapes chosen should have some relationship to the finished design or picture. Take one of the sticks and touch the printing end against the sponge. When the stick is pressed against the sponge, it will pick up paint. Remove the stick from the sponge and place it against the surface to be printed. Repeat the operation of applying paint to the stick and printing the shape. Try various shaped sticks in different combinations to form a design or picture. When printing with sticks, it is necessary to pick up the right amount of paint on the end. Too much paint will result in a blurred print. Again, as with any crafts technique, experimentation will assist the individual to learn the characteristics and properties of stick printing.

String Pulling

String pulling is a very simple technique that can be used to obtain attractive designs on paper. String, tempera paints, paper, and a wide-mouth container are the only materials needed for this activity. Select the desired colored tempera paint and place enough into the container to cover a piece of string. Cut a piece of string about the length of your arm. Take a piece of paper (newsprint, drawing, construction) and fold it in half. Holding the end of the string in one hand, dip the rest of it into the paint. A stick or pencil may be needed to make sure that the string is completely submerged. Place the end of the string between a piece of scrap paper and pull it from the paint, making sure that the string passes through the scrap paper. As the string moves through the piece of scrap paper, the excess paint will be removed. If the excess paint is not removed from the string, the design will have a blurred effect. Open the folded piece of paper and place the string on one side of the paper. The string is held above the piece of paper and allowed to drop in a circular and elliptical motion onto one side of the fold. The other half of the paper is folded over the top of the string. One hand is placed on top of the paper and the other is used to pull the string from between the folded paper. The string can be pulled straight out or from side to side. Before adding any additional paint, a second string pull can be tried. The second print will usually be lighter, but may have greater detail.

Different sized string can be used to change the texture and effect of the design. A second color can be included in the design by placing the string in a different colored paint and repeating the pulling operation. Another method of adding a second color is to add the paint to the string with the fingers before placing it between the folded paper. Both of these techniques for color variation require experimentation.

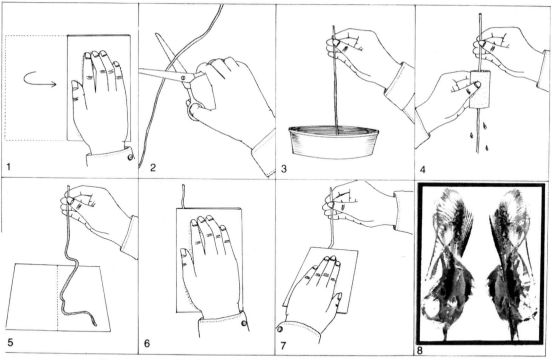

Figure 6-2 STRING PULLING

Materials: scissors, wide-mouth container, paint, string, scrap paper, paper.

1. Fold the piece of paper in half as illustrated.
2. Cut a piece of string the length of your arm.
3. Place the string in the container of paint.
4. Remove the string from the paint, wiping the excess paint from the string with a piece of scrap paper.
5. Drop the string on one half of the paper.
6. Fold the piece of paper together, forming a sandwich with the string as a filler.
7. Place one hand on top of the paper, and with the other hand pull the string from between the two surfaces.
8. Finished print.

Sponge Printing

Sponges can be purchased in a great variety of textures and then used to print curious designs or pictures. It is important to remember that the sponge was selected because of its texture and that this texture adds to the finished print.

Fill one wide-mouth container with water and another with the desired colored paint. With a knife or pair of scissors, cut the sponge into different shapes. After the sponge has been cut, moisten in water. Squeeze out any excess water. The sponge should be damp. Dip the moistened sponge into the container of paint and squeeze out the extra paint. The sponge is ready for printing. Dab the sponge against the surface to be printed. Too much pressure applied when dabbing will result in a blurred impression. Practice the technique, changing the amount of water and paint used. Notice the difference in the printed shapes. This activity can be stimulating

GRAPHIC AND
MANIPULATIVE
ART FORMS AND
INSTRUCTIONAL
METHODS

148

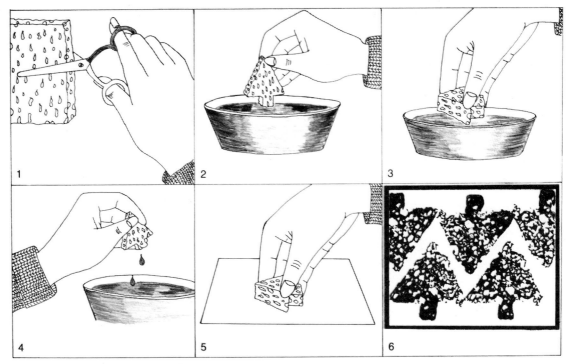

Figure 6-3 SPONGE PRINTING

Materials: sponge, paint, pan of water, scissors, paper.

1. Cut the sponge into different shapes.
2. Dip the sponge into a pan of water and squeeze out any excess water.
3. Dip the sponge into the paint.
4. Squeeze out any excess paint from the sponge.
5. Press the wet sponge against the surface to be imprinted.
6. Set the finished print aside to dry.

for children when they develop an understanding and feeling for the material utilized in this technique.

Surprise Printing

Surprise prints require only limited supplies and materials to provide children with an interesting crafts medium. Only tempera paints, watercolors, a paintbrush, and paper are needed for children to create some interesting designs. Children enjoy determining what the finished print looks like, giving their prints names, or writing stories about them.

To make a surprise print, select a piece of paper (newsprint, drawing) and fold it in half. With a paint brush, drop small spots of paint on one side of the folded paper. Tempera or watercolors can be used. More than one color can be used for variety. The paint should be watery so that it will spread easily. Fold the half with no paint over onto the side with the paint spots. Run the side of the hand over the face of the paper from the bottom to the top edge. Unfold the paper. If the spots have not spread, it is probable that the paint was not watery enough or too little paint was used. If the paint is too watery, it will run together to form a big blur. Prints should be

PRINT MAKING
AND BOOKBINDING

149

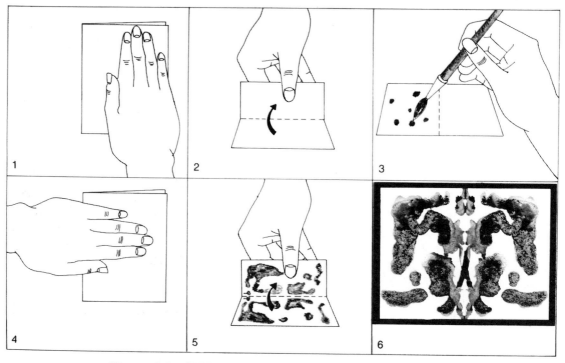

Figure 6-4 SURPRISE PRINT

Materials: paper, paint, paintbrush.
1. Fold the sheet of paper in half.
2. Unfold the sheet of paper.
3. Paint some spots of paint on one side of the paper.
4. Fold the sheet of paper and apply pressure to the top surface.
5. Unfold the sheet of paper.
6. Set the print aside to dry.

made combining different colors and consistencies of paint. Varying combinations of the size and location of the paint spots should also be tried.

Brayer Printing

The brayer can be used to apply printing inks to a surface that is placed over a piece of cardboard or string to obtain an unusual effect. The tones and shadows developed in this way can be utilized as a background for a picture or design.

Thin cardboard can be cut into geometric patterns for base material. Shapes can also be torn from a piece of cardboard, leaving irregular and frayed edges rather than straight and even edges. String, yarn, and bail wire cut into different lengths can also be used as base material. Twist the string or wire into various shapes. What other materials can be used as a base material? How about spaghetti, rice, and gravel! Try some of these materials alone and in combination. Place the selected base material on top of some newspaper. The shapes or material can be randomly dispersed or a planned format can be utilized for the base. A piece of drawing

GRAPHIC AND
MANIPULATIVE
ART FORMS AND
INSTRUCTIONAL
METHODS

150

paper or wrapping paper is used to cover the base materials. Care should be taken not to disturb the base design or arrangement. The corner should be taped down to prevent the paper from moving. Take a piece of metal or Masonite (smooth side up) and place a few drops of printing ink onto it. Roll the brayer over the drops of ink. The roller will pick up ink from one surface and allow it to be transferred to another. Care must be taken not to overwork the ink. The purpose of the brayer is to pick up, not spread, the ink. When the ink has coated the roller, the brayer is ready to run across the surface to be printed. Try running the brayer horizontally, and then change the piece of paper and run the brayer vertically across the surface. Add ink to the brayer to obtain the desired color and effect. Run the brayer across the surface in several directions. Change the arrangement of the base materials. Apply more than one color to the surface being printed. Combine more than one color at the same time. The possibilities are limited only by the imagination.

Leaf Printing

Almost any leaf can be used to print on paper or cloth. Collect different sized and shaped leaves and grass. Apply a few drops of printing ink to a piece of metal or Masonite (smooth side). Roll the brayer over the drops of ink. Select a leaf and place it on top of a piece of newspaper with the working surface (vein side) up. When the roller is coated with ink, apply the ink to the leaf by rolling it over the working surface. Pick up the leaf and place it onto a piece of paper with the inked surface down. A second piece of paper is put over the leaf and the side of the hand run from the bottom to the top edge of the paper. The top sheet is removed carefully, so as not to disturb the leaf. A print of the leaf remains on the bottom paper.

Some interesting effects can be obtained by mixing different sized and shaped leaves and grass together. Leaves can be inked with different colors and all printed on the surface at the same time. This technique requires experimentation to obtain the desired results. Too much ink can result in a blurred print. Evergreens, leaves with flowers, and vegetables also can be used to print a design or picture.

Vegetable Printing

Vegetable printing offers an opportunity to develop a design. A carrot or potato can be cut in half, creating two smooth surfaces on which to draw a design. The surfaces of either vegetable can be cut with a simple dull tool such as a paring knife. A melon spoon is also a useful tool for shaping the surface. Those parts of the design that are not to be printed are cut away, leaving only the surface to be printed. The surface to be printed should be put onto a padded surface of newspaper. Printing ink can be applied to the design with a brayer or the design can be painted, using tempera paints and brush. A stamp pad like the one made for stick printing can also be used. When the design has been inked or painted, it is ready for printing. The vegetable is held in the hand and the design is pressed against the surface to be printed on.

The design is not the most important aspect of vegetable printing.

Figure 6-5 SAMPLE PRINTS
1. Eraser print
2. Soap print
3. Stencil print
4. Stick print
5. Leaf print

A poor design can be both effective and attractive if printed rhythmically and systematically. However, children at an early age should begin to take pride in creating an aesthetically pleasing design. The child should be encouraged to try many techniques. For example, after printing a page of repeats in a light color, the surface can be wiped clean and a second color printed over a portion of each of the first prints. This process will create a multicolored print in a uniform fashion. Another method is to print a flower design three times before adding more ink or paint. Each print is repeated in the same spot, except that the design is turned slightly each time. The result is a flower with a shade and shadow effect.

Cardboard Printing
Cardboard from candy boxes and other types of packages can be used for printing. Corrugated cardboard should not be used for printing, because it is not strong enough to withstand the repeated pressure required to print a series of designs. For best results the cardboard should be solid.

Select a piece of cardboard and with a pencil draw a design on the

GRAPHIC AND
MANIPULATIVE
ART FORMS AND
INSTRUCTIONAL
METHODS

152

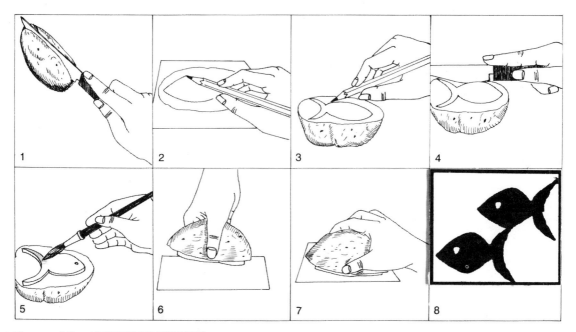

Figure 6-6 VEGETABLE PRINTING

Materials: uncooked vegetable, knife, pencil, paper, paint, paintbrush, surface to be imprinted.

1. Cut the vegetable in half and allow to dry.
2. Sketch a design on a piece of paper.
3. Transfer the design to the vegetable.
4. Carve out the design.
5. Apply paint to the design.
6. Place the vegetable and paper in position for printing.
7. Press the inked design against the surface to be imprinted.
8. Set the printed design aside to dry.

surface. A stencil or Exacto knife can be used to cut the design into the cardboard surface. The outline of the design is cut out with a pair of scissors, while interior lines and features are cut into the surface with a stencil or Exacto knife. When the design is finished, it can be mounted onto a piece of 3/4-inch plywood with one of the quick-drying glues. After the glue dries, the cardboard print is ready for inking. Printing ink can be applied to the surface with a brayer. The piece of material (paper or cloth) to be imprinted should be put onto a padded surface of old newspapers. The newspaper pad should be at least 1/2 inch thick. The inked cardboard print is placed against the material to be imprinted and pressure applied evenly to the block. The block should not be placed on a piece of paper on the floor and then stood upon, because the block and floor may not be flat and even. One misconception in printing is that greater pressure is required for the print to appear darker. Poor printing is usually caused by the design being incorrectly inked or the print being pressed against a surface that is not flat and even. The padded surface will compensate for differences that may exist between the printing block and the surface against which the imprinted material is held.

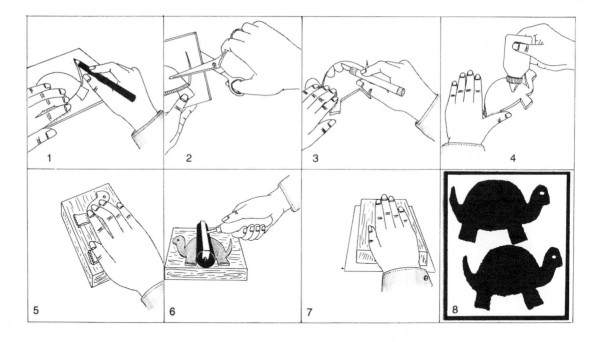

Figure 6-7 CARDBOARD PRINTING

Materials : cardboard, wooden block, pencil, stencil knife, paper, brayer, scissors, printing ink, and glue.

1. Sketch a design on a piece of heavy cardboard.
2. Cut around the outline of the design.
3. Use a stencil knife to remove interior sections from the design.
4. Apply glue to the back surface of the piece of cardboard.
5. Glue the cardboard to the wooden block.
6. Apply ink to the design.
7. Press the inked design against the surface to be imprinted.
8. Finished print.

Cardboard is made up of layers of paper which can be removed to form details and characteristics for the design being carved. To obtain skill in cardboard printing requires experimentation with the cutting and inking tools. This technique is excellent for a recreational program because it is inexpensive and easy.

String Printing

In string printing string is wrapped around a tin can and the wrapped can is then rolled over a piece of Masonite with printing ink on the surface. The string picks up the ink. Designs are formed by rolling the can horizontally, vertically, or diagonally across a sheet of paper. Different colors will also add to the aesthetic value of the design. Variation in the thickness of the string on different cans will change the texture of the print.

Glue Printing

An attractive print can be made using a piece of plywood on which glue has been dripped to create a raised design. The glue may be freely dripped directly from a squeeze bottle, or a design can be drawn on the wooden sur-

GRAPHIC AND
MANIPULATIVE
ART FORMS AND
INSTRUCTIONAL
METHODS

154

face with a pencil and the glue applied to these lines. Some children may prefer to work spontaneously. After the glue dries, the surface can be inked with a brayer in the same manner as with a block print. The ink has a tendency to adhere to the raised surface of the glue. A piece of paper is placed over the surface and carefully rubbed with the side of the hand. The paper is removed, and an impression of the design created by the glue appears. The texture of the design can be changed by varying the width of the glued lines that form the design. Variation in color can also be used to increase the quality of the finished design.

Metal-foil Printing
Flat aluminum foil cake pans can be used for printing. The flat foil is placed on a thick pad of newspaper and a pencil used to draw the design onto the surface. The pressure of the pencil raises a line on the reverse side of the foil. Because a fine-pointed tool is used to draw the design, detail is possible that cannot be obtained when utilizing other printing techniques. When the drawing is completed, the foil is attached to a piece of cardboard with the raised surface out. A brayer is used to apply the ink to the raised surface. The inked surface is then pressed against the surface to be imprinted. The finished print will be like a line drawing. Numerous effects can be obtained using this process alone or in combination with other printing techniques

Eraser Printing
A pencil eraser and a stamping pad can be used to print interesting and appealing pictures and designs. Ink on a slab can be used in place of a stamping pad. The small circles formed by the eraser create a picture or design like the half tone, a picture formed by a series of dots. Different colors and tones can be used to vary the design.

Soap Printing
A design can be carved on one of the surfaces of a bar of soap and then used for printing. Ivory soap is good for carving because it is soft and easy to work.

If either face surface is used, the lettering should be scraped off before starting to carve a design. The design can be drawn on the surface of the soap with a pencil. A knife and round stick sharpened at one end can be used to carve the design. The design can be inked with a brayer or painted. A stamp pad can be made by using a sponge in a container of paint. When the surface is inked or painted, it is ready to print. The surface to be imprinted should be placed on a padded surface made from about a 1-inch pile of old newspapers. The bar of soap is held by the edges and even pressure applied to the design against the surface to be imprinted. The desired amount of paint or ink can only be achieved through practice. Too much paint or ink causes a blurred design; an insufficiency produces a washed-out faded design.

Miscellaneous Types of Printing
Almost any type of material can be used for printing. Cork, Styrofoam, and carpet can provide the printing surface, and seeds, rice, straw, and

burlap can be glued to a piece of cardboard for different printing effects. New materials are always being developed for packaging that may be appropriate for printing. Old materials can be used with new materials to create a print.

Children should be encouraged to experiment with different materials and to combine different types of printing into a picture or design. The success of any program depends upon the utilization of scrap materials.

SILK-SCREEN PRINTING

Silk-screen printing is a process in which the stencil bearing the design to be reproduced is permanently affixed to a screen of silk, organdy, or some other meshed material. Colored paints, inks, or other printing mediums are forced through the screen with a squeegee and deposited on the printing surface, thus forming an impression of the original design. The technique is known as the silk-screen process because, originally, silk was exclusively used for the screen.

Materials

Silk-Screen Frames Silk-screen frames vary in size and are constructed from wood or cardboard. Some frames are hinged to a base of 3/4-inch plywood to control movement during printing. For simple printing operations, the frame does not need to be hinged to a base. The hinged frame is effective for stencil designs utilizing more than one color.

The frame is covered with a coarse or fine meshed material, usually silk, nylon, nylon hosiery, or organdy. The mesh of the material used for a screen should not be too fine or it will clog during printing.

A simple frame can be constructed by cutting away an area from the bottom or top of a cardboard candy box. This open area is covered with a piece of meshed material pulled smooth and stapled to the sides. The edges around the opening are taped to the meshed material with masking tape to prevent the paint or ink from seeping under the frame, thereby spoiling the design. The cardboard frame has only limited use and is not as durable as a wooden frame. However, with young children and crayon-and-paper stencil designs, the cardboard frame is satisfactory.

A wooden frame can be constructed from 1 x 2 inch wooden strips mitered at the corners and fastened together with glue and nails. The frame size may vary with the design to be printed. The frame is covered with a meshed material stretched smooth and tightened over the frame and secured with staples. To secure the screen evenly, begin at the center of one side; staple, pull the material tight, and staple the center on the opposite side. Repeat this process on each end of the frame. Then work the material from the centers toward the corners of the frame, stretching and stapling the material until the frame is covered.

Squeegee A squeegee is constructed by attaching a strip of rubber to a wooden handle. The squeegee is pulled across the stencil design, forcing the ink through the screen onto the surface to be decorated. Squeegees can be constructed or purchased and should be as wide as the frame being used.

Inks and Paints   Both oil- and water-base inks are available for silk screening a stencil design. Oil-base inks and paints require special solvents for thinning and cleaning, while water-base inks and paints require only water. Colors are opaque when thick and transparent when thinned. One color can be printed over another color when the first is dry. Dark colors are usually applied over light colors.

Fabrics   Any surface that will accept the paint or ink can be used for silk screening. Sized fabrics should be washed before they are imprinted; unwashed sized fabrics will not retain color when washed.

Procedure
How to Cut a Silk-Screen Stencil   Make an accurate drawing for the design on a piece of paper. With masking tape secure the four corners to a flat surface. Place a piece of lacquer film over the design with the lacquered side up and secure the corners with masking tape. The film should have a perimeter about 1 inch larger than the design. The design, clearly visible through the transparent lacquer film, is ready to be cut.

The design must be cut through the lacquer coating only. It should not be cut through the paper backing, which is a temporary carrier for the lacquer coating until it is transferred to the screen.

The stencil knife is used like a pen, and the operation is the same as tracing. A light even stroke is used. The stencil knife is held at an angle. A straightedge should be used· as a guide for cutting straight lines, while circles and arcs are cut with the aid of dividers. Irregular lines are cut freehand with a stencil knife, or a French curve can be used as a guide. Thin, straight, parallel lines are cut in one operation with a ruling pen. The points are set to the correct width and the lines are cut by pulling the pen along the straightedge. Square or sharply intersecting lines are cut across corners.

When the complete outline of any part of the design has been cut, that area of the film is carefully stripped from the paper backing. To strip the film from the backing, insert the point of the stencil knife under one corner of the cut portion and carefully peel off the lacquer film which is in the traced area. Continue cutting and peeling the film until the design is completed. If a completely outlined area is cut through the paper backing, that area will fall out.

Attaching Lacquer Film to Screen   To join the lacquer film to the screen, place the lacquer side up on a flat, smooth working surface. Then place the screen over the top of the film with the design in the desired position, so that the screen touches the film. Pour a small quantity of adhesive liquid (lacquer thinner) into a shallow tray or saucer. Moisten a cloth with the liquid and dampen a small portion of the screen. Immediately wipe this area dry with a second and larger cloth. If the adhesive liquid is allowed to settle, it will dissolve the lacquer film, thus ruining the design. Continue to moisten small areas of the screen and dry them immediately. Use a light rubbing motion to dry the screen and continue rubbing until the solution has evaporated. When the film has been attached to the screen, allow several minutes for drying.

Carefully place the stencil knife under one of the corners of the backing sheet and separate it from the film. Hold the paper backing with the fingers and slowly peel it off. Work slowly to prevent tearing. Should the film start to tear, stop and apply more adhesive liquid to that area. After the paper backing has been peeled off, check the design for any imperfections in the film. Imperfections are touched up by applying lacquer filler to the area with a brush or pen.

Mask out the open spaces between the edges of the film and the frame with paper and masking tape. The inside edges should be taped so that the tape, which is first creased in half lengthwise, is half on the wood and half on the screen. This will seal the inside edges of the frame and prevent any paint from seeping under the frame.

Printing a Silk-Screen Design A smooth, level, and clean surface covered with a sheet of heavy paper should be used for printing. Before starting to print, mark the position of the two upper corners of the frame on the surface. These marks are not necessary if the frame is hinged. The position of the sheets to be printed must be marked for the proper placement of the design. This will ensure that the design is printed in the same position on all the sheets. Raised guides may be used where they do not interfere with the design.

Place enough ink or paint for several impressions in the upper margin of the screen. Use a rubber squeegee of sufficient length to reach across the design and push the ink over the open design, pressing the ink through to the sheet below. The squeegee is slanted slightly toward the operator as it is pulled with a side-to-side or wavy motion across the screen. This technique produces a more uniform impression.

After the sheet is printed, remove it by lifting the frame and inserting a new sheet in position against the guides. Each printed sheet should be set aside to dry. Sheets should not be piled one over another, because they will "offset;" that is paint will be transferred from one sheet to the back of the sheet which is placed over the wet sheet.

Cleaning the Screen The frame and squeegee should be thoroughly cleaned when the printing operation is completed. Oil-base colors are cleaned with a solvent. Remove the excess color from the screen with a squeegee or rubber spatula and return to the original container. Place the screen on old newspapers and press the solvent through the screen onto the newspaper with the squeegee or cloth. Continue until the screen is free of all color particles. Check the mesh of the screen by holding it up to the light. Clear any clogged areas by rubbing the screen with a cloth soaked with a solvent. Soap and water can be used for the final cleaning.

To clean water-base colors, substitute cool water for the solvent and use the same procedures as for oil-base colors. Remove stubborn spots by scrubbing the spotted areas with soap and water. Some screens cannot be cleaned, and others are not worth cleaning. These screens should be removed from the frame and discarded.

GRAPHIC AND
MANIPULATIVE
ART FORMS AND
INSTRUCTIONAL
METHODS

158

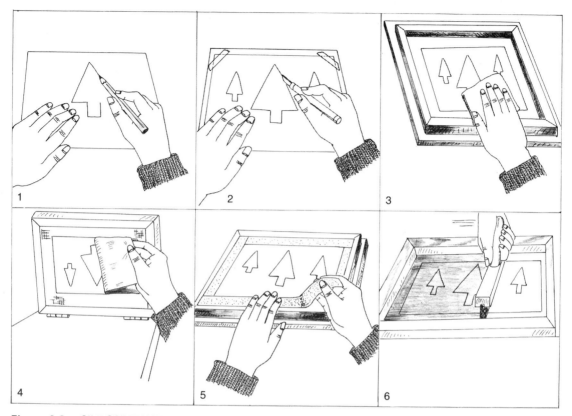

Figure 6-8 SILK-SCREEN PRINTING

Materials: pencil, lacquer film, inks or paints, squeegee, silk-screen frame, masking tape, stencil knife, lacquer thinner, scrap pieces of cloth, fabric or paper, mesh material (organdy).

1. Make an accurate drawing of the design to be printed.
2. Secure the design and film to a working surface and with a stencil knife cut the lacquer film.
3. Attach the lacquered film to the screen with adhering fluid.
4. Pull the paper backing from the lacquered film.
5. Seal the edges around the film and frame with masking tape.
6. Use even pressure to pull the squeegee across the screen. The paint is forced through the stencil onto the surface being imprinted.

Alternative Stencil Design Techniques

Stencil designs can be applied to the screen utilizing many different techniques. The process used to construct the stencil design depends upon the printing medium and the number of times it is to be used. The following techniques can be used to print an overall design or single impression.

Crayon Stencil Design   Crayon can be used to draw a stencil directly on a screen that can be printed with water-base paints or inks. The crayon is rubbed onto the surface, blocking the mesh in the screen and preventing the paint or ink from printing these areas. Place the frame over the design and with a crayon, trace the design onto the screen. Then fill in the design with a heavy coating of crayon.

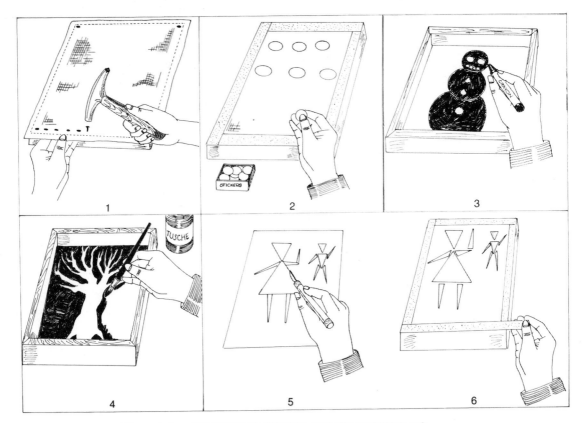

Figure 6-9   ALTERNATIVE STENCIL DESIGN TECHNIQUES

Materials: mesh material (organdy), silk-screen frame, gummed stickers, crayons, nail polish, shellac, stencil paper, masking tape.

1. Attach the mesh material to a frame.
2. Use gummed stickers to form a stencil design.
3. Use crayons to draw a stencil design on the mesh screen.
4. Use nail polish or shellac to paint a design on the mesh screen.
5. Use stencil paper to create a design on the mesh screen.
6. Seal the edges around the film, and frame with masking tape.

Stencil Paper Design   A design can be cut from stencil paper and attached to the bottom of the screen with masking tape. On a piece of paper, sketch or lay out a design. Transfer the design to a piece of stencil paper the same size as the frame opening. With a stencil knife, cut out the design. Secure the piece of stencil paper with the cut-out design to the bottom of the screen with masking tape.

Tracing paper, wax paper, and newsprint can be used to make a stencil design to be used for one run utilizing one color of an oil- or water-base ink or paint.

Gummed-Paper Stencil Design   A pattern can be formed by attaching gummed stickers to the bottom of the screen. Shapes can be punched or

GRAPHIC AND
MANIPULATIVE
ART FORMS AND
INSTRUCTIONAL
METHODS

160

cut from gummed paper and arranged in a design on the bottom of the screen.

Paint Stencil Design   Permanent stencil designs can be made by painting a design on the screen with house paints, spray paints, or lacquer. On a piece of paper, sketch or lay out a design. The design can be painted on the screen with a paintbrush, or a stencil can be used and the design sprayed.

Photo Stencil Design   Photo stencil designs are ideal for reproducing the very fine, delicate work which is too difficult to handle by any of the other techniques or wherever photographic accuracy is required. Only by the photo stencil process can very small lettering and fine pen drawings be reproduced. This technique is too difficult for young children. However, for some older children it may present a real challenge. Additional information can be obtained from reference books on the photo stencil design process of silk screening.

DRYPOINT ETCHING
Preparation of Copy
The copy for an etching should be composed of fine lines made by utilizing a pen or pencil sketching technique. A line sketch lends itself to etching, while a design with solid areas lends itself to either block or silk-screen printing. Photographs, illustrations, and pictures containing solid areas must be converted into a pen or pencil line sketch or printed using another medium. The design to be imprinted must be etched in the negative, that is, in reverse, in order to produce a positive impression. Hence, the original copy from which the etching will be traced must be transferred into the negative before it is copied. To make a negative sketch, place a sheet of carbon paper face up under the copy or design and fasten the corner with masking tape. Then trace all the lines. The carbon impression on the back of the sheet will be in the negative. The design will face in the opposite direction when the sheet is turned over. If the design is on transparent paper, it will need only to be turned over to be in the negative.

Place a piece of clear plastic over the design and secure the four corners with masking tape. With a sharp scribing tool, an awl, or a compass point, scratch the lines of the design into the plastic. For artistic effect a series of short lines should be used rather than a simple long line. The cuts are made by varying the pressure as the scriber is drawn over the plastic surfaces. Each line becomes a small trench with sidewalls to hold the ink.

The depth of the cut determines the intensity of the line printed. Deep cuts produce dark lines, while shallow ones result in light lines. Dark and shaded areas are obtained by carving and etching lines close together or cross-hatching an area. Cross-hatching consists of scribing a series of lines in one direction and then imposing a second series of lines in the opposite direction, crossing the first lines. Care should be taken not to remove the burrs formed as the lines are etched into the plastic. The burrs hold the ink in the etched lines. The progress and results of the etching may be observ-

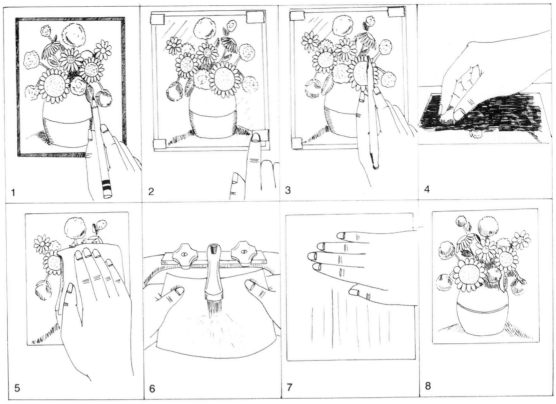

Figure 6-10   DRYPOINT ETCHING

Materials: sheet of plastic, masking tape, carbon paper, scribing tool, ink, piece of cloth, water, paper (uncoated).

1. Transfer a design into the negative by using a piece of carbon paper.
2. Secure the design and clear plastic to a working surface with masking tape.
3. Scratch the design into the plastic with a sharp scribing tool.
4. Press ink into the etched areas with a wadded cloth.
5. Wipe the surface clean, leaving only the etched areas filled with ink.
6. Wet a sheet of paper.
7. Place the paper over the inked surface and rub it to force the paper into the etched areas.
8. Finished print.

ed by sliding a sheet of colored paper between the plate and the copy. After the scribing is completed, the plastic plate is ready to be printed.

Printing a Drypoint Etching

The process of printing a drypoint etching is called "gravure" or printing from a recessed surface. It is the opposite of linoleum block printing, which is performed using a raised surface. Ink the plate by pressing the ink into the etched areas with a wadded cloth. Apply the ink in a circular motion, making sure that all the etched lines are filled with ink.

After the plate is inked, the surface of the plate should be wiped clean of ink and ink smudges, leaving only the etched areas filled with ink. This

GRAPHIC AND
MANIPULATIVE
ART FORMS AND
INSTRUCTIONAL
METHODS

162

will assure the print of having a clean background, with only the design actually printing.

Place the inked plate face up on a flat surface. Take a sheet of uncoated paper, which is first dampened with water to soften it, and place it over the plastic plate. The dampened surface makes it easier to pick up the ink from the etched surface, because the fibers are raised when wet. Place several sheets of blotting paper over the dampened paper and apply heavy pressure by rubbing the heel of the hand over the surface, forcing the paper into the scratches so that the sheet will pick up the ink. Separate the paper from the etched surface and check the print; additional lines may be added to the plate to obtain the desired effect. Two or three impressions may be made from one inking of the etched plate. The final print should be sharp and clear, free of any ink smudges. Set the prints aside to dry before handling.

Clean the plate with a solvent. Cleaning will prevent the ink from hardening in the etched surface, which would make it impossible to make any additional prints of the design.

BOOK BINDING

The art of bookbinding has infinite possibilities for any recreational and school crafts program. Periodicals, magazines, and typed pages can be bound together for easier handling and storage. It is an excellent method of restoring the appearance of old books. The basic techniques of bookbinding can be used to construct a photograph album, scrapbook, desk set, or portfolio. The possibilities of using many of these techniques in a crafts program are limited only by the individual's imagination.

Sewing Signatures

A signature is the arrangement of folded sheets of paper into groups. The folded sheets are inserted one inside of the other, forming sixteen to thirty-two pages of a book. The number of folded sheets inserted depends upon the thickness of the paper. However, four to eight is the number generally used.

With a ruler, mark off the folded edge every 3/4 inch and punch a hole at each mark with an awl. Holding the signature open with one hand, insert the needle through the first hole, and bring it out through the next hole. Continue until the opposite end is reached. Each signature is sewn using this technique before all are bound together.

Binding a Book by Side Sewing

The pages or signatures (sixteen- or thirty-two-page sections) for the book must be assembled in their proper order; a folded blank sheet of the same size is then placed at the front and back of the book. These folded sheets are called "end sheets" and are used for lining the covers. The completely assembled book is placed into a book press with a detachable guide and backstop for drilling the holes along the back of the book. This drill guide is a metal bar which has a series of small, evenly spaced holes across its entire length which serve as a guide for drilling through the pages.

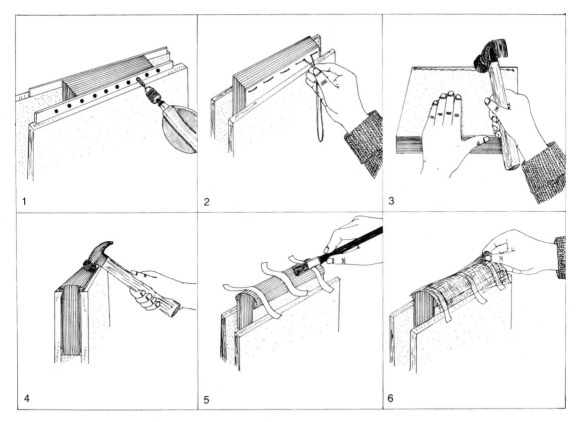

Figure 6-11 BOOKBINDING

Materials: hand drill, twist drill, needle and thread, hammer, book press, reinforcing tape, crinoline or organdy, glue.

1. Drill holes across the back of the book for sewing.
2. Sew the pages together as illustrated.
3. Round the back of the book by hammering.
4. Clamp the book in the press and flare the back edge of the book with a hammer.
5. While the book is still in the press, apply glue to the back surface and add reinforcing tapes.
6. Glue a piece of crinoline or organdy to the back surface.

The book is placed in the press with the back up, so that the holes in the drilling guide are about 1/8 inch from the top edge of the back of the book. If the holes are drilled too close to the back edge, strings might break through during the sewing operation.

With a drill, slightly smaller than the holes in the metal bar, bore a series of holes along the entire length of the back of the book. These holes will be used to sew the signatures together. When the drilling is completed, remove the guide and backstop from the press without disturbing the position of the pages. The book is ready for sewing.

Thread a large needle with heavy thread or lightweight string. Start the threaded needle through the first hole at the top end of the book, leaving a tail of about 2 or 3 inches. Bring the threaded needle back through

GRAPHIC AND
MANIPULATIVE
ART FORMS AND
INSTRUCTIONAL
METHODS

164

each succeeding hole the length of the book. Repeat the sewing operation by working the threaded needle back through the odd holes in the direction opposite to the starting position. Tie two ends of the string to prevent the string from loosening. The book is ready for the forwarding operations of trimming, rounding, gluing, and backing.

Rebinding an Old Book
Before an old book can be rebound, it must be stripped from the old cover. Remove cover by carefully cutting the cover at the hinges with a sharp knife. This will remove the cover boards, leaving only the back of the book with old binding. Care should be taken not to tear or soil the pages because of the added difficulty in repairing the book.

Place the book in the binder's press without destroying the original shape of the book. The back of the book should project about 1/4 inch above the top of the press to allow enough room for the back to be cut with a saw. Insert a piece of waxed paper on both sides of the book to prevent the pages from being glued to the press.

Clean the back of the book by removing the old super, a stiff crinoline cloth which was used to attach the book to the cover. Use a small hand scraper to scrape the surface smooth. Cleaning will provide a better adhesive surface for the glue. Make paired cuts across the back of the book about 1½ inches apart. The cuts are made about 1/8 inch deep and at an angle by slanting the saw. If the cuts are greater than 1/8 inch, they will show when the book is opened. The slanted cut will prevent the cords from working loose and weakening the book.

Insert cords made of heavy string in the grooves in the back of the book and brush glue over the entire back of the book. Glue must be brushed into the grooves holding the cords. The book should remain in the press until the glue is completely dry.

After the book dries, remove it and insert a folded sheet, the same size as the face of the book, on both the front and the back of the book. Attach these endsheets to the book by gluing a small 1/4 inch strip along one side of the folded edge of the back of the book. The book is then ready for the forwarding operations of trimming, rounding, gluing, and backing.

Forwarding a Book
Trimming   The three open sides of the book are trimmed on a print shop type of paper cutter after the book has been bound by either side sewing or grooves and cords. Place a piece of cardboard on top and beneath the book to prevent clamp marks or ragged edges from occurring. Place the bound edge of the book to the right of the cutter and hold firmly against the back and left guide to assure a straight even cut. If a print-shop paper cutter is not available, this operation can be omitted. The pages will not be as straight and even as when they are cut, but if care is taken to align the pages during the sewing operation, an acceptable finished product can be produced.
Rounding   The back of the book is rounded to offer a better appearance. Place the book on a flat clean surface with the bound side away from

the operator and hold firmly on the top surface with the left hand, while the thumb is pressed against the front edge. With a cobbler's hammer, tap the back edge lightly, while the left hand is pulling forward. The tapping is started at the center of the back edge and worked toward the ends. After one side is rounded, turn the book over and repeat the operation. Care should be taken not to tap too hard or the binding threads may be broken.

Backing   After rounding, the next step is to back the book. In this operation, the bound edges of the book are flared, forming an overhang or shoulder against which the cover board will fit. Place the book in a binder's press with the back of the book projecting about 1/4 inch above the beveled guides. Flare the edges of both sides of the book over the beveled guide by gently tapping along the edge with a cobbler's hammer. Reinforce the back of the book by gluing a piece of crinoline or super crinoline over the entire back of the book. Organdy can be substituted for the crinoline. The crinoline is used as a hinge for attaching the book to the cover and should overhang about 2 inches on each side.

Making a Cover for a Book
The cover for any book must be fitted to the assembled pages. For this reason, the pages must be bound before starting the cover. The correct dimensions are obtained by measuring the size and thickness of the bound pages.

Cutting the Cover Boards to Fit the Book   The material used to form the front and back covers of a book are cut from a heavy cardboard called binder's board. The measurements for the cover boards are obtained by measuring the distance from the front edge to the flared shoulder and adding 1/8 inch from the overhang. Add 1/4 inch to the length of the book to allow for a 1/8 inch overhang on the top and bottom edge of the book. The binder's board is cut with a knife and a metal straightedge. The cut-out cover boards are temporarily secured in place at the front and back of the book with two rubber bands.

Laying Out the Cover for the Book   Place a piece of fabric face down on a clean working surface. Place the book, with the cover boards attached, on the fabric and trace the outside edges with a pencil. After one side is traced, the book is carefully rolled over and the other side is marked off. Care should be taken to keep the book from slipping while being rolled or the measurements and guidelines will not be accurate. Rolling the book will provide the necessary space for the thickness of the book. An additional 3/4 inch is allowed on all four sides for overlapping the cover boards. The fabric is cut out along the outside guidelines with a pair of scissors.

GRAPHIC AND
MANIPULATIVE
ART FORMS AND
INSTRUCTIONAL
METHODS

166

Gluing the Cover Boards to the Fabric   The cover boards should be removed from the book and coated with a thin layer of glue. Place the glued cover boards in position on the fabric, using the pencil lines made when the cover was laid out as a guide. Test the tops of the cover boards

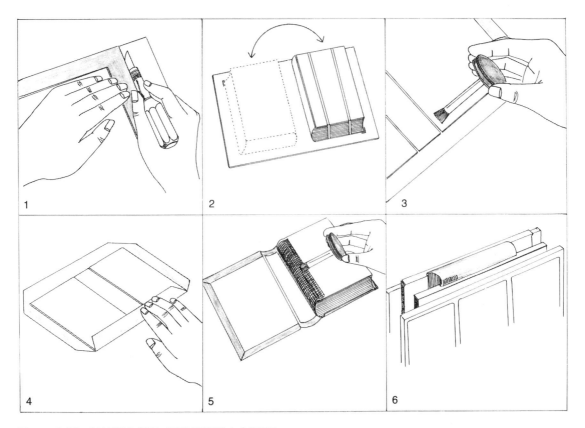

Figure 6-12 MAKING AND ATTACHING A COVER
Materials: binder's board, glue, cover fabric, square or straightedge, crinoline, book press, knife.

1. Cut the cover boards with a knife and straightedge.
2. Use the book to measure the cover material needed.
3. Apply glue to the edges of the cover material.
4. Turn in the edges and corners of the cover material and glue them to the cover boards.
5. Glue the crinoline to the cover.
6. Crease the shoulder in a book press.

with a straightedge to make sure they are straight and parallel. Turn the cover over and rub the surface with a clean cloth to prevent air bubbles and wrinkles from forming. Reverse the cover again and glue a strip of craft paper down the center between the cover boards. This strip of craft paper is called a lettering strip and is used for strengthening the back of the book.

Turning in the Edges and Corners of the Covers The corners of the fabric are cut off at a 45-degree angle about 1/4 inch from the corner of the cover boards. Turn the top and bottom edge of the fabric over the cover board and press down, securing it in place. Turn the sides over the cover boards and press the corners down tightly. Extra glue may be needed where the corners overlap. Place a piece of wax paper over the cover and slip it under a heavy weight until dry. The cover should be pressed for about twenty-four hours before being used to cover a book. The cover is ready to be attached to the book (casing in).

Attaching a Cover to a Book Place the book in position on the inside of the cover, making sure that the inner edges of the cover boards fit up into the shoulder of the back of the book. This will form a neat hinge for the cover. The cover should overhang the book evenly on all three sides. This will improve the appearance of the finished book. Glue the crinoline on the back of the book to the cover boards and glue the end sheets down on top of the crinoline. This operation will secure the book inside the cover. The end sheets should be smoothed by rubbing the surface with a clean cloth to remove any wrinkles and air bubbles. Place a sheet of waxed paper between the cover and the book before the cover is closed, to prevent the glue from getting on the clean pages. Turn the book over and repeat the process, gluing the crinoline first and then the end sheet. Place the book under heavy pressure for drying so that it will not warp.

Creasing the Shoulder of the Book Place the book in a press between two creasing boards, which have a projecting metal strip. These metal strips are located so that the metal projects into the cover of the book at the spot it hinges, forming a crease. The book should remain in the press for about twelve hours or overnight to ensure that a permanent crease is formed.

GRAPHIC AND
MANIPULATIVE
ART FORMS AND
INSTRUCTIONAL
METHODS

168

PAPER AND PAPIER-MÂCHÉ AS CRAFTS MEDIA

7

Most individuals think of paper in terms of two dimensions, such as flat cutout shapes fastened to a contrasting colored sheet of paper. It is very difficult for many individuals to visualize how this flat sheet of paper can be manipulated into a three-dimensional shape. Before starting to model with paper, it is important to experiment with the following processes: bending, curling, fluting, folding, fringing, joining or attaching several pieces together, perforating, pinking, scoring, and twisting.

PAPER PROCESSES

The properties and characteristics of different types of paper are important to this craft medium. Experimentation reveals the weaknesses and strengths of various types of paper. For example, tissue paper will not hold weight; stiff cardboard is difficult to roll and will crack when folded. It is important to create a form which shows the inherent qualities of the paper (stiffness, suppleness, fragility) or to select a paper that is suited to the shape being constructed. Experimentation will lead to the selection of the appropriate materials for a special purpose. What are the properties and characteristics of the following types of paper: newspaper, wrapping paper, facial tissues, paper bags, towels, napkins, drawing, and construction paper, oak tag, cardboard, newsprint, tracing tissue, oatmeal or rice paper, mimeograph paper, notebook paper, metallic paper, corrugated cardboard, stencil paper, parchment paper, crepe paper, cellophane, and such papers as watercolor and charcoal papers?

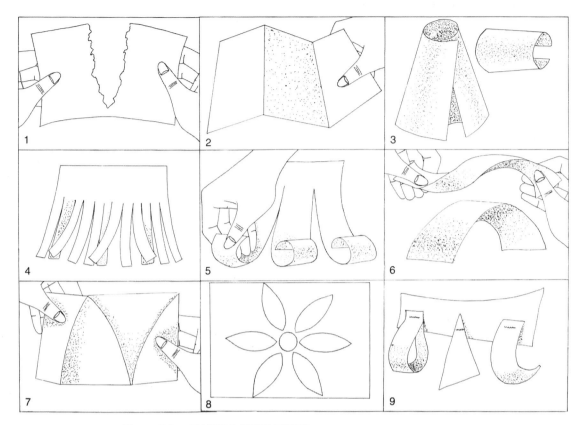

Figure 7-1   MANIPULATING PAPER
    1.   Cutting or tearing
    2.   Folding.
    3.   Rolling.
    4.   Fringing.
    5.   Curling.
    6.   Bending and twisting.
    7.   Scoring and folding.
    8.   Cutting out.
    9.   Fastening.

Curling

A pair of scissors or ruler can be used to stretch a piece of paper. Paper curls easiest when stretched in the same direction as the grain. Curled forms can be used as part of a paper sculpture.

Surface Texture

The surface of a piece of paper can be cut with a pair of scissors into a series of slits that vary in shape, length, and width. The tabs resulting from these cuts can be bent forward to produce a textured effect.

Fold a sheet of paper in half a number of times. With a pair of scissors make a series of straight and curved cuts along the folded edge, varying the cuts in width and length. Unfold the sheet of paper and bend the cut tabs outward.

GRAPHIC AND
MANIPULATIVE
ART FORMS AND
INSTRUCTIONAL
METHODS

170

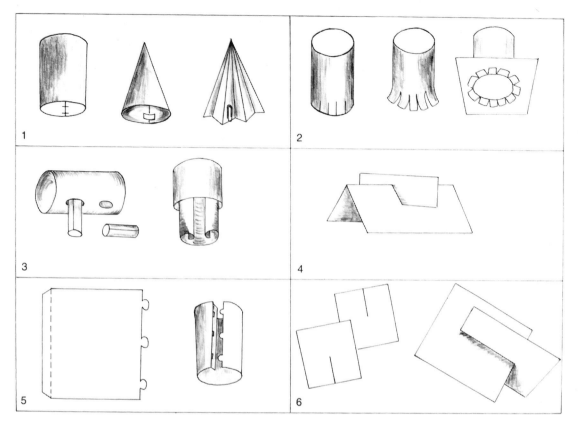

Figure 7-2 FASTENING PAPER
1. Use staples, tape, and paper clips to fasten paper shapes together.
2. Glue fringed edge to fasten surfaces together.
3. Use pressure to hold rolled paper shapes in a cylinder.
4. Use a shape cut from one piece of paper to hold the shape of a second piece.
5. Use tabs to fasten a cylinder together.
6. Use interlocking slits to hold two surfaces together.

Another technique used to obtain a textured surface is to cut out the desired shape or form. A knife or razor blade can be used to cut the slits in the surface.

Folding and Scoring

Folding and scoring are used in paper sculpture to obtain the same results. Folding is used with lightweight paper. Scoring is used with heavier paper that will crack or fold unevenly if not scored first. A knife, razor blade, compass point, or nail can be used to dent the surface of a piece of paper, allowing it to fold easily without cracking.

Geometric Shapes

Cylinder   A cylinder is constructed by rolling a flat sheet of paper and fastening the overlapping edges. The size of the cylinder is determined by the dimensions of the sheet of paper used.

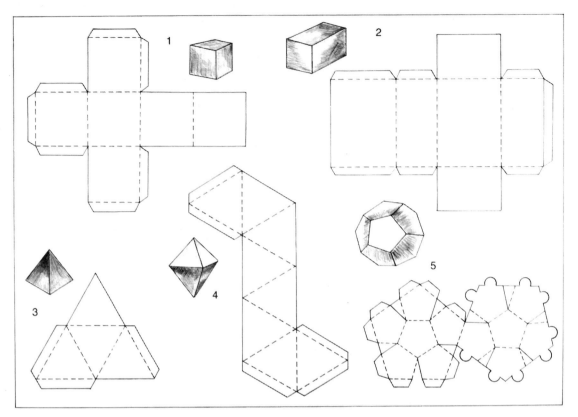

Figure 7-3 GEOMETRIC SHAPES
   1. Cube
   2. Rectangular prism
   3. Pyramid
   4. Octahedron
   5. Dodecahedron

Cone   A cone is constructed by cutting out a circle and making a slit from the outer edge along the radius to the center. Overlap the edges along the slit and fasten together. The cone can be made narrow by increasing the overlap or by removing an 1/8 or 1/4 inch before overlapping the cut edges.

Cube, Pyramid, Rectangular Prism, Octahedron, and Dodecahedron. A piece of paper can be laid out, cut, and folded to construct a cube, pyramid, rectangular prism, octahedron, and dodecahedron. See Figure 7-3 for example layout.

Three-dimensional Structure

A three-dimensional structure is constructed with flat sheets of paper by cutting two identical shapes and slitting each piece to the center. The two sheets of paper are interlocked by inserting each into the slit of the other at right angles. The size can be increased or decreased by varying the size and weight of the paper used.

GRAPHIC AND
MANIPULATIVE
ART FORMS AND
INSTRUCTIONAL
METHODS

172

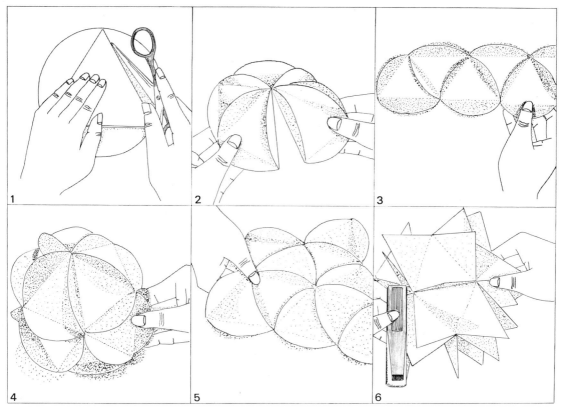

Figure 7-4   SPHERE MADE FROM CIRCLES

Materials: stapler, scissors, twenty paper circles, cardboard template (equilateral triangle), glue.

1.   Place the equilateral triangle template on top of one of the paper circles and trace around the edges with a scissor blade. Repeat for all twenty circles.
2.   The side flaps of the triangles are glued together for five circles to form the top. Repeat with five more circles to form the bottom.
3.   Glue the flaps of the remaining ten circles together to form a straight strip.
4.   Assemble by attaching the ten circles strips to the top and bottom sections.
5.   Making a flat structure instead of a sphere with the circles.
6.   Using triangular shapes instead of circles to make a sphere.

Sphere Made from Circles

With a compass draw twenty circles on a piece of paper and cut them out. Take a scrap piece of cardboard and draw a circle the same size as the first twenty. Lay out an equilateral triangle within the cardboard circle. The equilateral triangle is constructed by dividing the circumference of the circle into six equal parts by using the radius of a circle as a measurement. With a straightedge and pencil, draw lines connecting alternate points on the circumference to form an equilateral triangle. Cut out the triangle and use it as a pattern to trace an equilateral triangle on the other twenty circles.

Place a straightedge against one of the inside lines of the triangle and turn up the edge. Repeat this procedure for the three sides of each triangle on all twenty circles.

The side flaps of the triangle are glued together for five circles to form

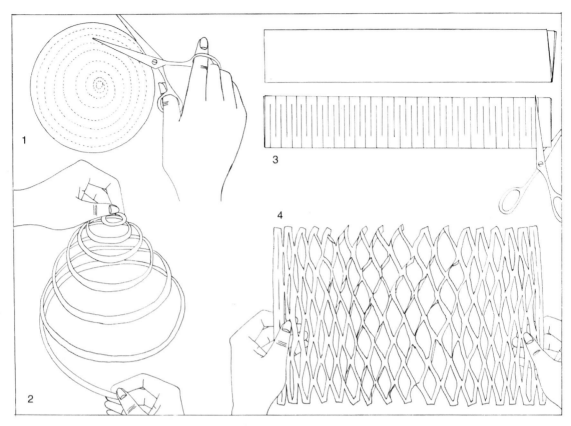

Figure 7-5   EXPANDING PAPER
1. Make a continuous cut from the outer edge to the center.
2. Pull the ends to expand the paper.
3. Fold a piece of paper in half two or three times. Cut paper from alternate sides to within 1/4-inch of the edge.
4. Unfold the paper and pull to expand.

the top. The top point of each triangle is connected to the next one. This procedure is repeated with five more circles to form the bottom. The flaps of the remaining ten circles are glued together to form a straight strip. The bases of the triangles are alternated with one on top and the next on the bottom.

The sphere is assembled by attaching the ten-circle strip to the top and bottom sections. The final shape can be modified by changing the number of circles used to construct the top, bottom, and center strips.

An alternative approach is to use equilateral triangles instead of circles to create the form. Each equilateral triangle is divided into four equilateral triangles. The three triangles around the center one are turned up to form the flaps that are glued or stapled together to create the new shape.

Expanded Paper

To expand a flat piece of paper, take any circular, square, or triangular shape and make a long continuous cut from the outer edge to the center.

GRAPHIC AND
MANIPULATIVE
ART FORMS AND
INSTRUCTIONAL
METHODS

174

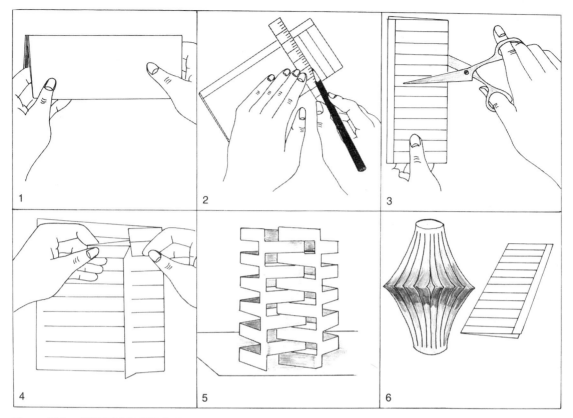

Figure 7-6 INTERLOCKING STRUCTURES
Materials: paper, ruler, pencil, scissors.
1. Fold a rectangle in half the short way: open it up and fold each outer edge to the center. Fold again on the center line.
2. With the paper folded in half, lay out a series of 1/2-inch lines parallel to the top edge on one side. These lines should run to within 1/2 inch of the center fold.
3. Fold the rectangle again on the center line and cut on the marked line from the edge to within 1/2-inch of the center fold.
4. Unfold the paper; starting at the upper left, push the first strip back and crease it. Push the second strip forward and crease it. Repeat for each strip, alternating the direction.
5. Completed structure.
6. A lantern shape can be created by folding the pieces of paper in half and making a series of 1/2-inch cuts parallel with the top edge.

Take the center of the resulting segmented paper and pull it outward. The cutout shape can be twisted into new forms or suspended by hanging it from a string.

An alternate technique is to fold a rectangular piece of paper lengthwise two or three times. Starting on the right side, cut a slit that is parallel to the top edge and stops 1/4 inch from the left side. A second parallel slit is cut starting from the left side and stopping 1/4 inch from the right edge. Continue to cut a series of parallel slits the length of the paper. Unfold the paper and stretch it out. The results should have a meshed wire effect.

A square can be folded diagonally two or three times to form a triangle and then parallel lines cut from alternating sides, to within 1/4 inch of the folded edge. Unfold and stretch out the segmented area.

Another method of expanding a flat surface is to cut out a circle and fold it in half two or three times. Cut a curved slit parallel to the outside circumference starting first from one side and then the other, to within 1/4 inch of the opposite edge. Unfold and stretch out the segmented area.

Interlocking Structures

Fold a rectangular piece of paper in half the short way. Unfold and fold each outer edge into the center. Place on a working surface with the center fold facing upward. Lay out a series of 1/2-inch lines parallel to the top edge on one side. These lines should run to within 1/2 inch of the center fold. Fold the rectangle again on the center line and cut on the marked line from the edge to within 1/2 inch of the center fold.

Unfold the paper and starting in the upper left, push the first strip back and crease it. Push the second strip forward to crease it. Alternate the direction each strip is pushed and creased until the end of the paper is reached. Starting in the upper right, push the first strip forward, while pushing the second forward and crease. Continue pushing each strip forward or back and creasing the length of the paper. The two halves are folded in reverse to one another and the strips are interlocked.

An alternative technique is to fold a rectangular shape in half and lay out a series of 1/2-inch lines parallel to the top edge on one side the length of the paper. These lines should run to within 1/2 inch of the unfolded edge. Cuts are made inward from the folded edge, allowing the paper to be pushed inward and outward at the fold and creased to form a structure.

A Paper Lantern

A lantern can be constructed by folding a rectangular shape in half and laying out a series of lines parallel to the top edge the length of the paper. These lines should run to within 1/2 inch of the unfolded edge. Starting at the folded edge, cut along the guidelines to within 1/2 inch of the unfolded edge. Unfold and fasten the outer edges together.

PAPER STRIPS

Paper strips can be used to construct a wide variety of paper forms. All types of paper trimmings can be used to create interesting sculptures and forms. Paper strips can be used for weaving (see Chapter 13).

Cut two strips of construction paper and staple them together at one end so that the opposite ends form a right angle. Fold the strips by lifting the bottom one straight back across the top one. Continue folding first one strip and then the other until the paper is entirely folded. This folded strip can be twisted, stretched, and bent in many ways to form a paper sculpture.

Paper strips can be used to form a ball. Place one strip on top of another to form a cross and staple together. Repeat this operation with another two strips. Place one cross on top of the other and rotate until the arms of the top one bisect the four 90-degree angles of the bottom one

GRAPHIC AND
MANIPULATIVE
ART FORMS AND
INSTRUCTIONAL
METHODS

176

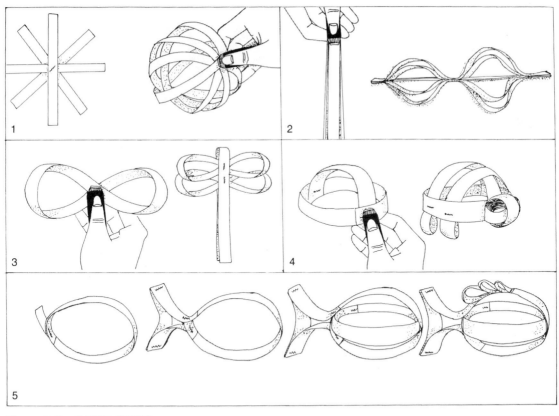

Figure 7-7 PAPER STRIPS
1. Using paper strips to form a ball.
2. Using paper strips to create loop designs.
3. Making an insect with paper strips.
4. Making a turtle with paper strips.
5. Using paper strips to make a fish.

and staple together. Lift one end at a time, placing it on top of the next one until all eight are together and staple. The size of the ball can be increased by using larger paper strips. A small ball can be placed into a large one. Experiment with different colored strips.

Paper strips can be used to construct loop forms. Staple five strips of equal length together at one end. Lift the two outside strips on both sides to form a loop and staple them to the center strip. Experiment with different methods of forming loops. For example, staple together at one end four paper strips of different lengths. Take the opposite end of each strip one at a time and bend it to form a loop. These ends should be stapled together at the base. A complete composition can be created by using forms created with paper strips.

POSITIVE AND NEGATIVE DESIGN

A design is produced when a form or shape is cut from a flat sheet of paper. The cutout portion and the section containing the opening form a positive and negative design.

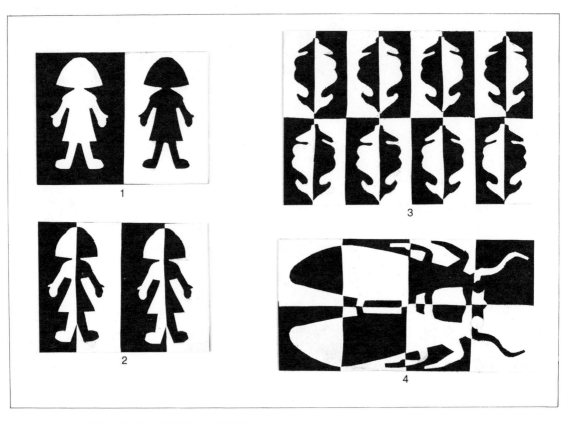

Figure 7-8 POSITIVE AND NEGATIVE DESIGNS
1. Paste negative and positive sections on a contrasting background.
2. Alternate positive and negative pieces and paste on contrasting colored paper.
3. Create an allover pattern with positive and negative sections.
4. Assembled design of positive and negative sections.

Simple Cutout Design

Select a sheet of paper and fold it in half. A simple symmetrical design can be cut directly from the folded material. The folded edge represents the center of the design. For some designs a pencil sketch will assist in the cutting procedure. The cutout shape is the positive, while the section containing the opening is the negative design. Unfold both pieces and place them on a sheet of paper of a contrasting color.

Another technique is to cut the negative and positive design in half. Place one half of the negative design on a piece of contrasting paper, while putting one half the positive design on the opposite half of this piece of paper. With some symmetrical shapes, it is easier to cut out the design if the sheet of paper is folded in half one way and then in the opposite direction. The design is cut in from the unfolded edge.

Overall Pattern

Select a sheet of paper and cut it into four or more equal parts. Take one of the parts and fold it in half. Sketch half of a design on one side and then cut it out. The cutout area is the positive and the section containing the

GRAPHIC AND
MANIPULATIVE
ART FORMS AND
INSTRUCTIONAL
METHODS

178

opening is the negative part of the design. If the same design is going to be used over the total surface, fold the remaining pieces in half and use the negative shape as a pattern to transfer the shape. Cut out each traced shape. Unfold all the designs and cut each one in half. Cement one-half of the negative shape in the upper left-hand corner of a large sheet of paper, while one-half of the positive is located so that the original design is completed. The total surface can be covered by alternating the positive and negative shapes until the total sheet of paper is covered.

Complex Cutout Designs

Take a rectangular piece of paper and fold it three or four times into a strip. Cut various sized shapes and contours from both edges. Unfold the piece of paper and place it over a surface with a contrasting color.

Another technique is to use a square piece of paper that is folded in half, quarters, and eighths. A wide variety of cuts are made from the folded side, open edge, center, and point. Unfold the paper and examine the results. The piece of paper can be refolded and new cuts made to improve the design.

To obtain a multiple cutout, fold a piece of lightweight paper in half several times. Each time the fold should be reversed to form a series of accordion pleats. Cut out shapes along the folded edges and in the center areas with a razor blade or sharp-pointed scissors. The bottom edge should not be cut, but left flat for a base. Unfold the paper and arrange so that the structure is free-standing.

PAPER CRAFTS PROJECTS
Paper Flowers

Attractive and interesting flowers can be constructed with some basic materials and tools. The finished flowers can be placed in a container and arranged into a bouquet. Six different types of flowers can be constructed from the following directions:

Flower A   Draw and cut out a 4-inch circle from bond or lighter paper. Using crayons or paints, color the circle. Some interesting effects can be obtained if the circle is shaded rather than colored a solid shade. With a pencil and straightedge, draw a straight line from the center of the circle to the outside edge. With a pair of scissors, cut along the line from the outside edge to the center of the circle. Curl the edge of the piece of paper around the center by overlapping the edges along the cut line. Select any color pipe cleaner and push it into the point at the top of the cone. Pinch the point of the cone around the pipe cleaner so that the paper flower will keep its shape. Set the finished flower to one side and start another flower. The second flower can be the same or one of the other five basic flowers.

Flower B   Draw and cut out a 4-inch circle from bond or lighter paper. Color the circle with either paints or crayons. Experiment with crayons and paints to obtain an interesting texture or shading effect.

With a pair of scissors, fringe the edge of the circle by cutting from the outer edge about 1 inch toward the center of the circle every 1/8 inch.

Draw and cut out a 3-inch circle from the same type of paper used for the 4-inch circle. Color this circle using either crayons or paints.

With a sharp pencil punch a small hole in the center of the flower. Select any color pipe cleaner and push it through the center hole of both circles. Knot the end of the pipe cleaner by bending it to a U shape and then twisting it. Set the finished flower to one side and start another flower. The second flower can be the same or one of the other five flowers.

Flower C   Draw and cut out a 4-inch circle from bond or lighter paper. Using crayons or paints color the circle. Experiment with different tones and shades to obtain an interesting effect. Some flowers can be left white.

Fold the circle in half, quarters, and eighths. While the circle is still folded in eighths, draw two curved lines forming a scalloped edge. With a pair of scissors, cut along these curved lines. Unfold the piece of paper and curl each one of the petals around a pencil to make the flower three-dimensional. With a sharp pencil, punch a small hole in the center of the flower. Select any color pipe cleaner and push it through the center hole of both circles. Knot the end of the pipe cleaner by bending it to a U shape and then twisting it. Set the finished flower to one side and start another flower. The next flower can be the same or one of the other five flowers. When three or more flowers have been made, they can be arranged into a centerpiece or bouquet.

Flower D   Draw and cut out a 4-inch circle from bond or lighter paper. Color the circle with either paints or crayons. Experiment with the crayons and paints to obtain variations in the texture and shading. Some flowers can be left the color of the paper used.

Fold the circle in half, quarters, and eighths. While the circle is still folded in eighths, draw two curved lines forming a scalloped edge. With a pair of scissors cut along these curved lines. Unfold the piece of paper and with a pencil and straightedge draw a line from the low point between the curved lines to the center of the circle. Take a pair of scissors and cut along the line between the petals to a point about 3/4 inch from the center of the flower. With a sharp pencil, punch a small hole in the center of the flower. Select any color pipe cleaner and push it through the center hole of the circles. Knot the end of the pipe cleaner by bending it to a U shape and then twisting it. Set the finished flower to one side and start another flower. The next flower can be the same or one of the other five flowers. When three or more flowers have been made, they can be arranged into a centerpiece or bouquet.

Flower E   Flower E is identical with flower C except the petals are not curled with a pencil.

Flower F   Draw and cut out a 4-inch circle from bond or lighter paper. Color the circle using crayons or paints. Some interesting effects can be obtained by experimenting with the crayons or paints. With a pencil and straightedge draw a straight line from the center of the circle to the out-

GRAPHIC AND
MANIPULATIVE
ART FORMS AND
INSTRUCTIONAL
METHODS

180

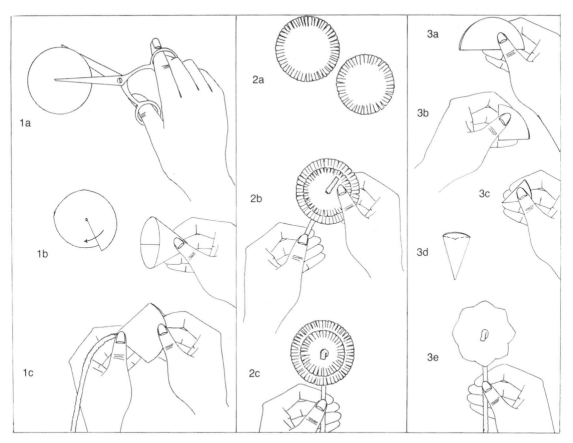

Figure 7-9 PAPER FLOWERS
1. Flower A
   a. Cut a straight line from the outer edge to the center of the circle.
   b. Overlap the cut edges to form a cone.
   c. Insert a pipe cleaner in the peak of the cone and pinch the paper.
2. Flower B
   a. Fringe the edges of a large and small circle.
   b. Put the smaller circle on the larger circle and push a pipe cleaner through both centers.
   c. Bend the end of the pipe cleaner.
3. Flower C
   a. Fold a circle in half.
   b. Fold the circle in quarters.
   c. Fold the circle in eighths.
   d. Cut a scalloped edge.
   e. Unfold and insert a pipe cleaner.

side edge. With a pair of scissors cut along the line from the outside edge to the center of the circle. Fringe the edge of the circle by cutting from the outer edge about 1 inch toward the center of the circle every 1/8 inch. Curl the circle around the center by overlapping the edges along the line cut from the edge to the center of the circle. Select any color pipe cleaner and push it into the point at the top of the cone. Pinch the point of the cone around the pipe cleaner so that the paper flower will keep its shape. Set the finished flower to one side and start another flower. The second flower can be the same or one of the other five basic flowers.

Making Leaves for the Different Flowers   On a piece of cardboard or oak tag draw some different shaped leaves. Select a piece of paper large enough to trace the leaf on. Cut out the leaf, being careful to cut the edge smoothly, because this shape is to be used as a template. A template is an outline of a basic shape useful for the tracing of designs that are going to be used more than once. Place the template on top of the piece of paper and with a pencil trace around the outline of the template. Cut out the traced shape of the leaf. If more than one leaf is needed, repeat the procedure. The leaf can be colored with crayons and paints. Place the leaf or leaves on the stem of the flower to locate their appropriate position. If the flowers are going to fit into a container, leaves located below a certain point will not be seen. Apply rubber cement to the leaf and stem and allow it to dry. When the cement is dry, twist the stem of the leaf around the stem of the flower. Leaves of more than one shape can be used.

Different Ways of Arranging Flowers   Select a container for holding the flowers. A piece of Styrofoam can be used in place of a container. Place a piece of crumpled newspaper or Styrofoam in the bottom of the container. Select a floral arrangement that is most appropriate for your container. Flowers can be arranged in a circle, diamond, oval, or modified crescent shape. With a pencil, punch holes in the Styrofoam or crushed paper so that the pipe cleaner stems can be inserted. Place each stem into one of the holes in the crushed paper or Styrofoam. The stems can be twisted or bent to obtain the desired arrangement.

Crepe Paper Flowers
Select a piece of crepe paper 5 X 30 inches and draw a line 1 inch from the top edge the length of the strip. Fold the crepe paper over along this line. Holding the folded edge inward and in an upward position, wrap the crepe paper loosely around the index finger until the end of the strip is reached. Remove the crepe paper from the index finger, being careful to keep the cylinder shape.

Take a pipe cleaner and insert it into the bottom of the rolled crepe paper. Pinch and twist the base of the crepe paper flower around the pipe cleaner and staple. Repeat this procedure until the desired number of flowers are obtained.

Sketch the appropriate shape for a leaf on a piece of oak tag and cut it out to use for a pattern. Place the pattern on a piece of green crepe paper, trace, and cut out. Repeat until the desired number of leaves are obtained. Arrange the leaves on the pipe cleaner and staple. Leaves can be cut from different shades of green, and the size may differ.

Shape the flowers by separating the layers of crepe paper or by twisting and stretching the crepe paper.

GRAPHIC AND
MANIPULATIVE
ART FORMS AND
INSTRUCTIONAL
METHODS

182

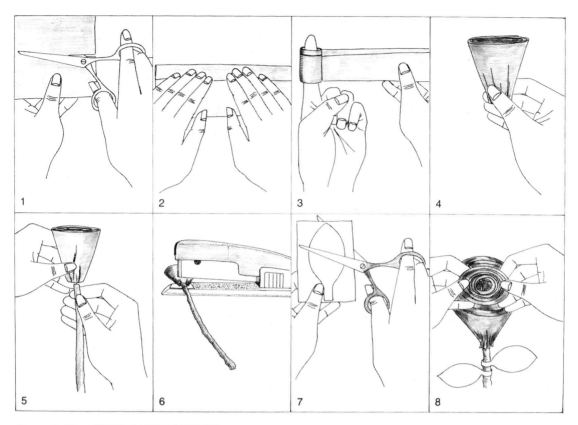

Figure 7-10 CREPE PAPER FLOWERS

Materials: crepe paper, pipe cleaner, stapler, scissors.

1. Cut a strip of crepe paper.
2. Fold over the top edge.
3. Wind the strip of crepe paper around a finger.
4. Remove the crepe paper from the finger and pinch the bottom.
5. Insert a pipe cleaner in the bottom.
6. Staple the pipe cleaner in place.
7. Cut out the leaves for the flower from a piece of crepe paper.
8. Shape the crepe paper flower to obtain the desired effect, and glue the crepe paper leaves to the pipe cleaner.

Paper Mosaic

A paper mosaic is a design that is constructed by the close arrangement of small pieces of different colored paper. Select a piece of background paper and sketch a light design or picture on the surface. Cut three or four different colored papers into small pieces of uniform size, but different shapes, and keep the pieces arranged by color. Glue the individual pieces in place on the sketch leaving a narrow space of background color between the paper shapes. Continue pasting the paper shapes in place until the design is completed. Variations in the shapes and color can be used to enhance the design.

Figure 7-11 TWO-DIMENSIONAL PICTURES FROM PAPER STRIPS

Torn Paper Pictures

Different types of paper can be torn into a wide variety of shapes that can be used to create a picture. Sketch a picture of the desired composition. This sketch can be used as a guide to the finished picture. The type of paper used should complement the subject and composition selected. Tear the paper into shapes adaptable to the subject. Select a piece of paper for the background and arrange the torn shapes to form a picture. When the desired arrangement is obtained, glue the torn paper shapes in place.

A Two-dimensional Picture from Paper Strips

Colored paper strips in varying lengths and widths can be used to create a design or picture. Select and cut three or four different colored pieces of construction paper into long strips 1/8 to 1/4 inch wide. On a piece of scrap paper sketch a pencil design or picture to use as a guide. The design or picture sketch should be composed of simple straight lines. Arrange the colored strips on a piece of contrasting colored paper. The paper strips should not be glued down until the desired arrangement is obtained.

An alternative technique is to use geometric shapes that vary in size and shape to create a design or picture. The geometric shapes are arranged

GRAPHIC AND
MANIPULATIVE
ART FORMS AND
INSTRUCTIONAL
METHODS

184

on a piece of background paper and are glued in place when the desired composition is obtained.

Colored Tissue Paper Painting

Select a tissue and sketch a number of different shapes on the surface. Cut out the shapes. Shapes can also be torn from the tissue. A number of different colored tissues can be used to create a design or picture. Place a piece of white mounting board or heavy cardboard flat on a working surface. Arrange tissue shapes on the surface, overlapping shapes and color to obtain the desired effects. Experiment with color, shapes, and technique before securing the materials to the base.

Apply rubber cement to the shapes and gently press them in place. Remove excess rubber cement by gently rubbing the area with a dried ball of rubber cement.

Paints can be used to highlight the finished composition, and it can be coated with clear plastic spray to protect the finished surface.

Corrugated Cardboard

Corrugated cardboard can be used to create two- and three-dimensional pictures and designs. It can be purchased or extracted from cardboard boxes by peeling off the top layer, exposing the corrugated surface. The corrugated surface can be colored with paints or crayons. Painting in the ridges, on top of the ridges, or across the ridges offers varying effects. Painting the inside ridge one color while using another color to paint the top ridges is interesting. Corrugated and plain cardboard combinations produce different effects.

Origami

Origami is the Japanese art of paper folding. This art has been handed down from generation to generation. The activity allows the individual to create imaginative shapes. Over a hundred objects can be created by folding a single piece of paper, without cutting or gluing it. This technique is illustrated in Figure 7-12.

Paper People

Paper and cardboard can be used to construct a wide variety of people. For example, a shape of a person can be torn from a piece of newspaper or cut from a heavier, stiffer material. Figure 7-13 illustrates some examples of paper people.

Foil Sculpture

Foil can be rolled, twisted, crushed, or crumpled into a wide variety of shapes. These shapes can be joined together to create an interesting sculpture. With tape or straight pins join the shapes together to form a sculpture. Color can be added to the sculpture by painting with tempera paint that has been mixed with two drops of liquid detergent.

The foil can be combined with paper or used to cover paper tubes

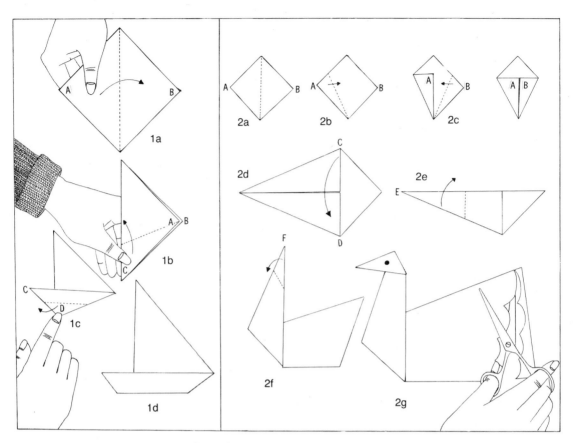

Figure 7-12 FOLDING PAPER
    1.   Sailboat
        a.   Fold A to B.
        b.   Fold C.
        c.   Fold D under.
        d.   Completed Sailboat.
    2.   Swan
        a.   Crease paper.
        b.   Fold A to the center.
        c.   Fold B to the center.
        d.   Turn sideways and fold C to D.
        e.   Fold E up.
        f.   Fold F down.
        g.   Cut scalloped edge.

or small boxes. These covered shapes can be used to add another dimension to the sculpture.

PAPIER-MÂCHÉ

Papier-mâché can be used to create interesting and beautiful objects. Many objects that are not well done with papier-mâché are the results of poor utilization of materials. This technique has been used for many centuries to create attractive jewelry boxes, trays, and other pieces. The

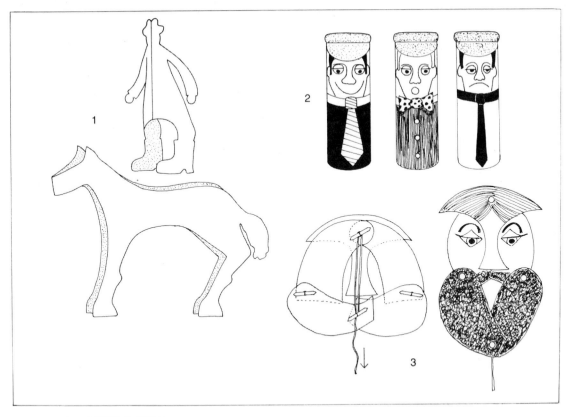

Figure 7-13   PAPER PEOPLE
   1.   Cut single-fold mounted figures from heavy paper and fold so that they are free standing.
   2.   Construct cylinder people from construction paper.
   3.   Faces with moveable features. The basic shapes are held together with a paper fastener. A rubber band can be added between the two center fasteners. The rubber band between the fasteners will stretch as the string is pulled.

ancient Chinese experimented with ways of tearing paper, mixing it with glue and shaping and molding the papier-mâché into interesting forms.

Today, Japan, Mexico, India, and Portugal produce large quantities of papier-mâché articles for export. Toys, vases, lamps, candle holders, and decorative furniture pieces are a few of the items made from papier-mâché and sold around the world.

Basic Materials
Paper   Almost any type of paper can be used to construct an object from papier-mâché. Newspaper, paper towels, tissue paper, or facial tissues are all suitable for use when making an object from papier-mâché. Cloth or an old bed sheet can be used to add strength and texture to an object. Cardboard and egg cartons may be cut up, soaked, and turned into paper pulp.

A wide variety of other kinds of paper are used for adding decorative touches. Wallpaper, gift-wrapping paper, magazine pictures, colored tissue, and colored comics can all be used in a number of ways to add to the appearance of an object.

Paste and Glue   A number of different paste mixtures can be used as the holding agent when constructing any object with papier-mâché. The selection of the paste mixture usually depends upon available materials and personal preference. Strong holding agents, such as wheat paste and diluted white glue, should be used for large and complex objects.

Basic Techniques

There are four basic techniques that can be used to construct an object from papier-mâché. The most common is the layer-on-layer technique. Strips of paper are dipped into a liquid paste and then pressed and formed over a base. A second technique utilizes several layers of paper pasted together to make one strong flexible sheet. These laminated sheets of paper can be shaped or molded over a base, or they can be shaped and formed separately. They can also be torn and applied to a base. The third technique utilizes a pulpy, claylike substance that can be molded like clay. The fourth technique utilizes pieces of yarn or string pasted over a removable base to form a cagelike shape.

Mixing Procedures

Flour Mixture   Mix 1 cup of flour with enough water to make a thin mixture. Heat over a low flame, stirring constantly, for a few minutes. When the mixture is cool, add a few drops of oil of wintergreen or formaldehyde as a preservative.

Wheat Paste Mixture   Add one part of commercial wallpaper paste or wheat paste to ten parts of water. Mix until the consistency of heavy cream.

Starch Paste   Mix 1 tablespoon of starch with 1 tablespoon of cold water. Add 1 cup of boiling water, while rapidly stirring the mixture. The mixture should be the consistency of heavy cream.

Liquid White Glue Paste   Mix one part of liquid white glue with one part of water.

Liquid Starch Paste   Mix 1 quart of liquid starch with 2 tablespoons of salt, sand, or plaster.

Selecting a Base   Papier-mâché can be used to cover a base made from almost any type of material. The importance of the base is directly related to how it minimizes the number of layers of pasted strips or paper pulp to obtain the desired finished shape. One of the following bases can be used to construct a papier-mâché object.

Removable Base   The base can be coated with a separator (petroleum jelly, waxedpaper, or a sheet of wet paper) to keep it from sticking to the

GRAPHIC AND
MANIPULATIVE
ART FORMS AND
INSTRUCTIONAL
METHODS

188

papier-mâché. If the base object is completely covered, it can be removed by cutting the papier-mâché in half and pasting the two halves together with masking tape or pasted paper strips.

Deflatable Base   An inflated balloon or beach ball can be used as a base and then removed from the core by deflating. When covering the base with pasted paper strips, leave an opening around the intake valve. The surface must be coated with a separator.

Permanent Base   A base may become an important part of the finished object. For example, a plastic bottle can be used as a base, but it also provides a waterproof lining for holding water.

Chicken Wire   Chicken wire is an excellent material to utilize as a base for papier-mâché objects because it can be bent and pressed into shape. When the desired shape is obtained, strips of dry newspaper are woven into the chicken wire to provide a base for the pasted strips.

Rolled or Crushed Paper   Paper can be rolled or crushed into balls, cylinders, and ovals and then held together with string or masking tape. These shapes can be fastened together with string or masking tape to form the base for a great number of papier-mâché objects.

Armature Base   Wood, cardboard, hardboard, or wire can be utilized to make a stick figure resemblance of the desired object. Plastic bottles, tin cans, and wire can be used to build up the armature.

Cardboard as a Base   Cardboard boxes of varying sizes can be cut and folded and pieces taped together to form a wide variety of shapes.

Modifying the Base Shape   The base shape can be modified by using rolled, crushed, or cut paper. A balloon can be made to take on the appearance of an animal by using one or a combination of the following techniques to obtain the desired features.

Rolled Paper   Strips of paper can be rolled into a cylinder to form legs, horns, or other necessary shapes. Take three or four strips of newspaper the required width and roll them into a cylinder. The diameter of the cylinder can be changed by increasing or decreasing the number of paper strips.

Crushed Paper   Newspaper can be crushed into a ball to form a head, cheeks, or jaw or any other desired shape. Take a sheet of newspaper and crush it into a ball. The size of the paper sheet and number of sheets will determine how large the ball will be.

Cut Paper   Layers of newspaper or cardboard can be cut into a variety of shapes and used to add a new dimension to the base. Take three or four layers of newspaper or a piece of cardboard and cut out the desired shape.

Attaching the Shape   With one hand hold the shape (leg, ear, jaw, etc.) while fixing it in place with a pasted strip of newspaper, string, or masking

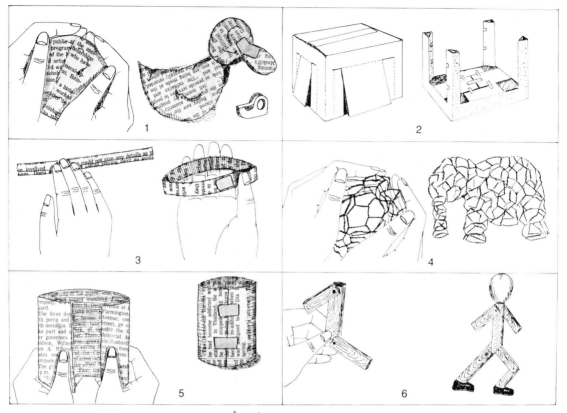

Figure 7-14 PAPIER-MÂCHÉ BASE
1. Crushed newspaper.
2. Cardboard box.
3. Rolled newspaper.
4. Chicken wire.
5. Laminated paper.
6. Wooden armature.

tape. Some shapes will require additional strips to hold them securely before the surface can be built up.

Once the rough shape is attached, additional strips can be applied to the surface to obtain the desired shape. These strips are added by running them from the base around the shape and back to the base in one direction and then in the opposite direction.

Layer-on-Layer Technique   Before starting to work with papier-mâché, cover the working surface with newspaper. A covered area protects the original surface and makes it easier to clean up after the project is finished.

Pick up a piece of newspaper and tear it into strips that are about 1 inch wide. Strips will tear evenly if the newspaper is torn with the grain. Torn strips are preferred to cut ones because the rough edges will mesh together forming a smoother surface. Tear about fifty strips and store them in a cardboard box for easy handling.

Prepare the paste. If the paste was mixed earlier, stir again before

GRAPHIC AND
MANIPULATIVE
ART FORMS AND
INSTRUCTIONAL
METHODS

190

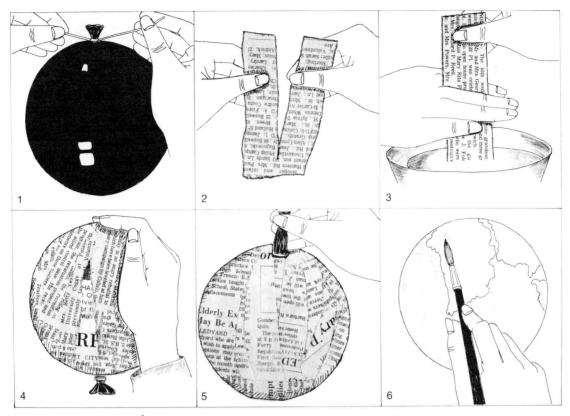

Figure 7-15 PAPIER-MÂCHE GLOBE

Materials: balloon, string, newspaper, wheat paste, paintbrush, paint, plastic container.

1. Inflate a balloon and tie the stem.
2. Tear newspaper into 1-inch strips.
3. Dip the strips in wheat paste and remove excess by running the pasted strips between the fingers.
4. Apply the strips to the surface of the balloon.
5. Remove the balloon from the newspaper sphere.
6. Paint the continents on the sphere.

using, because the flour will settle on the bottom of the mixture after standing for about twenty minutes.

Hold a strip of newspaper between the thumb and index finger. Dip the strip into the pan of paste, making sure that it is completely covered with the mixture. Lift the strip from the pan and run it gently between the index finger and the middle finger to remove any excess paste.

Take the prepared base—crushed paper, actual object, plastic container, chicken wire, armature, or cardboard box—and cover the surface with pasted strips. With your fingers smooth out the edges of the pasted newspaper strips. After the entire base has been covered, a second layer should be placed on top of this wet layer. The strips for the second layer should run in the opposite direction.

Add three more layers of pasted strips to the surface and be sure to

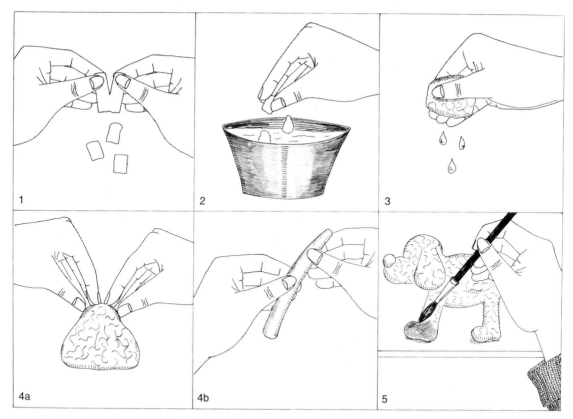

Figure 7-16 PAPER PULP

Materials: plastic container, paper toweling, facial tissues, wheat paste, water, paintbrush, paint.

1. Tear paper towels or facial tissues into small pieces.
2. Soak the small pieces of paper towel or tissue in a mixture of water and wheat paste.
3. Drain and squeeze out the excess water from the pulp.
4. Pinch the ball of pulp into a shape (*a* and *b*).
5. Paint the finished form.

run each layer in a different direction. The last layer can be strips of paper towel, cloth, or wrapping paper to obtain a different surface. Remember that strips should be smooth.

Paper Pulp Technique   Paper pulp is a claylike substance made from bits of paper that have been soaked in water and mixed with paste. The water-paste solution breaks down the paper and turns it into a pulpy, malleable substance. The paper pulp can be shaped or formed like clay and is very suitable for modeling small figurines and objects. It is also used to add texture to objects constructed by one of the other two techniques.

Tear newspaper, paper towels, facial tissues, egg cartons, or paper napkins into small bits and place them in water to soak overnight. The next day, pour off the water and squeeze the pulp until it is semimoist.

GRAPHIC AND
MANIPULATIVE
ART FORMS AND
INSTRUCTIONAL
METHODS

192

To this pulpy substance add enough paste to make a claylike mixture. Knead the mixture until the paste and paper fibers are thoroughly mixed. The paper pulp is ready to be worked into the desired shape. It can be formed or shaped by using the pinch method.

Set the finished object to one side to dry. A piece of screening or wire over a box makes a good drying rack for paper pulp objects. The wire rack allows air to circulate around all surfaces, resulting in even drying.

Laminated Sheet Technique   Laminated sheets or strips of paper can be used to form or shape an object where strength and durability are a factor. Newspaper, wrapping paper, or cloth can be glued together to form the laminations.

With a 3- to 5-inch paintbrush, apply paste between the sheets of paper. A lamination usually consists of four or more layers of paper. Paste should not be applied to the outside layer because it makes the surface too sticky to handle.

Allow the lamination to set for a few minutes until the paper becomes pliable. The lamination can be torn into strips or left in a whole sheet when applied to the base form. It also can be cut into a specific pattern and shaped, bent, or molded into a final form without a supporting base.

This technique requires that an individual experiment with the material before trying to obtain a finished product. Its potential is limited only by the individual's imagination.

String or Yarn Technique   Interesting shapes and designs can be constructed by forming pasted pieces of yarn or string over a removable base. Select a base and the appropriate yarn or string. The color and weight of the yarn or string depend upon the finished object.

Hold a piece of yarn or string between the thumb and index finger. Dip the yarn into the pan of paste, making sure that it is completely covered with the mixture. Lift the yarn from the pan, running it gently between the index finger and the middle finger to remove any excess paste.

Apply the yarn to the base. The yarn can be used to form a design. After the yarn dries, remove the base. If a beach ball or balloon was used, it can be deflated and removed, leaving a hollow shere.

Finishing Papier-mâché

The possibilities for finishing a papier-mâché object are almost endless. It is important to select materials and colors that complement the finished project. The surface can be covered with Suede Tex (a commercial product) where a durable suede finish is desired. A wide variety of other materials can be used to decorate a papier-mâché object—marbles for eyes, felt for ears, shirt stays for fangs, yarn for a lion's mane, or cotton for a rabbit's fur.

The dried surface should be sanded with fine sandpaper to smooth any rough edges before it is painted. Gesso is an opaque liquid that can be used as an undercoat to cover the paper surface. White latex paint can be used as a substitute for gesso. Gesso can be made by mixing 1 cup of evaporated milk with the powder from four sticks of chalk. Another

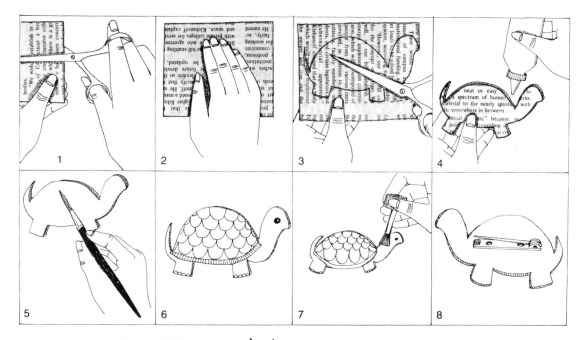

Figure 7-17 PAPIER-MÂCHÉ JEWELRY

Materials: newspaper, lightweight cardboard, clear nail polish, bar pin safety clasp, paint (tempera), paintbrush, scissors, wheat paste, glue, gesso.

1. Cut a piece of cardboard and four pieces of newspaper the approximate size of the pin.
2. Paste two pieces of newspaper to each side of the cardboard with wheat paste.
3. Cut out the design with a pair of scissors.
4. Apply glue to the outside edge.
5. Paint the shape with a thin coat of gesso.
6. Paint details on the surface.
7. Coat the surface with clear nail polish.
8. Attach the bar pin.

mixture combines one part of white powdered tempera paint with one part of evaporated milk. Both mixtures are stirred until creamy.

The paints most commonly used to decorate papier-mâché objects are tempera, poster paints, watercolors, acrylics, oil paints, latex paints, and enamels. Each of these paints has its own characteristics and quality. For example, tempera paints have good covering qualities and are easy for children to work with. Enamels give a surface a glossy finish. Water-base paints are easy to apply and dry fast, and they are easy to clean up after use. Oil paints and enamels are extremely durable and make the surface water resistant. It is important to select a paint for its particular effect, availability, or cost.

CARDBOARD-NEWSPAPER JEWELRY
Attractive jewelry can be constructed from a very simple papier-mâché process. Trace or sketch a design for a pin. Remember to think about the size and shape of the finished pin. Long, narrow designs or objects with

GRAPHIC AND
MANIPULATIVE
ART FORMS AND
INSTRUCTIONAL
METHODS

194

long, narrow protrusions should be avoided because they may break easily.

Cut a piece of cardboard from a cereal box approximately the same size as the design. With a piece of fine sandpaper lightly sand the shiny side of the cardboard to obtain a rough-dull surface. Glue holds better to a rough-dull surface than a shiny one. Cut four pieces of newspaper the same size as the cardboard. These will be used to build up both sides of the cardboard.

Mix 1/2 cup of flour with 1/2 cup of sugar. Add 2 ounces of water to the sugar-flour mixture and stir. Paste should be the consistency of pancake batter. Two tablespoons of glue will increase the holding power of the paste.

With a flat 1-inch brush, cover one side of the piece of cardboard with paste. Place a piece of newspaper on the cardboard and smooth the newspaper with palm of the hand, pressing from the center out toward the edges. Turn the cardboard over and repeat this procedure. Repeat this operation again on both sides. Stand the pasted piece on edge for approximately twenty to thirty minutes until nearly dry. Air should be allowed to circulate around the flat surfaces. This drying time can be used to add detail to the selected design. Sketch the outline of the design directly on the covered cardboard or transfer the design onto the surface using carbon paper.

The shape is cut out while the material is still damp. Material is more difficult to cut when completely dry. Scissors, tin snips, coping saw, or jig saw can be used to cut out the design. A generous amount of quick-drying glue should be applied to the edges. The edges should be pressed firmly together as the glue is applied. This will help to prevent the edges from unraveling. When the glue dries, paint the surface with a thin coat of gesso or white latex paint. Allow to dry for about ten minutes and then sketch the details on the front surface of the pin.

The details can be painted with tempera, watercolors, or acrylic paints. After the paints dry, clear nail polish can be used to protect the paints and give the surface a glossy finish. Apply a generous amount of nail polish, starting at one edge of the pin and working quickly to the other edge. Allow the nail polish to dry hard. Turn the pin over and glue the pin-back in place with Duco cement. Set the pin aside until the cement dries. The same technique can be used to construct key rings, tie bars, cuff links, and wall plaques.

SCULPTURING, CASTING, AND MOSAICS

Sculpturing, casting, and mosaics are three areas important to any crafts program. Wax, Zonalite, plaster, soap, and Styrofoam are inexpensive materials that can be used for subtractive sculpturing. Subtractive sculpturing is the process of cutting away those areas not essential to the finished form. It is one of the earliest forms of man's expression and dates back to his ability to fashion tools capable of carving wood and stone. Sculpturing need not be limited to solid forms; some interesting ones can be created from a piece of wire. Children enjoy manipulating wire, toothpicks, or wooden scraps into a wide variety of different forms. These materials enable children to explore in an entirely new and different direction.

Casting provides children with another process of reproducing a sculpture. A mold is made in sand or from rubber, and a liquid mixture is poured into the cavity. The mixture is allowed to harden, forming a reproduction of the original sculpture. Today many of the world's outstanding sculptures are cast from an original model carved from Styrofoam or other inexpensive material. Sir Henry Moore, the famous English sculptor, uses Styrofoam to carve many of his sculptures. These Styrofoam models are used to cast the finished sculpture from bronze.

Mosaics can be used to decorate a flat surface. Although they are not used to construct a three-dimensional sculpture, they can be used to form some attractive two-dimensional decorations.

SCULPTURING
Soap Carving

Carving with soap can be fun. It requires only a limited number of tools and materials (a bar of soap, pencil, carbon paper, knife, orangewood stick, and paints). Children will have fun carving a bar of soap into interesting shapes and objects.

Practice carving small pieces of soap with a knife into a circle, pyramid, oval, and square. It is important to acquire feel for the material before trying to carve an object or form that combines one or more of the basic shapes.

Think of a form or object to carve that will fit on the selected bar of soap. An animal, building, airplane, fish, or an unusual form can be carved from the soap. The design should be simple and clear. Small details are not important and are very difficult for the beginner to carve. Sketch the design onto a piece of paper that is the same size as the bar of soap.

Take a bar of Ivory soap and prepare it for carving. Letters and raised designs should be scraped off to form a flat surface. All other surfaces should be scraped to remove the outer coating. This outer coating is drier than the inner core, and its removal will prevent warping or bending during and after the carving of the object.

Place the carbon paper, carbon side down, on top of the wide surface of the bar of soap. Put the piece of paper with the design on top of the piece of carbon paper. Check to see that the soap, carbon paper, and design are in correct order and that the edges are even. Secure the carbon paper and design sheet to the soap with masking tape.

With a pencil, trace the design, being careful not to tear the paper or smear the carbon. Remove the design sheet and carbon paper from the top of the soap. The design should appear on the surface of the soap. If the design is not clear or is smeared, a thin layer of soap can be scraped off the surface and the tracing procedure repeated.

When the design has been successfully transferred to the soap, it is ready to be carved. Right-handers should start carving in the upper right-hand corner, while left-handers start in the upper left-hand corner. It is important to leave a 1/4-inch border around the design when cutting out the general outline.

Start carving by gently cutting away soap around the outline of the design with a knife. Cut down through the soap from the top to the bottom edge, being careful not to cut too close to the design. When the rough shape is obtained, the finished carving is ready to be started. Cut from the outer edge of the soap in toward the design. As the cuts get closer to the outline of the design, care should be taken not to cut into the finished shape.

Cuttings should be made on all sides of the shape so that the various parts of the object are gradually finished. Keep checking the design by rotating the object to be sure that it looks correct from all directions.

When you feel the form or object has the desired shape, it is time to start finishing the small details. Surface details can be added by using either a knife or an orangewood stick.

This is also a good time to smooth out any rough surfaces with a knife.

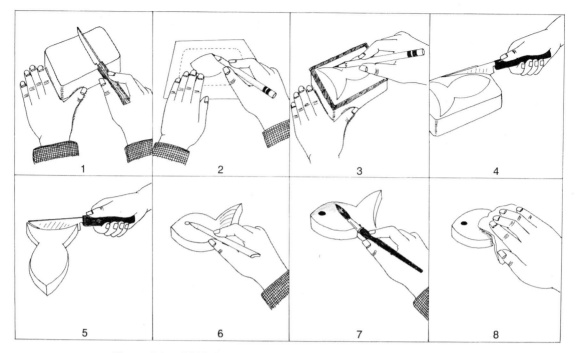

Figure 8-1   SOAP CARVING

Materials: bar of soap, pencil, knife, paintbrush, paint, paper napkins, orange-wood stick, paper, carbon paper.

1. Take a bar of soap and prepare it for carving. Letters and raised designs should be scraped off with a knife to form a flat surface.
2. Sketch a design on a piece of paper.
3. Place a piece of carbon paper on the bar of soap and trace over the design, pressing down lightly to prevent tearing the paper or smearing the carbon paper.
4. Start carving the bar of soap.
5. Gently carve the soap around the outline of the design.
6. Add small details with a orangewood stick.
7. Paint the surface.
8. Unpainted areas can be polished with a paper napkin.

Rough edges can also be removed by placing the soap under slowly running water and rubbing the edges with your fingers. If water is used to smooth the rough edges, set the carving aside for about a half hour to dry.

The finished object can be polished by rubbing the surface with a paper napkin, finger tips, or the palm of the hand. Polishing will give the finished object a shiny appearance. Color can be added by using tempera or acrylic paints. They also can be used to add detail to the finished object.

Styrofoam

Styrofoam is a light, pure white material that can easily be cut into a wide variety of shapes. Puppets, animals, sculptures, models, and decorations can be constructed from Styrofoam with a few simple tools.

Styrofoam can be purchased in many sizes and shapes. However, it is very expensive, so the funds available will determine the sizes and shapes

GRAPHIC AND
MANIPULATIVE
ART FORMS AND
INSTRUCTIONAL
METHODS

198

that will be used in the program. Sheets 12 X 36 X 1 inch and balls 1-1/8 and 2 inches in diameter will be very useful in a crafts program.

Styrofoam can be cut with a coping saw, knife, hot wire, and sandpaper. The easiest method for cutting Styrofoam is with a hot wire. A hot wire can be purchased or fabricated but is not essential. Indentions can be made with a hot soldering copper or iron. A knife also can be used to cut a cavity in the surface.

Styrofoam shapes can be glued together with one of the quick-drying glues or a special plastic adhesive. Some glues and cements will dissolve Styrofoam.

Styrofoam can be decorated with tempera, watercolors, acrylics, and oil paints. Some lacquer-based paints will dissolve the Styrofoam. These paints can be used to obtain some interesting effects.

Zonalite, Plaster, and Sand Sculpture

Before starting to work, it is important to cover the working surface with old newspapers. The Zonalite, plaster, and sand mixture will dry fast and will be difficult to remove from table tops.

Pour the necessary amount of water into a container. Mix one part of fine sand with one part of Zonalite and two parts of plaster. The dry mixture is added to the water by sifting it through the fingers or gently shaking it from a can. Keep adding the mixture to the water until it builds up above the surface. Stir the mixture thoroughly with the hands until it is smooth and creamy. Be sure that all the lumps of plaster are dissolved in the mixture. The mixture should be stirred gently to avoid bubbles. Once the ingredients are mixed, water should not be added to thin out the mixture or plaster to thicken it, because the correct consistency cannot be regained. Pour the mixture into a cardboard container.

Clean the mixing container and all tools with water. Plaster should not be washed down the sink. Set the mixture aside to dry for forty-eight hours. The material will remain damp for several days; this will not affect the finished sculpture. The block is ready to be shaped into the desired form with carving tools.

Carved Plaster Bas-Relief

Fill a mixing container with the necessary amount of water and add the plaster to the water by sifting it through the fingers. Continue adding the sifted plaster to the water until it builds up above the surface. Allow the plaster to soak for about twenty to thirty seconds and then stir the mixture thoroughly with the hands until it is smooth and creamy. Care should be taken to eliminate all lumps and to stir the mixture slowly to prevent air bubbles from forming. Water or plaster should not be added to the mixture once the correct consistency is obtained.

Pour the mixture into a cardboard mold and agitate to bring any bubbles to the surface. All tools and equipment should be cleaned immediately under running water. Large amounts of plaster should not be washed down the sink.

Set the plaster mold aside to harden and dry thoroughly before

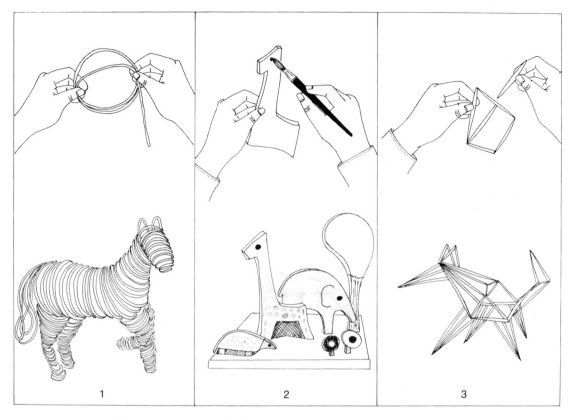

Figure 8-2 SCULPTURES
1. Wire sculpture
2. Scrap wood sculpture
3. Toothpick sculpture

removing the cardboard mold. The edges can be smoothed with any available tool, such as a knife, sandpaper, or file. Sketch a design or picture to be carved from the plaster. Transfer the design to the plaster and with any suitable carving tools, cut out the design. Soaking the plaster in water will facilitate the carving process. The plaster should be put on a soft padded surface before carving to prevent breakage.

The finished carving can be decorated with tempera, watercolors, or acrylic paints. Clear plastic spray or shellac can be used to protect the painted surface. Oil and enamel paints require no protective coat. A pure white, glossy finish can be obtained by soaking the plaster carving for thirty minutes in a solution of dissolved white soap flakes and then wiping the surface dry with a cloth. An antique finish is achieved by soaking the plaster in linseed oil and while still wet, dusting with dry yellow ochre or umber. The ochre or umber is wiped with a cloth until the desired color is obtained.

Wax Sculpture

Interesting objects can be carved from a block of paraffin wax. Melt the paraffin in a double boiler over a low heat. As a precautionary measure,

GRAPHIC AND
MANIPULATIVE
ART FORMS AND
INSTRUCTIONAL
METHODS

200

wax should always be heated in a double boiler. Select a container to use for a mold. Empty milk cartons make excellent molds. The wax can be colored by adding wax crayons or food coloring.

Pour the melted wax into the mold and allow to cool and harden. Remove the wax from the mold. Cardboard molds can be torn from the wax, while other types of molds are dipped in hot water until the paraffin drops out.

A knife, nail file, nail, hairpin, and orangewood stick can be used to carve the block of paraffin to the desired form. Before starting the carving, it is a good idea to make a sketch of how the finished object will look. Take a piece of scrap paraffin and practice carving different shapes with the various tools. When you have a feel for the material, start carving the object. Experiment with a knife heated over a low flame. The paraffin can be smoothed out by rubbing the surface with a cloth dampened in turpentine.

Wire Sculpture
Make a linear sketch of a design or figure that can be used as a plan for a wire sculpture. Take a piece of any substantial wire with some flexibility, such as heavy stove-pipe, copper, aluminum, or bailing wire and experiment bending and twisting it into various shapes. Some designs and figures may require the use of a coil. A wire coil can be made by wrapping the wire around a dowel, pencil, paper tube, or bottle. Be sure that the coil and base core can be separated.

Wire sculptures are usually conceived as one continuous length of wire, but they can be constructed from several lengths joined together. The pieces are hooked, twisted, or soldered together. The finished wire sculpture can be painted to improve its appearance. Wood, sponge, plastic, or paper can be combined with the wire to form an interesting sculpture.

Toothpick Sculpture
Toothpicks can be held together with Duco cement to form various three-dimensional structures. Styrofoam, paper, plastic, and wood can be used to enhance the sculpture. A pencil sketch should be made to assist in the planning of a sculpture.

Wood Scrap Sculpture
Scrap pieces of wood of various sizes, shapes, and colors can be placed together to create a sculpture. Collect a large variety of wooden shapes. Experiment putting the various pieces of wood together to create an interesting sculpture. When the desired arrangement is obtained, glue the pieces together. The sculpture should present an interesting view from all sides. Paint can be used to decorate the finished sculpture.

Mobiles
A mobile is a construction or sculpture of wire and a wide variety of shapes made from different materials that can be set in motion by air currents. They are created to produce movement with changing patterns. Constructing a mobile provides the individual with an experience in balance, design, sculpture, form, space, and color.

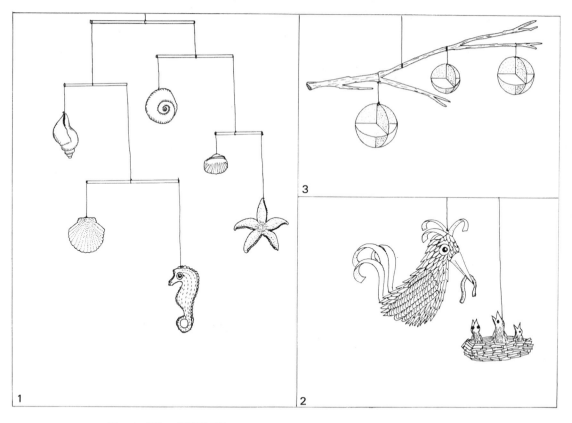

Figure 8-3 MOBILES

1. A simple mobile utilizing several suspended objects.
2. Two objects that are suspended and balanced to create a mobile.
3. Three objects that are suspended and balanced to create a mobile.

Decide on a theme for the mobile, the number of units, and the technique that will be utilized to construct the various objects. Wood, plastic, cloth, wire, paper, and numerous other materials can be used individually or in combination to construct parts of the mobile. There should be a relationship between the various objects that are used to make up the mobile.

Cut a piece of coat hanger wire or 1/8-inch wooden dowel, the length depending upon the size of the objects used to make up the mobile. Tie a piece of nylon thread to one of the objects so that it will balance when suspended. (This single object suspended from the ceiling would represent the simplest form of mobile and is an appropriate activity for very young children.) Tie the other end of the thread to the end of the piece of wire. A second object is tied to the opposite end of the wire. The objects should hang so that they do not touch. A small drop of glue or cement applied to the thread and wire will keep the thread from slipping. The thread used to hold the objects should not be too long, and the lengths should vary.

Tie another piece of thread to the center of the wire or dowel supporting the two objects. Move the thread back and forth on the wire or dowel until the point of balance is located. Apply a drop of glue to secure the thread

GRAPHIC AND
MANIPULATIVE
ART FORMS AND
INSTRUCTIONAL
METHODS

202

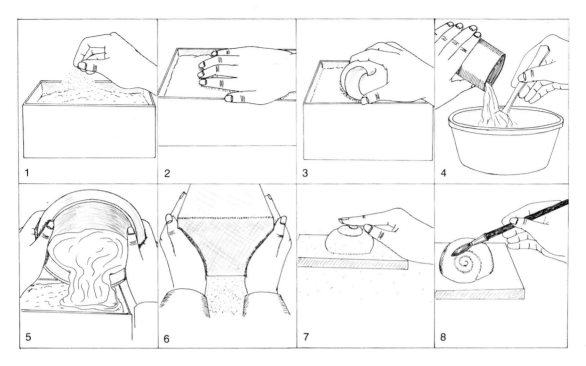

Figure 8-4 SAND CASTING

Materials : cardboard box, bowl, measuring cup, paint, sand, paintbrush, plaster of Paris or Keene's cement.

1. Place sand in a cardboard box.
2. Level off the sand.
3. Press an object into the sand to create an impression.
4. Mix plaster of Paris or Keene's cement.
5. Pour the mixture into the sand mold and set aside to harden.
6. Remove the casting from the sand mold by inverting the box.
7. Brush the sand from the casting.
8. Paint the casting with tempera, watercolors, or acrylics.

to the wire or dowel. This could be used as a simple mobile or additional pieces could be constructed and added to the mobile. Mobiles are constructed from the bottom up.

The thread holding the section can be attached to the end of the wire or dowel and secured with a drop of glue or cement. With a piece of thread, suspend another object from the other end of the wire or dowel. Attach a piece of thread to the center of the wire or dowel and balance both sections. Additional sections can be added as long as balance is maintained.

CASTING
Sand Casting

Sand sculpture is an inexpensive activity that can be used by children to create interesting wall plaques and other decorations. Plaster of Paris or Keene's cement are the only materials used that may not be considered common classroom supplies. Paints, cardboard boxes, and sand are found around most schools and homes.

Fill a small cardboard box with damp sand to within 1 inch of the top edge. With the edge of a piece of wood, level off the sand. Select an object that can be used to create an impression in the sand. It can be a seashell, a plastic object, ceramic figurine, or wooden shape. Press the object into the sand. Lift the object from the sand. The sand impression should be clean and smooth. If it is not, level the sand and make another impression.

Mix enough plaster of Paris or Keene's cement to form a 3/4-inch layer on top of the sand. Slowly pour the mixture over the sand. Make sure the surface of the mixture is smooth and level. A paper clip or bent piece of wire can be placed in the back of the plaque, while the mixture is wet. Allow the cement to dry overnight.

Spread a piece of newspaper over the working surface. With a knife, cut the sides of the box so that they can be folded over and the plaque lifted from the sand mold. Place the plaque on the newspaper and brush all the loose sand from the finished piece.

The plaque can be painted with tempera, watercolors, or acrylic paints. The painted surface can be sealed with a clear plastic spray.

Rubber Molds

Liquid rubber or latex can be painted over the surface of an object to make a mold that may be used to cast duplicates of the original form. Liquid rubber is very sensitive and when painted on the surface of the model, will pick up all the details in the original. Select a model or make one from clay or some other material. The model used should have a flat base and only a limited number of appendages. Too many appendages may make removing the finished rubber mold difficult and cause parts of the casted form to break off. For example, a dog with four legs could not be used for a model, unless the area between the legs was filled in. This area can be filled with clay and made to appear as grass.

Select a piece of plywood or hardboard to use as a base to hold the model. Choose a size 12 watercolor brush and dip it in a solution of soapy water. The soap will make cleaning the brush easier. Dip the brush into the liquid rubber and apply a small amount to the base of the model. Place the model on the plywood base; the liquid rubber will hold it in position while the surface is painted. Hold the top of the model with one hand, and with the paintbrush coat the surface with liquid rubber. Brush out the paint thoroughly to eliminate air bubbles. Apply two or three coats and allow to dry overnight. Another coat can be applied the next day. After the first three coats are applied, all other coats should be allowed to dry overnight. As the model is being painted, an area around the base should be covered forming a 1 inch lip. This lip will hold the mold when it is being filled with cement during the casting operation. Apply enough coats of liquid rubber to obtain the appropriate wall thickness for the size of the model. When the liquid rubber is dry, cover the outside surface with talcum powder to prevent it from sticking as the mold is removed. Pull the rubber away from the model and peel it back as though you were peeling an orange. Care should be taken when stretching the rubber not to tear the material. When the model is removed, the mold is ready to be used for casting.

GRAPHIC AND
MANIPULATIVE
ART FORMS AND
INSTRUCTIONAL
METHODS

204

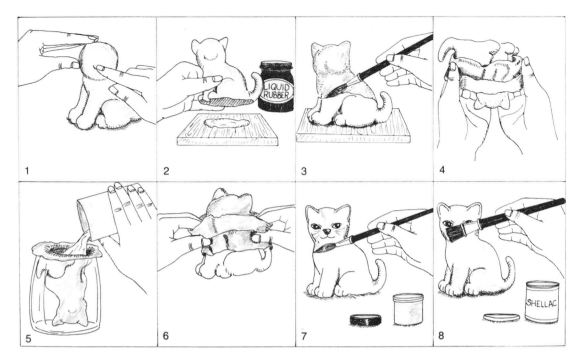

Figure 8-5 RUBBER MOLDS

Materials : clay, liquid rubber, shellac, plywood, paintbrush, paint, Keene's cement.
1. Form a model from clay.
2. Attach the model to a plywood base with liquid rubber.
3. Apply sufficient coats of liquid rubber to the model to obtain the desired wall thickness for the size of the model (eight to ten coats).
4. Remove the model from the rubber mold.
5. Fill the rubber mold with Keene's cement.
6. Remove the model.
7. Decorate the surface by painting with tempera, watercolors, or acrylics.
8. Seal the surface, if necessary, with shellac.

To cast with the rubber mold, take a cardboard box and cut a hole in the bottom large enough for the mold to slip through. The rubber lip around the base should keep the mold from falling through the hole. Tape the lip of the mold to the box with masking tape. Fill the mold with dry Keene's cement. Pour the dry cement into a container and slowly add water until the mixture is the same consistency as heavy cream. Slowly pour the mixture into the mold, while using a stick to move the cement around inside the mold. The stick will allow air bubbles to escape and to force the cement into the various parts of the mold. When the mold is filled with cement, pat the top of the surface to make sure all the air bubbles are removed. Set aside to allow the cement to harden overnight. The casting is removed using the same process as for the removal of the original model.

Making a Plaque A rubber mold can also be made of a plaque. Place the plaque on a piece of plywood with the back in a downward position. Paint the surface with three coats of liquid rubber and allow to dry overnight. The next day mix some liquid rubber with sawdust. Apply this mixture to the surface, building up the coating and the thickness of the walls of the mold. Fill in all the cavities, creating a surface that can support the weight of the cement when the mold is used for casting. The sawdust mixture will not interfere with the imprint made in the rubber surface. To cast the plaque, hold the rubber mold in a cardbox box in the same manner as described earlier. Molds for large plaques can be supported by building a cradle out of sand or cement.

The finished tooled or embossed design can be used as a mold for casting wall plaques. After the design is completed, turn up a 1/2-inch edge on all four sides to form a box. The corners can be sealed with masking tape.

Mix Keene's cement or plaster of Paris to the correct consistency and pour it into the mold. A piece of wood can be used to level off the cement or plaster of Paris. Set the material aside to dry.

The surface can be decorated by painting with tempera, watercolors, or acrylics. The painted surface can be protected with a clear plastic spray.

Spoon Molds

A spoon can be used as a mold to make the base shape for an attractive pin. Mix 4 teaspoons of plaster of Paris with 2 teaspoons of water into a creamy mixture. Coat the bowl of the spoon with petroleum jelly. Hold the spoon in a position so that the cavity can be filled without spilling the mixture. Pour the plaster mixture into the spoon and pat down and level it off with your fingers. Set aside to dry for about one hour. When the plaster is hardened, it can be removed by lightly tapping the spoon against the table.

With a piece of fine sandpaper, smooth off any rough edges. Paint the entire pin with white enamel, latex, or acrylic paint. When the paint dries, cement a pinback to the flat side of the pin and set aside to dry.

The pin is ready to be decorated. Use enamels, latex, or acrylic paints to create a colorful design. Watercolors or tempera paints can be used, but should be covered with a sealer to protect the design. Clear plastic spray or nail polish can be used to seal and protect the painted design. Glitter, sparkle, or other types of material can be used to make the pin more attractive. Use other small objects as molds to obtain variations in the base shape of the pin.

Moldless Casting

Plaster mixed into a paste consistency can be whirled on two fingers and then thrown onto a piece of paper. A wide variety of unusual shapes can be formed by using this technique. The shape is made into a pin using the method described for spoon mold pins.

MOSAICS

Mosaics are surface decorations made of small pieces of colored glass, stone, or ceramic tile. Sketch several designs on a piece of paper. Select the desired design and lay it out on a piece of cardboard, using crayon, paint, or cut paper to make a working model of the finished mosaic. If the design is one that utilizes only whole tiles, the design can be planned by arranging

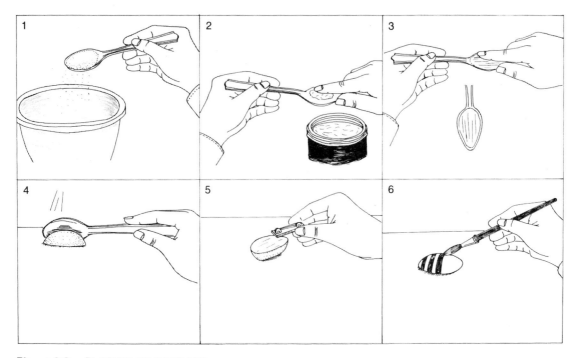

Figure 8-6 PLASTER OF PARIS PIN
Materials: plaster of Paris, spoon, bar pin safety clasp, paint, mixing bowl, paint-brush, Duco cement, petroleum jelly.

1. Mix 4 teaspoons of plaster of Paris with 2 teaspoons of water.
2. Coat a spoon with petroleum jelly.
3. Pour the plaster of Paris mixture into the spoon and pat down until it is level.
4. After the mixture has hardened, remove it by tapping the spoon on the table.
5. Cement the bar pin to the flat side of the form.
6. Decorate the surface by painting with tempera, watercolors, or acrylics.

the tiles. Transfer the design to a mounting surface. Hardboard can be used as a base for small mosaic projects, while plywood is used for larger activities. The thickness of the plywood depends upon the size of the finished mosaics (1/4-inch—up to 2 feet square; 1/2-inch—up to 4 feet square; 3/4-inch—larger).

Tiles are cut with nippers to fit the various areas of the design. Care should be taken when cutting tiles to shield the tile with a hand to prevent splinters from flying. Large tiles can be broken into smaller pieces by placing them in a burlap bag and smashing with a hammer.

Tiles are glued with Duco cement by spreading an even coating of glue over a small area. Care should be taken not to apply too much glue, because it will ooze up between the tiles making it difficult to apply the grout. Press the tiles in place allowing a 1/16- to 1/8-inch space between tiles for the grout. When the design is completed, it is set aside to dry.

The spaces between the tiles are filled with grout. Grout and grout coloring (dry pigments) can be purchased at a hardware store or building supply house. The grout is mixed by adding the dry powder to a small amount

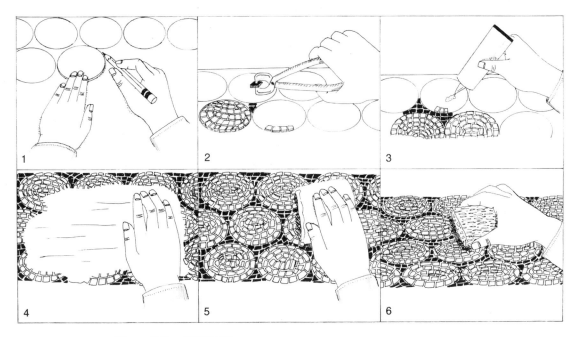

Figure 8-7   MOSAICS

Materials: plywood, rag, tile, grout, tile cutters, cement, sponge, silicone or wax.

1. Outline the design on a plywood base.
2. Cut the tiles to fit the various areas of the design.
3. Cement the tiles to the surface leaving a small space between each tile.
4. Rub grout into the spaces between the tiles and allow to set.
5. Remove the excess grout from the surface with a damp cloth.
6. Wash the surface clean with a sponge before sealing the surface with silicone or wax.

of water, while stirring until a consistency of heavy cream is obtained. It is spread over the surface and rubbed with the fingers into the spaces between the tiles. A small stick is helpful in forcing the grout into the spaces between the tiles. The grout is allowed to set before the excessive grout is removed from the surface with a sponge, damp cloth, or paper towel. Before applying a sealer (silicone, marble polish, or wax) to protect the grout, clean the surface with a damp cloth or sponge.

GRAPHIC AND
MANIPULATIVE
ART FORMS AND
INSTRUCTIONAL
METHODS

208

CERAMICS

Ceramics is a term applied to objects that are formed of clay and hardened by heat. Clay has been used by individuals in almost every civilization for aesthetic and/or practical purposes. In both ancient and modern times, clay has been molded or cast into forms both expressive and functional. Containers to store food, bricks to fabricate buildings, great sculptures, and decorative tiles are only a few ways individuals have utilized clay.

Essentially, the freehand methods used today are the same as those that have been used since primitive times. They are molding a form from a lump of clay, pinching a shape from a ball of clay with the thumb and fingers, twisting coils into a form, joining slabs into the desired shape, and forming a piece of clay over an object. These methods require only limited materials, tools, and equipment. Slip, which is a liquid clay, can be poured into a mold. The clay adheres to the walls and takes the shape of the mold. Another method is throwing on a wheel, a process of shaping a lump of moist clay while it is turning.

There are various clays, each with its own unique properties and characteristics. These clays are used to create objects with completely different textures and appearances. Certain clays, because of their qualities, are much more suitable for particular kinds of work.

Any ceramic program for children or adults should provide a period for exploration and experimentation. An orientation period is necessary to allow the individual to obtain an understanding of the properties and characteristics of different kinds of clay. Experimentation also enables the individual to feel his material, respect its limitations, and utilize it to build expressive forms.

Children enjoy patting, rolling, squeezing, thumping, pulling, and kneading clay. Doing so enables them to see and feel their ideas in three-dimensional form. Clay is malleable, flexible, and pliable, but it is also unpredictable, resisting, and often messy. However, it is economically feasible for use in any crafts program.

The material presented in this section will help to familiarize the reader with the techniques, materials, and tools needed to work with clay. Material is also presented describing those materials that can be used as substitutes for clay.

GLOSSARY OF TERMS

Biscuit   Clay pieces that have been fired once.

Bone-dry Clay   Clay that has become as dry as possible without firing. Bone-dry clay is very fragile.

Engobe or Colored Slip   Colored pigments added to slip and used for painting decorations on clay.

Firing   Baking the clay pieces in a kiln.

Glaze   A mixture of powdered glass and water which is applied to biscuit-fired ware.
   Underglaze   Dye stain used to decorate raw clay.
   Opaque Glaze   A thick mixture that produces a surface that cannot be seen through.
   Clear Transparent Glaze   A clear mixture used to cover surfaces painted with underglazes.
   Colored Transparent Glaze   A highly translucent mixture.

Green Ware   Unfired pieces of clay.

Kiln   Specially constructed oven in which clay pieces are fired.

Leather-hard Clay   Clay that is not completely dry, but is firm enough so that it cannot be modeled. It has the same color as moist clay.

Plaster Bat   A flat, pie-shaped slab made of plaster of Paris and used to absorb the moisture from wet clay.

Pyrometric Cone   A ceramic temperature gauge made from a combination of different clays that will bend at a certain temperature. The cone is used to determine the temperature inside the kiln. The larger the number of the cone, the lower the melting point. The most commonly used cones are $05 = 1886^{\circ}F$, $06 = 1841^{\circ}F$, $07 = 1787^{\circ}F$, and $08 = 1733^{\circ}F$.

Slip   Clay that is mixed with water to form a liquid substance.

Stacking   The arrangement of pieces in the kiln before firing.

GRAPHIC AND
MANIPULATIVE
ART FORMS AND
INSTRUCTIONAL
METHODS

210

Stilts Stands used to hold glazed pieces off the shelves or bottom of the kiln. They prevent the glazed pieces from sticking to the surfaces of the kiln.

Wedging Board A board with a wire stretched over it, with a plaster slab base on which to pound clay.

Wedging The conditioning of clay by hitting it against a surface to remove air pockets.

Welding A method of joining two pieces of clay together with slip.

CLAY
Types of Clay
Marblex is a gray plastic clay which hardens without firing. It is modeled like any other clay, but finished pieces resemble fired ware in hardness due to a chemical change which takes place as the clay dries in the air. Finished items can be decorated with show-card colors, enamels, latex paints, and lacquers. Clear lacquer, varnish, or shellac can be used as a protective coating over tempera and watercolor paints.

Mexican pottery clay is a strong durable pottery clay that hardens without firing. Air-dried pieces are a rich red color similar to Indian or Mexican pottery. Finished objects can be painted like Marblex clay.

Ceramite plastic clay or *Ceramite terra cotta* is a substance which can be worked like pottery and modeling clays. It bakes to durable hardness in twenty minutes in a kitchen oven at 250°F. Ceramite can be used over indefinitely if it is kept plastic by moistening with water. It becomes permanently hard and waterproof only after baking. Finished objects can be decorated with Ceramite glazes. Ceramite glaze is a glasslike fluid that can be obtained in a variety of beautiful colors and is applied by simply brushing onto the surface. The glazed surface becomes waterproof and durable when baked in a kitchen oven for twenty minutes.

White modeling clay is a gray-white color in its raw state and becomes pure white after being fired. It is an excellent clay for wheel throwing, sculpturing, and all other methods of hand modeling. Glazes are used to decorate the finished object.

Red clay is a rich red, before and after firing. Its excellent plasticity makes this clay suitable for wheel throwing, sculpturing, and all other methods of hand modeling. Glazes are used to decorate the surface of the finished item.

Pottery clay is a stoneware clay suitable for modeling, throwing, pressing, and slip painting. When fired at high temperatures, it becomes hard, dense, semivitreous, and buff color, while at low temperatures the color is light cream.

Terra cotta clay is a mixture of red and buff clay combined with a medium mesh grog (ground, screened, fired clay) to make fired pottery more porous and reduce cracking, shrinkage, and warpage. It has a rough texture that makes a very attractive finished product. At low temperatures the fired object is terra cotta color, while at high temperatures it has a rich red-brown color.

Casting clay contains a special substance called deflocculant which reduces the amount of water required and prevents rapid settling.

Clay is purchased in one of two forms: a dry powder referred to as "clay flour" or a prepared clay ready for use which is called "moist clay." Dry clay is more economical; however, the moist clay is more efficient and the additional cost is negligible when compared with the convenience of having clay that is ready to use.

Mixing Clay

Mixing clay can provide children with another experience. The dry clay is mixed by sifting the flour into water and stirring until the mixture is thick. The mixture is allowed to sit at least twenty-four hours before working it. Excess water and air bubbles are eliminated by kneading and beating the clay on a hard surface (plaster of Paris or Keene's cement). The clay should be worked until it is easy to manipulate and no longer sticky. A good consistency is one that allows the clay to be manipulated without cracking and stiff enough so that it does not stick to the hands.

An easy method of mixing clay is to put a pound of flour clay in a plastic bag and add a small amount of water. Press the air from the bag and secure the open end with a rubber band and allow one of the children to knead the mixture. If the clay is too dry, add more water; if too moist, add some dry clay. The mixture can be stored for an extended period of time in the plastic bag.

Clay should be workable, plastic, fine in texture, and possess good drying qualities. Clay of the proper consistency will not crumble and fall apart when being worked and will dry on the inner portions and outer surfaces in a reasonable length of time. If the correct consistency is not obtained and the clay is not workable or plastic, the next mixture can be improved by adding 40 percent talc and from 1 to 5 percent bentonite.

Fine texture can be determined by the satin smoothness of the clay flour or by rubbing moist clay between the fingers. If the clay is too coarse, the only alternative is to purchase a finer mesh clay.

WEDGING

Clay should be wedged before it is formed into any shape. Wedging eliminates air pockets in the clay and gives it an even consistency. Both these characteristics are very important if quality work is to be obtained in the finished product. Clay is wedged by throwing it against a wedging board or other solid surface such as a table or desk top. After throwing the clay vigorously against a flat surface a number of times, cut it with a wire or knife to determine if all the air pockets have disappeared. Take the two pieces of clay and slap them together as hard as possible to prevent any new air pockets from forming. Care should be taken not to put two halves together so the air will be trapped in old air pockets. If air pockets appear on the split surfaces, continue to throw the clay ball against the flat surface until they have disappeared. This is determined by cutting the ball of clay with a knife or wire.

GRAPHIC AND
MANIPULATIVE
ART FORMS AND
INSTRUCTIONAL
METHODS

212

STORING CLAY

Clay should be stored so that it will retain its proper moisture level. Plastic bags, crocks, garbage cans, and other airtight containers are excellent for this purpose. A wet cloth can be used to cover the stored clay to retard the loss of moisture. Water can be added to moist clay if it starts to dry.

Unused clay can be reclaimèd by wrapping it in a damp cloth and setting to one side for a few days. The clay can be returned to the main storage container when sufficiently wet again. Flour clay should be stored in a cool, dry place.

Unfinished work should be kept moist by wrapping in a damp cloth until it is finished. An old refrigerator makes an excellent storage area for unfinished projects.

MODELING

Success with clay or substitute clay can be enhanced if children understand the properties and characteristics of the material being modeled. Children should be encouraged to explore rather than create a finished product at first. They should learn that material can be returned to the clay container and reused to create a different form.

Children should be encouraged to pinch or pull their shapes from a ball, rather then just sticking shapes together. They should be provided an opportunity to see what happens when shapes are just put together. Children should experience how two pieces of clay can be worked together.

Making a Plan

Before modeling a dish, bowl, or sculpture, make some preliminary sketches of what the finished piece should look like. A sketch will assist the individual in planning the best method to construct the piece from clay. A template can be constructed from the sketches and used to check the inward or outward slopes of the walls of the piece under construction. Children will utilize the sketch to move from the play level to the craftsman level. The craftsman level requires controlling the clay to construct an object to certain specifications.

Pinch Method

The pinch method is the simplest method to use when forming simple sculptures or small bowls and dishes. The desired shape is actually pinched from a ball of clay. This method requires that a piece of clay be pinched, pulled, or pushed in a variety of ways to obtain the desired shape.

Making a Bowl or Low Dish   Form a ball of clay about the size of an apple and place it in the palm of your hand. Poke the thumb of the other hand into the top of the ball of clay. Continue to press the thumb into the center, while using the fingers to form the outer surface of the bowl. The wall of the bowl should be about 1/4 inch or more thick. Care should be taken to keep the walls uniform in thickness. The top of the walls should not be thinner than the other parts.

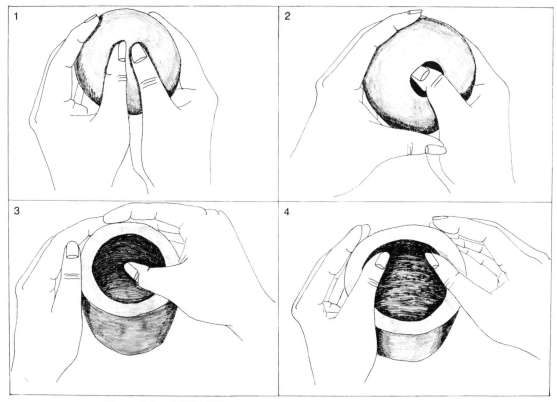

Figure 9-1 PINCH POT

Materials : clay.

1. Roll the wedged clay into a ball.
2. Press thumb into the ball.
3. Pinch the clay outward to form a pot.
4. Smooth the pot with the fingers.

Fingers can be used to smooth the inside and outside walls. Moisture can be added to clay by dipping fingers into water as the clay is being worked. This added moisture will help keep the clay in a workable condition. Too much water will make the clay difficult to model.

The finished shape can be round or a free form. If the finished object is not round, it should be free form enough to show that there was no intention to make it round.

Coil Method

This method utilizes coils of clay to model an object. This method is more difficult than the pinch method because it requires welding the coils into a uniform piece of material. Coils should be welded together so thoroughly that a seal is formed between them. The coil method can be utilized to create some sophisticated sculptures, bowls, plates, or pitchers.

To Form the Base The base can be oval or square; it does not have to be round. The base is formed by holding one end of the coil on a flat

GRAPHIC AND
MANIPULATIVE
ART FORMS AND
INSTRUCTIONAL
METHODS

214

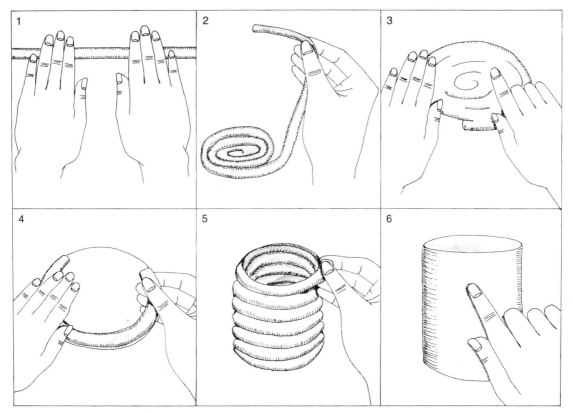

Figure 9-2   COIL METHOD
Materials : clay.

1. Roll a long coil for the base.
2. Wind the coil into the desired shape for the base.
3. Smooth the edges of the coil.
4. Place the coils on the base to form the sides.
5. Continue winding the coils until the desired height is reached.
6. Weld the coils together.

surface, while twisting the free end around the held end. Continue to twist in the same direction, being sure to push the coils close together. When the desired size of the base is obtained, press and smooth the coils together until the surface is flat. Turn the base over and flatten the opposite side.

If cracks appear as the coils are being worked, it may be that the clay is poorly wedged or too dry. This problem usually can be corrected by rewedging or adding water. Some clays are not plastic and will not bend without cracking. These clays are not suitable for modeling objects using the coil method.

The base can also be constructed by rolling out a flat piece of clay to the desired thickness and cutting out the desired shape.

Constructing the Walls   The walls of the object are also built up with coils. Coils should be firmly secured to the top edge of the base. Score

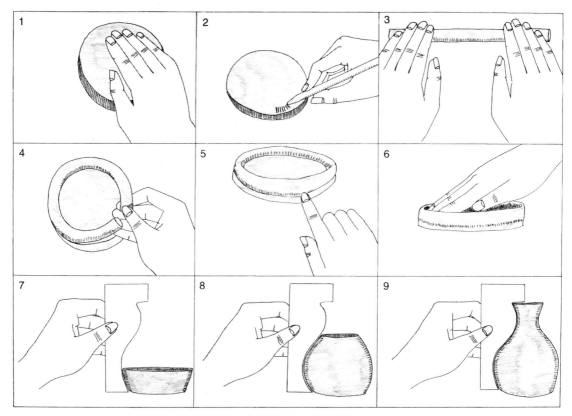

Figure 9-3 COIL BUILDING WITH A TEMPLATE

Materials: clay, 1/4-inch wooden dowel sharpened at one edge, cardboard template.

1. Form a base.
2. Score the base and moisten with slip.
3. Roll the clay into a coil.
4. Add the coil to the base.
5. Weld the outside.
6. Weld the inside.
7. Add another coil and check with a template.
8. Check the contour often with a template.
9. Completed project.

the surface of the base at the spot that the coil will be connected to the base. Apply slip to the scored area of the base before connecting the coil to it. Press the new coil very firmly to the base and cut off any extra material. The coil is welded to the base by working one hand on the inside of the wall, while using the other hand in the opposite position on the outside surface.

Before adding another coil, it should be decided if the walls are going to bulge outward or slope inward. An outward flare can be obtained by placing each additional coil toward the outer edge of the coil below. An inward curve can be obtained by putting each coil toward the inner edge of the coil below.

Score the top of the first coil and apply slip. A second coil is rolled and

GRAPHIC AND
MANIPULATIVE
ART FORMS AND
INSTRUCTIONAL
METHODS

216

welded in place. Add another coil to the wall. Then, check the slope of the wall with a template. The clay should be worked so that it conforms to the contour of the template. Only three coils can be added at one time without causing the walls to sag. This is very important for large objects or those that have walls that flare outward. The unfinished object should be covered with a damp cloth and stored until the next day. The clay should dry to leather hardness before more coils are added.

Before continuing to build the wall, moisten the top edge of the last coil. Add the desired number of coils to obtain the desired height. Remember that the coils should be welded together.

Rough edges can be smoothed with slip and later the finished piece can be sanded, sponged, or smoothed with the fingers. When the piece is bone dry, the base can be rotated on a piece of sandpaper and the side walls sanded smooth. The piece is ready to fire. If the piece is not going to be fired, it can be decorated with tempera paints.

Coil People and Animals   Young children can have fun forming and pressing coils together to construct animals, people, and abstract shapes. This activity is also an excellent experience for children to develop a feeling for working with coils.

Strip Method
This method uses flat strips instead of coils to model an object. The technique has advantages over the coil method when modeling cylindrical forms. The clay strips are rolled out with a rolling pin between two strips of wood to obtain the desired thickness and width. The thickness and width of the strips are determined by the size of the finished piece. The base is cut from a piece of rolled-out clay. The strips are welded together using the same technique as used for modeling with coils.

Sculpturing a Form
A sculpture can be pinched or pulled from a ball of clay. Free-form or abstract sculptures that do not resemble any particular object can be modeled. Animals, birds, people, and other interesting shapes can be formed by pinching and pulling shapes from a ball. Great satisfaction can be gained from a form that has rhythmic flow of lines related to each other.

Slab Method
The slab method lends itself to the construction of straight-sided geometric forms. This technique requires more skill than either the pinch or coil methods, therefore making it more appropriate to use with older children and adults.

The method requires rolling out the piece of clay with a rolling pin. Before constructing a form, the clay must be leather hard so that it will support its own weight when in a vertical position.

Clay Tiles   Tiles are shapes cut from a slab of clay that are glazed or decorated with a design and then glazed. Finished tiles can be used individually or combined to decorate a surface.

Take a piece of wedged clay and flatten it with a rolling pin on a piece of plastic or damp cloth. Thickness of the tile is controlled by rolling the clay between two 1/2-inch-thick sticks. Uniform thickness is obtained by rolling the clay in a crosswise and lengthwise direction.

Sketch a design for the tile on a piece of paper. Think of the method that will be used to bring the design out on the tile. Will the design be carved, embossed, or one of the other methods described under the section Techniques for Decorating Clay Objects? It is important to select a design and technique that will complement one another. Some designs can be enhanced by a decorating technique, while others will lose their appeal.

With a knife and straightedge, cut the slab into a tile that is suitable for the selected design. Set the tile aside until the clay becomes almost leather hard. Place the paper with the design over the tile and transfer the design by tracing the lines with a sharp pencil.

Set the tile aside to dry on a rack made from a piece of hardware cloth which will permit air to circulate around the bottom of the clay. This will prevent the clay tile from warping. When the clay is bone dry, the surface can be sanded smooth. The piece is ready to be glazed and fired.

Folded Clay Animals This technique utilizes a two-dimensional animal form cut from a slab of clay that is folded and twisted into a three-dimensional shape.

Take a piece of wedged clay and flatten it with a rolling pin on a piece of plastic or damp cloth. Thickness is controlled by rolling the clay between two 1/2-inch-thick sticks. The clay should be rolled in a crosswise and lengthwise direction to obtain a slab that has uniform thickness. The animal shape can be drawn directly on the slab of clay, or a sketch can be made on a piece of paper and cut out to be used as a pattern. Holding the pattern in place, trace around the shape with a pencil cutting slightly into the clay. With a knife, cut around the shape, applying enough pressure to cut through the clay.

Slip the knife under the cutout shape and lift it out from the slab. Fold the legs down into position so that they can support the body. Bend and twist the various parts of the body into the desired shape.

Smooth out rough edges and add texture or features with a modeling tool. If the clay is too soft to support itself, prop it up with a wire, crushed paper, or a ball of clay. Set the piece aside to dry. When the piece is bone dry, the surface can be sanded smooth. The piece is ready to be decorated and fired.

Constructing with Slabs Flatten a piece of wedged clay on the rough side of a piece of oil cloth with a rolling pin. The thickness of the slab depends upon the size of the form to be built. Thickness can be controlled by rolling the clay between two sticks of equal thickness. The clay should be rolled in a crosswise and lengthwise direction to obtain a slab that has uniform thickness.

If the clay cracks, it should be rewedged and moisture added. A limited

GRAPHIC AND
MANIPULATIVE
ART FORMS AND
INSTRUCTIONAL
METHODS

218

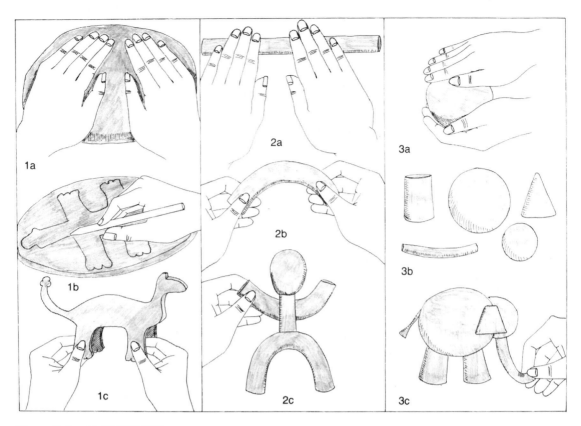

Figure 9-4 CLAY FIGURES
  1. Folded slab.
    a. Press the clay into a slab.
    b. Draw an outline of the figure.
    c. Fold the clay to form the figure.
  2. Coil.
    a. Roll out a coil of clay.
    b. Bend the coil to form a shape.
    c. Assemble coils to form a figure.
  3. Basic shapes.
    a. Model clay into basic shapes.
    b. Different shapes.
    c. Assemble shapes to form a figure.

number of small cracks can be filled with thick slip or smoothed with a modeling tool. Cracks can become air pockets that will result in problems when the object is being fired.

Lay a pattern on the slab of clay and trace the outline with a toothpick. With a knife cut out the shape. Slabs are joined together by applying a coating of thick slip around the outside edge of one of the pieces. Lift and set the other slab against the first one and weld the joint. Some corners may require a mitered joint to obtain a tight fit. The edges can be beveled with a knife when the clay is leather hard.

Some slabs may need to be supported during the construction and

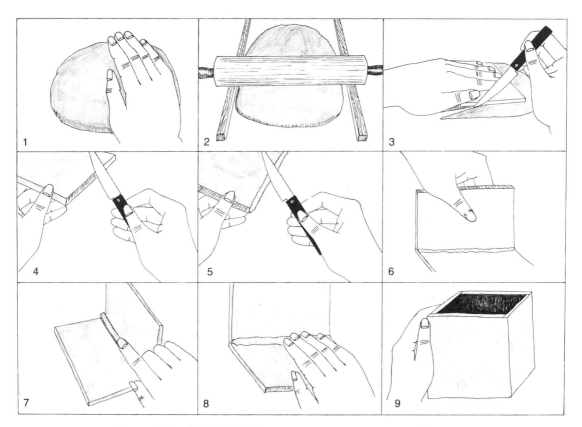

Figure 9-5 SLAB METHOD
Materials: clay, rolling pin, two wooden sticks of the same thickness, knife.

1. Flatten a piece of wedged clay.
2. Roll the clay between two sticks of equal thickness.
3. Use a pattern to cut out the shapes.
4. Score the edges of the slab.
5. Coat the edges with slip.
6. Join the side to the base.
7. Line the inside of the joint with a thin coil of clay.
8. Press the coil of clay into the joint.
9. Finished project.

drying period. Joints can be strengthened by coating the inside corners with a thick coating of slip. This extra slip should help to reinforce the joints. The joints can also be reinforced by lining the inside corners with a small thin coil of clay and then working the material into the corners with a modeling tool. If the clay is worked correctly, it should blend into the finished surfaces so that no trace of the coil remains.

The finished piece can be smoothed with a damp sponge or cloth. The piece should be set aside and allowed to dry slowly. Items constructed from slabs should not be allowed to dry on a plaster bat because it will cause them to warp. When the piece is bone dry, the surface can be sanded smooth. It is then ready to be decorated and fired.

Slabs can be rolled into tubular shapes and the edges sealed together.

GRAPHIC AND
MANIPULATIVE
ART FORMS AND
INSTRUCTIONAL
METHODS

220

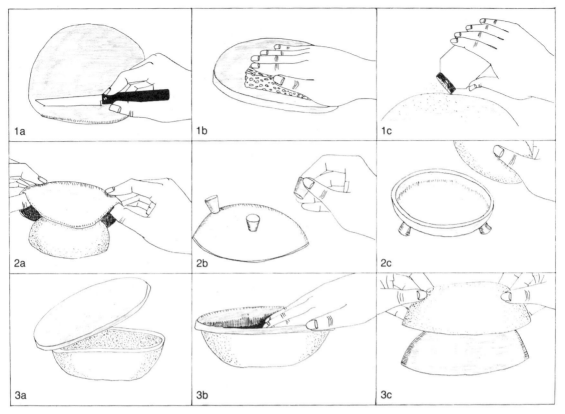

Figure 9-6 CONVEX AND CONCAVE DRAPING

Materials: clay, sponge, talcum powder, mold, knife.

1. Preparation of clay.
   a. Cut out the desired slab of clay.
   b. Sponge the slab smooth.
   c. Sprinkle the surface with talcum powder
2. Convex draping.
   a. Drape the slab of clay over a form.
   b. Add legs, footings, or appendages to the piece.
   c. Remove the clay piece from the mold.
3. Concave draping.
   a. Drape the slab over the mold carefully.
   b. Push the slab of clay into the cavity of the mold.
   c. Remove the clay piece from the mold.

A cone shape can also be formed utilizing the slab method. A paper pattern will assist in obtaining the desired size cylinder or cone.

Convex and Concave Draping

Convex draping is the process of forming a piece of pottery by covering the outside shape of a mold with a slab of clay. Concave draping is the process of duplicating a shape with a slab of clay by forming it to the inside contour of a mold. The molds can be made from plaster. Legs, footings, and appendages may be added to finish the piece. The finished piece can be decorated and fired.

CERAMICS

221

SLIP-MOLD CONSTRUCTION

A slip mold is a plaster form in which clay ware may be cast from slip. Molds can be constructed for casting vases, figurines, cups, and dishes. Select a model and carefully analyze it so that the intended mold is designed with a minimum number of pieces to permit the model and any subsequent castings to be removed without difficulty. Some models require only one-piece molds, while others require two- or three-piece molds.

One-piece Mold

A one-piece mold is constructed for objects that have straight walls with a mouth that is wider than the base. A model can be constructed by modeling a clay shape, or a commercial object can be used. Place the prepared model bottom up on a piece of plastic or oil cloth. Take a piece of thin sheet metal or heavy cardboard large enough to form a cylinder at least 4 inches greater than the diameter and at least 2 inches taller than the model. This is called a "cottle." If cardboard is used to construct the cottle, it should be sized with a heavy layer of soap size (a mixture of soap and water). Bend the material into a cylinder, sized surface in, allowing the surfaces to overlap 2 or 3 inches. Where the surfaces overlap, fasten the top and bottom edges together with paper clips. Seal the overlapping seam on the outside with masking tape. Rubber bands or string can be used to give the form added strength. With a coil of clay, seal the outside bottom edge of the cottle along the edge that touches the working surface.

Prepare the plaster of Paris, and then pour it into the cottle, filling it to the top edge. Allow the plaster to set and then remove the cottle. Round or taper the outside edges with a file or piece of sandpaper. Do not cut or mar any surfaces formed by the model. Remove the model by inverting the mold and tapping it lightly with a piece of wood until the model drops out. Allow the mold to air dry; be sure it is completely dried before using it for casting.

Two-piece Mold

Two-piece molds are constructed for models that require splitting the mold to remove the cast object. Select or construct a model to use in making a mold. The model selected for making a two-piece mold should not be complicated for the first attempt.

Take a piece of clay and construct a "spare." A spare is a clay form which will create passage in the finished mold through which the slip can be poured. Weld the spare to the model. Divide the model in half vertically with a try square. Rest the handle of the try square on a flat surface while the blade rests against the side of the model. Mark a line on the wall of the model using a brush and watercolors for green ware, a soft pencil for plaster, or a grease pencil for smooth, hard surfaces. Porous models should be sized thoroughly with soap size. Place the model in a bed of soft clay forming a clay cradle. The cradle should be 2 inches larger than the model on all sides. Level the clay surface of the cradle with a straightedge and sponge.

Construct a wooden form that will fit around the edges of the cradle and at least 2 inches higher than the side of the model which is imbedded in

GRAPHIC AND
MANIPULATIVE
ART FORMS AND
INSTRUCTIONAL
METHODS

222

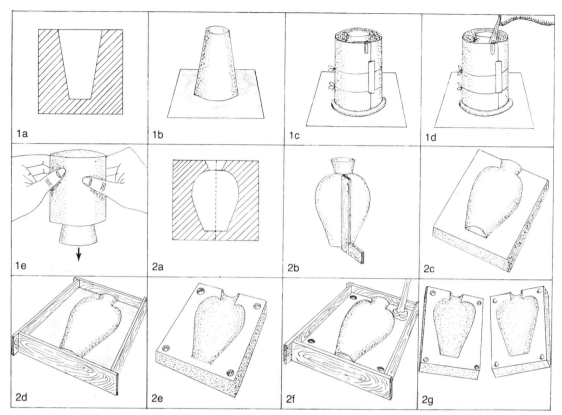

Figure 9-7   SLIP MOLD CONSTRUCTION

   Materials: model, cardboard, string, paper clip, clay, Scotch tape, plaster of Paris, try square, ply wood.

   1.   One-piece slip mold construction.
      a.   Sectional view of a one-piece mold.
      b.   Prepared model: bottom side up on nonabsorbent surface.
      c.   Bend, tie, and seal the cottle around the model with string, paper clip, clay coil, or Scotch tape.
      d.   Pour the plaster into the cottle.
      e.   Remove the model from the plaster mold.
   2.   Two-piece slip mold construction.
      a.   Sectional view of a two-piece mold.
      b.   Divide the model vertically with a try square.
      c.   Imbed the model in a soft clay cradle.
      d.   Build a wooden frame around the cradle.
      e.   One half of the two-piece mold.
      f.   Pour the other half of the mold.
      g.   Finished two-piece mold.

the clay. The corners of the frame should be sealed to prevent plaster from leaking out. Prepare the plaster of Paris and pour it into the form until it is even with the top edge. To prevent air bubbles from forming, pat the plaster surface with a stick, causing the air bubbles to rise to the surface.

   Allow the plaster to set and then remove the form. Clean away all the clay that served to hold the model. Turn the hardened plaster mold over to

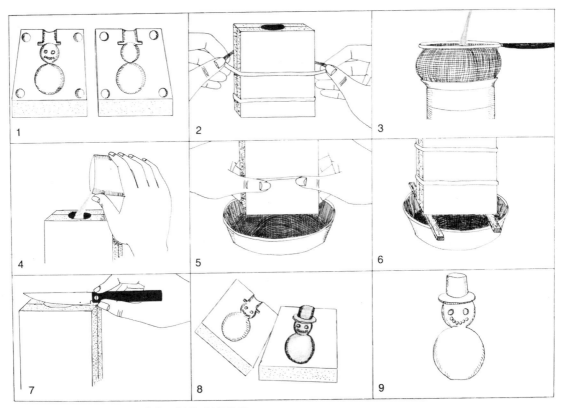

Figure 9-8 SLIP CASTING

Materials: plaster mold, rubber band, masking tape, slip, wide mouth pan, two wooden sticks, knife, sifter.

1. Two-piece plaster mold.
2. Tie the mold closed.
3. Strain the slip.
4. Pour the slip into the mold.
5. Empty the slip from the mold.
6. Drain the mold.
7. Trim the spare.
8. Remove the casting from the mold.
9. Finished casting.

act as the cradle instead of the clay. Cut four irregularly spaced holes or notches in the surface of the plaster. These holes will be nipples on the other half of the mold and are to help align the mold.

Be sure that the plaster surface is cleaned thoroughly and sized before pouring the second mold section. Secure the wooden form around the first section, making sure all corners are sealed. Prepare the plaster mixture and pour it into the form until level with the top edge. After the plaster hardens, remove the form. The mold halves are separated by gently tapping one section. Taper or round all the edges of the mold except those formed by the model. Allow the mold sections to air dry before using.

SLIP CASTING

Slip casting is the process of pouring a special composition of liquid clay into a plaster of Paris mold to form a ceramic piece. The molds can be constructed from plaster of Paris or precast molds and can be purchased in a wide variety of sizes and designs.

Dry the plaster mold thoroughly before pouring slip into it. The mold is usually separated in half to ensure that the inside surface is dry. Put the mold together and secure with tape, string, or rubber band.

Pour the slip into the mold until the slip is level with the top. The length of time the material remains in the mold depends upon the consistency of the slip, density of the mold, and desired thickness of the walls of the piece being cast.

When the correct time has elapsed to obtain the desired wall thickness, pour out the excess slip. Hold the mold with both hands over a bowl and rotate it slowly until almost upside down, allowing slip to run out. Place two sticks on the edge of the bowl; one stick should be thicker than the other. Set the mold on the sticks until the slip starts to harden. This step will prevent the slip from collecting on the inside of the bottom and forming lumps.

When the slip starts to harden, turn the right side up and clean the inside edge with a knife. As the slip dries, the walls of the object will shrink away from the mold. Allow the clay to dry an hour or so before trimming off the waste rim with a bent knife. Allow the mold and casting to dry until the clay begins to separate from the walls of the mold before removing the casting. Care should be taken when removing the piece from the mold since it is leather hard. Clean the mold with a sponge. The piece is finished using the same techniques as for any other ceramic piece.

THROWING ON THE POTTER'S WHEEL

Clay should be wedged thoroughly to remove all holes and air pockets before it can be thrown on a potter's wheel. Imperfections will result in the finished piece if these air pockets are not removed before working the clay.

The clay can be thrown on a plastic bat or directly on the bare wheel. If a plastic bat is used, it is secured to the wheel with small pieces of clay placed at 120-degree intervals. Slip spread evenly over the bottom of the plastic bat can also be used to secure it to the wheel.

The wedged clay is formed into a round ball and slapped onto the center of the wheel head. Place a container of water beside the wheel for wetting the clay as it is worked. Wet the clay. Center the clay by cupping it lightly in the hands as the wheel rapidly turns. When it stops thumping against the hands, it is centered.

Slow down the speed of the wheel and press both hands against the ball of clay to form a peak. Support the sides of the clay with one hand and press firmly down with the palm of the other hand on the peak.

Keep your fingers on the side of the clay while driving both thumbs into the center of the clay. Slowly separate the thumbs to form an opening in the center of the clay. Remember to maintain control over the outside contour

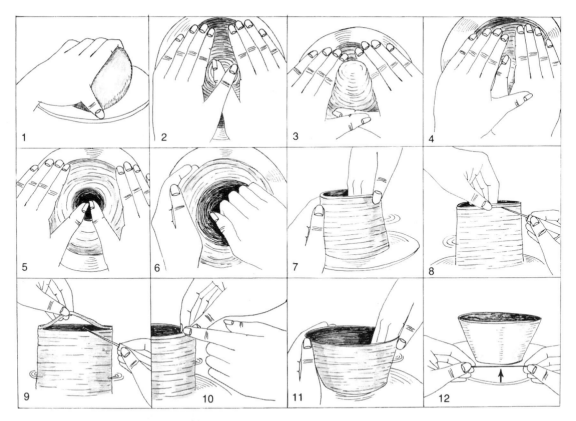

Figure 9-9 THROWING ON THE POTTER'S WHEEL

Materials: potter's wheel, clay, piece of wire, needlelike tool.

1. Slap a ball of wedged clay on the wheel.
2. Center the ball of clay.
3. Press both hands against the ball of clay to form a peak.
4. Flatten down the peak.
5. Make an opening in the ball of clay.
6. Widen the opening by pulling the clay wall outward.
7. Raise the clay wall.
8. Level the top of the piece with a needlelike tool.
9. Remove the sliced-off ring of clay.
10. Smooth the lip of the piece.
11. Continue the opening process until the desired shape is obtained.
12. Use a piece of wire to remove the piece from the wheel.

with your fingers or the piece will be shapeless. The bottom thickness is determined now because it is too late after the sides of the piece have been drawn and the top is formed. If the base is too thick, shrinkage of the base and sides will not be equal, causing the sides to split. If the base is too thin, it will split.

Place one hand inside the hole and try to keep the forearm as perpendicular as possible to the wheel. This hand is pressed firmly against the inside of the piece as the other hand supports the outside wall. An elephant's ear sponge may be used on the outside to obtain a smooth texture. Create

GRAPHIC AND
MANIPULATIVE
ART FORMS AND
INSTRUCTIONAL
METHODS

226

pressure on the sides between the two hands at the bottom of the piece and draw the clay upward to form the walls.

If the piece has a neck, it is formed by pressing inward with both hands in the desired position. Variations in the shape of the piece can be obtained by experimenting with different hand positions as the clay is worked. A needlelike tool is used to trim the top evenly. The piece is removed from the bat or directly off the wheel with a piece of wire. Stretch the wire taut and slide it underneath the piece. With careful handling, the piece can be removed from the wheel.

The piece should be set aside to dry. The neck of the vase should be covered to retard its drying, as the smaller diameter would cause less shrinkage and create cracks. When the piece is bone dry, it can be sanded, decorated, and fired.

DRYING FINISHED OBJECTS

An outstanding piece of modeling can be damaged if it is not properly dried. If thin edges and small parts dry faster than larger areas, they usually crack and fall off. This can be prevented by keeping these areas moistened during the drying process. A small brush can be used to apply water to these areas.

Objects with a flat base should not be placed on a table, but should be put on a surface that will allow air to circulate completely around all surfaces. This will result in a more even drying process.

Objects should not be placed directly over or near a heat source. The heat will cause the surface clay to dehydrate, while the core clay remains moist. The rapid shrinkage of the surface clay will result in cracks and small pieces falling off. Sufficient time must be allowed for clay to dry properly.

Some objects may need to be supported while drying. The heads and bodies of animals can be supported by wooden sticks or wire. The supports can be removed as soon as the clay is firm enough to hold its own weight.

WELDING WITH SLIP

The process of joining two parts of an object together with slip is called welding. The same clay that is used to form the object should be used to make the slip. Slip is made by mixing the clay with water to the consistency of heavy cream. Score both pieces at the point where they are to be joined. Apply slip to this point on both pieces, and press them together. The joint should be smoothed so that the weld will not show when the object dries. Care should be taken not to disturb the pieces until the joint is completely dry.

REPAIRING DEFECTS

Repairing a defect in a clay form or object is a very difficult process. Clay that is bone dry is impossible to repair, while leather-hard clay repairs will usually break again in the firing process. When repairing a clay object, it is important to use a minimum amount of water; too much water will weaken the areas around the defect. Repairs should be made with moistened clay shavings scraped from the piece being repaired.

Chips and broken edges cannot be placed back in place; instead the area should be rebuilt with shavings. Some cracks may need to be widened with a knife to obtain enough space for the moistened shavings. The moist-ened shavings are pressed into the crack and the surface smoothed and blended together. Put the object to one side to dry. Defective areas are built-up, not patched-up.

FIRING

Clay objects that are thoroughly dried are ready to be fired. These unfired pieces are called "green ware." Green ware can be stacked by putting the heavy pieces on the bottom and the lighter pieces on the top. When stacking green ware, small pieces can be placed inside larger objects. Clay pieces should be kept 1 inch or more from the side of the kiln.

Pyrometric cones (chemically prepared heat-measuring devices made to bend at certain temperatures) are inserted into small lumps of clay several days before firing to prevent them toppling over because the clay will shrink from the heat. Cones 08 and 07 are used for green ware. The cones should be located inside the kiln opposite the peep hole.

Procedure

Procedures for firing vary with the different types of kilns. No matter what type of kiln is used, the following procedures should be considered. Prefiring is an important process because it eliminates any moisture retained in the clay. Prefiring will usually prevent an explosion in the kiln caused by clay improperly wedged or welded. Wet clay should never be fired.

During the prefiring period the kiln lid is propped open and the switch turned onto the lowest temperature. The length of time for the prefiring depends upon the size of the kiln. The prefiring time required in a large kiln may be overnight; for a small kiln, only two or three hours are needed.

After the prefiring period the door of the kiln is closed and the heat slowly increased. The length of firing can be gauged by the use of a mechani-cal heat thermometer, pyrometric cones, or a pyrometer. Firing tempera-tures vary with the type of clay.

The cones are watched during the firing period. The number 08 cone should bend first. The other cones should be checked every twenty-five minutes because electric heat builds up rapidly toward the end of the firing period. The firing process for green ware is completed when all the cones are bent.

If the kiln has a pyrometer, the temperature should be checked to see if it coincides with the cone number. Any noted discrepancy should be corrected. The cone is a more reliable indicator of conditions inside the kiln than the pyrometer.

Fired ware should be allowed to cool in the kiln for as long as it takes to heat the kiln. Care should be taken in removing pieces because some may still be hot. The fired ware is now called "bisque."

Glazes

Bisque ware can be decorated with underglaze and then covered with transparent glaze, or it may be covered with a single glaze and then refired. Appropriate glazes should be purchased for the clay that is to be used. The glaze is mixed with water to a creamlike consistency and applied to the

GRAPHIC AND
MANIPULATIVE
ART FORMS AND
INSTRUCTIONAL
METHODS

228

bisque ware with a brush. More than one coat of glaze may be needed to obtain the thickness of the glaze coating. Glaze ware is stacked in the kiln on an individual stilt to prevent the glaze from fusing to the floor or shelf of the kiln. Pieces should be 1 inch apart to keep the glaze, which is a liquid glass, from fusing together. Cone numbers 08, 07, and 06 are usually used when firing glazed ware.

Some glazes can be used directly on green ware requiring only one firing. These glazes should be painted on heavily when the pieces are going to be fired once. The kiln is stacked the same as for glazed pieces.

Not all clay forms and objects should be fired. Clay figures and other objects for small-scale construction units, dioramas, and other such activities are usually not fired since they can be painted with tempera paints. Pottery, tiles, and figurines should be fired.

Kilns

A kiln is a specially constructed oven that is capable of reaching very high temperatures. Clay vitrifies at high temperatures, which means that the particles melt enough to seal together. The size of the kiln is determined by the inside dimensions of the firing chamber. The kiln usually operates on electric power, and the temperature range varies from about 1200 to 2000° F.

An area within the school should be provided for a large permanently installed electric kiln. If this is not possible, a small movable kiln on a platform can be used. This type of kiln can be moved into a classroom and plugged into the standard electric outlet.

If clay objects are going to be fired, children should be provided with an opportunity to observe the actual firing process by looking into the kiln through the peep hole.

Cleaning the Kiln Drops of glaze will spot the floor and shelves of the kiln during a firing. These spots can be removed by painting the floor and sides of the kiln with a special wash. The drops of glaze are then picked off the surface with a spatula. Kiln wash can be purchased in powdered form and mixed with water to a fairly thin consistency.

TECHNIQUES FOR DECORATING CLAY OBJECTS

Some objects constructed from clay may require no decorations because of the shape, design, or material, while others can be made attractive by using a transparent or colored glaze. A number of techniques can be used to enrich a ceramic piece. It is important to consider how the design or decoration adds to the finished product. The decoration should be suitable for the size and shape of the object. Experiment with the following techniques when the clay is damp.

Incising   This technique utilizes a sharp-pointed object to cut a line design into a damp clay surface.

Carving   This technique utilizes a sharp knife to cut out the design. Cuts should be made so that they slant from the outer edge to the center of the shape.

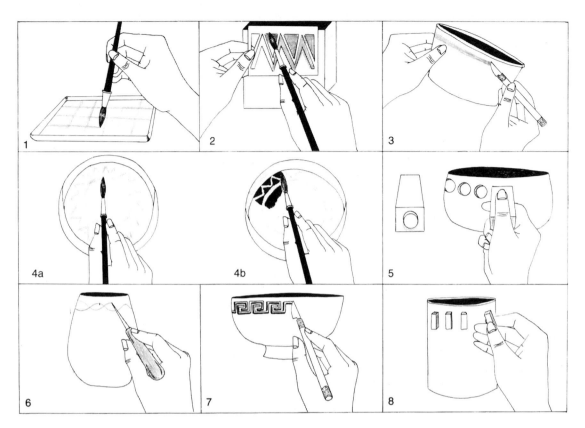

Figure 9-10 DECORATING TECHNIQUES
1. Paint: Paint the design on the surface with slip.
2. Stencil: Use a stencil as a guide to paint the design.
3. Sgraffito: Use a knife to scratch a design in the glaze.
4. Wax Resist: a. Paint the design with wax.
         b. Cover the surface with glaze.
5. Stamp: Stamp a design into the clay surface.
6. Incise: Use a sharp-pointed tool to cut a line design.
7. Carve: Use a knife to carve out a design.
8. Embossing or modeling-on: Add clay forms to create a design.

Embossing   This technique utilizes thin clay forms or coils. The forms are cut from slabs of clay, and the coils are formed from a ball of clay. They are arranged to form a design and are held in place with slip.

Stamping   This technique utilizes a variety of objects to make imprints in the clay surface.

Slip Painting   This technique utilizes contrasting clay to make the mixture of slip. The slip is used to paint the design on the ceramic piece.

SUBSTITUTES FOR CLAY
There are a number of excellent substitutes for clay and Plasticine. These substitute clays can be used to form and shape a wide variety of objects and figurines. Substitute clays are mixed by using common household items.

GRAPHIC AND
MANIPULATIVE
ART FORMS AND
INSTRUCTIONAL
METHODS

230

Children can cut, roll, and mold substitute clay into thousands of interesting objects like animals, flowers, boxes, and jewelry. The pinch, slab, or coil methods can be used to form or shape substitute clay.

Substitute clay objects should be placed on a screen or wire to allow the air to circulate around all surfaces. Finished objects should not be placed over heat or in bright sunlight because rapid drying may cause cracking.

Substitute clay can be decorated with tempera, watercolors, or acrylic paints. After the paints dry, dip objects into clear shellac, spray with clear plastic, or brush on clear nail polish. Substitute clay can be stored in a plastic bag and used the next day.

Sawdust Clay
Clean sawdust and wheat paste make an excellent claylike pliable substance. Sawdust is available from the industrial arts shop and local cabinet or woodworking shops.

If the sawdust is too coarse, it should be sifted through a screen. Coarse sawdust can be used to obtain a surface with a rough texture, while fine sawdust will produce a smooth finish.

Mix 5 cups of clean fine sawdust with 1/2 cup of dry wheat paste in a container. Be sure that the sawdust on the bottom has been mixed with the wheat paste. Slowly add water to the mixture until the material can be rolled into a ball. If water drips as the material is squeezed, add more sawdust and wheat paste. If the mixture crumbles, add more water.

Salt-Cornstarch Clay
Place 1 cup of table salt, 1/2 cup of cornstarch and 3/4 cup of water into the top part of a double boiler. Powdered tempera or food coloring can be added to obtain the desired color. The finished object also can be painted.

Put water in the lower half of the double boiler and then place the whole boiler over a low heat. Stir the mixture until it becomes thick and forms a lump. Place the lump onto a piece of aluminum foil until cool enough to handle. Knead the cooled mixture for a few minutes before forming or shaping it.

Salt-Flour Clay
Place 3/4 cup of salt in a saucepan; heat until piping hot and then remove from the heat. Mix 1 cup of flour with the salt in the saucepan. Gradually add the salt and flour mixture to 1 cup of water and stir thoroughly. Powdered tempera or food coloring can be added if color is desired. Color can be added by painting the finished object.

Place the saucepan over a low heat and stir the mixture constantly. Care should be taken to scrape along the sides and bottom as the mixture is being stirred. Continue to stir until the mixture has thickened and appears crumbly and dry. Scrape the mixture onto a piece of aluminum foil and allow to cool enough to handle.

Cornstarch-Baking Soda Clay
Mix in a saucepan until thoroughly blended 1 cup of cornstarch and 2 cups of baking soda. Mix 1-1/4 cups of cold water to these ingredients. Powdered

tempera or food coloring can be added if a tinted clay is desired. Paints can be used to decorate the finished object.

Place the saucepan over a medium heat and stir until the mixture has a moist mashed potato consistency. Cover the mixture with a damp cloth and allow to cool. Knead the cooled mixture for a few minutes before forming and shaping.

Uncooked Substitute Clays

The following mixtures can be used to make substitute clay without cooking the ingredients. Salt is used to obtain hardness, while cornstarch gives the mixture a glossy appearance.

1 Flour-Salt-Cornstarch Clay
   1 part flour
   1 part salt
   1 part cornstarch
   Water
2 Flour-Salt Clay
   a 2 parts flour
      1 part salt water
      Water
   b 2 parts salt
      1 part flour water
   c 1/2 cup flour
      1/2 cup salt water
      Water

Mix the ingredients together thoroughly. Slowly add water to the ingredients and stir until a ball of dough forms. The mixture should have a spongy consistency and should not be too soft. Tempera paint or food coloring can be added to the water to obtain a tinted clay. Finished objects can be decorated with paints.

Flour-Salt-Cornstarch Jewelry

Attractive pins, earrings, and medallions can be constructed from flour-salt-cornstarch clay. Plan a design for the piece of jewelry. Consideration should be given to the size and shape of the piece of jewelry. Long narrow protrusions should be avoided because they usually break easily.

With a rolling pin, roll out the clay to a thickness of 1/4 inch. Cut the clay into the desired shape. Geometric or flower shapes lend themselves to this type of material. The cutout shape can be rolled to distort the shape or the thumb can be used to press in a design. The edges can be trimmed with strips of clay. The strips are moistened and pressed in place. Place aside to dry.

The shapes can also be decorated with tinfoil, broken glass, and bits of gems glued to the surface. Pierce a hole in the edge and slip through a metal link. The link is then suspended from the earring backing or suspended on a chain as a medallion. The shape can be glued onto a clasp for a pin or slipped onto a wire for a ring.

The surface can be decorated with watercolors, tempera, or acrylic paints. After the paints are dry, dip into clear shellac and spray with clear plastic or brush on clear nail polish.

GRAPHIC AND
MANIPULATIVE
ART FORMS AND
INSTRUCTIONAL
METHODS

232

PART Ⅲ

CRAFT FORMS
AND INSTRUCTIONAL METHODS

LEATHER CRAFTS 10

Leather articles are durable and have a very pleasing appearance. Billfolds, key cases, purses, and belts are a few of the articles that can be made from leather. Calfskin, sheepskin, goatskin, cowhide, and pigskin are the most commonly used leathers. However, some articles can be enhanced through the use of deerskin, antelope, seal, lizard, or alligator.

Leather crafts include the process of cutting the leather, decorating the surface, and fastening the parts together with one of several techniques. These techniques are lacing, stitching, and riveting. It is not always necessary to decorate the surface, because leather contains its own intrinsic beauty that can be enhanced with oil or wax. Carving, stamping, punching, tooling, and embossing are the techniques used to decorate the surface of a piece of leather. These techniques can be used individually or in different combinations to obtain the desired effect. Nail heads, fasteners, buckles, and clasps are also used to decorate the finished articles.

TYPES OF CRAFT LEATHERS
Many different types of leather are available for any crafts program. Each type of leather has its own unique properties and characteristics. These qualities should be utilized to enhance the beauty and durability of any project constructed from leather. Leather is available for purchase in many different weights and colors. The weight is designated in ounces, with 1 ounce equal to 1/64 inch thickness.

Tooling and Carving Leathers

Calfskin is distinctly soft, fine-grained, and rich in appearance. It stains well and should be used for tooled articles where quality is required. Calfskin comes in natural colors. The weight varies from 1-1/2 to 3-1/2 ounces, and skin sizes vary from 9 to 16 square feet.

Cowhide or strap leather is excellent for carving and stamping and takes dye readily. It has a smooth grain and can be used for belts, handbags, and briefcases. It comes in natural colors. The weight varies from 2-1/2 to 10 ounces, and skin sizes vary from 18 to 23 square feet.

Sheepskin is a smooth-finished, inexpensive leather suitable for beginners and designed to simulate projects constructed from calf. It is not as strong nor as durable as calf, but it can be tooled. It comes in natural colors and only in skins of medium weight that vary in size from 7 to 12 square feet.

Steerhide is a soft, pliable leather with a very attractive crinkly grain effect. It is ideal for tooling and especially adaptable to use for handbags and wallets. Skins come in natural or two-toned colors and in weights that vary from 2-1/2 to 5 ounces, with sizes ranging from 20 to 28 square feet.

Pigskin is a very durable leather and is ideal for wallets, luggage, and novelties. Skins are natural in color and vary in size from 9 to 16 square feet, while the weight varies from 1-1/2 to 2-1/2 ounces.

Lining Leathers

Skiver is a very thin grain-split sheepskin, which when cemented to another leather makes a good lining. Skins range in size from 6 to 12 square feet and come in varying colors.

Lining calf is an excellent lining material with a smooth surface and comes in several colors. Skin sizes range from 7 to 12 square feet.

Suede has a soft furry finish. Skins come in a wide range of colors, and sizes vary from 5 to 9 square feet.

Miscellaneous Leathers

Reptiles: Alligator, snake, lizard. Some leathers are stamped to imitate reptile skins.

Hair calf: Hair calf is calf leather with the hair still on it. It may be used for small projects and garments. Skins come in sizes from 6 to 10 square feet.

Morocco goat: Morocco goat, which may be tooled, is used for linings, billfolds, and book bindings. Skins vary in size up to 10 square feet and come in several colors.

Seal, deerskin, and antelope are excellent leathers for making craft projects, but they are extremely expensive.

MAKING A LEATHER PROJECT

It is important for the beginner to practice cutting, stamping, tooling, and lacing leather before attempting to construct any complicated or large article. An understanding of how to use the various tools and materials is a requisite to the success of any leather craft activity. Small leather scraps are useful for practicing these operations.

Planning the Project
Before designing any leather project, it is important to study leather articles in catalogs, magazines, newspapers, or stores. Such an investigation will provide the individual with an understanding of how leather is used, decorated, and finished. A series of preliminary sketches should be made of the proposed item. When an acceptable sketch is obtained, a model of the finished project can be constructed from heavy paper. The paper model should be accurate because it will be used to lay out the templates for cutting the various parts from the leather.

To obtain accurate patterns, be sure to make all necessary allowances for bends, overlaps, folds, and sewing and lacing seams. One thickness of leather should be added to the length or width for each bend and seam, while twice the thickness is required for each fold. These allowances should be included in the lengths or widths of the paper patterns. Care should be taken when assembling the paper patterns to utilize the same bend, folds, and seams as those that will be used in the construction of the finished article from leather. For example, if the parts are laced, the paper model should be held together using a needle and thread in an over-and-over lacing method or buttonhole stitch to determine if the allowance is correct. The finished paper model should be checked for size to be sure the pattern pieces fit correctly.

Placing the Templates on the Skin
The templates should be moved around on the skin so that leather is cut to advantage. The back is the best part of the skin and should be used for tooling, while the legs and belly sections are used for gussets and linings. Parts with straight edges should be placed together so one cut is sufficient for both pieces.

Cutting the Leather
Place the leather on an old board or heavy cardboard and cut it with a sharp knife along the edge of a steel square or metal straightedge. Cut along the line to within 1 inch of the end. Reverse the knife and cut from the opposite direction to prevent overcutting and wasting leather.

Planning a Design
If the article is to be tooled, carved, or stamped, the design should be planned on scrap paper. Beginners should start with a simple design, with more difficult ones undertaken as skill and experience are gained.

The first step is to develop some preliminary sketches utilizing the principles of design described in Chapter 2. Select one of the designs and transfer it to a piece of paper the same size and shape as the leather surface it will be used to decorate. Plan to leave an undecorated border around the design at least 1/2 to 1 inch, depending on the size of the article. This allowance is needed for sewing, lacing, or just to offset the design. Lacing holes should be located one and one-half times the width of the lacing from

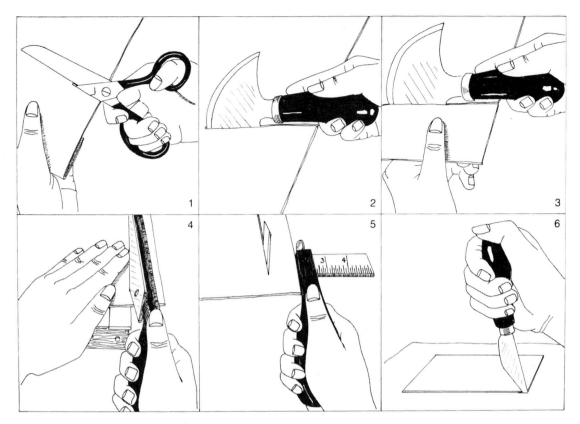

Figure 10-1 CUTTING LEATHER
   1. Using leather shears.
   2. Cutting a large piece of leather with a head knife.
   3. Cutting a small piece of leather with a head knife.
   4. Cutting leather with a paper cutter.
   5. Cutting a belt with a draw gauge.
   6. Cutting leather with a knife.

the edge of the leather. All tooling, carving, or stamping must be done before the various parts of the article are assembled.

Tracing the Design on a Leather Surface

Make sure the design is complete and correct before transferring it to the leather surface. Once the design has been transferred to the leather, it is almost impossible to remove any lines. Carbon paper should never be used to transfer a design to leather.

The leather must be moistened before the design is transferred. Lightweight leather is moistened on the flesh side with a clean sponge and water until the finished surface darkens. The entire piece should be moistened so that any shrinkage or color change will be uniform. Set the leather grain side up on a flat surface and allow to dry until it starts to resume its original color. The leather surface is now prepared to have the design traced on it.

Heavyweight leather is moistened by soaking the leather in water for a few minutes, removing, and wrapping in paper towels overnight. The soaking process will cause the fiber bundles to swell and makes the leather very pliable. Care should be taken in handling the leather once it has been moistened, because any undesirable impressions and marks will be impossible to remove. Set the leather grain side up on a flat surface and allow to dry until the surface shows traces of the original color. The leather is now prepared to receive the design.

Place the tracing paper with the design on top of the grain side of the leather and secure it with masking tape. The design and leather should be placed on a smooth, firm surface such as a piece of marble, hardwood (maple), hardboard (tempered), or metal.

With a tracing tool, a pencil, the small end of a modeler, or a stylus, trace the design. Care should be taken not to move the design paper or tear it during the tracing operation. Apply firm, even pressure as the design is being traced, and use a straightedge as a guide for tracing straight lines.

Raise one end of the design paper occasionally to check the impression. Make sure that impression lines are clear and that no lines have been skipped.

TOOLING LEATHER
Outline Tooling
Outline tooling is one of the simplest methods of decorating leather because it requires only the outline of the design being pressed down. Prepare the leather for tooling by moistening it as described above and then tracing the design on its surface. Place the piece of leather on a hard surface with design side face up. Holding the modeler like a pencil and using the small end, trace around the outline of the design. Increase the pressure each time the outline is retraced until the desired depth is obtained. Care should be taken to keep the depth of the depressed lines uniform.

If water oozes up from the leather as it is being tooled, it is too damp and should be set aside to dry. The impression will not hold if the leather is too wet. If the modeler breaks through or scratches the surface, the leather is too dry and should be moistened. Dry leather will not tool correctly.

A straightedge should be used for all straight lines. On lightweight leather straight lines should be tooled from the outer edge toward the center to prevent stretching the material.

Flat Modeling
Flat modeling is the process of depressing or beveling the background away from the design, making it stand out in bold relief. Prepare the leather for tooling. Place the leather design side up on a hard surface and trace around the design as in outline tooling. Using the broad end of the modeler, depress or bevel the background using a firm, even pressure. If the leather becomes too dry, a sponge can be used to moisten it slightly.

Embossing
Embossing is the process of raising the design, or part of it, above the surface of the leather by working it from the flesh side. Prepare the leather for tooling. Place the leather on a hard surface and trace around the design

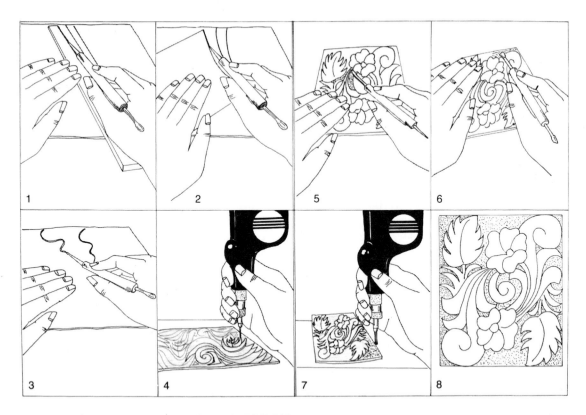

Figure 10-2   OUTLINE TOOLING

1.   Tool a straight line.
2.   Use a template as a guide.
3.   Draw irregular lines using the modeler.
4.   Use the Vibro-Tool for outline tooling.
     FLAT MODELING
5.   Bevel the background with a modeler.
6.   Use the deerfoot modeler.
7.   Push down the background with a Vibro-Tool.
8.   Design with the background tooled.

as in outline tooling. This should produce a clear outline of the design on the flesh side of the leather.

Pick up the piece of leather and hold it with the grain side against the palm of the hand. Using a ball-end modeler, raise the design by working the tool over the flesh side of the leather, forcing it down between the fingers. An alternative method of raising the surface of leather is to place it on a piece of sponge rubber and force the design down into the rubber using the ball-end modeler.

When the desired proportions of the design have been raised, place the leather grain side up on a hard surface. With the broad end of the modeler smooth down the background around the raised parts of the design. If the design is not raised enough, it can be reworked until the desired effect is obtained.

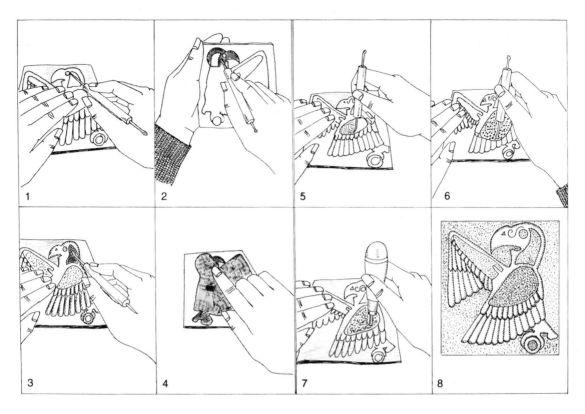

Figure 10-3 EMBOSSING
    1. Trace around the outline of the design.
    2. Emboss the back of the design with the ball-end modeler.
    3. Push down the background.
    4. Back the embossed areas.
    STIPPLING
    5. Stipple with a modeler.
    6. Stipple with a ball-end modeler.
    7. Using a stippler.
    8. Finished design with stippled areas.

When the leather dries, fill the embossed areas with kapok, plastic wood, or cotton to prevent the raised surface from being pushed in. Cover the flesh side of the leather with a piece of lining leather.

Stippling
Stippling is the process of decorating the background with a series of small, dotlike impressions. A tracer, stylus, small end of the modeler, or stippler can be used to make different size impressions on the background. Prepare the leather for tooling. Hold the tool vertically and apply uniform pressure to the tool, being careful not to break through the surface of the leather.

An embossing wheel or carriage is used to create a decorative border or design. The leather should be in the same condition as for tooling. Lay out the lines to be embossed. Apply even pressure to the carriage,

LEATHER CRAFTS

while pushing it along a straightedge. Sufficient pressure should be applied to ensure a clear, even impression the first time across the leather. It is impossible to go over the line a second time.

Curved lines can be embossed by using a template for a guide or by using the carriage freehand.

Stamping

Stamping is a technique that utilizes steel stamps to make simple patterns on a piece of leather. Craft catalogs list the different commercial stamps available for decorating a leather surface. Original stamps can be made by filing the ends of large-headed nails or the ends of 1/8- or 1/4-inch metal rods and bars. The design produced depends upon the stamp shapes available and the ingenuity of the individual. Stamping is one of the simple methods of decorating leather and is suitable for use by young children. It is important to experiment with the different stamps on a piece of scrap leather before attempting the finished design.

Moisten the leather as for tooling and allow to dry until the grain side of the leather has returned to its natural color. Leather that is too wet will not retain the impression.

Place the leather grain side up on a hard surface and select a stamp with the desired design. Hold the stamp vertically between the thumb and first and second finger, while resting the other fingers on the leather. With a mallet strike the end of the stamp sharply, being careful not to cut through the leather. Arrange stamps in a pattern or in combination with other stamps to create an interesting design.

CARVING LEATHER

Carving or incising is the process of cutting a design into the surface of a piece of leather, without actually removing or cutting away any material. The design is traced on the leather and the lines are cut with a swivel knife. Saddle stamps or a flat modeling tool are used to put down the background and decorate the design.

There is no definite procedure for carving leather. Each individual usually develops his own method and style of carving, but the fundamental process remains the same. Practice and experimentation are necessary if the individual is to become proficient in leather carving.

Prepare the leather for carving by moistening it and tracing the design on it. After the design has been transferred and before cutting, moisten the grain side of the leather with a sponge so that it is slightly wet.

Hold the swivel knife between the thumb and the middle and fourth fingers with the index finger resting on the yoke, while the little finger rests on the leather to help steady the hand. Practice making cuts on a piece of scrap leather. Cuts should be made with the corner of the blade and by pulling the knife. Light pressure is applied to the knife at the start and end of each cut, producing a shallow incision at both ends and a deep one in the center. The incision at the deepest point should not exceed one-half the thickness of the leather. Cuts should not be gone over a second time and should not cross one another. It is important to keep the knife

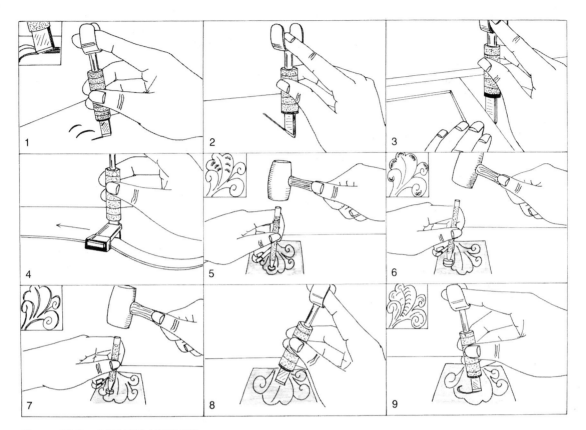

Figure 10-4 CARVING LEATHER
1. Using a swivel knife.
2. Hold the swivel knife at a right angle.
3. Using the swivel knife with a straightedge.
4. Using the Pro-gauge.
5. Using a camouflage tool.
6. Using a shader.
7. Using a veiner.
8. Making a dress cut with a swivel knife.
9. Finishing the dress cut.

in an upright position during the cutting operation. The design should be cut in the following order: border lines, flowers, stems, and leaves.

To obtain the desired effect, model those background areas that are to be depressed to make the design stand out in relief. This carved-out appearance is obtained by pressing the broad end of the modeling tool against the surface near the cut and working it back and forth.

Saddle stamps are also used to depress the background and decorate the design. If the impressions are stamped as close together as possible, a solid effect is produced. The raised areas contrast with the depressed ones to give a carved-out appearance. The following saddle stamps can be used: *Camouflage* stamps come in several sizes and shapes and are used to decorate flowers, leaves, and stones. *Pear* shaders comes in several sizes and are used to produce a shaded effect on leaves and flower petals. The working surface of the tool may be smooth, checked, or ribbed. The *beveler* is available in several sizes and is used to make areas of the design stand out in bold relief. The working surface of the tool may be smooth, checked, or lined. *Veiner* and *shell* tools vary in size and shape and are used to decorate plain areas on leaves, stems, and flowers. *Seeders* vary in size and shape and are used for the centers of flowers or swirls. *Background* tools come in several sizes and shapes and are used to decorate the background of a design.

These are the basic stamps and their purposes. It is impossible to illustrate all the ways in which they can be used. With experience and practice an individual can develop skill in adapting various combinations of stamps to create an interesting design.

EDGING TOOLS

Edging tools are used to round, level, and finish the edges of a piece of leather. They are available in different sizes for light and heavy leather, and in a variety of shapes.

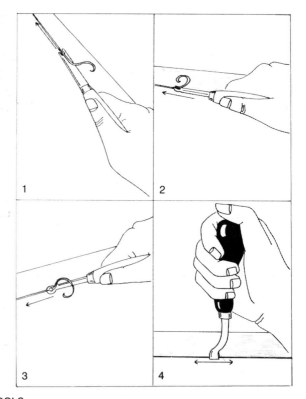

Figure 10-5 USING EDGE TOOLS
 1. Using the common edge tool.
 2. Using an edge beveler.
 3. Using a Bissonette edge tool.
 4. Using a single edge creaser.

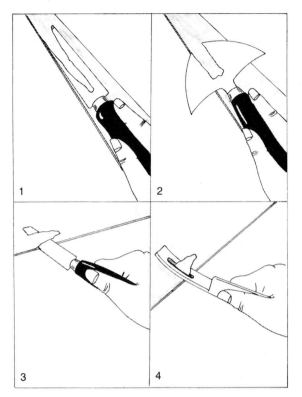

Figure 10-6   SKIVING

1. Skiving with a bevel-end knife.
2. Skiving with a head knife.
3. Skiving with a bevel-pointed knife.
4. Skiving with a Skife.

Leather to be edged should be in the same condition as for tooling, because the edger will produce a smoother cut on damp leather. However, if the leather is not going to be tooled or stamped, there is no need to wet the leather just to bevel or round the edge.

Edge Beveler   The edge beveler is used to bevel the edge on lightweight leather to prevent fraying, while the common edge tool is used to bevel or round edges on heavy leather. The tool is pushed along the edge, producing a uniform cut.

Edge Creasers   Edge creasers are used to crease lines along the edge of belts and open edges of pockets. A single or double metal edge creaser will produce the best results. The leather, in the same condition as for tooling, is held flat on a surface. Pressure is applied to the tool as it is pushed along the edge of the leather. Work the tool back and forth until the creased line is the desired depth.

Skiving Knife   A skiving knife is used to reduce the thickness of leather, making it more pliable. Skiving may be used to thin edges that will be sewed or laced later, or where the leather is going to be folded or bent.

Place the leather grain side down on a hard surface and with a skiving knife remove a few pieces at a time. Care should be taken not to cut off too much material at one time, because there is danger of cutting a hole through the leather. The depth of the cut depends on the number of pieces to be assembled. The assembled edges should equal the original thickness of the leather. The cut should be 1/2 inch in from the edge and down to one-half the thickness of the leather at the edge.

When used for skiving, the bevel-point knife, head knife, and bevel-end knife should be pushed away from the operator. The Skife, which is a patented skiving knife, is pulled toward the operator. It is an exceptional tool for cutting the edges of leather uniformly. Practice and experimentation are a must before skiving the pieces that are going to be used for the finished article.

CEMENTING LEATHER

Rubber cement can be used to hold linings, zippers, or edges in place for lacing or sewing. It can also be used to join two surfaces permanently.

Apply cement to both of the surfaces to be fastened together and allow to dry until shine disappears. If the surface is not to be folded, align the edges of the two pieces, while holding the other end. Slowly work the surfaces together by pressing and smoothing out the material.

For surfaces that are to be folded, align the two pieces at the fold and press one-half of the material in place, working from the center out to the edge, while the material is held in a folded position. Keeping the leather in a folded position, reverse the material and press the other half in place. After the surfaces are cemented together, they can be trimmed, laced, or sewed. Excessive cement on any of the surfaces or edges can be rubbed off with a cloth.

PUNCHES AND CHISELS

Round, oval, or oblong holes can be cut through a piece of leather using several different punches which come in various sizes.

Revolving and Round Drive Punches   Lay out the precise location of each hole to be punched. Center the correct size tube of the revolving punch over the mark and punch the hole.

Because of the shallow throat of the tool, the drive punch is substituted whenever the revolving punch cannot reach. With the leather flat on a piece of hardwood, hold the punch vertically over the mark and strike with a mallet.

Thonging Chisel   A thonging chisel with one to four prongs can be used to make a series of narrow slits along the edge of a piece of leather. To space holes for lacing, make a light mark with a pencil about 1/8 inch from the edge. Place the piece of leather on a piece of hardwood. Locate the chisel on the line 1/8 inch in from the edge and strike with a mallet. To space the slits evenly, lift the chisel and place the end prong in the last slit. Hold the chisel straight and strike with a mallet. Repeat this procedure until all slits are punched. Corners are rounded by using a one-prong chisel and placing one slit at an angle.

Other Punches   Oblong punches, tube belt punches, and strap end punches are also available for special purposes. These punches are not vital, but are very useful for some leather craft activities.

LACING TECHNIQUES

The major purpose of lacing is to fasten two pieces of leather together as well as to serve as a decoration. Lacing leather is made of calf or goat and comes in an assortment of colors. It can be purchased by the yard or spool. A 3/32-inch width is the most commonly used lacing, but a 1/8-inch width is best for large projects. The length of lacing needed for any article depends upon the size of the article and style of the stitch used. Because it is difficult to handle a piece of lacing about a yard long, it is advisable to add lace as it is needed. A new length of lacing can be spliced to the first one by skiving the top grain side about 1/2 inch or more at the end and skiving the underside of the new strip. Apply cement to the skived areas and overlap the pieces of lacing together.

A special lacing needle can be used for lacing the leather through the small slits, or the end of the lacing can be cut at an angle and stiffened by applying cement to it.

The end of the lacing is finished off by tucking 1/2 inch or so of the end back under the last few stitches.

Lay out and mark the guidelines for the lacing holes. One of the following stitches can be used to hold the edges together.

Running Stitch   Push the lacing through one hole and out through the next, continuing until the end is reached.

Whipstitch   Run the lacing through the end hole, over the top edge, and back through the next hole. Continue this procedure until the end is reached.

Double Whipstitch   Make in the same manner as the whipstitch, except that the lacing is placed through each hole twice.

Cross-stitch   Place the lacing through the end hole, over the top edge and back through the third hole. Continue running the lacing through the holes, skipping every other hole. When the end is reached, reverse the direction filling in the holes that were skipped.

Single Buttonhole Stitch   Start at the left end and run the lacing through the first hole, leaving a tail of about 1 inch. Bend the tail upward so that it extends above the edge and hold it in place with a thumb. Bring the lacing across the front of the tail, moving from right to left around the back of the tail, encircle it, and run the lacing through the second hole from the

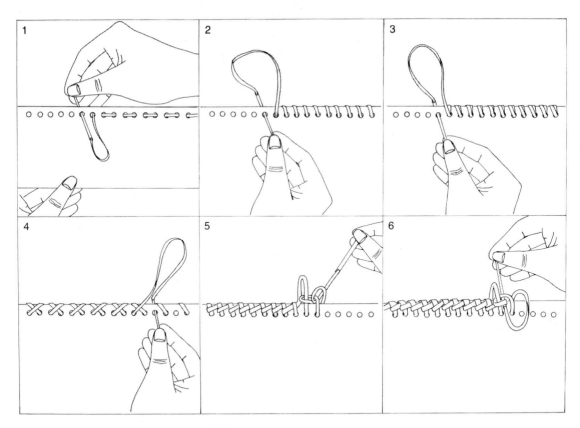

Figure 10-7   LACING
1. Running stitch
2. Whipstitch
3. Double whipstitch
4. Cross-stitch
5. Buttonhole stitch
6. Double buttonhole stitch

front to back. Bring the lacing over the top edge and under the loop already formed. Continue the process until the edge is completely laced. Although the stitch seems difficult, it is quite easy to perform once the idea is grasped.

Double Buttonhole Stitch   Make in the same way as the single buttonhole stitch, except that lacing is put under two loops instead of one.

HAND SEWING
Hand sewing is considered superior to machine sewing, because the stitches can be pulled tighter and will not loosen as easily as the machine lock stitch. For some articles, it is the only method that can be used to join leather together. Edges should be cemented before they are sewn together to prevent them from slipping. There are many kinds of needles (harness, sharps, or glover's) that can be used in sewing leather. These needles can be purchased in a wide variety of sizes at any notions counter. Waxed linen, nylon, or heavy cotton thread are all suitable for stitching leather.

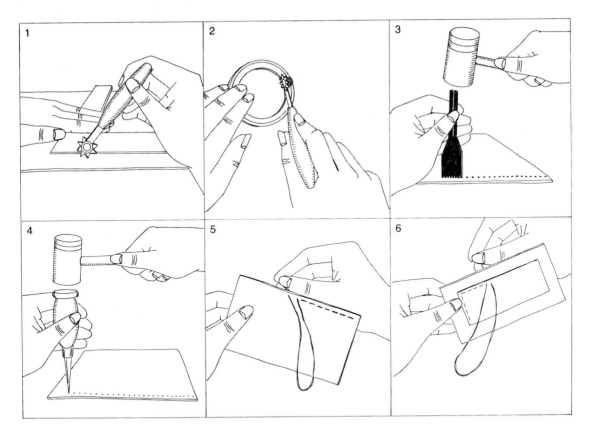

Figure 10-8   SEWING
1. Using a space marker with a straightedge.
2. Using a space marker with a template.
3. Using a stitching punch to make holes.
4. Using an awl to punch stitching holes.
5. Making a running stitch.
6. Sewing two pieces of material together.

Holes for sewing should be located 1/16 inch from the edge for light-weight leather and 1/16 to 1/4 inch from the edge for heavyweight leather. The type of construction used will help to determine the precise location of the stitching line. The number of stitches per inch should be fixed; for lightweight leather there should be from eight to twelve stitches. A space marker can be used to locate the holes for stitching. Holes can be punched with an awl, or slits for sewing can be made with a thonging chisel. Holes in thick leather can be drilled.

Running Stitch   A running stitch is preferred for use by beginners on lightweight leather. Start sewing in one direction by pushing the needle down and then up through the leather. Continue going down and up through the leather until the end is reached. Reverse the sewing procedure, filling in the alternate stitches. Pull each stitch tight, being careful not to cut the leather. When the sewing is completed, tie the ends of the thread and cut off any extra thread. A small amount of cement can be applied to

LEATHER CRAFTS

the knot. If nylon thread is used, the ends can be burned to prevent the knot from untying.

Saddlers Stitch   The saddlers stitch is used for heavy leather. Two threaded needles are used at one time, both going through the same hole from opposite sides of the leather. The positions of the needle are exchanged and returned through the next hole. This stitch fills in all spaces between the holes. Secure the end of the thread as for the running stitch.

SNAPS AND FASTENERS

Setting Snaps   Snaps are used to fasten together openings on purses, key cases, and other articles with an overlapping closure. Snaps consist of four parts, two of which go in an upper layer of leather and two of which go into the lower layer. These, in turn, snap into each other to hold the two layers of leather together.

There are two types of snap setters: the segma and birdcage. Care should be taken to use the correct part of the snap-setting device with the right part of the snap to prevent squeezing the wrong pieces.

Birdcage Snaps   Determine the correct size for the eyelet by punching a test hole in a piece of scrap leather. Place the eyelet over the anvil of the snap set. Push the leather down over the eyelet, grain side up, and place the cap over the eyelet. Place the concave part of the hammer over the cap and strike the tool with a mallet, setting the cap and eyelet.

Locate the hole for the post by aligning all parts and pressing the cap firmly against the surface. The eyelet will leave an impression on the surface, thus marking the position of the post. Punch a hole for the post. Place the post over the small anvil and then the leather over the post. The spring is situated over the post and leather.

Segma Snaps   Segma snaps are set in the same manner as birdcage snaps. The correct size of snap tool should be used for each size of segma snap.

Eyelets   Eyelets are used to fasten frames or metal plates to a leather surface and to reinforce or finish a hole. They can be purchased in sizes that vary from number 00 (large) to number 3 (small), with the number 1 eyelet the most common. Place the eyelet into the hole in the leather and then into the eyelet-setting device. Hold the eyelet setter over the eyelet in a vertical position and strike with a mallet.

Grommets   Where strength is needed, grommets, which are similar to eyelets, are used with washers.

Rivets   Rivets of tubular metal fit together to hold metal key sets onto a leather surface or to hold belt buckles in place. Place the rivet through the holes in the two pieces of leather or key holder and leather. The rivet is squeezed by hitting the rivet-setting device with a mallet so that one part spreads inside the other and holds it tight.

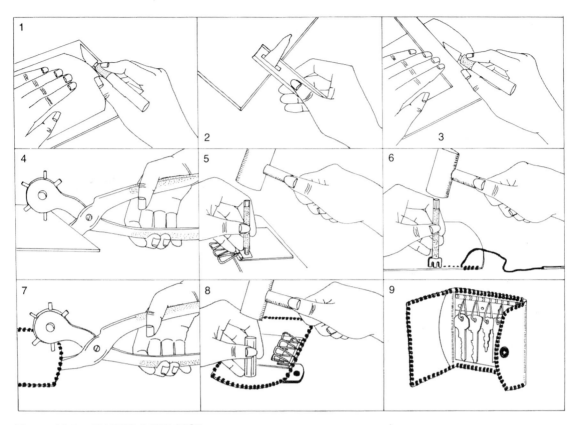

Figure 10-9 MAKING A KEY CASE

Materials: leather, template, key frame, rivets, thonging chisel, snaps, snap setter, lacing, revolving punch, drive punch, skiving knife, straight edge, rivet-setting device.

1. Carefully cut the leather, using a pattern as a guide.
2. Skive the edges of the leather.
3. Score the leather to facilitate folding.
4. Punch holes for the key frame.
5. Rivet the key frame in place.
6. Use the thonging chisel to punch holes for the lacing.
7. Punch the hole in the flap for the snap.
8. Set the snap.
9. Finished key case.

DYEING AND FINISHING LEATHERS

Dye is used to color the surface of leather, while a leather finish is applied over both natural and dyed surfaces to soften, protect, and condition the leather.

All tooling should be completed before dye is applied to the leather. Clean the leather to remove all dirt and grease so that the surface may be dyed uniformly. Dissolve 1 teaspoonful of oxalic acid crystals in 1 pint of water to make a cleaning solution or purchase a commercial leather-cleaning solution. Apply the cleaning solution with a cellulose sponge and allow the leather to dry thoroughly.

Pour a small amount of dye into a shallow container and with a

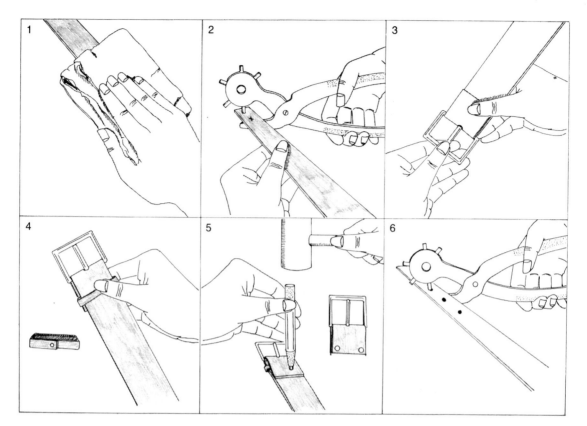

Figure 10-10 MAKING A LEATHER BELT
Materials: leather dye, revolving punch, buckle, belt leather, rivets, rivet-setting device.
1. Dye the leather.
2. Punch a hole for the tongue of the buckle.
3. Insert the tongue of the buckle in the hole.
4. Attach the loop to the belt.
5. Rivet the buckle in place.
6. Punch evenly spaced holes in the opposite end of the belt.

sheep's wool or cloth apply the dye in broad strokes and allow to dry. If the surface should dry streaky, a second coat of dye should be applied to the total surface. Small areas missed cannot be touched up. It is important to experiment on a scrap piece of leather before applying dye to the surfaces of the finished article. The scrap leather should be the same as that used in the finished article.

A small camel's hair brush can be used to apply dye to a carved background or small areas in a design. Care should be taken not to drip dye from the brush onto the leather surface, because it will cause spots.

Finishing Edges
Edges that are not going to be laced can be finished using one of the following techniques.

A small brush can be used to apply dye to the edges of colored leather; care should be taken not to get dye on the finished surface. A solution of gum tragacanth is used on natural leather.

A bone folder or the end of a modeler rubbed back and forth over a moistened surface will color the edge and set the fibers. Edges that receive excessive wear should be covered with an edge or casing compound.

Edge enamel or edge dye can also be used to coat edges that receive excessive wear.

Protective Finishes

A special leather lacquer can be used to preserve and protect leather. Antique finishes that produce highlights and shadows are available in a number of colors. Waxes in liquid, paste, or cake form can be used as a finish or protective coat. Saddle soap is a mild cleaner and dressing for leather. Neat's-foot oil is a good preservative which will darken and waterproof natural leather.

WOODCRAFTS

This chapter is devoted to a simple description of some of the basic wood-working tools and an explanation of how they are used. No attempt is made to include all those tools that could be used in any school or recreational crafts program. The materials presented are important to the individual planning a program that includes any aspect of the woodcraft area. It will assist him in considering the potential of woodcrafts and the dimension that they can add to the crafts program.

A detailed description of the basic hand tools necessary to construct simple wood projects is presented. The chapter also includes a description of an electric hand drill and jigsaw. The procedure for making a picture frame and the other basic joints are given. Picture frame construction has many implications to the other crafts areas such as silk-screen printing, copper embossing, and painting. The wood lathe and the techniques of faceplate and spindle turning are described in detail. The lathe provides a tool that can be used by the craftsman to construct a wide variety of novelty items.

BASIC WOODWORKING TOOLS
Measuring and Layout Tools
Bench Ruler   A bench ruler is made from hardwood with brass tips on the ends. One side is graduated in eighths, while the other is graduated in

sixteenths of an inch. The brass tips protect the ends from damage. Bench rulers can be purchased in 1-, 2-, and 3-foot lengths.

Zigzag Ruler The zigzag ruler is usually 6 or 8 feet long when open. It can be folded into 7-inch sections.

Push-Pull and Tape Rulers Tape rulers are usually made of flexible steel in lengths from 6 to 100 feet and are used to measure long distances.

Using the Ruler Hold the ruler on edge when laying out or making measurements. When marking the distance, do not use a dot, but use a line perpendicular to the graduation on the ruler. The point of a sharp knife is used to make accurate measurements.

Pencil Compass The pencil compass has one pencil leg and one leg with a sharp metal point. It is used to draw circles and arcs and to lay out geometric shapes or designs. The compass is set by marking off the distance directly on a sheet of paper or on the surface being laid out.

Dividers A divider is a tool that looks like a compass except that it has two metal legs. It is used to draw circles and arcs or for stepping off equal distances. The dividers are set by placing one leg over the inch mark on a ruler and adjusting the other leg to the correct measurement.

Scratch Awl The scratch awl is used for marking the center for holes to be drilled or bored. It can also be used to punch small holes for starting nails, screws, brads, and cup hooks. It is useful for punching holes in paper, cardboard, and leather. The awl is handy for scribing lines on wood and metal surfaces.

Using the Scratch Awl The tip of the awl is placed at the center point and forced into the wood with a twisting motion. If the awl is used too near the edge, it will split the wood fibers.

Try Square The try square has a metal blade and metal or wooden handle. The blade and handle are at right angles to each other. It is used to test the squareness of adjacent surfaces, draw guidelines, and lay out stock.

T Bevel The T bevel has an adjustable blade and is used for checking or transferring angles. The blade is adjusted by loosening the clamping screw and then setting to the desired angle with a protractor.

Combination Square The combination square consists of two major parts—a steel head and blade—and is used to perform many different operations. The blade has a groove cut along its length so that it can slide back and forth. One side of the head makes a 90-degree angle with the blade, while the other side forms a 45-degree angle. The head contains a level for

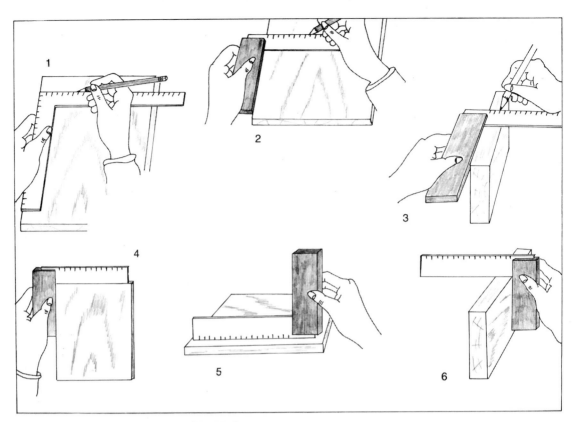

Figure 11-1 SQUARES

1. Scribing a line across the face of a board with a framing square and pencil.
2. Scribing a line across the face of a board with a try square and pencil.
3. Scribing a line across the edge of a board with a try square and pencil.
4. Testing an end for squareness with the edge.
5. Testing a flat surface.
6. Testing an edge for squareness with the face.

testing flat, horizontal surfaces. The combination square can be used as a depth gauge, marking gauge, try square, and miter square. The blade is graduated into eighths, sixteenths, thirty-seconds, and sixty-fourths of an inch.

Framing Square The framing square is a large steel square used for measuring and layout. The body is 2 X 24 inches and the tongue is 1½ X 16 inches. Four tables appear on the surface of the body and tongue of the framing square. They are a rafter or framing table for determining the length and angle of common, vally, hip, and jack rafters; an Essex board measure table, which lists board measure for standard lengths and widths; an octagon scale for laying out eight-sided figures; and a brace table for determining the lengths of common braces.

Using a Square To test adjacent surfaces, hold the handle of the square against the side of the stock, while moving the blade down to rest on the

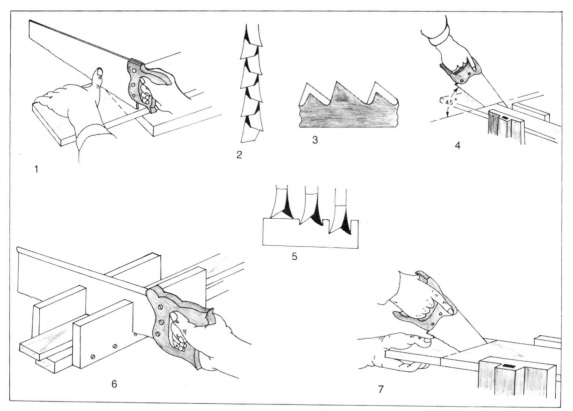

Figure 11-2 CROSSCUT SAW
1. Starting the cut across the grain.
2. Top view of crosscut teeth.
3. Side view of crosscut saw teeth.
4. Proper angle of the saw for crosscutting.
5. Cutting action of crosscut saw teeth (kerf).
6. Using a backsaw in a wooden miter box.
7. Supporting the board while finishing the cut.

end. If the surfaces are square, the blade will touch at all points. The blade can be used to test the flatness of a surface by laying the edge across the face of the stock. To draw a line, hold the handle of the square against the edge of the board with the left hand, and slide the square along the surface until the edge of the blade is aligned with the measurement mark. Draw a line with a sharp pencil, using the blade as a guide.

To use the combination square as a depth gauge or marking gauge, adjust the blade to the correct depth. This is the distance between the head and tip of the blade. The head rests on the edge of the stock, while a pencil rides along the tip of the blade to mark the surface.

Hand Saws

Hand saws are used to cut wood to different lengths, widths, and shapes. They are used to make joints to hold different members of a project together.

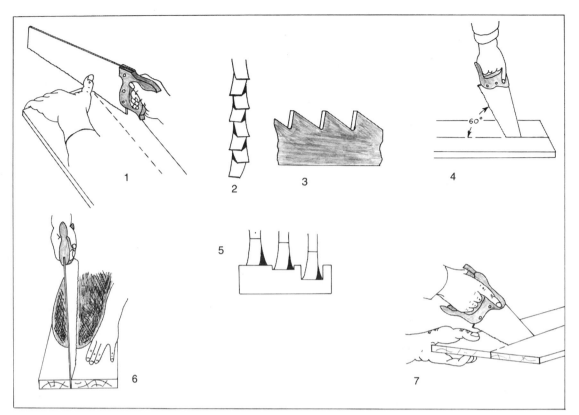

Figure 11-3   RIPSAW
  1.   Using your thumb as a guide to get the saw started.
  2.   Top view of ripsaw teeth.
  3.   Side view of ripsaw teeth.
  4.   Proper angle of the saw for ripping.
  5.   Cutting action of the ripsaw teeth.
  6.   Ripping a board held on a sawhorse.
  7.   Supporting the board while finishing the cut.

Crosscut Saw   The crosscut saw is used to cut across the grain. The teeth are knife-shaped and bent alternately to the right and left of the back of the blade. This is called "set" and allows the saw to make a cut wider than the blade, preventing the blade from binding during the cutting operation. The saw cut is called the "saw kerf." A crosscut saw, 20 inches in length with eight points to the inch, is a good general-purpose saw.

Ripsaw   The ripsaw is used for cutting with the grain. The teeth are chisel-shaped and are set alternately to the right and left of the back of the blade. A ripsaw, 20 inches in length with five and a half points to the inch, is appropriate for most work.

Using a Saw   Lay out a guideline with a pencil and square. Narrow pieces (4 inches and under) should be cut to the correct length in a miter box or held in a vise. Wide boards are placed on a stool or sawhorse to be cut. If sawhorses are used, the guideline should be placed outside the supports and not between. Hold the handle of the crosscut saw in the right hand, with the index finger extended to support it. Place the free hand on the board and use the knuckle of the thumb as a guide. Start the saw with two or three light, backward strokes to engage the saw teeth. Once the teeth are engaged, a few short strokes will deepen the groove, making it possible to remove the hand from the blade. Adjust the cutting angle to 45 degrees to the surface for the crosscut saw and 60 degrees to the surface for the ripsaw. Take long, uniform strokes, sighting along the saw to make sure the cut is square. If the saw moves off the line, take short strokes and twist the handle slightly to bring it back. When the cut nears the end, hold the piece being cut off to prevent the corner from splitting.

Backsaw   The backsaw is a fine-tooth crosscut saw, with a heavy metal band along the back edge to support the thin blade. It is used for fine work, especially for cutting molding joints and squaring up stock. The fine teeth and thin blade make a small saw kerf and leave a smooth surface.

Using the Backsaw   Lay out a guideline with a pencil and square. The piece to be cut is placed on a bench hook. A bench hook is a wooden board with a cleat nailed to the bottom and top surfaces. The bottom cleat hooks the edge of the bench, while the stock rests against the top one. The handle of the saw is held in the right hand, and the left hand holds the stock against the bench hook with the guideline to the right. Use the knuckle of the thumb of the left hand as a guide to start the cut. The saw is held high to start the cut, and as the cut is started, it is slowly lowered until the saw is parallel with the surface. Continue sawing until the correct depth is obtained or the waste stock is cut off. A small piece of scrap wood can be clamped to the stock and used as a guide for the blade of the saw. If a guide block is used, both hands can be used to control the saw. The right hand is used to hold the handle, while the left hand holds the back of the blade.

Coping Saw   A coping saw is used to cut out designs that have curved edges, very sharp corners, or angles that need to be cut with a thin saw blade. It can also be used to make interior cuts.

Exterior Cuts   Fasten the stock in a vise with the guideline slightly above the jaws of the vise. Install the teeth in the frame with the teeth pointing toward the handle. Hold the handle in the right hand, while the left hand holds the end of the frame. Cut along the line, applying pressure as the saw is pushed forward and releasing pressure as the saw is pulled back. The left hand is used to guide the frame so that the saw follows the line. Sharp curves are cut by slowly turning the frame as the saw is moved back and

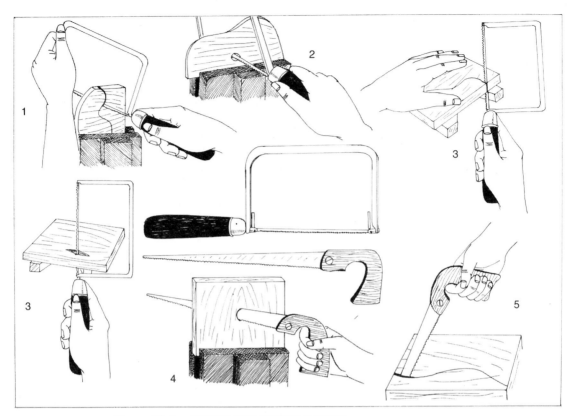

Figure 11-4   COPING AND KEYHOLE SAWS
1.   Using the coping saw for exterior cuts.
2.   Using the coping saw for interior cuts.
3.   Saw with a coping saw on a V-block.
4.   Using a keyhole saw for interior cuts.
5.   Cutting with a keyhole saw.

forth. Care should be taken not to twist the saw or the blade will break. The blade can be turned to any angle for cutting.

The coping saw can be used to saw material held on a V-block. Clamp the V-block to a bench or in a vise. The teeth are inserted in the frame facing the handle, because the cutting is done on the downstroke. Hold the work firmly on the block with the area to be cut near the base of the V. Pull down on the saw to cut, while adjusting the work as the stock is cut, keeping the cutting area near the bottom of the V.

Interior Cuts   Drill or bore a hole in the waste material. Remove the blade from the frame by unscrewing the handle and applying pressure to the frame. Slip the blade through the hole and fasten it in the frame again. Cut around the design. Remove the blade when the design is cut out.

Jigsaw

The jigsaw has a narrow blade held in a frame. The blade moves up and down and cuts the stock as it is fed across the cutting edge. It is used to

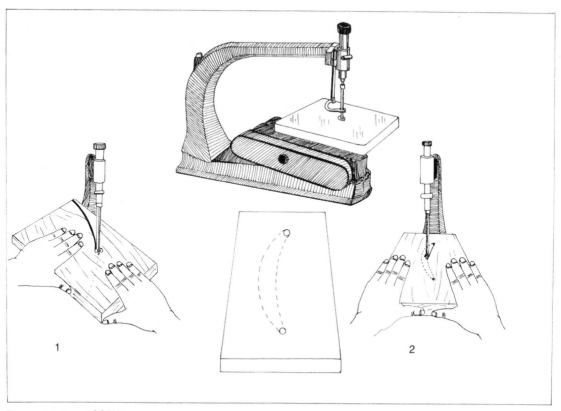

Figure 11-5 JIGSAW

    1. Cutting with a jigsaw. It is important to cut slowly and follow the layout line carefully.

    2. Internal cuts are made by drilling a 3/16-inch hole in the waste area for inserting the blade.

cut inside and outside curves and irregular shapes. It is an excellent and safe power tool for any crafts program.

Cutting with a Jigsaw Select a blade appropriate to the particular stock being cut. The blades vary in length, thickness, and number of teeth per inch. The greater the number of teeth per inch, the finer the cut. Blades vary from 7 teeth to the inch for cutting soft woods to 32 teeth per inch for cutting metals and other hard materials. A blade with 15 teeth per inch is a good general-purpose blade.

    The blade is inserted with the teeth pointing toward the table. Adjust the tension, using the upper chuck to keep the blade taut. The speed of the saw can be adjusted by changing the belt to the different pulleys. The speed ranges between 600 and 1750 rpm; low speeds make it easy to follow the guidelines, while high speeds produce a finer cut.

    The drive shaft should be turned one revolution by hand to check all adjustments. Place the work on the table and adjust the pressure foot so that it holds the stock down against the table. Turn on the machine and start to cut the stock by feeding it slowly into the blade. As the stock is manipulated, a downward pressure should be applied to the surface to prevent the stock from vibrating. When cutting around a corner, turn the stock slowly as a forward motion is maintained.

Cutting Inside Work   Drill a small hole in the waste stock and insert the blade through the drilled hole. Secure the top end of the blade in the chuck and proceed as in regular outside cutting. Remove the blade from the upper chuck to free the work.

Hand Plane
The hand plane is used to cut the surface of a piece of wood straight and smooth.

Types of Planes   There are four basic types of planes.

Jack Plane   (14 or 15 inches long with a 2-3/8-inch-wide blade) The most common plane, it is used to smooth rough surfaces requiring heavy cuts. It is also used to smooth and straighten the surface of a board.

Smooth Plane   (7 to 9 inches long with a 1-1/2-inch-wide blade) A good all-purpose plane, it is also used for small work.

Block Plane   A small plane that has a low-angle cutter, it is used to cut end grain and is also useful for general-purpose work.

Jointer Plane   (22 or 24 inches long with a 2-3/8-inch-wide blade) It is used for planing long boards, such as the edges of doors.

Assembling and Adjusting a Plane   Hold the single plane iron in the left hand with the bevel side of the blade down. Place the plane cap crosswise on top of the plane iron and drop the cap screw through the hole. Slide the plane-iron cap away from the cutting edge and rotate it one-quarter turn so that it is straight with the plane iron. Slowly slide the cap forward, guiding it with the left thumb and forefinger. Care should be taken not to slip the cap over the cutting edge, thereby damaging it. The edge of the cap should be about 1/16 inch from the cutting edge for most work and 1/32 inch for very fine work. Hold the two parts together and tighten the cap screw with the level cap. Make sure that the two parts are good and tight to prevent wood chips from getting between the plane iron and the cap.

Place the plane in an upright position on the bench with a piece of scrap wood under the toe to raise one end of the bottom. This will prevent the cutting edge from hitting the surface and becoming damaged. Hold the plane-iron cap assembly with the cap up and carefully slide the cutter into position. Be sure that the long slot in the plane iron fits over the roller of the lateral adjusting lever and the small slot in the plane-iron cap fits over the depth-of-cut lever. Place the lever cap over the plane-iron cap assembly and push the lever down, securing the plane-iron snugly in posi-

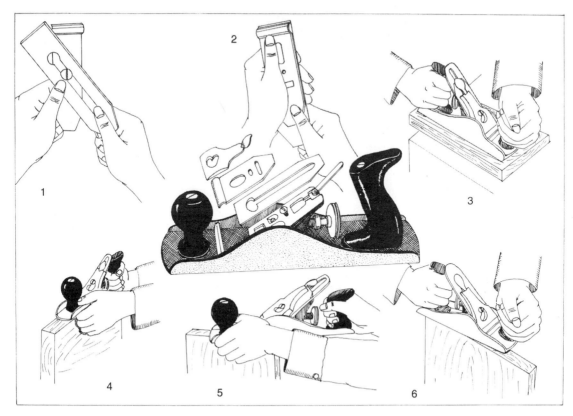

Figure 11-6 HAND PLANE
Parts of the plane: lever cap, plane-iron cap, plane iron, lateral adjusting lever, frog, handle, bottom.
1. Assembling the plane-iron cap and plane iron.
2. Aligning the plane-iron cap and plane iron.
3. Planing the working face.
4. Planing an edge.
5. Planing end grain. Note angle of plane.
6. Planing from the opposite edge to the center.

tion. If the lever cap is too tight, adjusting the plane is difficult; if it is too loose, the plane will not stay adjusted. Adjust the lever cap screw until the correct pressure is obtained.

Adjusting the Plane Iron Turn the plane upside down, holding the adjustment nut in the right hand, while the left hand holds the base of the plane. Sight along the bottom as the adjustment nut is turned until the cutting edge appears. Move the lateral adjusting lever to the right or left until the cutting edge is parallel to the bottom. Turn the adjustment nut again until the blade appears above the bottom. Test the plane on a piece of scrap stock. Adjust the depth of cut until the desired shaving is removed. The shaving should be smooth and uniform in thickness. When not using the plane, place it on its side.

Planing a Face True and Smooth   Select the largest surface with the fewest imperfections. Mark the direction of the grain, because the face should be planed with the grain. Clamp the board end-to-end between two pieces of stock; one piece should be thinner than the piece being planed. Another method of securing the board for planing the face is to use a bench stop and vise dog.

Take the plane and adjust the depth of the cut. Hold the knob firmly in the left hand and the handle in the right. As the stroke is started, apply pressure to the knob. When the whole plane comes into contact with the board, apply equal pressure to the handle and knob. As the front of the plane begins to pass off the board, relieve the pressure on the knob. Lift the plane on the return stroke; dragging it back will roughen the surface and dull the cutting edge. Start planing at one edge of the board and make a series of strokes moving across the surface until the opposite edge is reached. The surface should be tested frequently with a straightedge.

Planing an Edge   Clamp the board in a vise with the best edge up. Hold the handle of the plane with the right hand. The thumb of the left hand is placed on the base of the knob, while the fingers are placed on the bottom surface of the plane. The fingers are used to slide against the face surface and aid in keeping the plane parallel and steady. Take full-length strokes that will produce uniform shavings. Check the surface with a square for squareness and straightness.

Cutting or Planing an End   If the end grain is not going to show, the end can be squared by cutting the stock to length in a miter box.

To plane end grain, clamp the work in a vise with about 1 inch of the grain showing. If the stock is placed with the end too high, the material will vibrate, making it difficult to obtain a smooth cut. Start the planing stroke at one edge, moving half the distance across the surface, and then reverse the plane and start planing from the opposite side. If the plane is pushed all the way across the end grain, the back edge will split off. To plane, grasp the plane as for edge planing. However, the cutting edge is kept at an angle with the end of the stock. Holding the plane in this position will produce a shearing cut and smoother surface. The block plane works well to cut the end grain because the blade is held at a lower angle to the surface. Keep testing the surface with a square for straightness and squareness.

The other face, edge, and end can be planed using these same procedures.

Shaping with Chisel, Gouge, Carving Tools, and Knives
Chisels are used to shape the inside of a free-formed dish, the inside and outside shape of the hull of a model boat, or a carved figure. The cutting edge for all these tools should be kept extremely sharp. A smooth cut is obtained by operating the cutting tool in the same direction as the grain. When using a chisel or gouge, the work should be held securely with a vise or clamped to a sturdy surface so that both hands are free to control the cutting action.

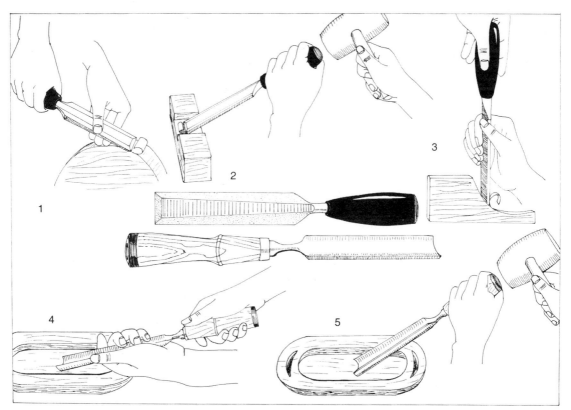

Figure 11-7 CHISELS AND GOUGES

    1.   Cutting a convex curve. Raise the handle a little to follow the curve.
    2.   Cutting a dado with a chisel and mallet.
    3.   Cutting a concave curve. Cut is made from the edge toward the end grain.
    4.   Final shaping of tray.
    5.   Remove waste stock by striking the gouge with a mallet.

Chisels   Chisels are cutting tools with a sharp beveled cutting edge used to shape and fit parts. The size of a chisel is determined by the width of the blade, and sizes range from 1/8 to 1 inch by eighths and 1 to 2 inches by fourths.

Horizontal Cutting across the Grain   Secure the stock in a vise or clamp it to a working surface. Cuts should be made with the grain and across the grain, but not against the grain. Large amounts of material are removed by holding the bevel side of the chisel down. Grasp the handle of the chisel with the left hand and strike it with a mallet. The surface should be cut from both sides toward the center. Cutting from one side will cause the material to chip on the opposite edge. When the cut is within 1/8 inch of the guideline, the chisel should be operated by hand.

Horizontal Cutting with the Grain   Secure the stock. Heavy cuts are made by holding the chisel bevel down and striking the handle with a mallet. Light paring cuts are made by holding the bevel up, while holding the blade with the left hand and the handle with the right. Apply pressure to the handle with the right hand so that the cutting edge cuts into the surface, while using the left hand to guide the blade from cutting too deeply and to maintain control of the tool. Swinging the handle back and forth slightly will assist in the cutting process.

Convex and Concave Surfaces   Secure the work in a vise so that the chisel is cutting with the grain. Hold the chisel with the bevel side up. Grasp the handle with the right hand, while holding the blade with the left hand, which is also resting against the stock. Raise the handle a little at a time, allowing the cutting edge of the tool to follow the curve of the surface. Concave surfaces are cut with the bevel of the chisel down and with the cut made from the edge toward the end grain.

Vertical Cutting across the Grain   Place the work over a scrap wooden block. Hold the chisel with the flat side against the wood. Rest one hand on the wood to guide the blade of the chisel, while the other hand applies pressure to the handle. Take light cuts. A shearing cut is made by moving the handle from side to side as pressure is applied to the chisel.

Gouge   A gouge is a chisel with a curved blade and is used to shape the surface of a piece of wood. The size is determined by the measurement between corners, and sizes range from 1/8 to 2 inches with an inside or outside bevel. The inside-bevel gouge is used to shape the edge of curved stock, while the outside-bevel gouge is used for making grooves and cavities.

Using the Gouge   Secure the piece of stock in a vise and select a gouge of the proper width for the cut to be made. Hold the blade of the gouge in one hand to guide the tool, while the other hand applies pressure to the handle. A mallet is used to strike the gouge when making heavy cuts or roughing out a shape. Finishing cuts should be light and with the grain.

Carving Tools   Carving tools are chisels and gouges with different shaped cutting edges for making angular and curved cuts. The set usually includes a straight chisel, skew chisel, straight bent chisel, parting tool, straight gouge, and veining tool. Carving tools are used to do fine, intricate work.

Using Carving Tools   The tools are held in a manner similar to that for using a chisel or gouge. When carving, control is the most important element to success and only small amounts of material should be removed in one cut. Make light, even cuts starting from the profile of the design and moving to the deepest recess.

Shaping Wood with a Knife   Select a piece of stock and lay out the general shape of the model. The rough shape is cut out on a jigsaw or with a coping saw. With a sharp knife, start the whittling in the corners or where the detail is most intricate. It is important to cut with the grain. Whenever

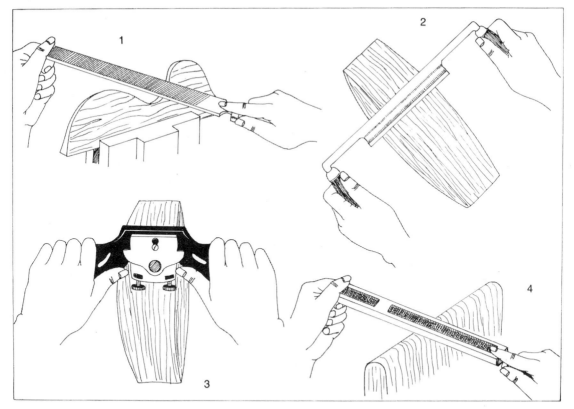

Figure 11-8   FILES, DRAWKNIFE, SPOKESHAVE, AND SURFORM TOOLS

    1.   Filing a curved edge.
    2.   Shaping a curved surface with a drawknife.
    3.   Pushing a spokeshave to shave a curved edge.
    4.   Shaping a surface with a surform tool.

possible, cuts should be away from the body. Some cuts will need to be made toward the operator. Care should be taken to keep the knife from slipping. Shape both sides, removing only small amounts of material with each cut.

Files, Rasps, and Forming Tools

Files   Files are used to remove burrs and sharp edges and remove large amounts of material from areas that are difficult to reach with other sharp-edged cutting tools. There are many shapes of files, but the common ones for woodcrafts are the half round cabinet and the flat wood file in lengths of 8 and 10 inches. The rasp is coarser than a file and is used for rough work.

Surform Tools   Surform tools are used to smooth, shape or form wood, plastic, leather, Keene's cement, soft metals, and composition board. They cut the surface more easily and faster, and the cutting edge stays sharper longer than on conventional surface-forming tools.

Using a File, Rasp, or Forming Tool Files and rasps should be used with a handle to protect the operator from being injured by the tang. Secure the stock in a vise or to the surface of a bench. Select the tool appropriate for the job. Grasp the handle of the tool in the right hand and the point in the left. Apply moderate pressure on the forward stroke. Long, rather slow and rhythmic strokes should be taken with the file lifted on the return stroke. The file should be at a slight angle to the cutting surface to obtain a shearing cut. Concave surfaces are filed with the round side of the file and with the tool held at right angles to the work. The tool is twisted as it is pushed across the surface. Sawdust is removed from the file by brushing the surface with a file card. A piece of sandpaper can be wrapped around the file and used to sand the surface smooth.

Drilling and Boring Holes

Twist Drills Twist drills are used to make small holes for installing screws, nails, dowels, and bolts. Small holes are also an important part of many woodcraft projects. Twist drills are purchased in fractional-sized sets from 1/64 to 1/2 inch in steps of 1/64th inch. They are used to drill either metal or wood.

Hand Drill The hand drill holds and drives a twist drill for drilling small holes. The size depends on the chuck diameter opening, which is usually 0 to 3/8 inch.

Using the Hand Drill Mark the location of the center point with a scratch awl. Secure the stock in a vise, or clamp it to a bench, adding a piece of scrap wood between the bench and stock to be drilled. Holes can be drilled with the hand drill held either vertically or horizontally with the stock. Grasp the chuck with the left hand and turn the crank counterclockwise until the jaws open wide enough to take the shank of the drill. Slip the drill into the chuck between the jaws and turn the crank in the opposite direction to tighten the jaws. Check to see that the drill is in the chuck securely and straight.

A depth gauge may be made from a piece of scrap wood to control the distance the drill travels into the stock. Masking tape wrapped around the drill can also be used for stop drilling. Put the point of the drill in the hole made with the scratch awl. Hold the drill straight and turn the crank evenly as a downward or inward pressure is applied to the handle. Continue to turn the crank until the necessary depth is reached. If the hole is going through the stock, let up on the pressure as the point of the drill starts to come out the opposite side to prevent splitting the fibers. The drill is removed by turning the crank in the same direction as the handle is withdrawn from the hole. Remove the twist drill and return it to the storage container.

Electric Hand Drill A small electric hand drill is also used to hold and drive a twist drill. The chuck opening determines the size twist drill that can be used to drill a hole.

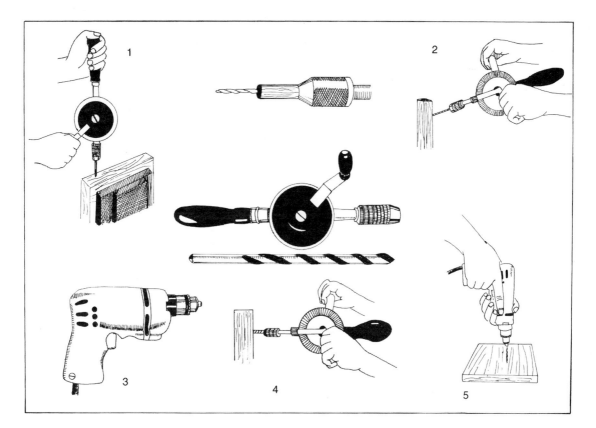

Figure 11-9   HAND DRILL AND TWIST DRILL
Hand drill parts: handle, crank, chuck.
Twist drill parts: shank, body, point.
Size is stamped on the shank.
1.   Drilling a hole in a vertical position with a hand drill.
2.   Drilling a slanted hole with a hand drill.
3.   Electric hand drill.
4.   Drilling a hole in a horizontal position with a hand drill.
5.   Drilling holes with an electric hand drill.

Using an Electric Hand Drill   Open the jaws of the chuck with a chuck key, before turning on the drill. Turn on the drill and check to see if the drill runs straight. Place the point of the drill into the hole made with the scratch awl to mark the center. Guide the drill with the left hand as the right hand applies pressure. Care should be taken because the drill will cut through the surface very quickly. It is important to hold the drill straight because a slight twist may cause the drill to break. A depth gauge can be used with an electric drill.

Auger Bits   Holes 1/4 inch or larger are bored in a wooden surface with an auger bit. They range in size from 1/4 inch (number 4) to 1 inch (number 16) by sixteenths. The number stamped on the shank of the bit indicates the size in sixteenths. For example, number 6 is 6/16 or 3/8 inch,

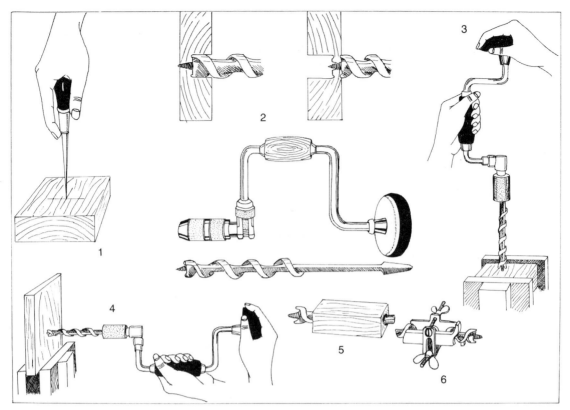

Figure 11-10   BIT BRACE AND AUGER BIT

Bit brace parts: chuck, ratchet, handle, head.
Auger bit parts: feed screw, spur, twist, shank, tang.
1. Starting the hole with an awl.
2. Correct procedure is to bore from one side until the screw appears and then reverse the auger bit and bore from the other side.
3. Vertical boring; check to make sure the auger bit is at right angle to the work.
4. Horizontal boring; check to make sure the auger bit is at right angle to the work.
5. Wooden depth gauge.
6. Adjustable metal depth gauge.

while number 10 bores a 5/8-inch hole. The screw on the end of the bit pulls it into the wood, while the spur scores the wood and the lips cut the material from within the scored circle.

Bit Brace   The bit brace is used for holding and driving all kinds of boring tools, countersinks, dowel pointers, and screwdriver bits. The two most common braces are the plain, or common, and the ratchet. The plain brace is used when a full swing of the handle can be made. The ratchet brace is used to bore a hole in a corner or in close quarters where a full swing of the handle cannot be made.

Using the Bit Brace   With a scratch awl, mark the center location of the hole to be drilled. Insert the correct size bit into the chuck of the brace.

Grasp the chuck firmly in the left hand, while the right hand rotates the handle to the left until the jaws are open wide enough to take the shank of the bit. Secure the stock in a vise or clamp it to a bench. If the stock is clamped to a bench, add a piece of scrap wood between the bench and piece being drilled. Guide the bit with the left hand until the screw point is located in the hole. Grasp the head with the left hand. Grasp the handle in the right hand. Be sure to hold the bit brace straight; it can be checked with a try square. Turn the handle as pressure is applied to the head. When the screw appears through the surface of the wood, reverse the bit and start from the opposite side to prevent splitting. A scrap block of wood clamped to the bottom surface will also prevent splitting.

Boring a hole to a predetermined depth is called "stop boring." A stop block can be made by boring a hole in a block of wood and placing it on the bit to cover the section that is not included in the measurement. Another method is to mark the bit at the correct depth with masking tape. The bit brace can be held in a vertical or horizontal position for boring holes. Remove the bit and return to the storage rack.

Expansion Bit   An expansion bit is used to bore a hole larger than 1 inch. The cutters of the bit can be adjusted to the desired size. A wide range of different-sized holes can be bored with an expansion bit.

Circle Cutter   A circle cutter is used to cut large round holes in wood. It can also be used to cut circles from a piece of wood.

Screwdriver Bit   The screwdriver bit fits into the chuck of the bit brace and is used to gain mechanical advantage in driving screws.

Countersink Bit   The countersink bit fits into the chuck of the bit brace and is used to taper a hole to the same shape as the head of a flathead screw.

Hand Screws
Hand screws are used to clamp surfaces together for nailing, gluing, or screwing. They are also used to clamp material in position for work.

Claw Hammer
The claw hammer is used for pulling or driving nails.

Using the Claw Hammer   The location of nails should be planned. They should be 3/4 inch from the end or edge of the stock. When located closer to the end or edge, a pilot hole slightly smaller than the diameter of the nail should be drilled. Knots should be avoided when nailing material together. Hold the hammer by the end of the handle, and hold the nail until it is secure in the material. Hit the nail flat on the head, starting with light taps and increasing the force as the nail penetrates the material. Care should be taken not to mark the surface. This is accomplished by decreasing the force of the blow as the nail head approaches the surface. Finish nails are set below the surface with a nail set. Other nails are driven so that the head is flush with the surface.

Nails are pulled with the claw hammer by placing the claws under

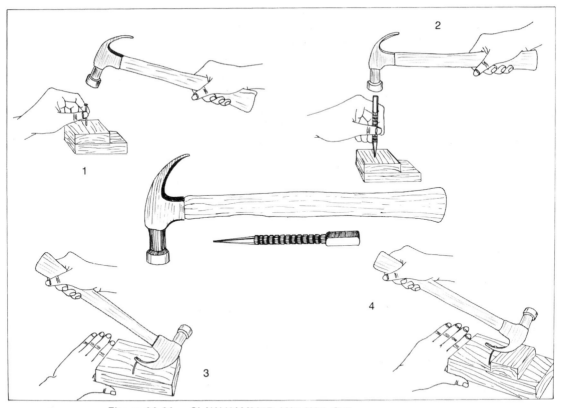

Figure 11-11   CLAW HAMMER AND NAIL SET
Hammer parts: head, face, claw, handle.
Nail set.
1. Starting to drive a nail.
2. Setting a nail.
3. Pulling a nail with a claw hammer.
4. Pulling a nail with a block of wood used to increase leverage.

the head of the nail and applying pressure to the handle. A block of wood can be placed under the head of the hammer to protect the surface and make it easier to remove the nail.

BASIC MATERIALS
Wood Screws
Wood screws are used to fasten together two pieces of material where strength is desired. They also allow the surfaces to be separated without damage to the stock. Wood screws are made from mild steel, brass, aluminum, and copper. The most common head shapes are slotted round, flat, and oval. Screws are manufactured in lengths from 1/4 to 5 inches and with a wire gauge that varies from 0 to 24. Wire gauge is the diameter size of the shank portion of the screw; the gauge number increases as the diameter of the screw increases. For example, a number 8 screw has a smaller shank diameter than a number 10 screw.

Fastening with Wood Screws   Select a screw with the correct wire gauge and length for the job. It should be long enough so that two-thirds of its length goes into the second part. The total length of the thread part of the screw should be in the second piece of stock. The wire gauge is selected according to the thickness of the wood. Locate the positions for the screws; they should not be closer than 1/2 inch from the end or edge of the stock. Mark the centers of the hole with a scratch awl. Select a twist drill equal to the shank diameter of the screw and drill a hole through the first part. Use another drill the size of the root diameter to drill a hole in the second part. Soft woods may not require a root diameter hole. When using flat or oval screws, the surface should be countersunk. Select a screwdriver that has a blade equal to the width of the screw head. If the screwdriver blade does not fit correctly, the tip will slip, resulting in damage to the slot and/or the operator. Hold the screw between the thumb and forefinger, and hold the handle of the screwdriver lightly in the right hand. Start the screw. Then slip the left hand up behind the tip of the screwdriver to guide the tool as the screw is driven into the surface. Care should be taken not to tighten the screw too much. Overtightening will break the screw or strip the threads in the wood.

Nails

Many different kinds of nails can be used in a crafts program. However, four basic nails are most commonly used. They are common, box, casing, and finishing. Common nails are for rough construction. Box nails are somewhat smaller and are used where common nails might split the wood. Casing nails have smaller heads and are used in cabinetwork. Finish nails have a small head and are excellent for cabinetwork and finished carpentry.

The size of a nail is specified by the term "penny" (d) prefixed by the number, such as 6d or 16d.

Wire Brads   Wire brads are small finishing nails. The size of wire nails and brads is specified by length and wire gauge. The wire gauge is the diameter size of the nail, and as the gauge number increases, the diameter of the brad decreases. For example, a number 20 wire brad is smaller in diameter than a number 16 wire brad.

Wood Glue

Glue is an adhesive used to fasten wood, paper, plastic, metal, or other materials together. A good glue joint is stronger than the original material.

Gluing Surfaces Together   Surfaces to be glued should be matched for correct fit. Glue will not compensate for those areas that do not fit. Glue will not act as a substitute for the material; the surfaces must fit together without any space between them.

A dry run can be performed before glue is applied to the surfaces to determine how the pieces fit together. The piece should be clamped in the same manner as it will be when glue is used. If clamps are not going to be used, the two surfaces can be rubbed together and then allowed to dry. A joint that is not clamped is not as strong as one made under pressure, but it is adequate for many woodcraft projects. Use a brush or stick to apply the glue in a thin layer to the surfaces. Place the pieces together and clamp. Protective blocks should be used to keep the clamps or hand screws from marking the surface. Wipe any excess glue from the surface with a damp paper towel before the glue hardens. Set the joint aside to dry for at least one hour.

Sandpaper

Sanding is the process of smoothing a surface with an abrasive and is an important operation in the finishing process. Each part of a project is sanded after it is cut to the final shape, and the total project is sanded after it is assembled. There are four common abrasives used in the manufacturing of sandpaper—flint quartz, garnet, aluminum oxide, and silicon carbide. The grit or degree of coarseness varies with the type of abrasive: flint, extra fine to extra coarse; garnet, 8/0 to 3 1/2; and aluminum oxide, 10/0 to 4 1/2. Sandpaper can be purchased in sheets, belts, disks, and rolls.

Before sanding any surface, consider the following points:

1   The basic material is an important factor in selecting the proper abrasive for the job. What type of material is going to be sanded, ferrous or nonferrous metal, hard or soft wood, glass, plastic, ceramic, rubber, etc.?

2   The shape, size, and condition of the material is important to the selection of an abrasive. Does the surface require the removal of a large amount of stock or merely blending and polishing?

3   The size of the piece often determines the type of equipment that will be used to sand the surface. A small part can be sanded by hand, while large pieces can be sanded with a portable machine.

4   What type of finish is desired—rough, polished, or high luster? This is important as it determines the grit or grit sequence used.

Different grit abrasives can be used for the following operations:

Roughing   Sanding a surface where a maximum amount of stock is removed with a coarse grit abrasive: flint, extra coarse, garnet, 2 1/2, 2, 1 1/2, and aluminum oxide, silicon carbide, 30, 36, 40.

Blending   Sanding a surface to prepare a stock for the application of a finish. Only a small amount of stock is removed with a medium grit abrasive: flint medium, garnet, 1, 1/2, 0, 2/0 and aluminum oxide, silicon carbide, 50, 80, 100.

Finishing   Sanding a surface that has been coated with a finishing material. The purpose is to smooth the surface and remove scratch patterns. The following grits should be used: aluminum oxide, silicon carbide, garnet 6/0.

Using Sandpaper   Large sheets of sandpaper should be cut into smaller pieces for hand or power sanding. To tear a piece of sandpaper, place the surface grit side down against the edge of the bench with half the sheet hanging off the bench. Tear by pulling down on the edge of the paper. It is important to use the smallest piece of sandpaper that will do the job.

Flat surfaces are sanded by clamping the stock to the bench. The piece of sandpaper is folded over the face and two edges of a block of wood. Grasp the edges of the block with the fingers of the right hand and push the block across the surface, taking long even strokes with the grain. Sand evenly from one edge to the opposite one, making sure to hold the block flat at all times.

Edges are sanded by securing the stock in a vise. The block is held on the edge and the fingers of both hands are used as a guide to keep it from rocking. All edges should be rounded slightly when the surface is sanded.

Concave surfaces can be sanded by wrapping a piece of sandpaper around a dowel or scrap wood shaped to fit the contour. The sandpaper can be folded for sanding small curves and corners. It is used folded for sanding a surface coated with a finished material.

FINISHING

The final satisfying step in the construction of any woodcraft project is applying a finish. The surface can be finished with stains, varnishes, paints, enamels, oil, or waxes. Finishes may be applied by brushing, spraying, dipping, wiping, rolling, or rubbing. There are many reasons for applying a finish to a surface. Finishes provide a protective coating and enable the craftsman to create a number of different effects. They help enhance the natural beauty of wood and conceal its blemishes.

Stains are used to color the surface and to bring out the natural beauty of fine woods. They are also used to change the tone or shade of the wood. Stains can be classified into four groups: water stains, non-grain-raising stains, oil stains, and spirit stains.

Varnishes are used to produce a relatively hard, though reasonably elastic finish, depending on the kind and grade. Varnish is an excellent transparent finish. The following types of varnish may be purchased: spar varnish, clear rubbing varnish, satin varnish, and varnish stain.

Lacquer is a synthetic, transparent, water-resistant finish which dries quickly. Brush and spray lacquers are available commercially.

Spray paints are available in many different colors and can be used on metals, wood, and other materials. They require no brushing and with little practice, some interesting effects may be obtained. However, spray paints are very expensive, both in price and in terms of the amount wasted.

Enamels are a mixture of varnish and paint. They are available in flat, semigloss, or gloss finish. They have poor covering qualities and require that the surface be prepared with an undercoating. Enamels can be purchased in a wide variety of colors that will produce a hard, long-wearing finish.

Latex paints, both interior and exterior, produce an excellent protec-

WOODCRAFTS

tive surface for projects that require a tough, durable, opaque finish. Latex paint can be purchased in a wide variety of colors. Tints may be added to change the shade of a color. Latex is an excellent finish to use with children because it dries quickly, and paint tools can be cleaned with soap and water.

Waxes provide an easy-to-apply surface coating that protects and polishes the surface.

Shellac is a transparent coating that can be applied by brush or sprayed. Shellac is ideal for sealing or protecting a surface. However, it turns white if exposed to moisture.

Oil provides an easy-to-apply finish that protects and polishes the surface. Mix the same amounts of turpentine and linseed oil together in a container. The mixture is rubbed on the surface and then allowed to sit for twenty minutes before it is wiped off with a cloth. Twenty or more coats can be applied to build up the oil finish. Coats should be allowed to dry overnight before the next one is applied.

To apply the different finishes, it is suggested that the directions on the side of the container be read and followed. These instructions may vary slightly with different manufacturers.

Paintbrushes
Paintbrushes can be purchased in a variety of sizes and shapes. Flat brushes are used for general work and can be obtained in sizes, ranging from 1/4 inch to 4 inches. To clean brushes, read the directions on the side of the paint container.

COMMON JOINTS AND THEIR USES
Butt Joint   The butt joint is used where great strength is required. It is constructed by planing the surfaces to be joined and then gluing them together. Dowels or splines can be used to give the joint added strength.

Rabbet Joint   The rabbet joint is used for simple drawer construction. The joint is constructed with a backsaw and then glued, nailed, or fastened with screws.

Dado Joint   The dado joint is used in the construction of shelves, steps, drawers, and bookcases. It is constructed with a backsaw and trimmed with a chisel. The second part of the joint is fitted to the first and then glued. The dado joint is not noticeable from the front.

Miter Joint   The miter joint is used in the construction of picture frames and the moldings around furniture. It is constructed by cutting the pieces with a miter box and then fitting the corners carefully. The pieces are fastened with glue, nails, or a spline.

Lap Joint   The lap joint is used to fasten the legs of furniture, molding, and braces. It is constructed with a backsaw and trimmed with a chisel. The two parts are cut like dadoes and then glued together.

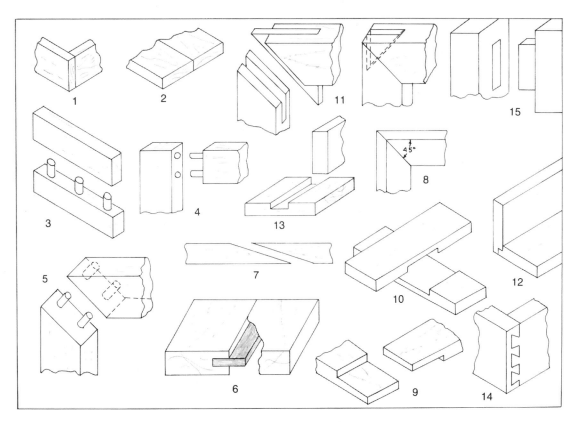

Figure 11-12   COMMON JOINTS

1. End butt
2. Edge butt joint
3. Doweled edge joint
4. Doweled end joint
5. Doweled miter joint
6. Splined edge joint
7. Scarf joint
8. Plain miter joint
9. End lap joint
10. Cross lap joint
11. Miter spline joint
12. Rabbet joint
13. Dado joint
14. Stop dovetail joint
15. Mortise and tenon joint

Mortise and Tenon Joint   The mortise and tenon joint is used for the construction of chairs and tables. The tenon is cut with a backsaw, and the mortise is drilled out and then trimmed with a chisel.

Dovetail Joint   The dovetail joint is used for drawer construction. It is cut on a jigsaw and then glued together.

MAKING PICTURE FRAMES

The purpose of a picture frame is to offset and enhance the picture within it. Most moldings serve as a decorative, as well as a protective element. Frame making is an art that requires great sensitivity in design and skills in carving and finishing a piece of wood. However, attractive picture frames can be constructed by the beginning craftsman. Picture frames are constructed in two operations: shaping the moldings and joining them with a miter joint.

A number of special tools can be used in picture frame construction, but the circular saw and a few hand tools are all that are needed to produce an infinite variety of differently shaped moldings. Picture frame molding can be purchased in different shapes and finishes in long strips. The molding needs only to be measured, mitered, and joined together. Almost any type of wood can be used to construct picture frames. White wood (yellow poplar) is a good wood for the beginner because it is not too hard, is close-grained, and does not split easily.

Planning the Frame

Determine the type of frame that will best suit the picture being framed. Framing photographs or prints is fairly easy because a narrow 1/2- or 3/4-inch flat frame can be used. The molding can be beveled, rounded, or grooved. Photographs and prints are often set off by a mat, a white or tinted cardboard frame with the center area cut out the exact size as, or slightly smaller than, the picture. The mat fits inside the frame. The proportions of the mat and frame will depend on their effect on the picture. Place the picture on a large piece of paper and mark off the margins of the mat and frame with a pencil. The proportions are altered until the design is satisfactory. A general rule is to make the bottom margin of the mat widest, the two sides equal, but slightly narrower, and the top the narrowest. Another method is to make the bottom margin the widest and all the other sides the same size, but slightly narrower than the bottom. Try different proportions to secure one that will enhance the appearance of the picture.

Designing a larger frame presents a more difficult problem, because of the size and the different shaped moldings that can be used to enhance the picture. Lay the print on a large sheet of paper as suggested for the smaller prints and experimentally plan the frame around it. Once the general proportions are determined, start planning the molding in terms of depth and width. It sometimes helps to draw a view of the molding as it would look if it was cut off squarely. When planning the rabbet for the back of the picture frame, remember to allow for the thickness of the print, mat, glass, and nails. All these should be slightly below the back of the picture frame. A canvas mounted on a stretcher does not need to be set flush with the back of the frame, but may extend above the rabbet.

Each picture requires its own individual treatment when being framed to bring out its full beauty. Pictures with delicate coloring or fine detail are enhanced with a blank mat that surrounds them inside the frame. A deep frame increases the illusion of distance or perspective in a picture.

Pictures that have a flat decorative effect usually require frames with little depth. Care should also be taken when finishing the molding. For most pictures, a natural wood finish is appropriate. Color may be applied to the whole surface or to molded lines or shapes of the frame, while the main segment of the surface is left natural. Rich colors should be avoided. It is advisable to use neutral colors, such as off-white or gray with a darker gray rubbed into sunken or incised areas. One of the colors in the picture can be repeated by rubbing it into an incised line in the molding. This technique will usually help to harmonize the frame with the picture.

Making the Molding

Determine the length of the molding needed to make the picture frame by using the following formula: two times the width, plus two times the length, plus eight times the molding width. Several extra inches should be allowed for mistakes and the width of the saw cut. If possible, the molding should be made out of a single length of wood to save time and to ensure accuracy. Only one performance of each operation is required to produce the desired shape of molding.

If a shaper is available, the different shapes of molding that can be produced are almost unlimited. This text will only describe how the circular saw and hand tools can be used to shape molding. A dado head attachment may be used to cut a rabbet or groove. A dado consists of two saws similar to a combination saw and a series of spacers, which act as waste cleaners, between the saws. Dado heads can be used to make a cut that varies in size from 1/8 to 1 inch.

The simplest type of molding is constructed by taking a flat piece of wood and cutting a rabbet in the back surface. A variation is to round the edges. Another technique is to cut a rabbet for the picture and glass and a second one on the face of the molding. The edges can be rounded with a file or sandpaper. Carving tools can be used to carve a bead or other shape in the molding.

The circular saw can be used to cut a bevel or chamfer. On most saws either the table or the saw may be tilted so that an angle cut between 45 and 90 degrees may be made. A tilting arbor saw is the most convenient to use for making these cuts. Adjust the saw to the proper angle and move the fence into position. The stock is pushed through, using the fence as a guide. The face of the molding can be decorated by making cuts of different widths at various intervals. Other variations are possible by combining the different cuts suggested or by devising new ones.

Cutting the Miter Joints

When the molding is finished, it is ready to be cut into the correct lengths for the picture to be framed. All measurements should be made accurately along the inside of the rabbet edge, because this is the surface that will be next to the picture. Allow 1/16 inch extra in the length and width so that the picture will fit freely. The mitered corners can be cut with a miter box and backsaw or table saw.

A mitered joint is an angle joint made by cutting the ends of two pieces of stock at equal slants. Mitered joints are usually made by cutting each piece at an angle of 45 degrees; when put together, they form a right angle. The most accurate method of cutting a miter is with a metal miter box.

The metal miter box is used to cut different angles. The backsaw is mounted on supports that allow it to be moved up and down and side to side to cut different angles. Most miter boxes cut from 0 through 45 degrees right or left at intervals of 15 degrees, while others cut from 0 through 45 degrees right or left but may be set at any angle within the range.

A miter guide may be purchased for use with a handsaw. Wood miter boxes may be purchased or constructed, but they are usually only a temporary measure and their accuracy is good for only a short time. To construct a wooden miter box, cut two pieces of hardwood for the sides; one 17 X 4 X 3/4 inch and the second 17 X 5 X 3/4 inch. Cut a piece of hardwood for the base 20 X 4 X 3/4 inch. Fasten the two side pieces to the base, forming a trough or U shape, with nails and glue. Drill holes in the side pieces to facilitate the nailing operation. The wide side of the miter box should extend 1 inch below the bottom base. This extension is used to hold the miter box against the edge of the working surface. Make a cardboard template with a base and height of 5 inches and a 45-degree angle. Lay out the lines for a 45-degree cut. Place one edge of the cardboard against the outer edge of the side and draw a line along the diagonal edge with a pencil. Using a try square, draw a perpendicular line from the ends of the diagonal line to the bottom edge on both sides. Clamp the miter box in a vise or hold it by hand and with a crosscut saw, cut a saw kerf down the sides to the inside base surface. Care should be taken to keep the saw straight on the line. With a try square and pencil, mark off a line at right angles to the side of the miter box across the top edges at a point that will not interfere with the 45-degree cut. Using a try square and pencil, draw a line down both sides of the miter box connecting this line with the base. Cut along the guidelines with a crosscut saw.

Cutting a Miter on the Circular Saw   Set the miter gauge at 45 degrees. The work to be cut is held against the miter gauge, and the cut is made by pushing the gauge and stock across the blade. A smooth cut is obtained by placing the angle points to the front of the table so that the cut is made with the grain.

Fitting the Joint   Place the cutout parts of the frame together on a working surface and with a try square or framing square, check the corners. Use a rule to measure across the length and width at the corners. Check to see if the miters fit properly. If the corner is slightly off, clamp the two pieces in a miter or corner clamp and with a very-fine-tooth saw, cut through the joint. A block plane can be used to remove high spots and make the corners fit snugly.

Assembling the Joint

Several different methods can be used to fasten a miter joint. The simplest is to glue and nail the corners together. Drive a nail into the first piece of molding until the point appears through the surface of the wood. Clamp the second piece in a vertical position in a vise and apply glue to the joint. Because the miter joint is end grain, it is a good idea to allow the first coating of glue to dry and then apply a second one. This will prevent the glue from being absorbed by the pores of the wood. Hold the first piece so that the corner is slightly over the top edge of the miter cut of the second piece. With a hammer, drive the nail into the wood. The second piece of molding should slip into place as the nail is set.

Another method is to clamp two pieces of molding in a miter or corner clamp. The joint is glued and then pulled tight by the clamp. Nails can be driven into the joint from both sides. Holes can be drilled for the nails to minimize splitting the molding.

A spline can be used to reinforce the miter joint. A saw kerf is cut in each member before the joint is assembled or in two members at the same time after they have been joined. In both methods, the grain of the piece of wood used for the spline should be at right angles to the face of the joint for added strength.

A dowel miter joint can be made by drilling a hole at right angles to each miter cut and a dowel glued in the hole across the corners.

Sometimes a half lap miter joint is used with the fasteners inserted from the back edge to increase the strength. When the moldings are assembled, they should be sanded and the appropriate finish applied.

WOOD TURNING

Wood turning introduces an experience that is entirely different from any offered in the other crafts areas. It increases the range of creative activities that can be produced in a crafts program. Bowls, plates, and trays can be turned on a lathe. The craftsman will enjoy the particular satisfaction of seeing his material take shape, from a rough block to a graceful finished form, under the control of his hands. The satisfaction is similar to that of the potter throwing on the potter's wheel. The difference is that the potter uses a plastic medium, which can be shaped over and over with his hands, while the wood craftsman works with chisels on a rigid material which cannot easily be altered once the shape is made.

A lathe is a special machine for holding and rotating a piece of wood while it is shaped with a chisel. There are eight chisels used for shaping the wood. They are the large-gouge chisels, medium-gouge chisels, small-gouge chisels, half-round scraper, diamond-point scraper, parting tool, medium skew chisel and large skew chisel. There are two main types of wood turning: spindle turning, in which the piece to be worked on is mounted and rotated between two centers, and faceplate turning, in which the work is mounted on a faceplate attached to the spindle of the head stock.

Faceplate Turning

In faceplate turning, the stock is mounted on a flat metal plate which fits onto the head stock of the lathe. As the faceplate revolves, the stock is shaped by the chisel scraping the surface. The round-nose chisel is used for concave cuts, the skew chisel for convex cuts, the square-nose chisel for straight cuts, the diamond-point chisel for V cuts, and the parting chisel for depth.

Select a piece of wood that is free of knots and other defects. With a compass, draw a circle 1/8 inch larger than the diameter of the finished turning. Cut the piece of wood with a handsaw. Select a faceplate smaller than the diameter of the work to be turned. Two methods may be used to attach the faceplate to the work. One is to screw the faceplate directly to the work, while the second is to glue a block of wood to the work and screw the faceplate to the wooden block. This method does not mark the base of the work with screw holes. The block of wood should be cut the same diameter as the faceplate. A heavy piece of paper should be glued between the wooden block and work to facilitate separating the surfaces when the turning is finished. Care should be taken when screwing the faceplate in position to make sure the centers coincide. The live center is removed from the head spindle and the faceplate screwed in place. A piece of paper placed between the shoulder of the spindle and the faceplate will facilitate removal when the turning is finished. Before starting the lathe, adjust the belt to obtain the proper speed. A slow speed of 600 rpm is usually used for large pieces, while a piece 3 inches in diameter or smaller may be turned at 1,200 rpm.

The tool rest is moved into position to cut the edge of the work straight and smooth. The tool rest should be parallel with the edge of the work and 1/8 inch below the center and 1/8 inch away from the work. Before starting the lathe, turn the work one revolution by hand to make sure it clears the tool rest. To operate the lathe, take a position facing the lathe at an angle of approximately 45 degrees to the bed. Select a skew and hold the end of the handle with the right hand, while the left hand holds the blade to guide the tool along the rest. It is a good idea to get a feel for holding the tool and manipulating it before starting the lathe.

Turn on the lathe. The edge is straightened and turned by holding the tool perpendicular to the edge of the work on the tool rest. Keep the full width of the blade against the work while moving the tool across the thickness of the stock, taking small cuts until the shape is true.

On faceplate turning, the outside shape or form is usually turned before the inside. Concave cuts are made by holding the skew perpendicular to the work on the tool rest, while the handle is pivoted to form the desired arc. Concave cuts on the edge are made by using a round-nose tool. The tool is also held perpendicular to the work and pivoted to make a concave cut.

Convex cuts on the face surface are made by turning the tool rest so that it is parallel with the surface, 1/8 inch below the center and 1/8 inch away from the work. Place the skew chisel on the tool rest and pivot the cutting edge from the center out. Concave cuts on the face surface are

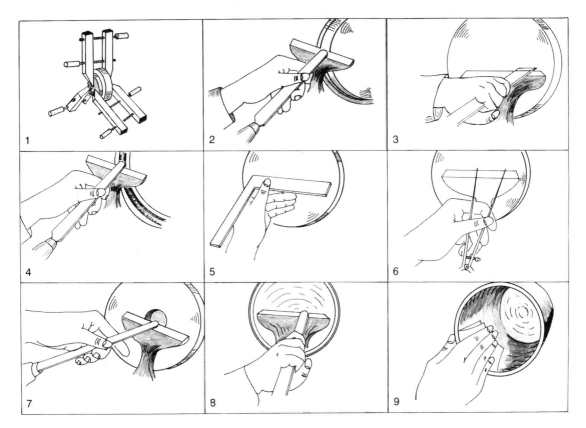

Figure 11-13   FACEPLATE TURNING

1. Gluing the disk to a mounting block.
2. Cutting the edge of the disk straight with a round-nose chisel.
3. Smoothing the face of the disk with a skew chisel.
4. Shaping the edge of the disk with a round-nose chisel.
5. Testing the face of the disk for flatness with a square.
6. Marking circle with dividers set to the radius.
7. Cutting a hole with a round-nose chisel.
8. Shaping the inside of a bowl by scraping with the round-nose chisel.
9. Sanding a concave surface on a faceplate. Sanding is done below the center and on the down slope of the rotation of the stock.

made with the round-nose tool. Cuts are made by holding the tool perpendicular to the surface at the center of the work and moving toward the outer edge. It is important that the tool be held straight and level with the tool rest so that the end of the tool is doing the cutting. As the work takes form, the tool rest is advanced and adjusted to keep the proper working distance between the two surfaces.

The base and wall thickness of bowls and trays should be 3/16 inch. The depth of an inside form can be measured by placing a straightedge across the opening and using a rule to measure the distance between the base of the object and the straightedge. The wall thickness can be measured with outside calipers.

When the work is the desired shape, it should be sanded. Move the tool rest out of the way before starting to sand. Start sanding with 1/2 garnet cabinet paper to remove chisel marks and then use 2/0 garnet paper for the final sanding. When the surface is sanded free of all scratches and rough areas, the faceplate is removed from the lathe. If a wooden backing block was used, it is removed with a mallet and chisel. The chisel is placed at the glued joint between the wooden block and the finished turning and tapped lightly. Care should be taken not to damage the finished product. Apply the desired finish to the surface.

Spindle or Between-Center Turning

Select a piece of wood free of defects and cut to size, allowing 1 inch extra in the length and 1/4 inch extra in the diameter for waste. Cut both ends of the stock square. Locate the centers of both ends by drawing diagonal lines across the corners. Place the stock in a vise and, using the diagonal lines, cut two saw kerfs 1/8 inch deep with a backsaw. On the opposite end, punch a hole at the center. For hardwoods, it is advisable to drill a 1/8-inch hole at the center of both ends. Remove the live center from the spindle by pushing a metal rod through the head stock. Place the stock in an upright position and, with a wooden mallet, drive the live center into the wood, making sure that the spurs enter the saw kerfs. Holding the live center in position, insert it into the spindle and slide the tail stock toward the head of the lathe until the point of the dead center enters the hole in the stock. Lock the tail stock in position and turn the spindle speed feed handle until the dead center is seated in the wood. Back off on the spindle feed handle to release the pressure slightly and apply a little wax, oil, or soap to the impression made by the dead center. Tighten the handle until the center is back in the original position. Adjust the tool rest by rotating the stock, making sure that the corners of the stock clear the edges of the rest by 1/8 inch. The height of the tool rest should be 1/8 inch below the center. The tool rest should be adjusted as the stock takes shape, and the gap between the two surfaces should not exceed 3/8 inch. Stock larger than 2 inches square should have the corners removed before it is inserted in the lathe. Corners can be removed with a plane, spoke shave, or draw knife. Adjust the belt to obtain the correct speed; when the stock is square, the lathe should run at a slow speed of about 600 rpm.

Select a large gouge and with the right hand grasp the handle toward the end. The left hand is used to hold the blade and guide the tool along the tool rest. A scraping cut is made by holding the gouge in a perpendicular position with the stock so that the tip end of the tool is doing the cutting. This method of turning will produce a rough cut. A shearing cut is made by lowering the right hand 10 degrees and turning the gouge slightly toward the direction of the cut. The gouge is moved along the tool rest, taking a fine cut. Scraping and shearing cuts are started in the center and the tool is worked toward the edge. Continue to turn with a gouge until the stock is cylindrical.

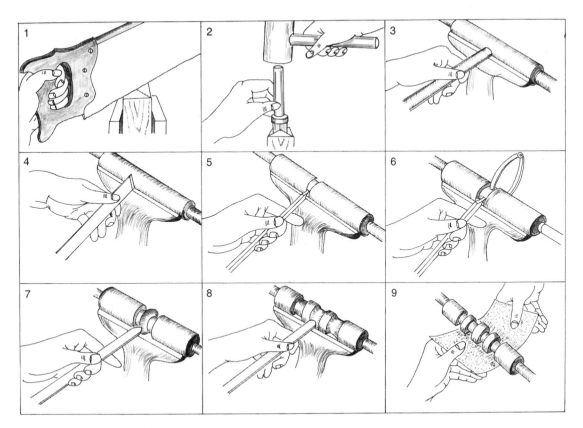

Figure 11-14 SPINDLE OR BETWEEN-CENTER TURNING

1. Using the backsaw to cut diagonal lines 1/8 inch deep for the spurs of the live center.
2. Using a wooden mallet to drive the live center into the wood so the spurs enter the kerf made by the saw.
3. Rough turning with a gouge using a scraping cut. Note the horizontal position of the tool.
4. Scraping with the skew chisel.
5. Using a parting tool to make a depth cut.
6. Using calipers to check the diameter of the turning.
7. Scraping a large bead with the diamond-point tool.
8. Scraping a concave surface with a round-nose tool. Hold the chisel flat on the tool rest and pivot the handle to form an arc.
9. Sanding in the lathe. Sanding is done by holding the paper either above or below the turning.

The higher the speed, the smoother the cut. The speed should be increased to 1,600 or 1,800 rpm. Use the large skew to smooth the surface. Hold the handle of the skew close to the end with the right hand, while the left hand is placed on the blade. The slope of the bevel should be pointing in the direction of the cut to be made and resting against the stock. Adjust the tool by moving the right hand until the blade is at an angle of about 120 degrees to the axis of the stock. Raise the tool until the blade starts to cut a shaving. Slide the tool along the rest, keeping the proper angle. Reverse and repeat until the stock is the correct diameter. The stock is ready to be shaped.

Making V Cuts   Mark the center line and the width of the V with a rule and pencil. Place the pencil against the surface and rotate the stock, making a mark around the cylinder for each measurement. Score the center line by placing the edge of the skew on the tool rest with the head down and the cutting edge on the center line of the V. Move the skew over about 1/8 inch from the center line and turn it at a slight angle toward the center line. Cut into the center line. Repeat this operation on the other side of the center line. Continue this operation until the correct V is formed. A V shape may also be made by using a diamond-point chisel to scrape the surface into the desired width and depth. The tool is held horizontally and at right angles to the stock, while being pushed against the surface.

Cutting Beads   Lay out the width of the beads with a pencil and rule. Rest the pencil point against the surface and rotate the stock, marking a guideline around the cylinder. For wide beads, a center line is helpful. The bead is shaped by placing the edge of the skew on the tool rest with the heel down. The cutting edge is rested against one of the lines that marks the width of the bead and pushed against the surface, scoring it. This operation is repeated on the other width line of the bead. Move the skew 1/8 inch along the tool rest toward the center of the bead. With the heel of the skew doing the cutting, roll the tool toward the width line. Repeat this cut on the other side. Continue this process until the correct shape bead is formed. Calipers can be used to test the diameters of the crest and base of the beads.

Making Concave or Cove Cuts   Lay out the surface with a pencil and rule, marking the center and width measurements of the concave shape. With a pencil against one of the measurement marks, rotate the spindle, marking a guideline around the cylinder. This operation should be repeated for each mark. With a parting tool, cut a groove to within 1/16 inch of the desired depth. Calipers are used to test the diameter of the cut.

The round-nose tool can be used to form a concave shape, using a scraping cut. Place the round-nose tool on the tool rest, with the bevel side down and in a horizontal position. Hold the handle with the right hand and the blade with the left hand, while sweeping the tool from side to side, forming the desired concave shape.

A gouge can also be used to form a concave shape, using a shearing cut. Place the gouge on its side on the tool rest about 1/8 inch from the groove made with the parting tool. Roll tool toward the center, cutting the surface of the stock. Repeat this operation on the other side. Continue cutting the surface on both sides of the center groove until the correct shape is obtained.

Cutting a Long Taper   Lay out the points for the largest and smallest diameter with a pencil and rule. Make a full-size drawing on a piece of wrapping paper so that the diameter dimensions can be determined at several points. These points should be marked on the stock. With a parting tool, cut these depths on the side of the line with the smaller diameter. Calipers can be used to test the size of the diameter at these points. With a gouge, cut off the surplus stock. Adjust the tool rest so that it is parallel with the taper and, with a skew chisel, cut the stock to the finished dimensions, using either a scraping or shearing cut.

Sanding   Remove the tool rest for sanding. If the surface was scraped to the desired shape, use number 1, 1/2, and 2/0 garnet paper to sand the surface. For a shearing cut, 2/0 garnet paper should be sufficient to obtain a smooth surface. Cylinders are sanded from above the work by holding a long piece of sandpaper between both hands and at right angles to the stock. Apply even pressure as the paper is moved back and forth the length of the stock.

Beads, V-grooves, and coves are sanded by forming the paper to fit small sections of the contour of the turning; sand from the bottom side so that the operation can be observed.

12 METALCRAFTS

Copper, aluminum, and brass are metals that can be used to create a wide variety of decorative objects. Jewelry, trays, candle holders, dishes, and plaques are a few of the items that can be made utilizing the metalcrafts techniques described in this chapter. Easy to work with, durable, and highly decorative, these metals are the most widely used in recreational and school crafts. Precious metals (gold, silver, and platinum) and their use are not discussed because of their expense. Copper, man's first metal, is still one of the warmest and most pleasing, and for workability, it is difficult to equal. However, both brass and aluminum have excellent properties and characteristics for use in any metalcrafts activity.

Embossing is a simple activity that can be performed by very young children, but can also challenge the most accomplished craftsman. Hammering, a craft used by early man to create many of his utensils, represents another interesting technique for the young craftsman. The forming of a flat sheet of metal into a three-dimensional form over a sandbag gives an individual a feeling of accomplishment. Etching and the decorating of a metal surface with a chemical process are most intriguing to the young craftsman. Enameling, a highly artistic endeavor, is another that offers the individual a great deal of satisfaction as the powdered glass used to coat the copper surface changes appearance as it is heated.

TOOLING OR EMBOSSING

Tooling or embossing is a technique used to decorate the surface of a thin piece of metal with a design. Copper, brass, and aluminum foil are available in sheets or rolls 12 inches wide and with a thickness of 36 gauge (0.005 B & S). Tools needed are a liner, or french molder, wide and narrow wooden spatulas, orangewood sticks of different sizes and shapes, a large felt pad 1/2 to 3/4 inch thick, a piece of Masonite, and steel wool number 000.

Modeling Tool

A modeling tool can be made from a wooden dowel by sharpening one end to a point and cutting the opposite end to a 45-degree bevel. Old book mailers or newspapers can be used to substitute for the felt pad.

Planning a Design

Select or draw a suitable design, keeping in mind how and where it is going to be used. The surface of the foil is raised to bring out the features of the design. Some designs and objects lend themselves to tooling more than others. Animals, sailboats, and geometric forms make good copy for tooling.

Procedure

Select a piece of copper, brass, or aluminum foil. Place the tracing paper on top of the metal foil and secure it with masking tape. Put the metal foil on top of the felt pad and trace the design onto the foil using a hard number 6 pencil. Remove the tracing paper and masking tape from the foil and retrace the design on the foil with a liner or the pointed end of the wooden modeling tool.

Turn the foil over with the face side down against the padded surface and with a tracing tool draw a line about 1/32 inch on the inside of the traced design. This line should be slightly heavier than the first line. Should the tool accidentally slip and hit the line turn the foil over and tool the line again from the right side.

Place the foil face down on a felt pad and press the design out with a wooden spatula or an orangewood stick, pushing out those areas that are going to be raised. Light, firm strokes should be used starting at the outline of the design and working toward the center.

Turn the piece of foil over and examine the tooled surface. If the surface is not raised to the desired height, turn the foil over and rework these areas. When the surface is raised to the correct height, place the foil face side up on the felt pad and retrace the design lines.

One of the following techniques can be used to tool the background. A plain background is obtained by placing the foil on a piece of Masonite and smoothing the background around the design with a flat wooden tool. After depressing the area close to the design with a small flat tool, take the larger wooden tool and finish smoothing the background.

The background should be flat without bulges or scratches. All the stretch should be taken out of the foil in one direction, either up and down

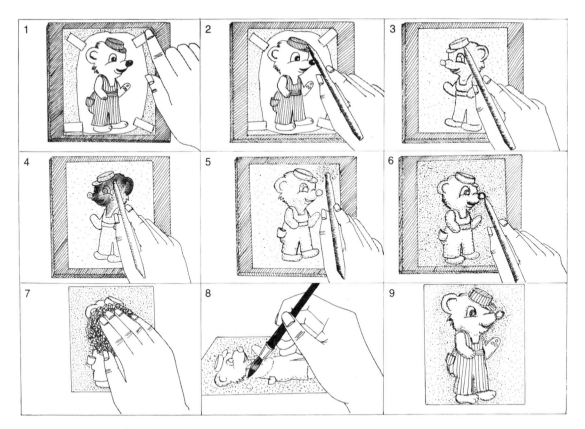

Figure 12-1   TOOLING AND EMBOSSING METAL
Materials: masking tape, copper foil, modeling tool (wooden dowel), felt pad, number 000 steel wool, clear lacquer, paintbrush.

1. Place the design on the metal and secure it with masking tape.
2. Put the metal foil on top of a felt pad and outline the design with a sharp-pointed instrument.
3. Turn the copper over and trace around the inside of the original line.
4. Start tooling by pressing out those areas to be emphasized.
5. Turn the design over and push down the background areas.
6. Decorate the background.
7. Clean the surface with number 000 steel wool.
8. Coat the surface with clear lacquer.
9. Finished tooled design.

or from side to side always starting close to the center of the design and working toward the edges. If the background is smoothed in both directions, the foil will buckle. Care should be taken not to overwork the metal because it will become brittle and hard.

If desired, a stippled background can be obtained. First take out any bad bumps or rough spots with the wide spatula. Start as near the center of the background and as close to the design as possible. A 3/8-inch center punch can be used to obtain a fine stippled background. A ball point pen also can be used to produce a very interesting pattern. Start stippling around the design and working toward the edge of the foil. This will stretch the metal in the same direction the surface is being worked. The amount of stretching can be reduced by making 1-inch circles and filling them in.

The design is ready to be finished. A bright shiny surface can be obtained by polishing the foil with number 000 steel wool and sealing it with a protective coating of plastic spray or wax.

An antique finish can be obtained on a copper foil by mixing a small piece of liver of sulphur in 1/2 pint of water. Apply a small amount of the solution to the surface with a piece of steel wool. The surface should turn black almost immediately. Wipe off any extra solution with a towel. With a piece of dry steel wool, polish the areas that should be highlighted. The dark areas give the design depth. The surface can be coated with more liver of sulphur to obtain the desired effect. Liver of sulphur liberates hydrogen sulphide, which is poisonous. Do not use it in a closed area. If the solution dries too long before the surface is highlighted it becomes almost impossible to rub off. Silver of sulphur can be used to loosen and remove the liver of sulphur if it becomes too dry. When appropriate effects have been obtained, seal the surface with a plastic spray or wax.

Copper and brass, when heated over a Bunsen burner or in an oven, will produce a spectrum of colors varying with the length of time heated. The range starts with reddish orange and moves through bluish purple, brassy yellow, dark red, dark purple, and eventually chestnut brown.

Sharp indentations and raised surfaces can be supported with Plasticine or soft clay. This will protect raised edges from being pushed in. The clay or Plasticine should be worked into the cavities and impressions from the back of the foil. Care should be taken not to damage the design when working the Plasticine into position.

Tooling can be used to make plaques, jewelry, and decorated metal facings. The finished foil can be mounted on a piece of wood with escutcheon pins, or it can be framed.

HAMMERING

Forming by beating may be accomplished in two ways: beating over a stake and beating into a form. Forms of hardwood are used when only a limited number of articles are to be produced. Wooden forms can be purchased or are made by turning or carving into the wood a recess of the shape and depth desired. For beating down, a ball peen hammer or a mallet made of horn or wood should be used. To protect the metal surface, the peen faces are covered with a piece of leather or a rubber crutch tip.

Beating into a Form

Select or design a suitable form. Prepare or purchase a suitable form by turning or carving a recess of the shape and size desired from a 2-inch piece of wood. Lay out and cut a piece of 10- to 18-gauge copper or aluminum. When cutting the metal, every effort should be made to minimize the amount of material wasted. Cut the piece in rectangular form, allowing a little surplus for distortion when the metal is hammered into the form. The amount of surplus needed depends upon the depth the material is beaten down and the size of the object. For example, for an article 6 inches

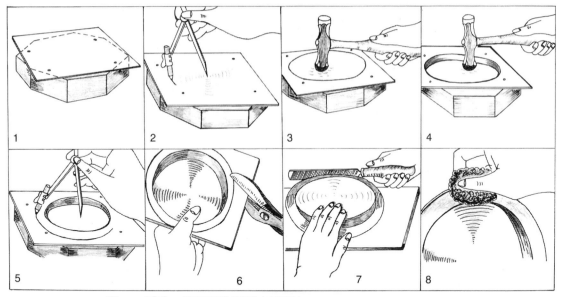

Figure 12-2 BEATING INTO A FORM

Materials : wooden form, steel wool, planishing hammer, tin snips, compass, file, sheet of copper or aluminum.
1. Fasten the metal to the wooden form.
2. Draw guidelines with a compass.
3. Hammer in center, working in circles to the outer edge.
4. Continue hammering the metal until it is the shape of the wooden form.
5. Lay out the guidelines for the finished form.
6. Cut around the guidelines with the snips.
7. File the edges smooth.
8. Polish with fine steel wool.

in diameter with a 3/4-inch dip, 3/16-inch allowance on each side will be sufficient. The amount of surplus will increase with the size and depth of the article being formed.

The piece of metal is centered over the form and fastened in place with brads driven through the corners into the wooden form. Locate the center, and with a compass draw the outline of the recess on the face of the metal. This line indicates the area that should be beaten down and the area that should not be hit.

Place the form on a solid surface. With a medium-size ball peen hammer or mallet start forming the metal by striking overlapping, light blows and working in circles out toward the edges. Heavy blows are not needed; however, it is important to keep the handle of the hammer and the arm in a straight line, with the elbow close to the side. The hand is raised just enough to elevate the hammer head a few inches and on the downstroke exert little force. The hammer should hit the metal surface squarely.

Start again at the center and work in circles toward the outer edge. Be sure to use light, overlapping blows. Start from the outer edge and work toward the center. Alternating the direction tends to equalize the internal strains which develop as the metal is stretched to form the requir-

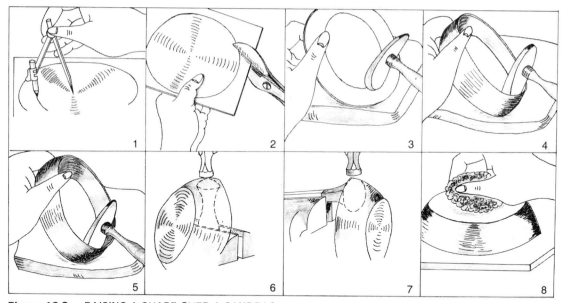

Figure 12-3   RAISING A SHAPE OVER A SANDBAG

                Materials: sandbag, round-face wooden mallet, tin snips, planishing hammer, compass, stake, sheet of copper or aluminum.

1. Draw guidelines with a compass.
2. Remove surplus stock with the snips.
3. Start hammering along the guidelines.
4. Increase the angle as forming progresses.
5. Continue to increase the angle until the correct form is obtained.
6. Planish the surface over the stake.
7. The stake should fit the contour of the bowl.
8. Finish the surface by rubbing it with steel wool.

ed shape. Continue beating down the metal until it assumes the shape of the form. If the metal (copper or brass) begins to work hard, it should be annealed. Annealing is the process of softening metal by heating. The copper is heated evenly to a salmon red color and allowed to cool.

Raising a Shape over a Sandbag

A sandbag does not have the same limitations as a wooden mold. It allows for greater flexibility in the size and shape of the finished product. It can be used to form a great variety of shapes and sizes.

    Make a sketch of how the finished product should look. Select, lay out, and cut a piece of 10- to 18-gauge copper or aluminum to the correct size. The size of the metal can be determined by bending a piece of wire to form a cross section of the finished shape. A cardboard template should be made to check the shape as it is being formed.

    Place the piece of metal on the sandbag with the guideline over the approximate center of the bag. Raise the rear of the metal about 2 or 3 inches, and with a horn or round-face wooden mallet strike the metal a light blow near the guideline. Rotate the metal slowly toward the right, striking another blow overlapping the previous one. Hold the metal at the

METALCRAFTS

same height and continue striking the surface with light blows until a complete circle has been made around the guideline. Move the metal back slightly on the sandbag so that another series of blows can be made that will slightly overlap the first ones. The height of the metal should be increased slightly.

Continue to move the metal back on the sandbag, while increasing the height. Care should be taken not to increase the height too fast because wrinkles will form. Wrinkles should be hammered out immediately. If the metal is formed gradually and carefully, wrinkles should not develop.

As the metal is being formed, the template should be used frequently to check the shape of the object. Continue to hammer and manipulate the metal on the sandbag until a suitable shape is obtained. If the metal is overworked, it will become hard and brittle and should be softened by annealing.

When the correct shape is obtained, slight irregularities in the shape and indentations made during the forming should be removed by planishing. Planishing is the process of smoothing and stiffening metal by hammering the surface over a stake with a smooth-faced planishing hammer. If a planishing hammer is not available, a round-faced raising hammer or the ball end of a ball peen hammer can be used.

The top edge can be cut straight with a pair of tin snips and then smoothed with a mill file. A guideline may help and be necessary to obtain a straight edge. The finished product can be polished with fine steel wool or pumice.

Beating over a Stake

Select or design a shape to be formed. Select, lay out, and cut a piece of metal to the desired shape. Make a template of the inside shape.

Secure a suitable wooden stake in a machinist's vise. The top of the stake should not be higher than elbow height from the floor. The metal is held flat against the top of the stake, with the guideline about 1/8 inch away from the edge of the block. The metal is held with one hand, while the other is used to strike the surface with a round-face forming hammer or the peen of a ball peen hammer. The blows should be struck just inside the guideline. Strike one or two medium blows, rotate the metal to the right, and then strike one or two more blows. Continue this procedure until a complete circle has been made around the inside of the guideline. The direction of rotation is changed to the left and another series of blows made so that they slightly overlap the first ones. The direction of rotation is alternated until the desired shape is obtained.

At various intervals and in several spots, test the shape with the template. Should the rim or the bottom warp, place the object on a flat surface and with a flat piece of wood on the metal, strike it vigorously with a hammer. The rim can be trimmed with a pair of snips and the edge smoothed with a mill file. Polish the surface with fine steel wool or rubbing compound.

Raising a Shape over a Recess

Select a block of hardwood 5 X 3 X 2 inches or log of hardwood from a tree. Secure the piece in a vise and bore or gouge out a recess in the center, edge, or corner to fit the curvature of the form to be produced.

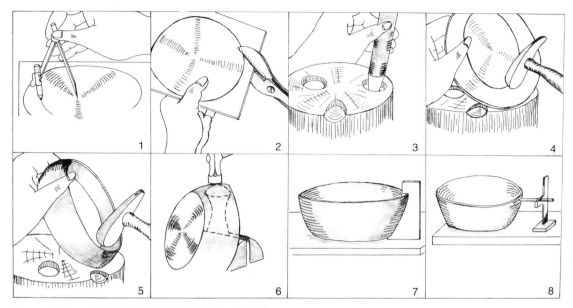

Figure 12-4   RAISING A SHAPE OVER A RECESS
   Materials: round-face wooden mallet, tin snips, planishing hammer, compass, height gauge, file, stake, sheet of copper or aluminum, wooden log.

1. Draw guidelines with a compass.
2. Cut the shape out with the snips.
3. Gouge out a recess in the center, edge, or corner of the end of a hardwood log that fits the curvature of the form to be produced.
4. Place the piece of metal on the block of wood so that the guideline is over the center of the recess and at an angle of 20 to 30 degrees. Strike along the guideline with a round mallet.
5. Move the metal back and strike another series of hammer blows that slightly overlap those in the first row. The hammer blows should be just above the point where the metal and block touch.
6. Planish the surface over the stake.
7. Check the contour of the side with a template.
8. Mark the height of the finished bowl.

Select a piece of metal and lay out the point where the curvature of the shape begins. A cardboard template is helpful to check the finished shape.

Place the piece of metal on the block so that the guideline is over the recess and at an angle of 20 to 30 degrees. While in this position, the metal is formed by striking light overlapping blows with a round mallet, the peen of a ball peen hammer, or a suitable raising hammer. Rotate the metal to the right and continue to strike overlapping hammer blows along the guideline that indicates the point where the curvature begins.

After a complete circuit of hammer blows has been made along the guideline, move the metal back to allow another series of hammer blows that slightly overlap those in the first row. The hammer blows should be just above the point where the metal and block touch.

The metal should be manipulated on the block and over the recess to obtain the desired shape. The shape of the recess may require some adjustment to obtain the desired curvature for the finished form.

With a template, check the shape during the forming operation. Wrinkles should be hammered out when they form. However, if the piece is formed gradually and carefully, wrinkles will not develop.

The metal should be manipulated and worked until the appropriate shape is formed. On shallow shapes only a few complete circuits of hammer blows will be required to raise the side of an object to the desired height. Trim the top edge and file smooth with a mill file. Polish the surface with fine steel wool or rubbing compound.

STAMPING

Stamping is a technique that utilizes steel dies to make simple patterns on a piece of metal. The design produced depends upon the die shapes available and the ingenuity of the individual.

A pattern or design should be developed on a piece of cardboard. When the sketch is completed, transfer it to the piece of metal being used for the finished product. The design can be drawn freehand or traced by using a piece of carbon paper under the tracing paper.

Place the piece of metal being stamped on a polished steel plate. Hold the die shape tool perpendicular to the working surface and strike the tool a sharp blow with a ball peen hammer. The design should be cut into the metal to a depth of about 1/32 inch. Check the design for the quality of the various stamped impressions. When the stamping is completed, the piece of metal is ready to be formed or shaped.

CHASING

Chasing is a technique that utilizes blunt tools of various shapes to depress the metal on one side, while raising it on the opposite side in the form of a design. No metal is removed in this process. The tools and devices essential for chasing are a chasing hammer, chisels, punches, and a pitch block. The piece of metal is held in a bowl of pitch or on a block of lead to allow the metal to be pushed into it when chased. Chasing is similar to stamping except that the design is cut into the surface to a much greater depth. It is also similar to embossing, except that the 24-gauge metal is so thick that metal tools are required to form a design.

Chasing can be used to model a metal surface that is going to be used to make a piece of jewelry. Design and cut out the desired shape from a piece of metal. With a scriber or pencil lay out the outline of the design to be chased. Some designs that are raised above the background must be drawn in reverse if they are not symmetrical. Select a container that is suitable in size for the metal surface being chased and fill it with chaser's pitch. The pitch surface is heated and the metal pressed into it. A thin coat of machine oil on the metal makes it easier to remove the pitch after it has been chased.

Chasing chisels and punches are not cutting tools, but are pieces of hardened steel with smooth, somewhat rounded, and highly polished tips. They are used to drive portions of the metal back to form a design. Chasing tools are manufactured in a wide variety of sizes and shapes.

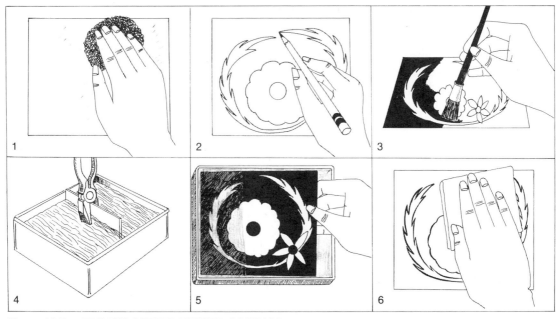

Figure 12-5 ETCHING COPPER, BRONZE, OR BRASS
Materials: sheet of copper, bronze, or brass, pliers, steel wool, turpentine, resist (asphaltum), paintbrush, acid bath.

1. Clean and polish the surface.
2. Transfer the design to the metal surface.
3. Paint unetched areas of the design with resist.
4. Use pliers to place the metal into the acid bath.
5. Wash off the acid in a pan of water.
6. Clean the resist from the surface with turpentine.

Select a suitable tool, usually a tracer, and when the pitch has taken hold of the metal, set the tool on one of the lines to be chased. Hold the tool so that it is slanted slightly backward, and with a chasing hammer punch the tool along the drawn lines of the design. The chasing tool is always advanced toward the operator half the length of the edge and a second blow struck. This procedure is continued until the line is completed. A curved chasing tool is used for curved lines. Sufficient pressure should be applied to make the line protrude on the opposite side to the necessary degree of sharpness. When the design is completed, remove the piece from the pitch and clean with turpentine. The metal surface can be polished with fine steel wool or pumice.

ETCHING COPPER, BRONZE, AND BRASS
Etching is a process that utilizes a chemical action to remove metal from the unprotected areas on the metal surface when placed in an acid bath. This technique is used to decorate bookends, paper knives, bowls, boxes, and jewelry.

Select or draw a design for the item to be etched. Cut and shape the piece to the preferred dimensions. It is a good practice to leave a little waste stock around the outline of the object, because the resist material has a tendency to crack and peel off along the edges allowing the acid to eat into the metal and produce uneven edges.

The metal surface should be cleaned with fine steel wool. With masking tape secure the design in position on the metal with a piece of carbon paper between the design and metal, carbon side down. Trace around the design with a pencil. When the design has been transferred to the metal surface, remove the design paper and carbon paper.

With a small brush, cover the areas from which no metal is to be removed with a resist material, usually black asphaltum, varnish, or stovepipe enamel. The areas from which the metal is to be removed are left unprotected. Allow the protective coating to dry a few hours, and with a knife, carefully remove any of the resist material that may have smeared onto the design.

Prepare the etching bath in a shallow glass or porcelain container. Mix one part nitric acid with two parts water. With a pair of tongs, slowly place the piece of metal into the nitric acid bath for from a half to three hours to obtain the desired depth, usually about 0.005 to 0.010 inch. After the metal is in the acid solution a few minutes, the acid will start to eat away the unprotected areas. The acid is working when small bubbles begin rising from the unprotected metal areas. With a pair of tongs remove the piece of metal from the acid and wash under running water. Care should be taken not to handle the metal until the acid is washed off.

The resist material is removed by soaking the piece of metal in turpentine or naphtha for about forty-five minutes and then wiping it clean with a cloth.

The piece of metal can be formed to the desired shape if this was not done before starting the etching process. Etched areas can be oxidized to make them stand out. A ball peen hammer can be used to decorate unetched areas.

ETCHING ALUMINUM

The design is traced on the metal surface in the same manner as for etching on copper. The difference is that the protected areas on aluminum are coated with orange shellac. The shellac is allowed to dry for three hours. When the shellac is dry, use a knife to remove any shellac that may have flowed onto those areas to be etched.

Prepare an etching bath of concentrated hydrochloric acid in a glass container. With a pair of tongs place the piece of aluminum in the bath. Allow it to remain in the acid until the metal surface has been eaten away to the desired depth, which is usually 0.005 to 0.010 inch. Take the metal from the bath with tongs and wash under running water until the acid is entirely removed.

The shellac is removed by washing the surface with a cloth well moistened with denatured alcohol. The metal surface is etched and ready to use.

ENAMELING

Enameling is the process of fusing a powdered, glasslike material to a metal surface. Enameling is used in metal work to add color, texture, variety, and permanence. To enamel a surface, select a piece of 18- to 20-gauge copper. Thoroughly clean the surface to be enameled and spread the powdered enamel over it. The piece is then fired for two to four minutes at 1300 to 1500° F. The heat melts the enamel, resulting in a glassy film covering the metal surface. The piece is removed from the heat when it becomes red hot and glossy and allowed to cool. When the piece is cool enough to be handled, the areas not covered with enamel can be filed and polished.

Equipment and Materials

Kilns are used to fire the pieces. A torch can be used, but is primitive. The hot-plate kiln is inexpensive and made for small pieces. The chamber kilns are larger, more versatile, and equipped with temperature gauges.

Sheets of 18- to 20-gauge copper are purchased and then cut and shaped. A wide variety of preshaped pieces can be purchased from most crafts supply houses. Copper is easy to work and is much less expensive than precious metals. Gold and silver can also be used but are very expensive.

Nitric acid is used for pickling the work. Pickling cleans off the fire scale. When pickling, use a covered heat-resistant dish and copper tongs.

Long and short metal spatulas are used to lift enameled pieces in and out of the kiln.

Tin snips are used to cut the desired shape.

Glass salt shakers are used to store and dust the enamel colors on the metal surface.

Small paintbrushes are used for brushing a thin layer of oil or gum solution onto the metal before dusting with enamel. They are also used to add decorations to the enameled piece.

Tweezers are used to add enamel lumps, threads, and bits of stained glass to decorate the enameled piece.

Files are needed to clean and smooth edges before and after firing.

Stilts are bent metal pieces with prongs that point upward to support the copper in the kiln.

A trivet is a piece of Monel metal bent to a U shape and used as a rack. Monel is used because the other metals will flake off when fired.

Enamels are purchased in powder form. The size of the mesh is controlled by the screening through which it must pass when being applied to a surface. For most work 80 mesh is satisfactory, while 60 mesh is used for large pieces and 150 mesh for very fine jewelry. Colors are opaque or transparent and the following are recommended for a beginning program:

Opaques—red, medium blue, white, gray, black, medium chartreuse, light green, turquoise, lemon yellow

Transparents (colorless, soft or medium fusing)—red, yellow, green, dark blue, lavender, gray, aqua
Enamel decoration may be enamel lumps, threads, bits of stained glass, glass cloth, clean sand, tiny glass beads, marbles, and buttons. Overglaze decorating colors may be added for special effects.

Flux is a colorless transparent enamel which fires to a luminous gold. It is not acid-proof and does not make a good counter enamel. Transparent colors fired over flux have more life than when fired directly on the copper surface. Reds become very dark and almost opaque if they are not fired over a flux.

Agar, gum arabic, and gum tragacanth solutions are all used to hold the enamel in place until fired.

Solder or glue are used to attach the enamel pieces to earring wires, pin findings, and cuff links.

Clear lacquer is used to protect polished edges and findings from tarnishing.

Cleaning the Metal
Before a piece of metal can be enameled, it should be thoroughly cleaned of oxidation, grease, and dirt. Fine steel wool dipped into a paste of vinegar and salt, baking powder and water, or metal cleaner can be used to clean a metal surface. The cleaning operation should not take place in the same area where the enamel powders are applied to the metal surface. This is necessary to prevent foreign particles from mixing with the enamels. Care should be taken not to scratch the surface when using transparent enamels.

Metal pieces should be enameled the same day they are cleaned. Long delays will cause the metal surface to oxidize and may require that the cleaning procedure be repeated. Discoloration can be retarded by coating the surface with one of the gum solutions. Tongs or spatula, not bare hands, should be used to manipulate the cleaned piece of metal in order to protect it from oil and grease.

Applying the Enamel
Cover the working surface with newspaper. Place the cleaned piece of metal on a wire rack and put both on a 9 X 12 inch piece of coated paper. The coated paper is used to collect the enamel as it is dusted onto the metal surface.

With a paintbrush apply a coat of gum solution to the metal surface. The gum solution is made by adding 1/2 ounce powder or flaked agar to 1 gallon of water. Bring the mixture to a boil, while stirring constantly. Set aside to cool overnight, and the next day squeeze the thick gelatine through a nylon stocking. Add 2 quarts of water and 3 drops of carbolic acid to prevent souring.

The enamels should be stored in salt shakers with a piece of nylon stocking under the cap or in containers with a fine screen covering the top. The sieve allows a fine even dusting of enamel powder to be applied to the

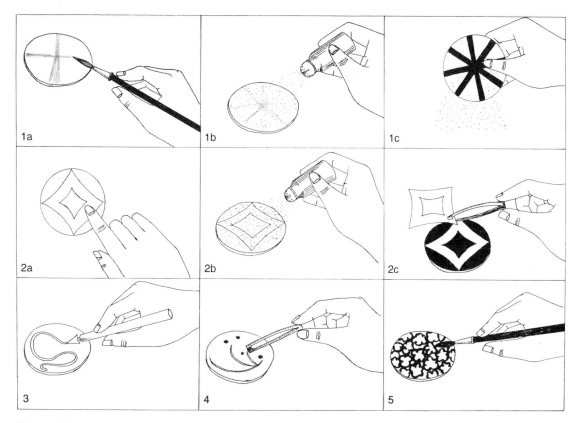

Figure 12-6   DECORATING TECHNIQUES
    1.   Paint a design.
        a.   Paint the design with a brush, using gum arabic.
        b.   Dust evenly with powdered enamel.
        c.   Tap gently to remove excess enamel.
    2.   Use a stencil.
        a.   Place the stencil on the surface to be enameled.
        b.   Dust the surface with powdered enamel.
        c.   Use tweezers to remove the stencil.
    3.   Use a pointed tool to scratch a design on the powdered enamel.
    4.   Use glass (beads, fragments, or threads) to decorate a surface.
    5.   Overglaze painting.

metal surface. Shift the enamel onto the metal until a thin even layer of powder covers the entire surface. Care should be taken to ensure that the edges are covered. Return the enamel on the coated paper to the storage container before using another color. Discard any enamel with impurities such as fire scale and steel wool particles.

Alternative Techniques for Applying Enamel
There are many ways to apply enamels to a surface. The most difficult part of enameling for the beginner, one which is usually overlooked in the mechanics, is designing for the medium. The design can be enhanced by understanding the properties and characteristics of the materials being

used. Experimentation is important to any crafts activity. For example, all transparent enamels improve with successive firings.

Stencil and Sift A stencil cut from a paper towel can be moistened with water to make it adhere to the metal surface. A gum solution is then applied to the uncovered metal surface and enamel sifted over this area. The stencil is removed and the piece is fired.

Wet Inlay The gum solution is mixed with enamel to a runny paste. Separate areas of color are formed and allowed to dry slightly before they are pushed together. The enamels can be rolled in different directions to give the metal an even covering. When the enamel is smooth, place to one side to dry before firing.

Lines Marks or lines can be made through wet or dry inlay, exposing the undercoating color previously applied and fired.

Fences A series of lines may be made by applying wet or dry enamel to the surface and then firing the piece. After the first firing, the areas bound by the lines are filled in with enamel and the piece is refired.

Counter Enameling This is the process of coating the back surface of the piece of metal. Counter enameling gives the piece a finished appearance. However, if pins or clasps are to be soldered to the surface a small area should be left bare for this purpose.

Special Effects

Bubbling Counter-enamel a piece of metal. After the piece has been counter-enameled, apply a heavy coat of a soft opaque enamel and fire. A thin layer of a transparent enamel is added and fired, giving it extra heat and extra time in the kiln until the opaque enamel pops up through the transparent enamel.

Dots Drops of enamel can be used effectively as colorful accents in a design. Drops are formed by mixing a gum solution with the powdered enamels. The piece is cleaned and counter-enameled, and the front is coated in position on the preenameled surface with an enameling spatula. The proper amount of heat will prevent the drops from flattening out and give them a hob-nail appearance.

Crackle A commercial prepared liquid is applied over a prefired base coat of enamel and then fired. During the firing process the base coat crackles, because the copper expands and so does the slush. The base coat fuses or heals, but the slush does not. Slush is available in a wide range of colors.

Luster Crackle A metallic crackle is used under certain transparent colors. Metallic crackle can be used to cover the entire surface or selected areas. A heavy coat of soft opaque black enamel is applied to a clean metal surface and then fired. When it has cooled, brush on the liquid metal and allow to dry thoroughly overnight in a warm spot and then fire. Sift a thin

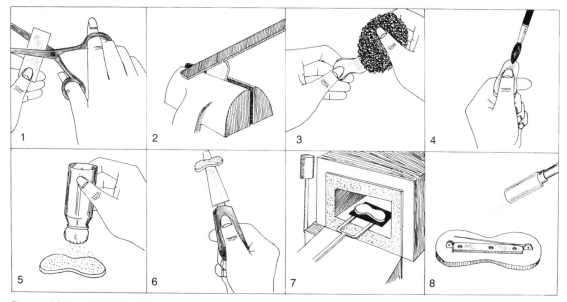

Figure 12-7 COPPER ENAMELING

Materials : bar pin, spatula, file, enamel, salt water, copper, steel wool, solder, propane torch.

1. Cut the desired shape from a piece of copper.
2. File the edges smooth.
3. Steel wool the surface clean.
4. Coat the surface with salt water.
5. Apply the enamel to the surface.
6. Use a spatula to place the metal on the firing screen.
7. Place the screen in the kiln with a loading fork.
8. Solder the bar pin to the back surface.

coat of flux over the area. During the firing process a rich metallic crackle appears. A very rich appearance will result if a transparent color is used instead of the flux.

Separation Enamel A commercial prepared material that sinks into previously applied enamel and spreads when fired, revealing a combination of all the colors used. Coat a clean piece of metal with flux and then fire. Brush the surface with a coat of transparent enamel and then fire the piece. With a brush draw a series of lines on the surface with separation enamel. The piece is placed in the kiln and fired for four minutes at 1600° F. Experiment with different combinations; use two or three layers of transparent enamels. Try one opaque enamel as a base coat, with one or two coats of transparent enamel over it, and then apply separation enamel over this surface.

Firing the Kiln

The manufacturer's directions for operating the kiln should be read before it is fired. Chamber kilns are usually preheated to 1500° F.

Tongs or a spatula should be used to manipulate the copper pieces in and out of the kiln. Take a thoroughly dried piece of copper that has been coated with enamel and place it in the firing chamber for two to three minutes at 1350 to 1450° F. The firing time depends upon the size and thickness of the metal piece and the color and thickness of the enamel being fired.

The kiln should be put in a position so that the firing process can be observed. During the first minute, the piece takes on a dark appearance and slowly turns to a bright red, while the enamel softens in the second minute. The surface first takes on a rough appearance, which is transformed into a smooth, glossy finish as the firing time is increased. Care should be taken not to overfire the piece because cracks, tiny holes, fire scale, and other flaws will occur.

The fired piece is removed from the kiln and placed on a piece of asbestos to cool. If a smooth, glossy surface is not obtained, the piece may require a second or third coating of enamel.

Cleaning and Polishing the Enameled Piece

Areas not covered with enamel or flux will oxidize during the firing process and become covered with fire scale. This black covering is removed by filing the surface with a carborundum hand stone. Fire scale can also be removed by using a file, sandpaper, scouring powder, and steel wool. The fire scale can be removed by soaking the piece for several hours in a vinegar and salt solution. Care should be taken when filing; always work away from the enameled edge. If too much pressure is applied to the surface, the enamel may chip or crack.

Attaching Findings to Jewelry

Duco cement or liquid solder can be used to attach pin or earring backs and cuff links to pieces of metal jewelry. These jewelry findings can be soldered in place. The area where the finding is to be attached should be thoroughly clean. With a pair of tweezers or tongs hold the finding in place while the enameled piece is slowly heated with a soldering copper. Apply the solder to the heated joint and allow it to melt. It should form a bright line around the finding. Hold the finding in place until the piece cools.

WEAVING, SEWING, AND HOOKING 13

WEAVING

No attempt can be made here to present all the intricate ramifications of weaving. It must suffice that elementary weaving forms, with some variations, are presented. The potential student should be persuaded to seek a recreational outlet through this craft. If the urge to create can be aroused, if curiosity about advanced weaving techniques and designs is stimulated, this chapter will have served its purpose. There are many volumes, which the interested person can read, that delve into the mysteries of the loom and its extensive modifications. While the principles of weaving remain fairly constant, the technical aspects insofar as pattern and loom are concerned require thorough investigation. The general concept of weaving with fiber, cloth, paper, and reed materials is offered on the following pages. More significant, however, is the basic premise that weaving can be performed with or without a frame or loom.

Simple Looms

To rig a good, basic loom requires only a few pieces of wood, some small nails, and string. Weaving can be performed on any frame capable of withstanding the tension placed upon it by the warp. Take two strips of wood approximately 1/2 X 1 X 12 inches, and two pieces about 20 inches long. Nail the two shorter strips to the longer ones to form a rectangle. This is the frame. Drive several nails into each corner to strengthen it. At 1/2-inch inter-

305

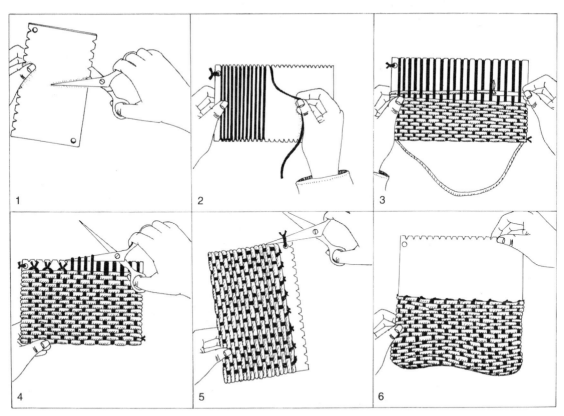

Figure 13-1   CARDBOARD LOOM AND WEAVING
Materials: cardboard, scissors, yarn, Popsicle-stick shuttle.

1. Cut notches on edge of cardboard.
2. Warp cardboard face.
3. Weave yarn through warp.
4. Cut warp ends and tie off.
5. Cut end knot and tie off.
6. Remove cardboard loom.

vals along the center line of the shorter wooden pieces, drive 3/4-inch finishing nails halfway into the wood and slant them toward the outside of the frame. The loom is now ready to be strung by warp strands.

Tie the end of the warp to any corner nail. Putting tension on the warp, carry it to the opposite side of the frame and bend it around the back of two nails, carry it back to the starting side and bend it around the second two nails, then back to the opposite side in a continuous pattern until the entire loom has been warped. This will place the warp strands parallel to one another at 1/2-inch intervals. The loom is easy to use, particularly for children. The process of weaving is simply to alternate the weft under and over the warp, packing each line tightly down, until the material is of a size which the weaver desires. When the weaving is completed, it may be removed from the loom, and the ends can be knotted and trimmed.

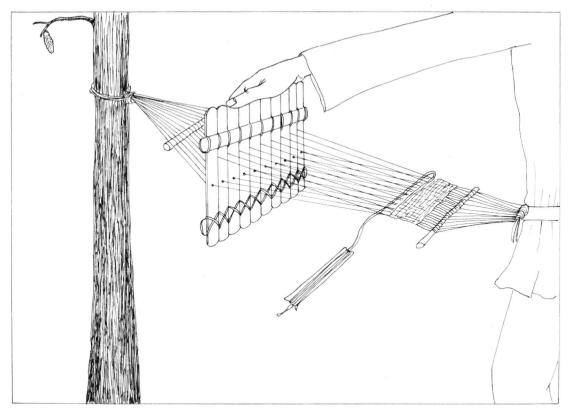

Figure 13-2 INDIAN LOOM WEAVING
Materials: wooden spatulas or Popsicle-sticks, fishing line, yarn, two dowels, wooden shuttle bobbin.
1. Heddles are raised and lowered to form shed.
2. Weft is fed through the shed.

Cardboard Loom   The cardboard loom consists of a piece of stiff cardboard cut to a size approximating the completed weaving. On the top and bottom edges of the cardboard an odd number of notches, spaced 1/2 inch apart, should be cut. These will serve to hold the warp strands. Punch a hole in the upper left-hand corner of the loom and another at the lower right-hand corner. The warp thread is knotted so that it cannot slide through the hole, passed through the top left-hand hole, and wound around the notches of the loom. The thread is pulled through the bottom right-hand hole and tied off. The entire card is now covered with vertical warp threads.

To weave, thread the woof thread through a large needle or shuttle and begin at the lower right of the cardboard loom by using a simple over and under pattern. Continue until the woof is across. Make sure that the woof is continually pushed down so that threads are tightly packed. This packing process may be done with a beater so that the work remains firm and even. When a line is completed in front, turn the loom over and weave again, until the starting point is reached. Continue this procedure until the weaving has reached to approximately 1/2 inch of the top. The warp threads should then be cut and knotted two by two on each side. The warp knots may then be cut at the upper left and lower right. The weaving can then be taken from the loom intact.

Indian Weaving Loom   This loom is the type found among a variety of Indian tribes. The major part of this loom is a heddle. It is constructed from a number of small flat sticks lashed together vertically and held in a frame by two pieces of wood or cross sticks. The frame may be made to whatever length is desired. Indians used lashing techniques to fasten the frame. Thus, diamond lashing secured the vertical sticks to the cross bar, while a series of clove hitches fastened the horizontal piece to the vertical sticks. A hole is bored through the center of each vertical stick.

Warp strands are threaded alternately through the holes and between the sticks. Both ends of the warp are secured to sticks. The far end of the warp is attached to some stationary object, typically a tree or post, and the nearer end to the weaver's waist. To maintain tension and thereby keep the warp taut, the weaver must sit well back. The woof is wound around a bobbin, a reel to hold the length of yarn to be used in the project, and fastened to an outer warp strand. The bobbin is then passed between the two rows of warp threads formed by the heddle. By alternately pressing the heddle down and then lifting it up again, a shed or weaving space is formed, so that the weaver simply must pass the woof back and forth. Thus the weaving is performed quite automatically. After each threading of the wood, a beater should be used to compact the thread and make it even. The weaver continues raising and lowering the heddle and threading woof through the shed until the weaving is completed.

Cannister Loom   One who has developed skill with the cardboard loom will find this technique simple as it is but a variation of the former. Take any cylindrical box, such as an empty oatmeal carton, and make an odd number of notches in the top and bottom of the box. To warp the loom, knot one end of the warp around any of the notches at the top and pass the thread down the sides, under the bottom, up the other side into a notch, around the notch next to it, down the side, under and across the bottom, and up the other side. This procedure is carried on until the loom is strung. The weaving process is much easier than with the cardboard loom because the loom does not have to be turned over when the end is reached. On the circular frame of a cannister loom, there is continuous weaving until the top is reached. When the weaving is completed, the tabs are cut off, the loops are loosened, and the box is removed.

Circle Loom   The circle loom, as its name implies, is used for weaving round objects. The loom can be suspended from any convenient branch, pole, or hook. Because it is so lightweight, it may be comfortable for the weaver to hold the loom in one hand with the lower half resting in the lap. Almost any material may be used for warp. Whatever is used for the warp, lighter material should be used for the woof. A barrel hoop is used

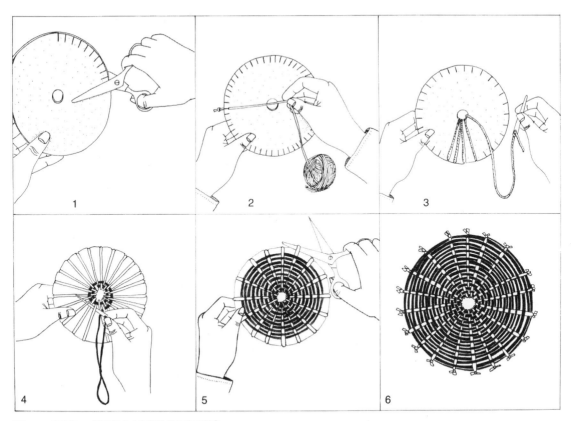

Figure 13-3 CIRCLE LOOM WEAVING
Materials: cardboard, scissors, yarn, large steel needle or Popsicle-stick shuttle.

1. Notch edge of cardboard circle.
2. Warp strand from edge through center hole.
3. Continue warping circle.
4. Weave weft through spokes.
5. Cut weft and tie off.
6. Remove cardboard loom.

as the basic frame for the loom. If a hoop cannot be found, a circle may be cut from a piece of 1/2-inch plywood as a substitute. Holes are bored around the circumference of the circle frame. They should be 2 to 3 inches apart, directly opposite one another, and of an odd number so that continuous weaving may be accomplished.

To thread the loom, pass the warp through a hole and knot the end. Carry the warp strand across the center and to the hole directly opposite; pass the thread through the circumference over the hole adjacent to it on the right, coming back through the circle from the outside to the hole on the opposite side of the circle to the left of the original warp strand. This process is repeated until the loom is strung or warped. The appearance of the circle loom completely strung is that of a wheel with radii or spokes. The last warp strand end should be fastened to the first.

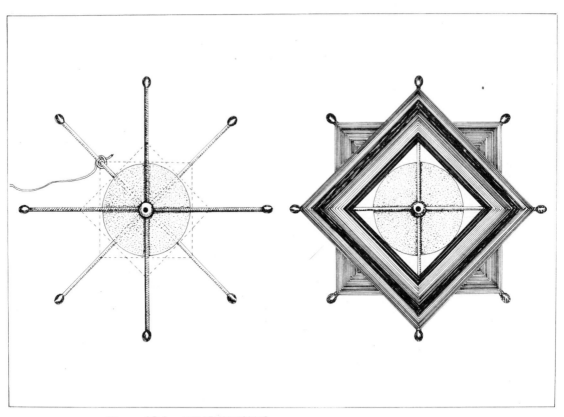

Figure 13-4 WRAP WEAVING

Materials: twine, yarn, thread, twigs, Popsicle-sticks or thin dowels, acorns, buttons, wax (if desired), cardboard, scissors, glue.

1. Take a piece of cardboard and cut in a circular shape.
2. Take wooden sticks or thin dowels and cross them over the cardboard base.
3. Secure the sticks to the cardboard.
4. Make a simple knot at a point one-half the distance between the base and the tip of the spoke.
5. Weave over the alternating spokes.
6. A combined weaving effect may be achieved by turning the frame over and weaving around the spokes bypassed in the initial operation.

To weave on the circle loom, simply knot the woof strands at the point where all the warp strands cross. Holding the frame securely, begin to interlace the woof. Initially, the warp should be divided into four segments where it cuts across the center. These parts will serve as the core and should be woven around three or four lines until the midsection is even and tight. The warp should then be subdivided into eight sections, woven around three or four lines, and subdivided again until the woof is being threaded under and over each alternate warp strand. The weaving should continue until the fabric reaches the desired size. On the final line, weave between the warp threads. Remove the material from the loom by cutting the outside threads. There should be several inches of warp remaining. Place the material on a flat surface and tie each warp end with a double knot. The ends may then be woven several inches into the material. The material is now ready for whatever purpose the weaver has in mind. If it is to be a mat, it may be lined with long-lasting and heavy fiber. The material should be steamed so that it will lie flat.

A Weaving Project

To produce a bag or other carryall from a woven piece, double it and sew the edges together. Line or finish it at the top with a variety of fasteners, including a zipper, a cord and button, or a drawstring. The material could be folded in thirds, sewing two sides together and using the last section as a flap. A loop is braided, crocheted, or formed with a buttonhole stitch over strands of yarn and attached to the flap so that it can be secured over a button. Make a bag by weaving around a cardboard loom so that it is closed on the sides and bottom and open at the top. The cardboard is removed when the weaving is finished. Warp threads are retained in position and the crafts project is prepared as previously indicated in the section dealing with the cardboard loom.

Wrap Weaving

Almost any fiber may be used in wrap weaving. Typically, remnants or left-over threads are the basis for creating attractive handwoven forms. A variation on the circular loom process of weaving is achieved by wrapping a number of threads around interesting pieces of wood or other small-diameter rigid materials. Tongue depressors, dowels, Popsicle sticks, and slightly longer pieces of wood may best be used for this weaving method.

The wrapping technique requires the thread to be passed from one spoke to another. To begin, place a solid circle of thick cardboard in the center of the crossed sticks. All the spokes are secured to the hub. The thread is then wound over alternating spokes. Threads may be wound so that the lines will cover the top or the bottom of the frame. Combination weaving may also be performed, thereby giving the finished project a three-dimensional effect. The fabric may be doubled by first wrapping the thread around alternating spokes and then turning the frame over to work on the spokes that were passed during the initial operation. Almost any pattern may be developed, depending only upon the ingenuity of the weaver.

Card Weaving

Card weaving is a fairly simple technique which requires few pieces of equipment. The warp is secured at both ends to a stationary dowel which will hold the strands under even tension while the work proceeds. The cards become heddles, with each turn providing shed space. The texture of the fabric woven through the use of cards is quite different from that of the typical loom. Generally, weaving is performed with an over-and-under pattern of warp and woof. In card weaving the warp strands are twisted as the cards rotate while the woof threaded through the sheds holds the warp in place, producing a smooth finish. The pattern is developed from the warp. A small, flat shuttle is used for threading the woof strands as well as for beating. The shuttle should be strong and even-surfaced so that it will not snag or otherwise disturb the warp.

Although beautiful patterns can be obtained from specific library collections, there is a definite satisfaction to be gained from innovation and an attempt to create a distinctive pattern of one's own. Pattern design may be made by the use of the strip method. If twenty cards are to be used, draw four lines of twenty squares each on a strip of paper. Number the squares from left to right one through ten and then ten through one. Letter the lines A, B, C, and D. Each number corresponds to one card, while each letter corresponds to a hole punched in the card on a clockwise basis. Essentially, the strongest colors should be used, and striking designs are most satisfying. In this technique brilliant hues are more effective than softer shades.

Decide how many colors will be used in the pattern. Each color block represents one unit and is almost inconsequential from a total project point of view. However, each block contributes to an overall pattern. The diagram merely illustrates the areas in which different colors will appear. The actual design becomes interesting insofar as the direction in which the threads twist as the material is woven.

Inspection of the diagram in Figure 13-5 shows that forty strands of yarn are required—four to a single card. Of these, twenty are blue, eight are white, and twelve are red. Each strand is passed through the proper card hole. At the bottom of the pattern are small slanting lines which indicate whether the cards are threaded from face to back or from back to face. To warp cards for the design shown, the following order is necessary.

Card 1. A blue, B blue, C blue, D blue
Card 2. A blue, B blue, C blue, D blue
Card 3. A white, B red, C red, D white
Card 4. A blue, B red, C white, D red
Card 5. A blue, B white, C red, D red
Card 6. A blue, B white, C red, D red
Card 7. A blue, B red, C white, D red
Card 8. A white, B red, C red, D white
Card 9. A blue, B blue, C blue, D blue
Card 10. A blue, B blue, C blue, D blue

Cards may be made from playing cards or stiff cardboard. The cards themselves are approximately 3 inches square, with holes punched in about 1/2 inch from each corner. The holes should be at least 1/4 inch in diameter to permit easy passage of the warp strands. Cards should be numbered consecutively from one to whatever is half of the total number of cards used. If twenty cards are to be used for a pattern, cards should be numbered from one to ten and from ten to one. The holes are lettered A, B, C, and D in a clockwise position, as on the paper strip showing the design. The A position is the guide position, from which the card rotations are counted.

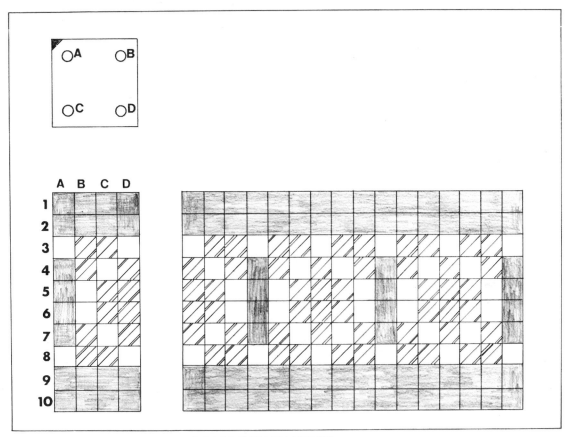

Figure 13-5   CARD WEAVING DESIGN OR PATTERN MAKING
Materials: blank paper, ruler, colored pencils.

After the pattern strips are made, colored warp strands are laid out in preparation for threading the cards. The warp strands should be at least three times the proposed finished length with 7 inches added on for fastening the strands to the frame. The pattern strip should be scrupulously followed as the cards are threaded. The threads should be passed through the cards, lying face up, one on top of the other. Approximately 18 inches of thread should remain on the shorter or left-hand side. Card number 1 must be on the bottom of the pile when the strands are completely threaded. Each card must have all strands going the same way.

When the cards have been threaded and are correctly aligned in sequence, the warp should be straightened out. The cards may be held together by some fastening arrangement, perhaps rubber bands, during this process. When the left-hand warp has been combed straight, it should be secured to the frame. The other strands should also be straightened and attached to the opposite side of the frame under considerable tension. The cards should be at the center of the warp and capable of moving freely along the warp. Properly set up, the cards carrying the warp will produce a clear shed.

Spreaders should be used to maintain the shed. These may be any

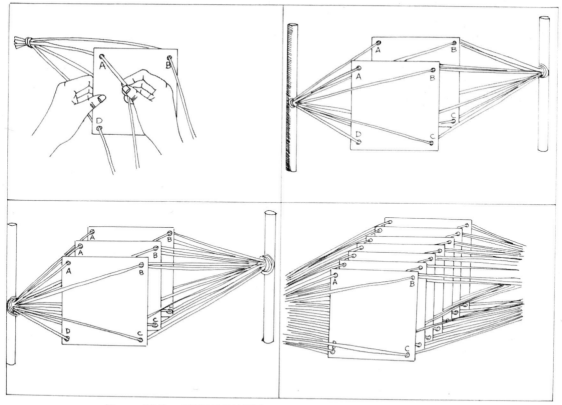

Figure 13-6   CARD WEAVING

Materials: old playing cards or square pieces of stiffened cardboard, paper punch, yarn or thread, wooden spatulas, colored pencils or crayons, rubber bands.

1. Take cards and punch holes 1/2 inch from each corner.
2. Letter each hole A, B, C, D clockwise.
3. Number each card consecutively to one-half the number of cards used.
4. Number the latter cards in declining order to one.
5. Tie warp thread to retainer and pass colored fiber through the appropriate holes according to the pattern.
6. Threads should be passed through cards, lying face up, one on top of the other.
7. Thread all cards and align in sequence.
8. Straighten warp.
9. Hold cards together with rubber bands.
10. Comb left-hand warp to straighten and fasten to frame.
11. Comb right-hand warp to straighten and fasten to opposite side of frame under tension.
12. Cards should be at center of warp and freely movable.
13. Use spreaders to maintain shed.
14. Place spreader close to bar and rotate cards once to the left.
15. Place each successive spreader and rotate cards each time.
16. Pass the shuttle through the shed near the last spreader.
17. Rotate cards from A to B position.
18. Pass the shuttle through the second, third, and fourth shed and beat each line as completed.
19. Rotate the cards each time until the A position is again reached.
20. Reverse procedure after every four turns.

smooth rigid piece of wood or cardboard. A tongue depresser will serve admirably. Place the spreader at the left as close to the bar as possible and rotate the cards once to the left. Place the second spreader and repeat the process. Place the third and fourth spreaders in the same way. Now the weaving may begin.

The shuttle should carry enough thread to complete the project. The woof can be the color of the border if it is to be hidden. Pass the woof through the shed near the last spreader. Rotate the cards from the A to the B position. Pass the shuttle through the second shed. Beat each line as it is completed. Continue this procedure until the cards have been rotated to the first, or A, position. Reverse the procedure after every four turns. Make sure that all cards turn together and that they are in proper position. Reversing the weaving process after every four turns keeps the warp straight. As always with creative enterprises, the weaver may decide against a formal pattern and simply thread the loom with oddly drawn fibers. In this instance the outcome will certainly come as a surprise. Only after the strands are woven will any pattern be discernible.

Spool Weaving

A large empty spool, four brads, and some kind of flexible material are all that are required for this type of weaving. String, gimp, woolen yarn, or other fibers may be suitable. Hammer four nails halfway into the top of a spool, as close to the hole as possible without splitting the wood. Place the nails so that they form a perfect square. Pass the thread through the spool until it is hanging out the bottom. At the top, bend the thread around one nail, and carry it across to the nail immediately to the right and then back, using a figure-eight loop. The material will now be outside the first nail. Pass it on the outside to the next adjacent nail and return using a figure-eight loop. Repeat the procedure for the nail opposite the first. Now the weaving process may begin. Simply pick up the outside strand from the first nail, raise it over the nail and drop it. Repeat with all other nails in turn. A woven strip will soon appear at the bottom of the spool.

Solid-Core Weaving

Among the variations on weaving is the utilization of a semibraiding technique, worked on a solid base or core without a loom or frame. The warp strands, sometimes made out of plastic lace, are fastened to one end of an oblong piece of metal. The strands are permitted to overlap the edge and are then secured by some kind of tape (masking tape will do) or a paper clip. The flat metal blank may become a bracelet or, if square, a brooch.

The warp strands are stretched from the point of attachment down to the opposite end, where they hang freely. The weaving or braiding design may be checkerboard weave, inverted V's, or other geometric shapes which please the designer. Weft threads or strands may be twisted or placed flat, depending upon the effect desired. The weft strands are woven in the same under-and-over manner as in any weaving. They are drawn tightly across the surface of the metal blank and passed around the under

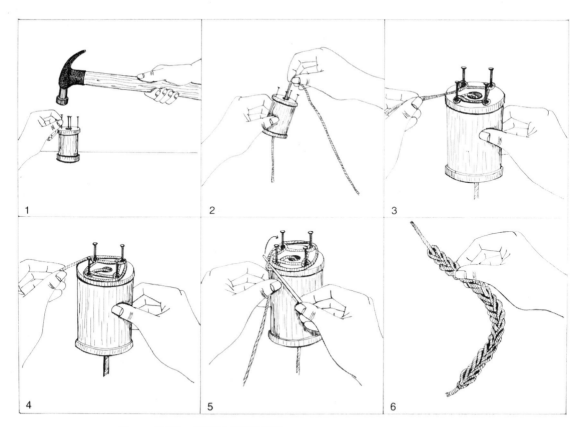

Figure 13-7 SPOOL WEAVING

Materials: spool, four nails, string, needle, hammer.

1. Hammer four nails into the top of the spool so as to form a square.
2. Drop string through center or spool.
3. Bend string around one nail.
4. Carry string to the nail immediately to the right.
5. Use figure eight loop and bring string back.
6. Carry string to second nail, bend around adjacent nail in figure eight loop, and bring back.
7. Repeat procedure with other two nails.
8. Pick up outside strand from first nail, raise it over the nail, and drop.
9. Repeat procedure with all nails in turn.
10. Woven strip appears at bottom of spool.

part. Continued tension should be maintained upon the cross strands, and each successive strand must be positioned next to the strand that preceded it so that the two actually touch where the warp strands permit. Continue the procedure until the design and the blank are finished. Tuck the end strands into the weft and clip for a neat finish. The single weft strand is tucked in under itself at the last line of the finished blank.

To make a bracelet, simply bend the metal oblong around some rounded object; a metal pipe will serve for this task. The metal blanks are flexible enough so that they may be bent around the human wrist to produce the kind of fit desired. Since the blank is flexible, it may be enlarged or made smaller as the wearer demands.

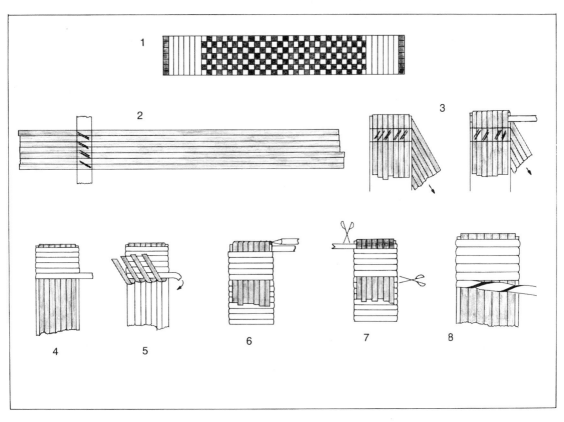

Figure 13-8   SOLID CORE WEAVING
Materials: oblong aluminum strip, gimp or pyrolace in various colors, masking or Scotch tape, scissors, paper clip.
1. Finished product.
2. Warp strands are taped to metal blank.
3. Weft strands are folded under metal blank.
4. Wrap weft strands to begin weaving.
5. Tuck end under warp.
6. Tuck end strand into the weft.
7. Clip ends for neat finish.
8. Twisting effect.

Where a complete circlet, without break, is worked, the following procedure may be employed. Cut three or more strips of flat plastic lacing long enough to go around the circumference of the band with approximately 1/2 inch extra. Secure these to the base by means of a paper clip. The working strand or weft should be five or six times the length of the warp strands and is woven in the typical alternate pattern of weaving. Pass the weft through the ring, and continue weaving until the core is covered. Remove the paper clip, and carry the weaving directly over the loose ends which it was retaining. When the pattern is finished, the working strand end is sliced to a sharp point and threaded through the first row of weaving taken. It is then tucked under a strand on the inside of the ring, drawn taut, and cut off.

Paper Weaving

Almost any kind of paper may be woven: crepe, cellophane, tissue, blotting, wallpaper, and so forth. Textured papers, papers with hard or soft finishes, and varicolored papers may be utilized for this easiest of all weaving crafts. Paper weaving can be started as early as kindergarten grades and extended to arts and crafts courses through the college years. It is a fruitful and enjoyable activity which introduces the tyro to the weaving craft and also permits the expert the full range of creative and artistic endeavors. Nothing is as simple to weave as paper, but intricate patterns, lines and designs can be produced by a master craftsman.

The fundamental procedures concerning cutting and weaving warp and woof may introduce the beginner to the entire weaving process, thereby developing an appreciation for the simplicity of weaving. The more sophisticated worker, on the other hand, may be able to develop highly advanced and detailed designs by altering the method in which the warp and woof are formed, modifying the manner in which the strands are interwoven, and combining the weaver's technique with other art forms.

Paper may be cut in a variety of lines so that other strips may be woven into it. Vertically cut strips serve as the warp, while strips that are cut across serve as woof. An interesting technique for making the warp is to fold a sheet of paper in half, folding a margin across the paper approximately 1/2 inch down from the open edges, and slicing strips of differing width or curving lines, and stopping at the fold. Another method for warp making is to rule a line approximately 1/2 inch down from the top of a sheet of paper and cut strips from one edge to the ruled line. The woof strips are then threaded across the warp to form a woven pattern.

Bead Weaving

To construct a loom for bead weaving, butt-joint two pieces of 4 X 14 inch plywood to a 14 X 18 inch base. Take 3 pieces of wood and notch the top edge of the 3-foot-long sticks into 1/8-inch segments. Attach the yardsticks to the inside top of the frame sides, with notched edges raised and showing over the sides. Pass a brad through a large bead and hammer into each side of the base.

To warp the loom, estimate the completed length of the project and add additional length for knotting the ends. Thread is generally used for warping this loom. Tie one end of the thread bundle to a nail at the bottom of the loom, and wind the warp around the loom until the correct number of strands is achieved for the desired project. Pull the warp taut and wind the extra thread around a nail at the opposite end of the loom.

There must be one more warp thread than there are beads in a row. For symmetrical designs there must be an odd number of beads in a row so that there will be the same number of beads on each side of a center point. The outer warp threads should be doubled for a strong border.

Take a thread approximately 36 inches long and tie it to the left side of the warp with a lark's-head knot. Tighten the knot, leaving at least 4 inches on the short end. Thread beads under the warp and push them up

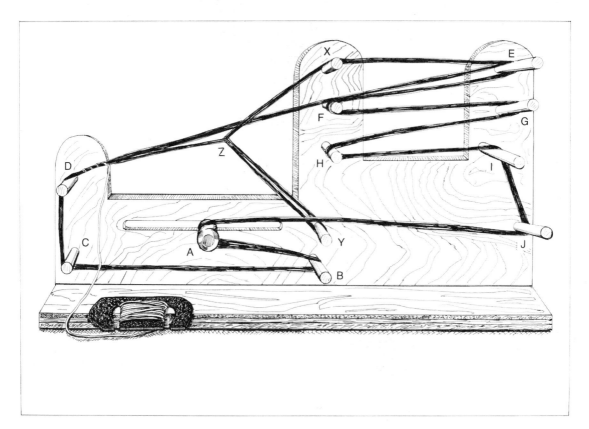

Figure 13-9   INKLE LOOM WARPED FOR WEAVING

Materials: five wooden boards, one 2 x 2 x 30 inches, two 2 x 2 x 9-1/2 inches, and two 1 x 2 x 8 inches long; five 3/4 x 7 inch dowels, saw, chisel, drill, 1/2-inch screw, one shuttle 1/2 x 2 x 6 inches long, yarn, scissors, bobbin, spreaders, string.

1. Select yarn needed.
2. Loop yarn around tension control A.
3. Pass yarn around dowels B, C, and D.
4. Make string heddles and loop around dowel Y.
5. Carry one-half of warp from dowel D to dowel X and pass around dowel E.
6. Carry one-half of warp from dowel D to dowel E.
7. Pass warp from dowel D to dowel E.
8. At point Z loop the heddle over the up-warped strand and place the looped ends over dowel Y, knot down.
9. To change shed, lift or lower the down warp (line DE).
10. Depress down warp and insert one spreader.
11. Raise down warp and insert second spreader.
12. Start to weave by alternately raising and lowering the shed and shooting the shuttle carrying the woof. Continue until fabric is complete.

so that they are positioned between the warp threads. Bring the woof up over the right border, and then pass it through the beads on top of the warp to lock the line in place. Continue this process and arrange beads evenly. On narrow strips, the entire row can be pushed between the warp threads and secured with the insertion of the needle. On wide strips, pass the woof through only five or six beads in an adjacent row and trim. All loose ends should be rewoven. In order to decrease the width of a line or split it into a V, step it down one bead at a time, tying in the warp thread as the work continues. Always work a few inches of straight strips first and then return and work slanted strips.

Inkle Loom Weaving

The inkle loom produces a narrow strip or band of material. The width of the strips varies from very narrow to 3 or 4 inches. On this loom the shed is made with the assistance of string heddles attached to the arms of the loom. The warp is passed continuously around the loom. The fabric resulting from this procedure is warp-faced; that is, the woof does not show in the body of the fabric. The pattern is built up entirely with the warp. The warp may be made of almost any fiber, but cotton, linen, wool, or nylon are preferred. For beginners, three-ply wool is the easiest to weave. The woven strips can be used for neckties or belts and are often sewn together to produce fabric for rugs, scarves, slipcovers, throws, jackets, coats, capes, kilts, skirts, or wall hangings.

The inkle loom is easily made of any kind of wood, although hardwood assures the longest wear. The parts should be screwed together for strength and durability. Materials required to construct a loom consist of five variable-length boards. The length of the main beam will govern the length of the strips produced through weaving. Five dowels, a saw, chisel, drill, 1/2-inch screw, and one shuttle 1/2 X 2 X 6 inches are required. The inkle loom illustrated in Figure 13-9 will weave strips 50 inches in length.

On the loom, temporarily tie the first warp to tension control A. Pass the warp over dowel B and around dowel C. From this point, warp the remainder, using only the dowels required for the length of the desired project. Thus, the length of the weave may be determined in the following manner:

Dowels used	Length of woven piece, feet
All	8-1/2
C, 1, 4, 5	6-1/2
C, 3, 4, 5	7
C, 4, 5	5

The second warp strand is carried directly to dowel C and does not loop around dowel B. From dowel C, both strands are warped in the same manner. Using the same procedure and alternately going over dowel B and bypassing dowel B, the loom is completely warped.

Each time the warp thread color is changed, the new warp strand should be tied to the last warp strand at tension control. When the warping is completed, the first warp strand should be untied from the tension control and knotted to the last warp thread. Heddles retain the threads. These may be made of string or rug warp. Tie string around dowels 1 or 5. Place each warp strand that passes over dowel B through one of the heddles as the loom is warped. When the heddles are tied on, maintain the evenness of the line and tie it in a definite alternate pattern. Other patterns may also be established, for example, 2-1-2 or 3-2-3. There are three basic patterns in inkle weaving: vertical stripes, horizontal stripes, and checkerboard. For classical patterns and methods of innovating, an excellent source is *Crafts Design.*[1]

Position the loom so that it is directly in front of the weaver, with tension control facing the weaver. With the left hand, lift up all free warp strands directly in back of the heddles until a shed appears. Slide a spreader between the layers of threads to the tension control and hold the shed open. Insert the end of the woof near the tension control at the left side and pass it across. With the left hand, push the free warp threads down behind the heddles until the strands are positioned between the heddles. The down shed should then appear. As pressure is exerted downward, insert a beater between the warp threads in front of the heddles, and beat the woof until it is firmly in place. Then reverse the woof thread to throw another line by making a down shed and an up shed. Each time the woof is inserted to make a line, an up shed and a down shed must be woven to lock the woof in place. The lines should be kept even and straight, with the tension control maintained relatively taut, although it may occasionally be loosened to permit winding of weave under the tension bar. To change the woof strand, weave the end into the last line and insert a new thread.

Simple Tapestry Weaving

Looms may be purchased or constructed. An elementary loom may be made from the end of an orange crate with the depressed section removed. A small picture frame will serve equally well. The loom should be sandpapered to a smooth finish. Drive in small brads approximately 1/2 inch apart at one end. The tapestry will be about 3/4 of an inch smaller than the inside measurement of the loom. A design must now be created. Since curved lines cannot be woven, the design must consist of only straight lines. Transfer the design to colored paper, cut it out, and cement it on heavy paper.

The loom is strung with strong warp strands. Secure the warp around the first brad and wind it tightly around the loom, with two threads in line with each nail. There should be an odd number of threads. The best method is to wind the warp completely around the loom. This will assure a secure warp. By double warping, a tapestry may be woven on each side of the loom. The two may then be cut apart when the work is completed. The warp must be under sufficient tension to maintain tautness. Tie the warp thread around the last brad.

A variety of needles may be used as shuttles. They may be of wood or of the heavy type used in furniture upholstery work. Insert the design behind the warp, where it will remain secured in position by the back threads. Approximately eight lines of warp should be woven in an alternating over-and-under pattern before beginning the design. As the weaving commences, it should be beaten to ensure evenness and firmness. A medium-weight yarn can be used for the woof. The design may be woven first, and the background filled in afterward. It is advisable to weave the

[1]Spencer Moseley, Pauline Johnson, and Hazel Koenig, *Crafts Design* (Belmont, Calif.: Wadsworth Publishing Company, Inc., 1962), pp 130-139, 144-145, 173-177, 188-193.

entire project line by line. When filling in one color next to another, where vertical lines are being shown, the two woof strands must pass over the same warp thread. Several small needles threaded with all the colors being used should be kept handy so that the woof threads remain unbroken until each color segment is finished.

Basketry as Weaving

Although natural plant reeds are available and can be gathered for use, it is to commercial reed that most people turn when basketry is considered for crafts. Commercial availability and convenience permit a wide range of reeds to be selected. Thus, flat and round strands of different widths and diameters are readily accessible. Commercial reeds frequently come in skeins and are typically dry and, therefore, brittle. However, soaking the reeds in water makes them pliable and easy to handle. Working strands of reed should be bundled into a loose coil before soaking. When preparing for use as spokes or handles reed may be cut to short lengths before soaking. The reeds should be kept damp through the application of moist cloths.

Basketry is sufficiently different from flat weaving to have some terms with which the potential craftsman should become familiar. The "base" is the solid or woven core around and on which the basket will be developed. From the base there protrude "spokes." The spokes may be made by inserting several strands of reed through other strands when the base is woven. Spokes always lie flat and radiate from the center of the base. Reeds which are inserted into a solid base and stand vertically are called "stakes."

Round Bases   Using pliable reeds, select eight which will be used for the base. Slit four of the reeds slightly to the left and right of the center of each read so that the cuts are capable of accommodating transverse reeds. The other four reeds are then inserted into the lengthwise openings. Align these four spokes so that they touch on the edges. When these eight reeds are arranged properly, they should form a symmetrical cross. The weaving process is initiated around these eight reeds.

To begin the weaving, take a thinner reed strand than was used for the spokes and loop it around one of the cross arms so that the ends of the strand are free. Push the strand close to the midsection of the cross. Weave the two free ends around the next cross arm so that one end goes over the spokes while the other goes under the same spokes. Cross the ends and weave them around the third cross arm. Continue this procedure until the working reed has run about four lines. Finish this core weave by tucking the working strands over or under the next arm. The base is enlarged by pairing the cross strands. Instead of having two cross pieces of four strands apiece, each bar will be divided into pairs so that eight spokes will emerge. This is accomplished in the same way that the core was created. Weave reed ends over and under these pairs until the spokes are held securely in place.

Now, the paired spokes must be divided to provide single spokes. This is achieved by separating the double strands and weaving around the

Figure 13-10 BASKET WEAVING

Materials: reeds of appropriate length, wooden base (if necessary).

1. Slit four reeds slightly to the left and right of center and insert four transverse reeds.
2. Loop a weaving reed around one cross arm, pass one end over the next four, and pass the other end under the same four. Continue this procedure until all cross arms are secure. Tuck the working strands over or under the next arm.
3. Divide the four arms into eight pairs by looping a weaving reed around two strands and following step 2.
4. Divide the pairs again by looping a weaving reed around one strand and following step 2 to obtain sixteen spokes.
5. Bend the spokes upward and weave a working reed over and under each spoke.
6. Continue the weaving process until the desired height is reached.

individual spokes until the base is of the size desired. It will be circular in shape and may be completed by finishing the edge. The edge can be finished by weaving each spoke around the other spokes or by bending each spoke and inserting the end into the base weave so that a series of closed curves are presented to view.

Oval or Oblong Bases   The oblong base may be made with any number of reeds, but eight are generally used. Lay four reed strands side by side. Take

WEAVING, SEWING,
AND HOOKING

four shorter strands and slice the center section so that the longer strands may be inserted through them. Make sure that the shorter strands are well spaced and not touching at all. The weaving process is now begun by taking a thinner working reed and looping it around one bar of the lengthwise reeds. This strand is then crossed and each end is woven under and over each of the shorter width reeds and then all four of the lengthwise reeds on each side. Two lines of tight weaving should suffice to secure the core of the base.

As the weaving continues, separate the groups of reeds into individual spokes, drawing the spokes farther apart with each line of weaving. This will produce an oval shape. When the base has attained the desired size the edges may be finished as previously described.

Solid Bases Plywood bases of almost any shape, but usually round, may be purchased commercially or they may be handcrafted. The commercial bases generally have drilled holes into which the vertical reeds or stakes are pushed. When the height of the sides has been decided, weaving may commence. The sides of the basket are an extension of the base. Almost any weaving design may be utilized for constructing sides. Stakes may be made by inserting reeds of a specific length into the edges of the base and bending them so that they rise perpendicular to the base. Of course, such reeds must be pliable when bent. Another method is to insert the stakes through the woven matting of the base. These underbase stakes may themselves be woven by first bending one down and weaving it around the next three adjacent stakes. Continue this procedure until all under stakes are intertwined. Any excess reed may then be clipped off for an even finish.

A variety of weaves may be used on the sides. Close weaving, which includes alternate under-and-over patterns, may be combined with open work. One form of simple weaving which is used to give shape to the rising sides is called "waling." Waling requires three strands of reed. Position two strands on opposite sides of a stake; cross them and then bend them around the next stake. Repeat this procedure for one row. The third strand is then insinuated into the previous pattern by threading it over the top of the two crossed strands, then in front of the two next stakes, then under the next cross, and so on.

Sewing

Sewing is the attachment of one piece of material to another by means of inserting flexible fiber (thread) through the materials to be joined. The implement used for passing the thread through material is a needle. Needles are generally made of steel and have a pointed end for quick penetration and an eye at the opposite end so that the thread may be passed through and secured. Almost any material can be sewn if it can be penetrated by the needle and if the thread can maintain the attachment of closure. Sewing may be simple or complex, depending upon the need, the project contemplated, and the skill and artistic sense of the sewer. Sewing may be very practical, producing useful items, or it may have no utilitarian value, but great artistic or aesthetic value.

Stitches

A variety of stiches are used in sewing, and each one is useful for certain purposes. Among the stiches are:

1   Basting stitch: A large straight-line stitch used to temporarily hold material in place until a finer and more permanent stitch may be used. Basting stitches are removed after the project is finished.
2   Running stitch: A tiny straight line stitch used for seams which are not put under any strain. The needle is passed through the material and back again, taking up a very small amount of material for each stitch.
3   Gathering or shirring stitch: This stitch is performed as for running stitches. After the thread is knotted, fill the needle with stitches and draw them back on the thread. After all the material which is to be shirred is on the thread, pull the thread to the desired length and secure.
4   Overcasting stitch: This stitch is used to secure a rough edge. If two pieces are to be attached, baste them in position and take stitches over the seam edge, holding the needle in a slanted position. All stitches must be of the same length.
5   Whipping stitch: A shallow overcasting stitch. Using the same kind of stitch as in overcasting, make smaller stitches closer together.

Without stitches there could be no needlecraft. Stitching is the technique by which thoughts, plans, and art may be transmitted to fabric. Stitches are selected because they suit the design. There are a variety of stitches which can be used in almost any given piece of needlework; however, there are some stitches that are admirably suited to the theme being worked upon. All stitches will attach one surface to another or permit the development of some idea with the insertion of thread through fabric; but a stitch becomes eminently appropriate for use when it expresses or reflects absolutely the subject to be worked. For this reason the craftsman must have a good knowledge of the stitches which are available and the skill to use and select the right one for the subject matter at hand. There are literally hundreds of stitches which can be used for needlecraft. A few examples should serve to indicate the variety of techniques available.

The Satin Stitch   The satin stitch is composed of a number of flat stitches laid side by side in close parallel lines. Satin stitches should not be long. When a surface is broken up and worked in flat satin, the change of direction of the threads causes an interesting play of light upon the color.

Roumanian Stitch   The Roumanian stitch makes an excellent filling for a broad stem or border. There are several variations of this stitch, but fundamentally it consists of one long stitch tied down by a shorter one taken across it. The tying-down stitch may be taken either at right angles or as an oblique transverse. To make the stitch, take the thread through at the top left-hand area of the space to be covered. Pass it through to the

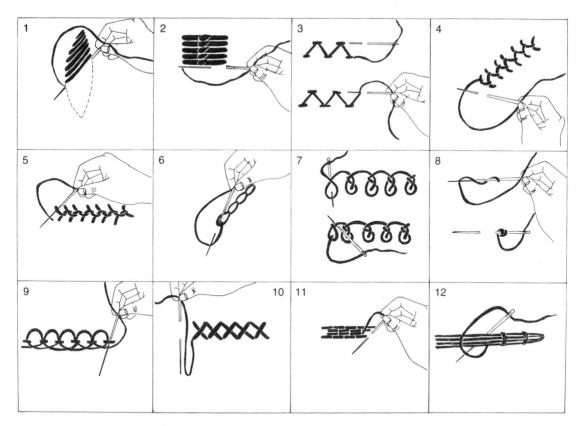

Figure 13-11 DIFFERENT STITCHES
1. Satin
2. Roumanian
3. Chevron
4. Feather
5. Looped
6. Chain
7. Rosette chain
8. French knot
9. Pekinese
10. Cross
11. Chain border
12. Couching

back and bring the needle out again slightly in front of the center, and above the half-worked stitch. Pass it to the back, below the stitch now laid upon the surface. For the next stitch, pass the thread through to the surface upon the left-hand side, just below where it emerged originally. Always bring the transverse stitch through the middle of the crossing stitch above.

Chevron Stitch The chevron stitch, as its name suggests, is a series of inverted V's used chiefly for borders. To work the stitch pass the thread through on the lower line, insert the needle approximately 1/8 inch to the right of the start, and press it through to the surface slightly above and at the midpoint of the stitch in progress. Thereafter, pass the needle at the upper edge to the right, and bring it through to the surface a little to the left of the point where entrance was just made. Then take the needle to the back, slightly to the right and bring it to the front again at the midpoint of the stitch. Continue the process by taking alternate stitches at the upper and lower lines as previously described.

Looped Stitches   Looped stitches are deviations of flat stitches where the flat stitch is pulled out and forced into a loop by another passing across it. Among the loop stitches is the feather stitch. The feather is formed in several ways and is appropriate for carrying outlines. It may also be profitably used for executing any type of light all-over pattern upon some background. To work the stitch, pass the thread through at the top of the left-hand pattern and throw the working thread to the right. Insert the needle slightly higher than the starting point, and push it through a little below. Pull the needle through over the working thread. Each new stitch should begin at a point opposite the middle of the last one completed.

The looped stitch is useful for light filling for a leaf or broad line. To initiate, draw the thread through at the right-hand end of whatever edges are used at the midpoint. Push the needle on the upper line and slightly to the left of the starting point and work it through again on the lower line directly below. The needle should never be permitted to pierce the ground stuff underneath while looping through the thread.

Chain Stitch   Chain stitching is most generally used for the execution of solid filling. Almost all the historical embroidery of value was carried out in this technique. The chain stitch is especially well suited to the execution of curved or spiral lines. For each successive stitch the needle picks up a small piece of ground material, about equal in size to the stitch, each time penetrating where it last emerged and keeping scrupulously to the prepared line. If the stitch is performed correctly, a neat series of back stitches should appear on the reverse side.

Rosette Chain Stitch   The rosette chain is useful for working small flowers. For a sophisticated finish to collar or cuff, to edge a circle, or for executing upon the edge of a band design, it is most appropriate. To perform the stitch, push the needle through at the right-hand end of the line to be followed. Pass the thread across to the left side and hold it on the material with the left thumb. Pass the needle through the ground and draw the thread through over the loop. Pass the needle under the thread and continue the process until the line is completed.

Knotted Stitches   The knotted stitches form a special group which has particular use for solid fillings. The irregular texture that the knotted stitch develops on the surface of the material sewn provides a distinct contrast to the evenness of the flat stitches. Among the most typical of the knotted stitches is the French knot. Correctly made knots are neat and taut. French knots are frequently used to depict the center of flowers and, as such, are massed together. Separate knots are also utilized for decoration. To begin a French knot, pass the thread through at the desired point. Hold it tautly between thumb and forefinger of the left hand, approximately 1-1/2 inches from the initial point of emergence. Allow the point of the needle to be doubly entwined as in Figure 13-11 and while retaining tension upon the thread, rotate the needle until the point is close to where the thread first appeared. Draw the needle and thread through the twists to the back of the material. The finished knot should resemble a bead standing on end upon the material.

Composite Stitches A large number of stitches belong to the group known as composites. Usually two or more stitches are necessary to their formation. The base stitch lays the foundation and the over stitch is often a surface interlacing for decorative or stress purposes. Among the composite stitches the Pekinese is justly noted. This stitch is frequently used for working complete embroideries. It makes an excellent line or outline stitch. To make the stitch, a line of close back stitches must be made. The thread is then drawn through this foundation. The lower portion of each loop is pulled fairly tight, although for clarity the illustration indicates loose loops. All or any succeeding lines should be executed closely above the first. The adaptability of this stitch for working with difficult thread, such as metallic substances, is apparent.

Cross Stitch Perhaps the most familiar and widely used of canvas stitches is the cross stitch. It can be used for fine or coarse work and is most applicable when double-thread canvas is used as the ground. To work the cross stitch, the thread is drawn through the ground and the needle emerges on a straight line slightly to the left of the point of entry. The needle is inserted down and to the right directly opposite the starting point. The thread is drawn on a slant to the right. The needle is then passed directly to the left and emerges below and directly opposite the second point of entry. The thread is carried under the ground while the needle penetrates the material up and to the right of the original point of entry. The needle is inserted underneath and brought up at the lower right-hand corner, carried around and inserted at the upper left-hand corner, and emerges again at the lower left-hand corner.

Chain Border Stitch Among the variety of drawn fabric stitches is the chain border stitch. Such stitching is used in white embroidery. To execute the stitch, begin by bringing the needle through at the point indicated in Figure 13-11. Turn and reverse the material because the stitch is made from left to right. Pass the working thread to the back four threads in front, and permit it to emerge on the line below: two threads closer to the point of origin. The action of the needle indicates the technique involved. Constant repetition on one line or the other completes the process. When the work is finished in one section, reverse the material so that the stitch may continue in the left-to-right pattern.

Couching The tying down of one or more threads upon material by means of another thread is couching. Some threads are too rough, too fragile, or too delicate to be drawn continuously through the ground material. Therefore, couching has developed. The chief problem with couching is to execute the fastening stitch secure enough to do the job without spoiling the appearance of the surface. Ordinary couching is used for solid fillings, outline work, applied edging, and so on. Most forms of couching require a frame for ease of handling. When clusters of threads are couched down together, they are frequently laid loosely on the material and the securing thread is pulled tightly. Many stitches can be utilized for tying down surface threads. One couching technique is simply securing threads by means of a single traverse stitch. The simplest method of tying a single thread or clusters of threads to material is to pass a working thread in and out of the material across the laid threads. The fastening thread may be of contrasting color or material, and it may occur at varying intervals or in some repetitious pattern.

Now that a variety of stitches have been explained and illustrated, the application of stitchery to different situations might be feasible. Surely the dressmaker's craft is the widest form of use for needlework, whether of machine origin or the painstaking effort of a seamstress, but this volume is not designed, to offer, nor is it capable of offering, instruction in this area. Rather, we merely suggest a couple of areas in which crafts groups may profitably experiment.

Quilting

Among the more pleasurable social crafts activities which have been traditional in the United States and elsewhere is the quilting bee. During long winters, when frozen rivers and high drifting snow did not permit travel, families would gather about the central fireplace of the home and sort through various pieces of cloth. Putting them together in interesting patterns or with no pattern at all provided the participant with a recreational activity that was diverting, satisfying, promoted conversation, and still enabled the creative person to exhibit special talent and inventive ideas.

For any patchwork quilt, select fabric scraps of the same type and weight. The pieces in each figure can be all different or show color variations. To design the quilt, cut two squares of cardboard and mark the desired figure on each one. Each square is approximately 12-1/2 inches. Leave one whole to show the design and cut the other up to use as a pattern. Cut out pieces of fabric around cardboard patterns, allowing about 1/4 inch on all edges. Sew the pieces into squares and press the seams open. Embroider over the seams on the right side with six-strand embroidery floss in a herringbone or other stitch. For cotton quilts, use two to three strands of floss. Join completed squares into strips with 1/4-inch seams and embroider over the seams in the same decorative stitch. Connect crosswise strips of squares and embroider seams. For the lining of a double size quilt, cut two pieces of fabric 40 X 104 inches; for the border, cut two pieces 4 X 80 inches and two pieces 4 X 104 inches. Join lining pieces with a 1/2-inch seam and press. Sew border pieces to squares with 1/2-inch seams, mitering corners. Place the lining wrong side up on a flat surface and spread two layers of batting over it, trimming wherever necessary. Press the quilt top carefully and place it over the batting, right side up. Turn under 1/2-inch seam on the lining and quilt top edges and fasten together. Baste to keep batting in place. Whipstitch the lining and quilt edges. For decorative purposes, quilt along ornamental square edges, gathering in all thicknesses.

Appliqué
Appliqué is a technique which fastens pieces of a fabric to a ground. Almost any material can be used. Fastening may be done by sewing, pasting, or tacking. For the crafts instructor, there are unlimited opportunities to introduce appliqué work to youngsters as well as to the more mature individual. Children enjoy sewing if exposed to the process at an early age. In fact, young boys show a remarkable aptitude for it. All that is required are large quantities of scrap materials of various colors, sizes, and textures. Because applique is concerned with two-dimensional shapes, preliminary designs can be worked out with drawings, paintings, or colored paper before the actual cutting and sewing are undertaken.

Instruction should encourage spontaneity, surprise, and the ideas which come to mind as the work continues. Themes for appliqué may be derived from fantasy, history, everyday life, books that have been read, schoolwork, or any of the myriad ideas which contemporary life urges upon the individual. Environmental concerns and objects in their natural state may all serve as stimuli for this craft. When the design has been decided upon, pieces of fabric representative of the spaces in the design are chosen and cut to size. Initially, the pieces of stuff are tacked onto the ground and then sewed securely in place. Even at this stage, the instructor should encourage modifications of the basic scheme and changes in texture, color, and stitching if the student is so inclined.

HOOKING
Hooking employs a tool with a curved end to draw and press flexible material alternately in and out through some background material. It permits the combined use of weaving and stitchery and offers the participant an opportunity to experience the joy and satisfaction of creating a unique piece of work which is a delight to the eye as well as to the sense of touch. Arranging color, pattern, and texture in a satisfactory design challenge the ingenuity and technical skill of the craftsman. Hooking is simple enough to be performed by a child, yet its advanced forms require the greatest skill and talent of the artist. A variety of products from rugs to wall hangings of intricate design and great beauty may be produced in a range of textures from shag to sculptural effects.

Hooking requires a fabric to be pulled and pushed alternately through a ground. Two fundamental techniques are utilized in hooking. One uses a backing of burlap or other such material and a hooked tool; the second employs the loop latch hook and a backing material of scrim. Generally,

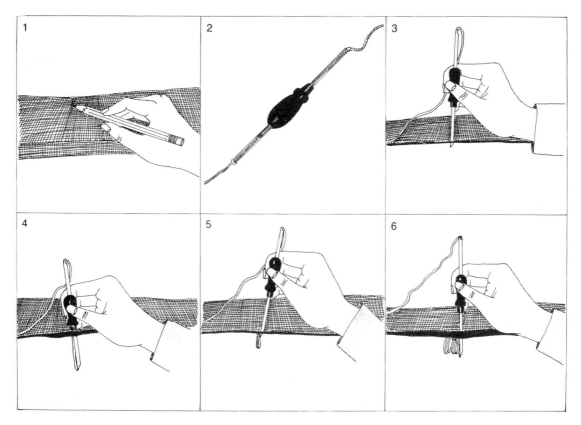

Figure 13-12   HOOKING

Materials: burlap, yarn, hooking tool, pencil, scissors.

1. Lay out design on ground.
2. Thread punch needle.
3. Insert needle into ground.
4. Push needle through ground.
5. Make pile loop beneath ground.
6. Repeat hooking process until completed.

the former method is preferred. In the hook-and-burlap method, yarn or other material is held underneath the ground with one hand; the hooked tool is inserted through the ground and catches the yarn which is then drawn up into a loop at the top. The process is repeated until ten or twelve strands have been pulled up. The hooking must be done in such a manner that the loops are tightly bunched together to prevent their being pulled out. Of necessity, each loop should be at the same height. Different yarns or fibers may be used to create a mixture of colors, piles, and textures which adds to the effect.

Among the tools used for hooking are the punch needle, shuttle hooker, and hand hook. A crocheting needle may also be used advantageously. When a rug is to be hooked, a design should be made. Burlap is stretched on a frame (which may be constructed or purchased commercially) and secured with tacking so that it remains taut. The design should then be transferred to the burlap with charcoal, paint, dye, colored paper, or chalk.

To use the punch needle, pass the yarn through the eye of the tool and through the inside point. Pull approximately 12 inches of yarn through the needle; then draw the yarn back with sufficient tension so that it will slowly slide into the tube and handle. Set the loop gauge for the desired loop length. Slant the needle in the direction the hooking will incline. Press the needle through the backing until it meets the handle. Keep the hand holding the tool firmly on the backing. Draw the needle to the surface and smoothly move from loop to loop. Continue the procedure as the clustering loops now secure one another in place. When all sections of the design have been completed, remove the material from the frame. Fold the edge back and apply appropriate stitching for an even and neat finish.

The second method of hooking employs a scrim background and the loop latch hook. Since scrim is a stiffened material, there is no need for a frame. The design should be transferred to the scrim before the hooking is started. The loop latch hook actually knots the yarn into the backing. The desired length of yarn for this technique is about 2 inches. Enough threads should be cut and piled so that at least one section of the design may be completed before more yarn must be cut to size. Join the two ends of yarn so that a loose loop is formed and hold together between the fingers. Insert the loop latch through the loop and under one strand of scrim. Draw the two ends of the yarn up to the tip of the hook and position them between the hook and latch. Close the latch and draw the tool back through the scrim and through the first loop. Continue to hold the ends of the yarn so that a knot is formed. Repeat this procedure while making sure that the loops are close together.

NATURE CRAFTS FROM NATURAL MATERIALS 14

Naturecrafts have traditionally been associated with camping activities. But these simple crafts suggestions are but a few of literally thousands of crafts ideas which can be programmed and offered to those who are interested in basic crafts forms. Most outdoor settings, whether at school or camp, furnish many natural materials that can be used for crafts purposes. Such materials may be utilized for individual needs or may contribute to overall community satisfaction. Nature souvenirs from the woods or seashore are valuable as gifts or as remembrances of happy times.

EASY PROJECTS

Among the various plants that can be gathered and used for crafts purposes are freshwater rushes. These may be used in making mats, flat bags, and chair seats. Normally, rushes are best obtained in August and hung out to dry, cut end up, in a storage area away from light. Dried rushes will keep indefinitely. When rushes are being utilized for any crafts project, they should be dampened so that they may be worked. Mats may be woven on any flat surface. The easiest weave is an under-and-over pattern, although more intricate patterns can be attempted, depending on the craftsman's level of skill.

Willow withes, stems of bittersweet, honeysuckle, goldenrod, and splints of maple, hickory, and white oak can be used for crafting baskets. Rough twig baskets are decorative. Even cured corn husks may be the raw material out of which baskets may be fashioned.

Wherever birch trees grow, there are likely to be fallen branches or logs from which a variety of useful articles may be made. Thin sheets of birch serve as writing paper; small holders can be made by cutting a rectangular piece of birch and folding the ends. The ends are held together with string or twigs. Decorations may be made by exposing the underlayers of bark. A 4-inch section of a birch log can be turned into a candle holder if an appropriate size hole is drilled part way through the middle of the section. The item may then be sanded and shellacked.

Along the seashore one may sometimes discover various materials which can be put to crafts use. Oddly shaped driftwood may serve as ornaments; with a small amount of shaping by carving, an abstract form becomes more familiar to the viewer and thereby more satisfying.

Many species of trees and nuts which can be gathered offer the craftsman innumerable opportunities to convert raw material into useful and/or artistic creations. Sawing thin cross sections of branches, large pits, or nuts and then carefully sanding them so that the natural grain is fully revealed is the first step in making earrings, brooches, buttons, pendants, or pins. These objects may be mounted on wood or metal backings or worn from leather thongs or other stringed arrangements.

Shells offer an almost infinite variety of uses. Large seashells may be used as utensils, candle holders, dishes, cookingware, etc. Small shells, dried sea horses, starfish, and other debris usually found along the shore may be used to construct decorative arrangements for the table or home. Such natural arrangements are limited only by the creativity of the individual who puts them together.

Seed pods, acorns, small fungi, hemlock cones, and seeds from watermelons, pumpkins, or sunflowers can be utilized for a variety of ornaments or decorations. Pins, necklaces, buttons, or bouquets can be the end product when these items are pierced and strung together. Flowers, place cards, centerpieces and other imaginative settings may be arranged when these natural materials are glued together, combined with pipe cleaners, or drilled and strung. Almost any of these things may be colored with natural dyes made from berry juice or other plants, clays, or ores. The outer skin of the yellow onion makes an excellent yellow dye.

Candles can be made from bayberries. Berries are collected, washed, and then boiled. The melted wax derived from this process is then skimmed off and collected in a tin can which is heated by means of a double-boiler process. The pith of the common rush, gathered during the summer, may be used as wicking. The pith is most easily removed immediately after the rushes are harvested. Two pins are pushed through the center of the blossom end and crisscrossed. The blossom end is held while the two pins are forced to the bottom of the rush, separating the peel from the pith. Holding the pith so that it dangles from one hand, dip the wicking into the molten wax so that layers are formed to build up into a candle.

Natural dyestuffs offer a wonderful opportunity for experimentation. With the current fad for tie dying, here is an excellent chance to do what comes naturally. Fruits, berries, roots, leaves, hulls, bark, flowers, and nuts are all possible sources for dyes. However, it is necessary to develop mor-

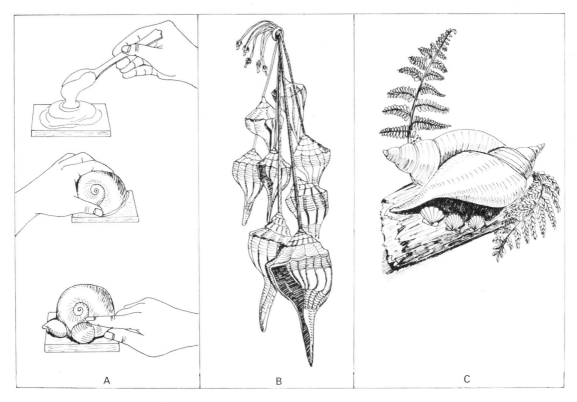

Figure 14-1   SHELL CRAFTS
Materials: wooden base 1/2 x 3 x 4 inches, plaster of Paris, spoon, pan, water, shells, string, reed, yarn, driftwood, ferns, leather thongs, glue.

A.   1. Mix a batch of plaster of Paris and spread on wooden base.
    2. Place large shell on congealing plaster.
    3. Place various shells in different attitudes for effect.
    4. Allow plaster to set.

B.   1. String a variety of conch or other notable shells together with string, yarn, or leather thongs.
    2. Attach string to top of shell with glue.
    3. Knot strands together with a simple knot.
    4. Knot ends.

C.   1. Mix a batch of plaster of Paris and spread on driftwood base.
    2. Place large shells or shell on congealing plaster.
    3. Place various shells in different attitudes for effect.
    4. Place fern ends in plaster to enhance aquatic effect.
    5. Allow plaster to set.

dants which act to fix the resultant dye because some dyes have a tendency to fade out in sunlight or at the first washing. To make mordants, make separate saturated solutions of soda, salt, and alum. Soak several strips of cotton cloth in each of these solutions for at least two hours, and then squeeze excess fluid out and hang up to dry. Soak other strips in light vinegar, squeeze, and hang up. Each strip should be labled so that precise colors may be guaranteed for future use.

    Collect whatever berry or root is to be used for the base of the dye

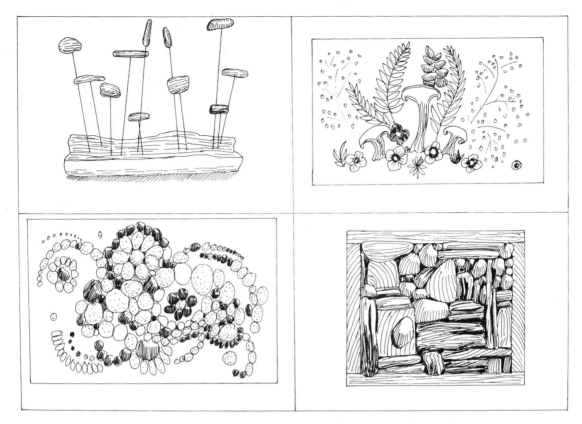

Figure 14-2 VARIOUS ARRANGEMENTS OF NATURAL OBJECTS

and brew it. Let the brew come slowly to a boil and maintain boiling for one-half hour. The resulting dye should be strained. One of the mordanted samples may then be dipped in the dye. Dip the material several times, letting it get air between dips. Rinse the material in cold water until bleeding has ceased and then hang to dry. The outcome should be very colorful.

Clay is a natural product that may be collected from lake or stream beds or from excavations. Although clay may be found in almost any color, it is usual to see it as buff, gray, terra cotta, or olive green. Sometimes clay is found almost entirely free of foreign matter, but if small objects are embedded in it these should be removed. Once this initial cleaning is performed, the clay is set aside to age or dry in the air for several days. When it is dry, it must be broken into powder. The powdered clay is then placed into a pail or tub, covered with water, and allowed to soak until it is soft enough to be stirred. After stirring, the resultant thick liquid should be poured through a coarse and then a fine filter to remove any foreign matter. Permit the mixture to stand until the clay settles to the bottom of the container. When all the clay has settled, pour off the water, spread the clay out to dry, and permit to stand until most of the excess water has evaporated. The clay is now ready for use.

The suggestions offered above are a mere sampling of what can be offered in the way of naturecrafts from natural materials. Projects that untrained hands may undertake with materials easily obtained abound. Here there will be no attempt to provide an exhaustive series of projects, but rather to illustrate the possibilities that are available to anyone who has any interest. Many simple offerings will be made to stimulate interest in the fascinating realm of naturecrafts. There will be some overlapping of crafts activities with other forms which have been presented in detail, but this only serves to point out the ease with which natural objects can be adapted to the most intricate crafts activities.

Spore Prints

To make a spore print, cut a mushroom from its stem, close to the gills. Coat a hard-surfaced sheet of paper with gum arabic. Place the mushroom cap, gill side down, on the paper and cover with a dish to prevent air currents from moving the spores as they drop from the gills. A perfect reproduction of gills will be made if ordinary precautions are taken. Since fungi may be identified from their gills, collections have biological value as well as offering participation in a satisfying craft.

Fungi Etchings

Some of the bracket fungi are very suitable for etching. The common fungus that is typically found extending horizontally from the trunks of trees has a surface texture which indicates its years of growth. Its coloring ranges from gray to brown, tan, and ochre. The undersurface is creamy white, and it is this surface which can be etched. Almost any sharpened instrument may be used for making a design. The design will be indelibly drawn in against the unetched background and will keep indefinitely. Fungus must be handled carefully, because every pressure or scratch mark will show up on the sensitive undersurface. In order to construct fungus bookends, etch the fungus and then dry it. When the fungus is completely dried, saw the edge of the fungus at right angles. The flat edge may then be screwed to any flat base. The underside of the fungus becomes the outside of the bookends, facing away from the books.

Fungi Ornaments

The shell-like polyphore fungus can be arranged to form a flower with an acorn or small evergreen cone as its center. The polyphore fungus comes in a variety of colors including gray, green, violet, and some white. The fungi can be made into table wreath decorations or lapel rosettes. Whether the fungi will become a table decoration, place mat, rosette, or wall hanging simply depends upon the number gathered and the intent of the designer. To make the fungus ornament, one only needs a base, some needle and thread, and a discerning eye.

First cut a disk or other geometric pattern from cardboard. For absolute naturalness, a base of bark may be used. The base provides the outline to which the fungi will be attached. With needle and thread, sew on one polyphore with several firm stitches. The next polyphore should be

NATURE CRAFTS
FROM NATURAL
MATERIALS

337

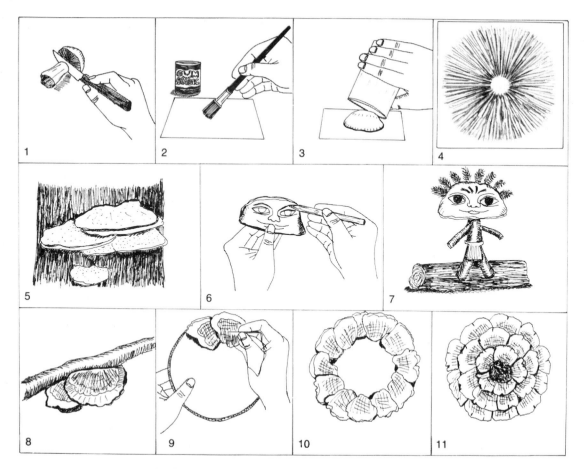

Figure 14-3 SPORE PRINTS, FUNGI SCULPTURE, FUNGUS ORNAMENTS

Materials: Exacto knife or pen knife, glue, brush, sheet of white paper, needle, thread, scissors, cardboard, acorns, twigs of various lengths and size, drinking glass, pine cone, fungi, toadstool.

1. Cut mushroom from stem at cap.
2. Coat paper with gum Arabic.
3. Place mushroom cap on paper and cover with dish.
4. Finished spore print.
5. Obtain bracket fungi.
6. Etch design on fungus.
7. Finished sculpture.
8. Obtain polyphore fungi.
9. Place overlapping fungi on circular cardboard base.
10. Sew fungi to base.
11. Finished flower.

sewn on by overlapping the first a little. By using this method the entire periphery of the base is covered. Just inside this initial border, an inner fungi line is begun and completed in the same way. Depending upon the size of the ornament, there may be a need for more inner lines. When these lines are completed, there will be a small central space open. To complete the ornament, sew a pine cone or other berry or nut into the center.

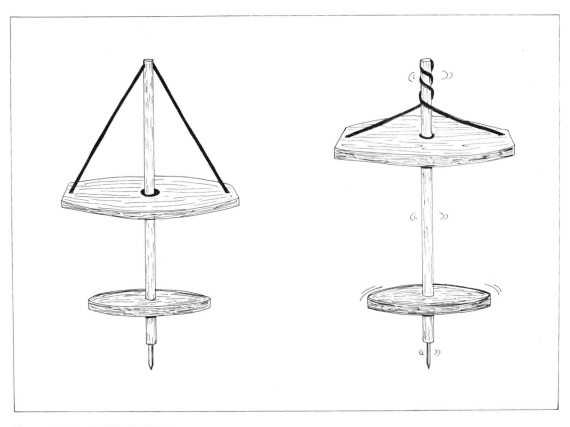

Figure 14-4 NATURAL DRILL
Materials: one dowel 1/2 x 16 inches, one piece of wood approximately 7 inches square, one piece of wood 1/2 x 12 inches, a drill and bit, rawhide thong, glue.

The polyphore fungi become dry and brittle after collection. They should be kept moist so they may be worked. Care must be taken not to wet them too much or they will tear. Almost any pattern may be cut out to serve as a base, thus providing an infinite source of designs which can be continued with as many varicolored fungi as can be gathered. Since the fungi grow in great profusion, the collector has a large stock from which to make selections.

Pump Drills

A pump drill can be manufactured easily for fire making or drilling any natural material. This versatile tool requires few materials and can prove invaluable to the camper or craftsman.

To construct a pump drill, take a dowel 1/2 X 16 inches or longer and roughly sharpen one end. Then bore a hole about 3/16 inch in diameter 1/2 inch from the opposite end. Cut a circular piece of wood about 5 or 6 inches in diameter, and bore a hole in its center to fit the dowel. Shape a crossbar from another piece of wood so that it is tapered toward the ends. Its dimensions should be approximately 1/2 X 2 X 11 inches and about 1 inch wide at the ends. Bore holes 3/16 inch in diameter approximately 1 inch from each end. A hole 5/8 or 3/4 inch should be bored in the center of this wooden piece. Take a rawhide thong and tie a knot at the end of it. Then thread it up through one end of the crossbar, through the central vertical dowel, and down to within 1 inch of the circular wooden piece (wheel). Complete the sequence by carrying the thong through the hole at the other end of the crossbar and tie and knot it on the underside of the crossbar. Glue the wheel to the vertical dowel 3 inches from the pointed end.

The operation of the pump drill is quite simple and efficient. Holding the drill in a perpendicular position, with its sharpened end resting on a precut wooden slab into which a hole has been bored, spin the crossbar until it is wound to its highest possible position. With both hands on the crossbar, make a determined and quick downward stroke causing the thong first to unwind, then to rewind. Repeat this movement until there is a continuous rhythmic winding and unwinding of the thong. The drill should revolve smoothly and easily. Continuous rubbing produced by the motion of the drill will cause buildup of heat through friction. A spark should develop as a result of the activity. When the spark comes, let it drop into some very dry shredded cedar bark or other fuel. Gently blow it into a flame.

When the pump drill is utilized for boring holes in wood or shells when making bracelets, necklaces, or belts, the drill point may be made by driving a nail into the base of the dowel, after sawing off the sharpened end so that it is flat enough to receive the nail. The nail head may be either cut off with a hacksaw or filed off. The remaining exposed metal is then filed into a three-cornered point which becomes the bit of the drill.

A simple vise may be constructed to contain whatever is to be bored by splitting a thick stick half way, inserting the object to be drilled, and tying the open end securely with any fastening material.

Shell belts, bracelets, pendants, or necklaces may be made by boring holes at appropriate places in the shells and threading thongs through the holes. Seashells come in such variety and color that they may be crafted to produce exquisite jewelry.

Natural Baskets

A coil basket from spruce and willow products is a simple craft of attractive and durable design. Evergreen roots are collected in long strings, soaked in hot water, and then peeled. When the bark is removed, the roots are continually soaked so that they remain pliable for working. The bark of the willow is stripped and soaked to separate the inner bark from the outer. When the inner bark is removed, it is hung in strands until used.

The basket is made by wrapping the end of an evergreen root with the inner willow bark (see Figure 14-5). The wrapped end is bent back on itself as the willow bark is continuously wound around it. This process is continued while stitches are taken at regular intervals so that the coil remains fastened. When the base coil has reached a desired size, the side walls of the basket are formed by setting the side coil on top of the last base coil.

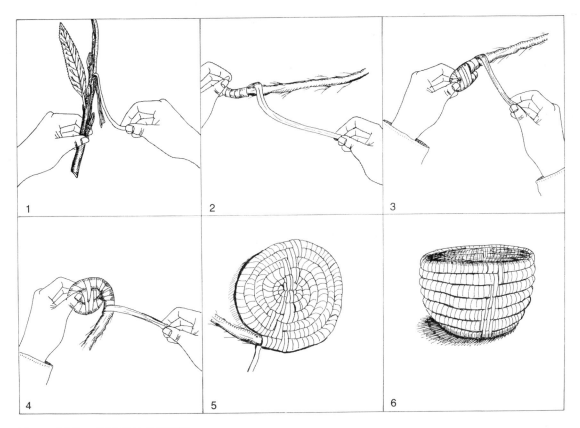

Figure 14-5 NATURAL BASKET
Materials: evergreen roots, water bucket, willow branches, needle, thread.

 1. Peel bark from roots.
 2. Wrap evergreen root with willow bark.
 3. Bend wrapped end back upon itself.
 4. Continue to wrap willow around root.
 5. Form circular base.
 6. Build sides by coiling.

Stitching is continued as before. The basket sides are gradually raised until the desired height has been attained.

Corn Husk Sandals

Corn husks should be gathered and dried carefully to prevent rotting. They should be bundled tightly together and kept in a dry place until used. Before using them, it may be necessary to soak them so that they become pliable for working.

Select husks and then fold and braid them together. When the strands become short, braid in longer ones. To estimate the needed length of the braid, coil the strand to determine the size of the sole. Once the husk braid has been finished, the sandal may be started. Fold one end of the braided husk back on itself. Once the core is formed by this method, the rest of the sandle sole is coiled around the core until completion. The coils should be

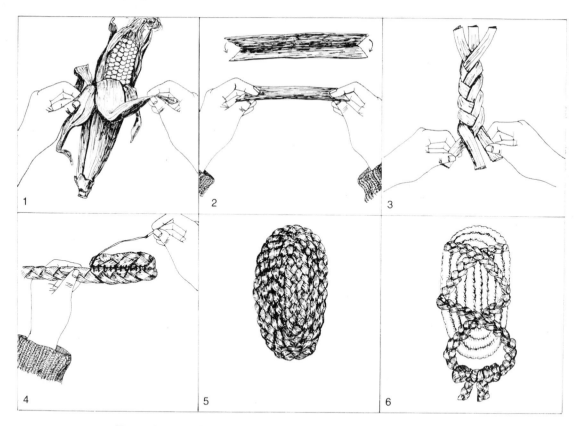

Figure 14-6   CORNHUSK SANDALS
Materials: cornhusks, needle, thread.
1. Collect corn husks.
2. Strip husks and fold.
3. Braid husks.
4. Bend husk back on itself and sew in place.
5. Continue coiling and sewing to necessary size.
6. Make braided sandal straps and attach.

stitched to each other as each coil is made. The coils are set flat against each other so that the edges form the top and bottom of the sole. Various shaped sandals may be made by shortening the central coil or beginning with a rounded coil and continuing until a satisfactory size is attained. All coils must be stitched together as they are formed.

Sandal straps are made of braided husks and are sewed to the sides of the sole in a crisscross pattern. The tie strands coming from the heel of the sandal must be long enough so that they can be tied around the ankle.

CANDLEMAKING
Candlemaking is an ancient art which still has great appeal to all ages. Children enjoy dipping or pouring candles.

Preparing the Wax   Paraffin is a very satisfactory substitute for candle wax. It is less expensive than candle wax and easier to obtain. Discarded candle ends also can be used in making new candles. Place the wax in a can and set the can in a pan of boiling water. Wax is extremely flammable and should be heated in a double boiler over a low heat. Heat the paraffin until it is melted. If old candles are used, melted wax should be strained through cheese cloth or old nylon hose to remove short lengths of wick and other impurities. Stearic acid can be added to liquid wax to prevent the finished candle from drooping at high room temperatures. It also increases the intensity of any color added to the wax.

Wicking   Wicking can be purchased from a hobby shop, department store, or made from chalk line or soft white string. Cut the chalk line or string into 6-yard lengths and soak overnight in a solution of 1 tablespoon of salt, 2 tablespoons of borax, and 1 cup of water. Hang the potential wicking up to dry. This treatment retards the rate at which the wick burns. Cut a piece of wick 2 inches longer than needed for the candle and dip it into the melted wax a few times. Hang the dipping up to dry, keeping the wick straight. The larger the candle, the heavier will be the wick required to prevent excessive dripping. Too heavy a wick will cause smoking. Two or more strands can be braided together to obtain the desired size wick.

Molds and Their Preparation   Almost any type of container can be used as a mold for casting wax candles. Waxed cardboard containers, plastic containers of all types, glass tumblers, mailing tubes, gelatin molds, and cones or other shaped paper cups all can be used as molds for casting liquid wax. It is important to remember, when selecting a mold, that solidified wax must be removed from a mold in one piece. If the mold is not to be destroyed, the opening must be at the largest point. All molds, except wax-coated paper containers, should be greased with colorless vegetable oil and chilled before pouring the heated wax into them.

The sides of a cardboard container should be supported with string before wax is poured so as to prevent buckling. When using a mold with an opening at both ends, seal the bottom end by pouring 1/4 inch of wax in a small plate. Set the mold in the puddle and allow it to solidify before filling the mold.

Inserting the Wick   The wick can be fastened in place before the wax is poured into the mold or it can be inserted after the wax has solidified. When using paper containers, plastic containers, and rubber molds, the material can be pierced to allow the wick to be inserted. A knot is tied at one end of the wick, while the other end is passed through the hole and tied to a stick placed across the opening of the mold.

For other molds, tie one end of the wick to a pencil or wooden dowel that is longer than the diameter of the opening. Fasten a small weight, such as a metal nut, to the other end of the wick so that it will hang down into the center of the mold.

The wick can be inserted into a solid candle by melting a hole in the center with a heated piece of metal. The metal may need to be heated several times to obtain the desired depth. The hole does not need to go all the way through, because the candle is usually burned only 2/3 of the way

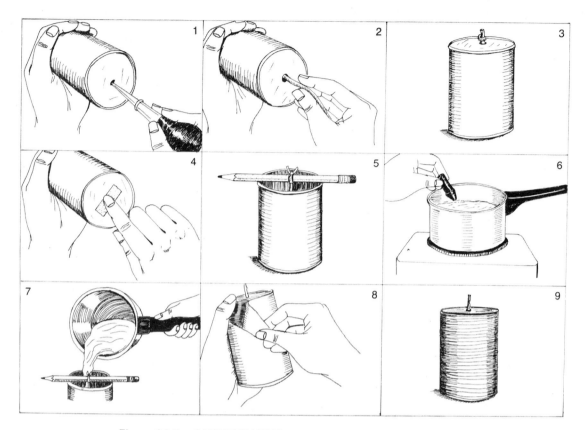

Figure 14-7   CANDLE MAKING

Materials: paraffin or candle ends, three large tin cans (juice cans), one large pan, water, old nylon hose, stearic acid, crayons, soft white string, salt, borax, pencil or thin dowel, metal nut, fork, metal punch, masking tape.

1.   Bore hole in bottom of cardboard mold.
2.   Insert wick.
3.   Knot wick.
4.   Seal knotted end.
5.   Tie opposite wick end to transverse pencil.
6.   Heat wax and add coloring.
7.   Pour melted wax into mold.
8.   Remove mold.
9.   Finished candle.

down. Thread the wick into the hole and pour a little melted wax around it. A hand or electric drill can be used to make a hole in the center of the wax candle for the wick.

Coloring the Wax   Each of the following can be used to add color: candle dye, artist's oil paints thinned with turpentine, powdered paint, powdered fabric dye, and old wax crayons melted down. One wax crayon will color about 1 quart of wax. A stronger color can be obtained by adding additional crayons. To color paraffin with the other materials, add the powder or liquid gradually to the melted paraffin, stirring until the desired depth of color is reached.

Pouring the Wax   Allow the wax to cool slightly before pouring it into a mold. Hold the container about 1 inch above the mold to prevent air bubbles from forming in the wax and marring the surface of the finished candle. Wax, as it cools in the mold, will shrink in the center. Additional wax can be added to the mold as the surface starts to solidify.

Removing the Mold   Care should be exercised when removing the candle from the mold. Tapping the mold may cause colored candles to whiten. Cardboard molds can be gently torn away from the candle, while other types of molds can be removed by placing them under hot running water. Care must be taken not to melt the wax, but only to loosen it from the mold. Cooling the wax in a refrigerator will also cause it to separate from the mold.

Dipped Candles   Select two large juice cans and remove the tops from both. Fill one with cold water and pour approximately 1 inch of hot water into the other one. Pour melted wax into the container with the hot water filling it to the top.

Tie a weight (metal nut) to one end of the wick. Dip the weighted end into the melted wax once or twice quickly while holding the other end. Lift the coated wick out of the wax and lower it into the cold water for a quick bath. The cold water is used to harden the wax swiftly in preparation for the next dipping. After the first dip or two, it is advisable to straighten out the wick by pulling on the weighted end. Between twenty and thirty dips are required to form a full-sized candle. When the desired size is obtained, the candle should be hung by the wick until the wax solidifies.

Floating Candles   Floating candles are easy to make. They can be made from melted used candle ends, because only a small amount of wax is required. Pour the melted wax into a gelatin mold, muffin tin, or any other shallow container of similar size. When the wax solidifies, remove it from the container and insert the wick.

Sand Mold Candles   A sand mold can be constructed to cast an unlimited number of different shaped candles. Pour sand into a pail until the pail is almost filled. Slowly add water to the sand until the sand can be molded. Scoop out some sand to form a depression; fingers, spoons, or sticks can be used to create an interesting form.

Tie one end of the wick to a stick that is longer than the diameter of the pail and allow the other end to extend the depth of the mold. Slowly pour the melted wax into the mold. After the wax solidifies, remove it from the sand and untie the wick from the stick.

Decorating the Candle   Melted wax that has cooled until a thin skin forms on the top can be whipped with an egg beater or fork until it becomes fluffy. Quickly apply the warm, whipped wax to the candle with a fork. Glitter can be sprinkled on the whipped wax while it is still soft. Sequins are fastened with straight pins or can be pushed into the soft wax.

Candles can be painted with colored wax. Hold the candle at an angle over a large pan to catch the drippings and with a pastry brush apply several coats of the desired color wax. Different colored wax drippings permitted to run down the sides of a candle will create an interesting effect. Hold the candle in an upright position over a pan and with a spoon drip the cool wax so that it will run down the surface. Keep turning the surfaces, allowing the drippings to cool after each application.

Solidified wax can be carved with some simple household tools, and soft wax can be molded into a wide variety of shapes. Flower petals and other decorations can be pressed from the wax while it is warm and pliable. The wax can be kept warm and workable by keeping it in a pan over hot water.

Multicolored candles are constructed by building up layers of different colored wax. Pour one color into a mold and allow to solidify before adding the next color. Scented candles are developed by adding a few drops of perfume, oil of pine, or any other scent to the melted wax. A special candle scent, in a wide variety of different odors, is available commercially.

WOODCRAFTS

This is not an exhaustive treatment of crafts which can be exemplified in wood. Rather, it is a selection of crafts activities which can be performed with one of the most common natural materials with very simple tools. It is not intended as an illustration of cabinetmaking, woodworking, furniture designing, or other complicated wood products fabrications. It is a general indication of how raw wood, in its natural state, can be utilized for a variety of crafts projects.

Whittling

Whittling is an old custom that requires only a pocket knife and any piece of wood at hand. Sometimes whittling is done solely for relaxation, and the whittler makes little shavings out of sticks, blocks, or chunks of wood. However, a wide variety of objects can be carved with a small knife and a piece of wood.

Almost any well-seasoned wood can be carved or whittled. Some woods are known for their softness and are well suited for beginners. Other woods are better known for color, texture, or grain. Some woods are very hard and, while long-lasting, are difficult to carve. Probably white pine is as good a wood as any with which to attempt whittling. It is soft, has little grain, and works well.

All whittling is performed with well-known knife cuts. The most typical of all is the full-hand grip. This cut quickly removes waste, but is difficult to control. Many whittlers guide the blade by placing their thumb along the back of the blade. The knife may be drawn toward the body with the thumb braced on the material. For stop cuts, the blade is guided by the forefinger. The stop cut is the single most important technique in whittling. Essentially, it is a deep vertical incision with or against the grain. It is utilized to restrict splintering of wood in an area from which material is to be removed.

Canes, letter openers, eating utensils, and similar objects can be whittled from saplings or branches and decorated by bark whittling. This con-

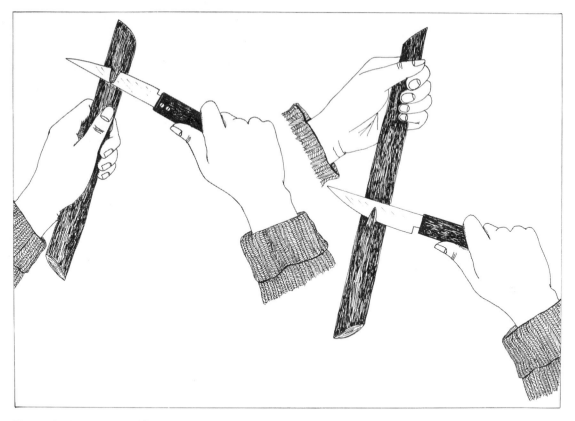

Figure 14-8 WHITTLING
Materials: any length of soft wood, jackknife or penknife.

sists of cutting away portions of the bark, exposing the wood underneath in some kind of design. Any tree with a smooth bark can be used. The branch should be permitted to dry for a few days before whittling is attempted. Oddly shaped pieces of wood can often be used for a variety of forms or grotesqueries by exaggerating the unusual shape of the branch. Driftwood is especially suitable for this type of whittling.

Bird Feeders
From tree trimmings, select several large sections of limbs. Drill several holes of varying sizes, although holes 1 inch in diameter and 1 inch deep will serve very well. After the section of the limb has been drilled insert screw eyes or other appropriate fasteners to which thongs, braided rushes, or willows can be tied for hanging purposes. Two to four fasteners should be used. Melt bayberry wax over low heat; while this is cooling, add to it bird seeds or other suitable food. When this mixture is quite thick, fill the holes in the limbs with it. This should be done while the mixture is still pliable. The feeder is now ready for hanging.

Hanging Flower Baskets
An attractive decoration for any human habitation is a hanging flower basket made from a section of well-seasoned wood. Baskets can be of al-

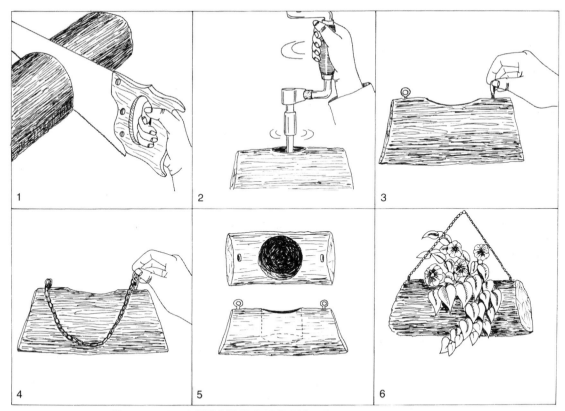

Figure 14-9   HANGING FLOWER BASKET

Materials: cut section of log, rough sandpaper, brace and bit, two screw eyes, length of chain.

1. Saw appropriate log.
2. Bore hole in log.
3. Insert screw eyes.
4. Attach chain.
5. Fill hole with soil and nutrients.
6. Finished product.

most any shape, depending upon the imagination of the carver and the measurements of the piece of wood. A section of log should be cut and the ends sanded to eliminate slivers. Drill a hole in the top of the log at least 3 inches deep and 3 inches wide. Fasten two screw eyes in such a position that the basket will hang straight, and attach a chain to the screw eyes to hang the basket from. Fill the hole with the kind of soil and nutrients that will promote growth, and plant whatever flower or vine is appropriate to the environment. Such flower baskets must be securely fastened so that they will not fall.

Log Stools

Seating is easy to construct when the individual is outdoors and has access to rough wood. Any good-sized log may be used for the seat, while the legs are smaller branches or tree limbs which have been chopped when the original tree was felled. With a few carpentering tools a commendable bench or stool can be easily constructed.

Select a log of appropriate length and four smaller pieces of wood. The log should probably be not less than 2 feet long and at least 6 inches wide. The bark may be left on the underside of the seat as well as on the potential legs if a rough appearance is desired. Split the log and plane the flat surface to a smooth finish with a drawknife. The surface may be sanded to eliminate the marks of the tool or left in a marked condition. Through the underside of the slab, drill four holes at equal distances from the four corners. A 1-inch bit and brace will produce a hole of necessary size. The drilled holes should be made at a slight angle. To ensure that each hole is drilled at the same angle, a jig can be used. The jig consists of a base board and a second board whose side has been cut at a predetermined angle nailed to the base. Place the jig against the edge of the wood slab and hold it firmly. Then rest the bit against this angle so that each hole is drilled in the same manner. The holes should be bored through the slab. Whittle the pieces of wood which will serve as legs. One end of each leg should be cut down until it fits the drilled holes tightly. Push the legs through the holes until 2 inches protrude through the seat. Either cut or saw a notch into the leg where it has been pushed through the holes and fit a wooden wedge into the leg at the top. Hammer the wedge firmly into the leg. This will cause the leg to spread and fit more snugly. The protruding part of the leg and wedge should then be cut off even with the surface of the seat. The legs should be evened off at the bottom so that the stool stands straight. The surface of the seat may be finished off by rough sanding and waxing.

KNOTTING, HITCHES, AND LASHING

Everyone who works or lives in the outdoors should be capable of using knots and all those fibers by which joinings or combinations may be made. Knots are the means of tying together the parts of one or more flexible materials such as rope, line, plastic, leather, or other fiber. Knotting crafts include bends, hitches, and splices. The skills of fastening materials together can produce fascinating projects for those who become adept. Such activities are relatively inexpensive, requiring few tools and little space; yet they offer the participant a wide variety of experiences ranging from manipulation of materials to the production of decorations, receptacles and articles of clothing, and they may even ensure survival. Knowing how to use flexible materials for attaching objects, hauling materials, constructing utensils and clothing, or building shelters depends to a considerable degree upon the individual's ability to utilize the correct knot for the particular task involved. In learning to tie knots, cord at least 1/8 inch in diameter should be used. The parts of cord to be used for knotting have names. The main or long section of cord is called the "standing part." Any looped or curved section of cord reversed on the standing part is called a "bight." The tips of any material used in knotting are called "ends."

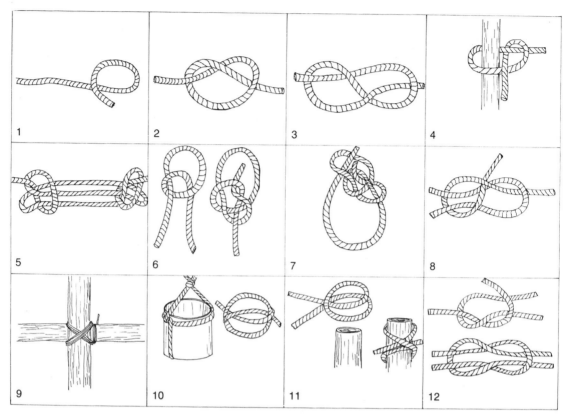

Figure 14-10   KNOTTING

  1. Parts of rope: standing part, end, bight
  2. Plain knot
  3. Figure-eight knot
  4. Half hitch
  5. Sheepshank
  6. Bowline knot
  7. Running bowline
  8. Weaver's knot
  9. Ledger lashing
  10. Can sling
  11. Clove hitch, over post
  12. Reef knot

Knots

The important thing about tying knots is to form them correctly and secure them tightly. They must be pulled slowly, steadily, and firmly. Heavy cord or rope may be utilized for practice purposes so that the user can see how the parts are joined and formed. All knots reduce the strength of any material; therefore knots which provide maximum holding power should be used rather than easy or less secure knots. There are a variety of useful knots, each having a specific strength or value. In some instances, it is not always possible to employ the best knot for a particular purpose because of its bulk, rigidity, or tendency to slip when tied in various materials. For example, knots which retain from 85 to 90 percent of the breaking strength of the material used may not be helpful in flytying if such knots are too bulky. Knots commonly used in craft projects will be presented here along with their major uses and disadvantages.

Plain Knot   The simplest knot to tie is the plain knot. It is most frequently used as a basic part of other knots. It is formed by passing one end over the standing part to make a bight and slipping the end through the bight. The knot is difficult to untie and remains firm when pulled. Plain knots are used to keep a rope or cord from moving beyond a desired point. The stopper knot is made at any section of the standing part to prevent the material from moving through any aperture. These knots may also be utilized to prevent the unraveling of strands at the ends.

Figure-Eight Knot   This knot is bigger than the plain knot. It is formed by passing the bight under the standing part, reversing the bight over the standing part and tucking the end through the circle made by the upper bight. This is a good angling knot.

Reef Knot   The reef knot is used to connect materials of equal size or thickness. To make the reef, cross the ends of two cords so that the first cord, A, slides under the bight of cord B, and then over and under the standing part of B. Bring the two ends up, away from the body, cross A under B, turn B under A, and tighten by pulling on the two ends simultaneously.

Weaver's Knot   For joining two ends of different sizes together this knot provides the strength and security as well as the quickest method. Cross the ends of two ropes. The right end should be placed underneath the left and held at the point where they cross. With the free hand bring the standing part of the right piece up and over the left and then down around its own end, which should be protruding to the left. Bring the right piece back between the two ends on top of the cross, holding it with the left hand. The loop that has been placed around the left hand should be slipped forward over the end of the left rope. The knot may be tightened by pulling simultaneously on the standing parts. The weaver's knot is very useful for making nets and hammocks.

Perfection Loop Knot   The perfection loop knot is useful in angling when it is desirable to tie a loop at the end of a synthetic leader, typically made of nylon. The loop serves the purpose of connecting the line and the leader. Hold the nylon between thumb and forefinger, permitting 4 to 5 inches of material to project upward. With the right hand make a bight behind the standing part and hold the intersection between the fingers. Make a second bight in front of the first, and bring the end around between the two that have been formed. Holding it firmly at the base, bring the second or front bight through the first bight. Pull the second bight steadily upward while holding the free end of the nylon and simultaneously close the knot portion.

Blood Knot　The blood knot is useful for connecting two strands of material when the diameters of both strands are approximately the same size. To make the knot, cross the two strands and hold between thumb and forefinger, permitting at least 3 inches of each section to extend. Grasping the near strand extension, twist around the standing part of the opposite strand four or five times. Pass the end through the bight formed by the two strands and hold the intersecting pieces together firmly with the other hand. Twist the other strand extension around the standing part four or five times in the opposite direction, and pass the free end through the bight so that it comes through from the opposite side. Holding both free ends between thumbs and forefingers, tighten the knot by slowly drawing on all four parts simultaneously. Any excess material can be clipped off after the knot has been correctly formed.

Bowline　The most widely used of all loop knots, the bowline has an almost infinite number of uses because it is absolutely dependable. It will not slip, cannot jam, and is fairly easy to untie. To form a bowline, make a small bight, permitting a long loose end of sufficient size for a loop. Bring the end downward through the loop. Carry the end under and around the standing part. Reverse the end over and then under the bight. In order to tighten the knot, pull on the standing part. The bowline can be used to moor any aquacraft to a dock or wherever a loop is required.

Running Bowline　The running bowline is formed by making a bowline initially and then putting the main rope back through the large bight to form a slip knot that is more effective than any other knot of its kind.

Hitches

A hitch is nothing more than a twist or combination of twists in a line to attach a rope or cord to some rigid object. There are a number of hitches, of which the half and clove hitches are best known. The half hitch is made by turning in the end of a line. The clove hitch binds fast to any surface. It is superior when a quick hitch is needed. It has the advantage of being able to take a strain while being prepared, cannot slip along whatever it is fastened to, and will permit easy unloosening when desired. A clove hitch is easily formed by dropping two half hitches over or around the object to which the line is being connected. Bend one end around any object to which a desired attachment is to be made. Pass the end over its own standing part and around the object and then under its standing part.

Taut-Line Hitch　This is one of the more important knots for use by anyone living off the land or camping out. This knot is essential for all lines slung between two objects. The taut-line hitch permits adjustments to be made in the lines after the shelter has been set up. The knot will not slip accidentally, but it can be worked up or down manually along the tight part of the rope to any desired point. This offers a technique for lengthening or shortening the ropes which, for example, may be guyed from tent to stake.

Bale Hitch   The standing part of the line should be passed over the back of any object that is to be carried. The ends are brought up over the front of the back and out under the bend. The two long ends may be used to raise or lower the object. In portaging, the two ends are brought forward over the packer's shoulders and held with the hands. Thus, the pack can be dropped instantly if necessary.

Bucket Hitch   The bucket hitch is useful for suspending any vessel that does not have a handle. To form the hitch, set the container on the line and pass the two ends up to make a loose plain knot. Draw the two ends down until they bend around the upper edge of the container. Tighten the line and knot the ends together over the vessel.

Sheepshank   The sheepshank permits any line to be shortened without cutting the material. Even when both ends are fastened to some object the sheepshank can be used. It can be connected without having to whip the line. Make a simple running loop and press a bight through this loop. Tighten the loop.

Lashing

Lashing is a technique that uses binding materials to hold wooden objects or other fibers together when other fastening equipment either is unavailable or would be useless. When wooden objects are to be held together, it is preferred that notches be made at the points where they are to be joined. The joint thus made will be less liable to slip and provide a more compact fit. In making a birchbark canoe, for example, it is unlikely that glue, nails, staples, or other fasteners would work as well as lashing to attach the ribs to the gunwales. In lashing, it is the standing part of the line that is manipulated rather than the ends. Almost all lashing is started by forming a clove hitch around one or more of the objects to be joined. Another clove hitch completes the method.

Diamond Lashing   When wooden beams, poles, or braces are to be joined at right angles, a clove hitch is made around one of the pieces. Wrap the standing part across the joint on an angle and continue wrapping along the joint on the opposite angle until a tightly secured joint has been made. Finish off the process with a clove hitch.

Shear Lashing   This method is utilized to make a supporting device. Wooden parts are laid parallel to each other and lashed together. When spread, they form a base. Two pairs will serve as a trestle; three poles lashed together from a tripod. Place the desired lengths of wood side by side and make a clove hitch around one piece near one end. Bend three to five loose turns about the poles. Wind the line between the poles so that the lashing is more firmly held together and complete the shear with another clove hitch. In this manner the framework of a shelter can be made.

NATURE CRAFTS
FROM NATURAL
MATERIALS

Pole Splice Lashing   When a piece of wood or pole is short and it is desirable to add length to it, the pole splice technique is used. This process may also be valuable in repairing any fractured spar, pole, mast, or beam. Place two pieces of wood of approximately the same diameter end to end. Lay other pieces of wood alongside of the ends so that these extend beyond the fracture or point to be lengthened. Make a clove hitch around the top of the splint sticks and the pole and wrap the standing part securely around the hitch. Pass the standing part down from the initial winding, make another clove hitch and wrap the line firmly around the second hitch. Repeat this procedure at the juncture where the wooden pieces meet and again just below. Finish the process with a final clove hitch.

Malay Winding   This method is used to fasten fiber materials, typically reeds, straw, clumps of grass, pine boughs, or other soft substances. It is merely a series of figure-eight windings about bunches of fibers. The finished product can be shaken apart without too much difficulty and without leaving any knots in the line.

Continuous Lashing   This technique is used when shorter sticks are needed to connect larger or longer poles, as in a ladder. Generally, the larger poles are notched to receive the smaller ones. The lashing is begun with a clove hitch at one end of a long pole. The hitch is made in the middle of the line so that the two ends are even. The rope is then passed across the back of the long pole and up and over the first short stick. This procedure is repeated until all the short sticks have been attached to the long pole—as though the short sticks were laced to the longer ones. Complete the lashing with a clove hitch or two half hitches. The ends should be tucked in carefully. This procedure is performed on the second pole. The result of this effort may become a wooden walkway, tabletop, stretcher, ladder, or drying rack.

Splicing   This is a method for joining two pieces of binding material together. Correctly made, a splice can be stronger than any knot, and may be preferred for use with loads, when a knot might prevent a line from sliding, or for a neat end. Take the materials to be spliced together and lay them side by side. Twist the first line around the standing part of the second about five times. Pass the end through the loop made by the two strands while holding the lines firmly. Twist the other strand around the free standing part at least five times in the opposite direction, and pass the free end through the loop so that it returns from the opposite side. Draw ends together and clip away excess material. For further security, the splice may be wrapped.

FLYTYING

The skill of imitating natural foods eaten by fish through the artful application of natural or artificial materials to an appropriate hook is called fly dressing or tying. Precise imitations of the natural food at which fish strike are less important than something the fish will accept as an enticing sub-

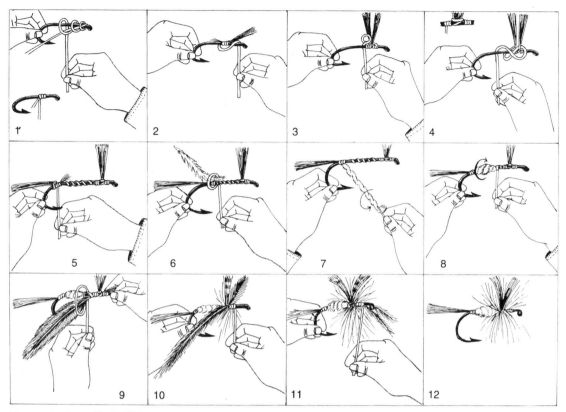

Figure 14-11 FLYTYING

Materials: waterfowl feathers, dry fly fishing hooks, silk thread, scissors, yarn, toothpick.

1. Attach thread to hook with half hitch and pull taut.
2. Tie on one wing with jam knot and pass thread to front.
3. Tie on second wing and bring thread between wings so that they stand up.
4. Crisscross windings to set wings permanently.
5. Tie on tail with half hitch.
6. Catch woolen fiber in loop of thread and pull taut to firmly attach.
7. Twirl fiber counter clockwise around thread.
8. Wind body fiber and thread around hook shank.
9. Wind in hackle and secure with half hitch.
10. Pull half hitch taut and secure hackle.
11. Finish fly with whip knot neatly in front of hook eye.
12. Completed dry fly.

stitute. The most successful flies are those which suggest something edible. Here, we will offer a method for tying dry flies which is fairly well standardized, thereby permitting the amateur to learn quickly the procedure for making flies that will catch fish. All flies should be attached to hooks made specifically for flytying. Dry-fly hooks should be light and fine with needle-sharp points for quick penetration. A dry fly is designed to float.

A fly has five major parts: the tail, body, ribbing, wings, and hackle. The tail of the typical dry fly should approximate the hook shank and be sparse rather than full. Preferably, it should be made from naturally water-resistant waterfowl feathers. The body should be firm and slim to prevent or reduce water absorption. The ribbing on dry-fly bodies may be of any strong, flexible, and fine material. The wings of a dry fly are also made from waterfowl feathers and should be the length of the hook shank. The hackle of the dry fly provides wind resistance and buoyancy on the water. See Figure 14-11 for the steps to follow in tying a fly.

MACRAME
The artistic method for using knots to convey designs and carry out practical crafts products is called macrame. Although it looks extremely complicated, the entire process is based upon a few simple knot forms. The procedure begins with the attachment of a series of clove hitches around some rigid object from which the design or project develops. Perhaps some series of knots are arranged if the craftsman wants a patterning effect. In many cases, however, the object becomes a spontaneous intermingling of knots, lines, swirls, and curves which are improvised.

Among the many projects which can be constructed using the ancient art of knotting are wall hangings, place mats, book bags, belts, purses, runners, and rugs. The materials involved are inexpensive and sturdy. Some macrame work lasts indefinitely. There are infinite designs to attempt, limited only by the artistry and ingenuity of the individual involved. Macrame takes up little or no space and may be worked on routinely or at odd moments. It is a superior craft for those who want the spontaneity of instant pattern change, yet it may also provide many happy hours for those who desire the experience of following some prearranged sequence.

Perhaps the best way to begin is to determine the way in which the macrame is to be used. If the object is to receive hard wear, the material to be used must be strong and durable. Projects expected to endure constant rough use or to maintain a certain shape require strong cord with a hard twist. Wall hangings with swirls and feathery designs should probably be made of a thinner material, have flexibility, but also contain the strength of twine.

Pattern is the single observable effect of most macrame. Dominating every other aspect of the craft, bold designs are what the viewer perceives initially. Varying textures, colors, and materials carry out the theme. Among the materials required are the fabric to be knotted, such as cord, twine, lines, yarn, or hemp. Pins are useful to secure the knotted material to a working surface, which may be anything into which pins can be easily inserted. If the project is to be one of a large design, there may have to be used some form of rod or hanger to suspend the work and thus provide the craftsman with space necessary to execute the pattern.

Project Construction
The length of the completed design must be known because cord length must be appropriate to the pattern. The cords involved will be three to four times the length of the finished design. Since the cords are doubled

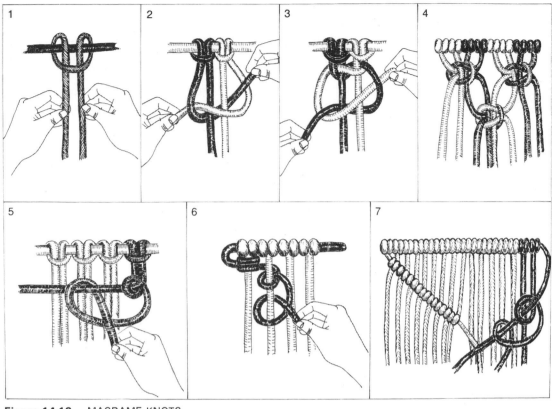

Figure 14-12 MACRAME KNOTS
Materials: any fibrous material (usually cord), retaining rod.
1. Lark's head knot.
2. Square knot.
3. Alternating square knot.
4. Horizontal double half hitch.
5. Vertical double half hitch.
6. Diagonal double half hitch.

when attached to the suspending rod or holding line, the actual length of the cords should be six to eight times the length of the expected design. Outer cords, which are the knot-bearing or holding cords, must be double the length of the others. If all the cords are 10 feet long, the end cords should be 20 feet.

The holding line, to which all cords are attached, should be approximately 6 inches longer than the finished width of the design. To make sure that the cords will not slide off, small knots should be formed at the end of each line and pinned to the working surface. If a rod is used in place of a holding line, it should be at least 6 inches wider than the design. Some knots, because of their convolutions, require more than the cord length generally given. Among these are the diagonal double half hitch, vertical double half hitch, and bowlines. Some of these knots need at least double the length of cord for good execution of the knot.

Basic Knots

The *lark's-head knot* is used for attaching cords to the holding line. Bend the cord in half, then pass the top of the loop down over the cords to form two loops. Bend the new loops back so that they touch one another. Draw over the holding line and tighten.

The *half knot* is formed from four cords that have been passed around the holding line. The two center, or filler, cords must remain stationary while the outer cords are knotted around them. The filler cords may be held in place by either pins or tape while the work proceeds. Bend the right outer cord over the filler cords. Bend the left outer cord over the right one, under the filler cords, and over the right cord. A sennit or series of half knots are produced in this manner and develop a twisting spiral design.

The *square knot* is formed from a half knot. After the half knot has been made, bend the right outer cord under the filler cords. Bend the left outer cord under the right cord, over the filler cords, and under the right cord.

The *alternating square knot* requires a multiple of four cords for execution. A row of square knots should be made leaving some extra cord space between it and the row above. For the alternating procedure to occur, let the two far left cords remain unused while the next four cords are knotted together in a square knot. The third row should be a counterpart of the first. It will contain the two outer right and left cords that row two did not use.

The *horizontal double half hitch* is begun at the far right edge. The far right cord then becomes the knot bearer, as all other cords are knotted over it. During the knotting process, this cord must be maintained in a taut and horizontal position over the other cords. Knot the next cord, second from the far right, over it, passing the loop in a clockwise direction. Make two loops with each cord and knot securely. When the left edge is reached, reverse the procedure by using the far left cord as the knot bearer, passing the loop in a counterclockwise direction.

The *vertical double half hitch* is executed around the hanging lines. The far left cord should be pinned. Slide the cord under the adjacent one and bend it twice around in a clockwise direction. Reverse the procedure when the far right side is reached by utilizing the right outer cord to knot. This is performed by looping in a counterclockwise direction.

The *diagonal double half hitch* requires the division of all cords into two groups. The far right and the far left cords are used as the knot bearers. The procedure is identical with the two groups. Maintain tension on the knot-bearing cord and hold it at an angle of 45 degrees over the cords. Make double loops over it on each cord. The loops are wound clockwise in the right group and counterclockwise in the left group. At the intersection of the cords, double-loop the left knot-bearing cord over the right cord. Continue double half hitches until the cross is finished.

Making a Wall Hanging

A wall hanging may be completed with a little time and effort and some imagination on the part of the performer. Any rigid material or rod may be secured for this purpose. The rod should be 3/4 inch, and the cord used will be seine twine. At least 500 feet of cord, some rubber bands, and white glue will be necessary for the completion of the project.

To begin the project, bend sixty-two cords, 48 feet in length, over a rod and attach with lark's head knots. Pull the far right cord horizontally across the other cords and maintain tension. On the line, make a row of horizontal double half hitches. For the next several inches of the hanging, this type of knot is to be used, but it should not be permitted to cross in a straight line. Only sections of the cords are used, some in diagonals and some in curves. Periodically, leave spaces where the cords are open and pull some cords across or twist them around into a series of half hitches. Use the rubber bands to restrain the lengths of cord which are not being worked.

Since the hanging is of the free-form variety, spontaneity is the key to its design. Several of the knots may be used as the craftsman feels his way during the process. Improvisation contributes more to the overall pattern than rigidly following a set model. Vertical flat braids may be introduced through a series of double half hitches. By holding one or more vertical cords taut and alternately looping double half hitches around them this effect may be obtained. The twisted braids are nothing more than half hitches in series. As the knotting continues, the series twists automatically. Finally, loop all the cords around the rod at the bottom. Three rows of alternating square knots should be added to finish off the design. The fringe must be trimmed as evenly as possible at the bottom. The result is a free-form hanging suitable for interior decoration.

NETTING

Netting is an old craft which antedates the Bible. Fishermen have long used netting as a strong and inexpensive way to rest themselves, catch their fish, or hold tools and other utensils. Hunters who trapped birds for food and entertainment often did so through the use of nets. In fact, the word "fowler" is derived from the type of knots that were used in making the nets by which birds or other animals could be caught. Netting itself became a household art hundreds of years ago and was used to make catchalls for storage purposes as well as to decorate walls and furniture. In some cases, netting was used for clothing.

Netting is both a useful and decorative craft. Netting is durable because each stitch is perfect in itself, and if it breaks, the web is not loosened. It is inexpensive because it needs only cord or thread as its basic material. The shuttles or needles utilized in this craft may be homemade from wood. A hardwood needle may be easily fashioned from a piece of wood. It should be at least 3/16 inch in thickness. The mesh stick or block may be of any desired width, although 1 inch is preferable for hammock making.

Making a Hammock
The cord used in hammock making varies in weight, but 2 pounds are sufficient for the project. Approximately 5 yards of side cord will also be necessary for the completion of the hammock.

Once the requisite materials are obtained, the cord should be wound into balls and the needles filled. The simplest method for making a hammock is to put the required number of stitches on a cord stretched between two nails. This makes it easy for the craftsman to see the meshes and to avoid mistakes when working in a horizontal line. Forty-two stitches provide sufficient width for an adequate hammock. The needle carrying the cord is inserted between the sheds created by the lines hanging from their respective knots and looped around the bottom rod. Care must be taken to draw up the thread rapidly and tightly so as to avoid a slip knot. The worker must exercise extreme care never to slip a knot.

When the first row is completed, the mesh stick is moved along so that it retains not less than six stitches on it. The end loop is permitted to be quite long and the new row is begun. If necessary, the work may be untied and turned inside out so that the craftsman is always working from left to right. However, it seems better to be able to work in either direction. The thread must be connected with care when the needle has to be refilled. This is done by lapping the threads at the center of the knot. When the hammock reaches sufficient length, about 7 feet, the ends should be finished without slicing the cords at the last mesh. The hammock is laid on a long working surface, so that the end meshes extend straight across it 2 feet from the end. A tack can be driven under the working surface at the edge to retain the ring. The needle should then be passed from the end through the ring and back, then through two meshes, where it is caught with a stitch, through the ring again, back through two more meshes, and so on. If the thread needs lengthening, a new piece may be tied in with a weaver's knot, quite close to the ring. The thread should finally go up to the ring, and all the threads near the ring should be securely wound. A piece of cord approximately 5 yards long should be set aside for this function.

Side cords should be put in place before finishing. They are intertwined through each side of the hammock, so that they pass through all the rings, and are loosely knotted around the bunch of threads. The side cords should be under a certain amount of tension to hold the hammock taut without letting it sag too much in the middle. In winding the ends, the same process as that of splicing is brought into play. The remaining ends must be left so that they can be pulled under the twist. To do this, lay the end through a loop of cord of sufficient length that the ends extend 8 or 9 inches along the threads. As the twist is only 6 inches long, ends are dangling. When the twist is long enough, the end may be passed through the loop and these ends pulled until the end is inserted far along the twist. Both ends of the hammock should be finished in this manner. The end product will be more satisfying if the rings are buttonholed with cord.

BRAIDING

Braiding and knotting are related activities which can easily be performed by the merest tyro. They have the greatest advantage of requiring no special tools; all that is needed is the flexible material to make the product. Material for knotting and braiding, as has been previously indicated, may be of any flexible strands such as rope, cord, string, wire, raffia, paper, yarn, cloth, plastic, or leather. The techniques described below may be used in numerous crafts projects, such as decorations and articles of clothing, as part of outdoor gear, and for everything from bracelets to dog leashes. A variety of projects can be undertaken, and while there are fundamental procedures for braiding and knotting, both functional and ornamental patterns and decorations may be combined through the expedient of vari-colored strands or different styles of braid, loops, and knots.

The initial step for any kind of braiding is to hold the ends firmly so that they will not unravel. This can be done by securing one end in any number of ways. If one end is to be attached to a fastener of some sort, the end may be knotted or secured to the fastener. Other methods include doubling the length of material required and bending it around a peg or nail hammered into position for that purpose. Naturally, a third strand must also be secured so that simple braiding can be done. A more complex braid calls for doubling three strands over a fastener, or any holding device, so that six strips can be worked. All braidwork requires a firmly secured set of strands so that even tension may be maintained as braiding continues. Braiding may be done either loosely or closely, but the tension must be even throughout.

In estimating the length of strands required for the completion of any project, it is well to remember that the braid takes not less than two thirds of the length of the material used. Considerable variation as to length occurs, depending upon the slackness or tightness of the braid and the numbers of strips utilized in the project.

Flat Braiding The easiest and most widely recognized form of braiding is flat braiding with three strands. The strands are held securely at one end with each strand laid alongside the others. Whichever side is more convenient, take an outside strand and pass it over the middle one. Take the opposite outside strand and pass it over the first outer strand which has since become the middle one. This procedure is repeated until the braid is completed.

This technique may be used for all braiding where there are an odd number of strands. Simply determine the center strand, then weave an outer strand over and under the other strands on that side until it passes over the middle one. Take the opposite outer strand and pass it over and under the other strands on the same side until it crosses the middle one. Braiding is always done with the outer strands, which are passed over and under the adjacent ones until they cross the center strand.

The method used for an even number of strands in flat braiding is similar. Here, however, the first outer strand used always goes *over* the strand next to it while the opposite outer strand always goes *under* its neighbor and then *over* the next one. The procedure is continued with the starting outer strand always passing over one and the opposite outer strand always passing over and under two. It makes no difference how many strands there are. The second outer strand will always pass through one more strand than the outer strand which is first used to start the braid. To complete the flat braid, reverse the ends and pass them through the braid.

Square Braiding Square braiding is typically performed with four strands. It may be used to complete a round braid or, and most generally, be used for lanyard design. The four ends are held firmly together by knotting or with a clip of some kind. The four strands are held so that the strands are laid out in four opposite directions. Any strand may then be selected to start the braid. A strand is passed between two strands opposite it and held so that a small bight is formed. A second strand is looped over the first and passed between the two strands opposite. A third strand, which was crossed by the first, is brought over the second strand. The fourth strand is passed over the third and through the bight formed by the first strand. All strands are then tightened evenly and the process is repeated until the braid is completed.

To finish off the square braid, a knot may be made. The knot is completed by taking one strand, bending it around the next strand, and passing it through the loop securing that strand. This sequence is repeated for all ends. This centers all four strands in the knot. When the strands are pulled tight, the braid is sealed. The ends may then be trimmed or left to form a tuft for decoration.

Spiral Braiding Spiral braiding is a variation of square braiding. The resulting spiral pattern is formed after the first row is braided as in square braiding. In making the spiral pattern thereafter, the strands are passed diagonally across rather than straight across until the braid is finished. The knot may then be used to seal the braid.

Round Braiding Round braiding is usually made with an even number of strands. We will discuss a four-strand braid. The initial procedure is to arrange the strands parallel to one another. Take the second strand from either side and pass it over its neighbor, away from the outer side on which it is situated, and thence under the outer strand. Pass the outermost strand, on the same side as the one with which the work was begun, under what is in effect the third strand and over the fourth strand. Thus, the two formerly left-side strands are now at the right, and vice versa.

The outer left strand is bent around and under the others through the space between the strips at the right. This strand is then bent back to the left so that it parallels the strip on the left. The outer right strand is then bent under and around the others and through the space between the strips at the left. The strand is then bent back to the right so that it lies parallel to the strip on the right. The sequence is continued until the braid is completed. The project may be completed by doing two or three square braids and then sealing the braid with a knot.

Round braiding may be performed with any even number of strands, with six- and eight-strand braids being most popular. When working with six or eight strands, the first maneuver is to cross the strands as in the four-

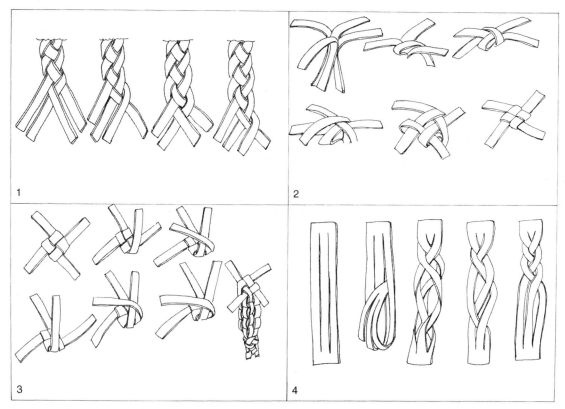

Figure 14-13 BRAIDING
Materials: any fibrous materials (usually leather thongs), pyrolace, cord, twine, yarn, wire.

1. Round braiding.
2. Square braiding.
3. Spiral braiding.
4. Flat braiding with closed materials.

strand braid until all the left-hand strands are on the right. In six-strand braiding, the innermost left strip is bent around and under all strands and then passed between the last two left-hand strands. In eight-strand braiding the innermost left strip is bent around and under all strands, passed up between the second and third strips of the right side, and passed over and then under the remaining two strands. These sequences are repeated until completion of the braid.

WEAVING WITH NATURAL MATERIALS
Although weaving has been taken up elsewhere in this book in considerable detail, there remains a form of naturecrafts which uses the weaving process. Woven and braided mats can be processed on looms. Weave a border warp 1/2 to 1 inch in width before beginning the straw or cattail weave. Complete the other end with the same border. The pattern will depend upon the choice of materials used and the rhythm followed in over-and-under

alternates. The weave can be mixed with grasses, straw, corn husk cat-tails, or stripped willow, to vary the texture and change the pattern. Remove the finished mat from the loom when it is dry and knot the ends.

Mat Weaving

This is the most primitive and simplest of all weaving procedures. No frame or loom is required, only the materials which will be woven. Almost any fiber can be used, including strips of cloth, newspapers, or linoleum. The end product is used for outdoor seats, sleeping mats, etc. Natural materials such as grasses, palmetto, raffia, rushes, or corn husks may be used. As with all weaving warp strands are necessary. Lay approximately half the strands of the material vertically, side by side. This will form the warp. Secure the top of each strip to a stationary object. This may be done by tacking the strips to a flat stick or other surface. Take a strand and with an alternating under and over pattern, weave the weft through the warp and then push the line up to the end that has been secured. Continue this method until all the weft strands are interwoven.

To finish off the project, fold each strand over the end strand and bend the end under the same strip. The first strand is bent back over and under the first side strand. The second strand is bent forward over and under the first side strand. This procedure is continued until all strips are secured in this manner. The same bending and alternate folding front and back are used along the sides until all strands are tucked in and secure.

Chair Caning

Chair caning may be looked upon as a form of weaving that uses natural fibers (cane), and for this reason it is placed in this chapter. When caning a chair, use fine or extra fine cane. The cane should be dampened to make it pliable throughout the procedure. Bore a series of twenty-four holes through the edge of the seat approximately 1/2 inch from the inner edge. Begin caning at hole one. Secure the strand in the hole with a 1/4-inch dowel. Pass the strand across to hole number 2, bend underneath and across to hole number 3, and then take it transversely to hole number 4, underneath to hole number 5, and so on. Maintain tension on the strand and use wooden plugs to keep it in place. Fasten a second layer of strands perpendicular to the first set as before. Remove plugs from chair and se-cure loose strands beneath chair frame in knots around strands that extend from hole to hole. Pass the next layer of strands parallel to the first, over first and second layers, in the same manner.

Begin the weaving process, using a caning needle to assist with the under and over weaves. Each time the strand is passed through the hole, thread it through the needle and weave it across to the opposite side. Ar-range the wet pliable strands in two, forcing them into tight, straight parallel strips. Diagonal weaving follows. Thread the diagonal strands through each corner hole, working the strand under and over the intersecting strands until the third hole is reached. Carry the strand underneath and through the second hole, back under the vertical lines at the third hole, and diagonally weave the strand into the corner hole. Weave remaining strands diagonally

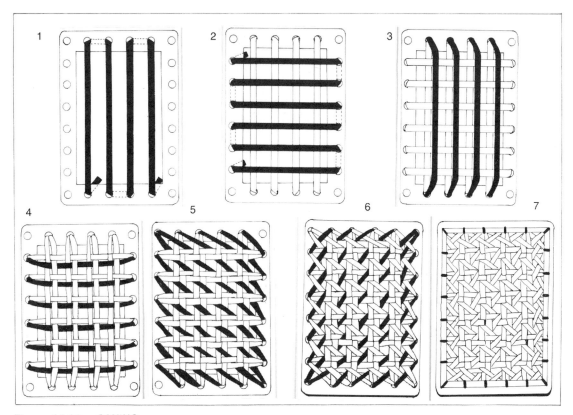

Figure 14-14 CANING
Materials: cut-out chair seat, drill and bit, a number of wooden dowels for plugs, caning needle, caning, binder caning, scissors.

1. Warp vertical strands.
2. Warp horizontal strands.
3. Warp second layer of vertical strands.
4. Warp second layer of horizontal strands.
5. Begin weaving cane under and over the warp.
6. Continue weaving cane diagonally.
7. Finish caning.

from the opposite direction. Pass two diagonals into the four corner holes and continue the process until all side and corner holes are connected.

Using binder caning, frame the edges of the woven caning. Lay the binder over the holes and bend fine cane through each or alternate holes, catching in the binder. Stretch the caning tightly so that the binder fits closely. To complete the seat, permit the binder to overlap two or three holes. Tie these ends together. After the final loop is made, secure the end of the strand by plugging the hole from beneath or with a knot.

15 THEATER CRAFTS

Puppetry is an ancient art which has been utilized in all parts of the world to entertain people. During the first part of the twentieth century, the Punch and Judy show was still part of the European and American tradition. Puppetry declined in popularity with the invention of animated cartoons, motion pictures, and television. However, this trend has reversed itself with the use of puppets on television.

Very simple stick or paper bag puppets can be constructed by very young children, while more elaborate ones may require the skill of a craftsman. Puppets are a very versatile tool and their implications to learning are endless. They afford a wide variety of opportunities for individual expression and group activity. The experiences for the individual include making the puppets, making the stage, arranging the props, assigning the parts, and dramatization of a play.

Puppetry is a form of dramatization that is especially helpful for some children and offers the individual countless opportunities not found in similar activities. For the shy, introverted child, puppetry can be just the experience needed to make him feel at ease. This type of dramatization allows the child to assume the identity of the puppet. In this way, the child's own limitations and feelings are minimized, and his expressions are not forced but are spontaneous and natural.

Puppetry in the classroom can be applied to almost any subject area. Historical events come alive when presented through puppets. Children learn while researching and developing the script for the puppet show. They are exposed to the more personal aspects of history—for example, why some individual performed a specific deed and how he felt as a result of his participation in the event. Language arts skills of writing, reading, speaking, and listening are reinforced through puppetry. Opportunities are available to vocalize for an audience and articulate words so that they can be understood at all times.

A puppet show also helps to elicit the creativity that is generally stifled by less interesting classroom experiences. When either writing or improving a script, children are creating and expressing their ideas. Puppetry can make the child's day more stimulating and colorful. It encourages learning and promotes good classroom atmosphere.

There are four basic types of puppets: the hand puppet, rod puppet, marionette, and shadow puppet, each of which has innumerable variations. Before attempting to make any puppet, the individual should know the difficulty in the construction. Consideration of the motor coordination required to manipulate the puppet is also necessary. Some rod puppets and marionettes require two operators to handle the body parts.

Hand puppets slip over the puppeteer's hand and are sometimes referred to as fist or mitten puppets. They usually consist of a head and a loose-fitting garment similar to a nightgown. The head and arms of the puppet are operated by placing the forefinger into the hole at the bottom of the head, while placing the thumb and little finger into the sleeves. The thumb and little finger simulate arms for the puppet. The puppet comes to life when the thumb and little finger are wiggled. After completing the hand puppet, experiment with different ways to move your fingers and thumb to make the puppet perform. Try to make the puppet nod and wave, brush his hair, and take a bow. Hand puppets usually hop across the stage rather than walk. This hopping action can be accomplished by a swaying motion of the fingers and thumb. Hand puppets are worked from below the stage opening.

The rod puppet is constructed on a rigid rod (1/4-inch dowel), and movement is created by one or more rods attached to the various body parts. Rod puppets, like hand puppets, are worked by the puppeteer from below the stage opening. The single rod puppet is very easy to construct and maneuver. For this reason it is adaptable for school use at all age levels.

The marionette, unlike hand and rod puppets, is manipulated from above the stage opening by strings. Marionettes are usually more difficult to construct and manipulate. Some elaborate marionettes have been constructed that require more than a dozen strings for their operation.

The shadow puppet is also manipulated from below the stage opening. Shadow puppets are flat two-dimensional cutouts fastened to a thin wire or rod, which is used to manipulate the puppet. Shadow puppets usually have arms, legs, and mouths that are movable. They are usually jointed with a paper fastener to provide free movement of the various body parts. A light is placed behind a tightly stretched cloth that has been painted with the desired scene. The puppet is held against the cloth on the lighted side and appears as a silhouette to the audience.

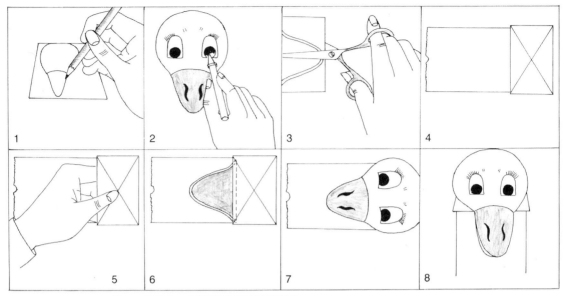

Figure 15-1   PAPER BAG PUPPETS

Materials: paper bag, pencil, scissors, glue, construction paper, drawing paper, crayons.

1. Draw the head and chin of the puppet on a piece of construction paper.
2. Cut out and color the head.
3. Cut out and color the chin.
4. Place the bag down on the table with the bottom fold up.
5. Lift the bottom of the folded bag up.
6. Glue the chin in place under the bottom fold.
7. Glue the head to the bottom of the bag.
8. Insert a hand and manipulate the puppet.

PUPPETS
Paper Bag Puppets

A simple paper bag puppet can be constructed by painting a face or head onto the side of a bag. To construct this type of puppet, take a small paper bag (number —5 X 9-3/4 inches) and with a pencil and ruler, draw a line 3 inches from the top edge of the bag. Then, with a pencil, sketch in a face for the puppet. It is important to encourage children to use their imagination when sketching their puppet's face. Colored crayons or watercolors can be used to paint the face. Yarn or cotton can be glued to the bottom of the bag for hair. Other accessories can be added to the face of the puppet. When the head is completed, gather in the bag where the line was drawn, and tie a string loosely around it. The string should be loose enough to allow the hand to slip into the bag. The puppet is completed and ready to use.

A second type of paper bag puppet utilizes the bottom flap of the bag as the upper portion of the face, while the side of the bag is the lower jaw. See Figure 15-1. With a pencil, sketch the face of the puppet onto the bag. The upper segment of the face should appear on the bottom of the bag, while other parts will be on the side. Crayons or watercolors can be used to add color to the puppet's face. String, yarn, or cotton can be used as hair or eyebrows. Buttons, bottle tops, toothpicks, or other materials can be used to make the puppet more attractive. When the puppet is finished, slip the bag over the hand and place the forefingers into the bottom flap. If the fingers are placed in this position, it becomes easier to manipulate the bottom of the bag and gives the puppet a more realistic appearance, since the mouth can open and close.

A third type of paper bag puppet utilizes construction paper glued to the paper bag for the head and body. With a pencil or crayon, sketch the head and body features of the desired character on a piece of construction paper. Try to create an interesting character. It is good practice to experiment with different lines and shapes on a piece of scrap paper.

The upper part of the head should be separated from the lower jaw. Paint or color the head and body of the puppet. Eyes, ears, hair, and other features can be added to the puppet. A wide variety of accessories can be used to identify the character. When the head and body are completed, they can be glued to the paper bag. Attach the body to the elongated portion of the bag. The upper portion of the head is attached to the bottom flap of the bag, while the lower jaw is placed in position under the bottom flap. It is important to design the upper and lower jaws of the puppet so that the mouth can be opened and closed.

The puppet is completed and is ready for use. Slip the bag over the hand and place the finger into the bottom fold. Opening and closing the hand allows the puppeteer to give the appearance that the puppet is speaking.

Stick Puppets

A stick puppet can be made from stiff paper or cardboard and attached to a stick. To construct a stick puppet, place a 6-inch paper plate on a piece of cardboard and trace around the outline of the plate with a crayon. Then draw a 10-inch circle using a 10-inch paper plate as a pattern; the smaller circle is the head of the puppet, while the larger circle is used as the body.

Glue the smaller circle to the larger circle with about 1 inch of each circle overlapping. Before attaching the stick to the body of the puppet, one should decide whether the character is an animal or person. If the character is an animal, the head should be tilted to the side. For a person, the small circle or head circle is located in an upright position. Place some glue onto the end of the stick and attach the large circle to the stick. The puppet is ready to be decorated. Sketch in the eyes, nose, and other features. Buttons can be used for the eyes, or they can be drawn with crayons or paints. If the puppet needs hair, yarn or cotton can be used. Legs, ears, arms, and even a tail can be cut from cardboard and glued to the puppet's body.

Stick puppets can also be constructed by cutting out pictures from magazines and gluing them to stiff paper. A small stick is attached to the bottom of the cardboard by paper staples or glue. Old ice cream sticks are perfect for this purpose.

Stick puppets are operated from below the stage. Each child makes

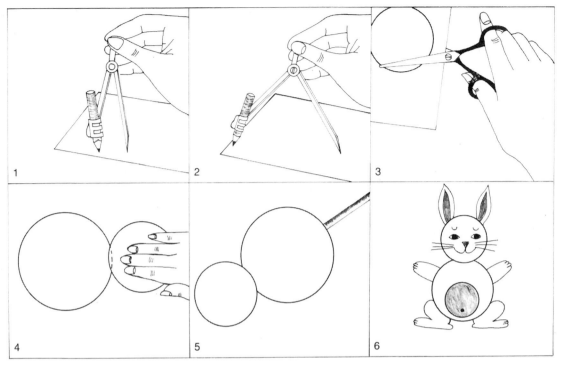

Figure 15-2 STICK PUPPETS
Materials: compass, crayons, paint, pencil, stick, scissors, construction paper, glue, oak tag.

1. Draw a 6-inch circle on a piece of oak tag.
2. Draw a 10-inch circle on a piece of oak tag.
3. Cut out both circles.
4. Glue the small and large circles together.
5. Glue a stick to the back of the large circle.
6. Cut out the features and glue in place.

and moves his own puppet. Some stick puppets are placed in a groove and moved back and forth along the groove. String attached to the sides of the puppet's body and head can be used to manipulate the puppet in a forward or backward direction.

Many other variations can be used to make the puppet's head, arms, and legs move. The head or arms can be attached with paper fasteners. Different sized circles and variations in the shapes to create odd-looking puppets should be tried.

Styrofoam Puppets

Another form of stick puppet can be constructed by using Styrofoam for the head and hands instead of paper. Styrofoam has many advantages. It can be shaped to give the puppet a three-dimensional appearance and is much more durable. The material is light and easily worked with a knife, coping saw, hot wire, and sandpaper.

Sketch the head and hands for the puppet on a piece of scrap paper. It

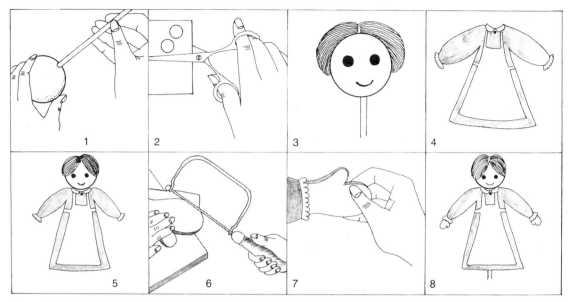

Figure 15-3 STYROFOAM PUPPETS
Materials: Styrofoam ball, wooden dowel, scissors, yarn, felt, construction paper, cloth, glue.
1. Insert the dowel into the Styrofoam ball.
2. Cut out the features for the puppet.
3. Glue the features to the ball.
4. Make a costume for the puppet.
5. Glue the costume to the head.
6. Cut out the hands.
7. Glue the hands to the costume.
8. Finished puppet.

is important that the head have a neck and the hands have wrists for the purpose of attaching them to the costume. Cut out these shapes and use them as patterns for tracing the head and hands onto the Styrofoam. Sand the edges with sandpaper.

At the center of the base of the neck, push a pencil 2 inches into the Styrofoam. Apply glue to one end of a 1/4-inch dowel and insert it into the neck hole and allow to dry.

Features and detail lines on the face and hands can be cut or shaped out of the Styrofoam with a knife and/or sandpaper. Felt, construction paper, Styrofoam, yarn, or felt-tip markers may also be used to add facial features.

Draw a pattern for the puppet's costume on a piece of paper. The sleeves must be long enough to allow the hands to be attached. Cut out the pattern. Fold a piece of cloth in half and pin the pattern to the material. Cut the material by cutting around the pattern. Take the pins off when the pattern is cut. There should be two identical pieces of material. Take one piece of material and turn it to the wrong side (dull side) and apply a thin strip of glue around the edge. Place the second piece of material wrong side down on top of the glued surface. Press the edges together and allow to dry. Place the 1/4-inch dowel through the neck opening and press the top of the costume to the glued portion of the neck. Glue the wrists to the sleeves.

The puppet may need a hat or hair. Try different materials. Different effects can be achieved by using odds and ends to dress up the puppet. By using straight pins to attach facial features, the characteristics of the puppet could be changed in seconds.

An alternative Styrofoam puppet can be constructed by cutting out the arms, legs, body, and head as one complete unit. Sandpaper, a knife, coping saw, and hot wire can be used to obtain the desired shape. This simple stick puppet does not require a dress. The various parts of the body and costume can be painted or pinned directly on the Styrofoam surface.

A more elaborate Styrofoam puppet can be constructed by cutting all the body parts separately. After the arms, legs, body, and head have been shaped and sanded, they can be connected for manipulation. Wooden dowels can be used to join the arms, legs, and head to the body. The dowel should be inserted so that it acts as a pivot for the moving parts. Wire or metal can be used to connect the parts. Different materials are employed to obtain the desired movement or create a new motion. These techniques can be used in combination to develop different effects.

A combination of the complete unit and the cutout parts of the body can be used to produce a unique puppet. Part of the body could be made as a total unit, while some of the limbs or head would be cut out separately. The jaw might be separated and hinged in place to allow it to move up and down. One arm and leg could be cut and jointed to allow movement. The fun is to create a puppet that is unlike any other.

Cereal Box Puppets

A small (one-serving size) cereal box can be used as a base to construct a puppet. When the box is opened to remove the cereal, it should be cut across the middle, and down the side. If the cereal box has been opened by using the dotted lines on the back of the package, masking tape can be used to join these pieces together. After the box is cut, it is placed on the table with the cut side face down. One end of the box is held against the table, while the other side is bent until the top and bottom surfaces meet.

The cereal box is ready to be turned from an empty box into an interesting character. A sketch on a piece of scrap paper may be helpful to plan how the puppet can be made realistic or funny.

Select the desired color of tempera paint and paint the entire outside surface of the box. More than one coat of paint may be required to cover the original lettering on the box. Tempera paint will not cover masking tape unless a small amount of soap is added to the paintbrush before dipping it into the paint. After the box has been painted, it is ready for the face features of the puppet. With a pencil, sketch in the features for the face on the bottom and top ends of the box. The upper section of the face (ears, eyes, and nose) should appear on one end of the box, while the lower portion of the face (mouth, teeth, and jaw) should appear on the opposite end. This arrange-

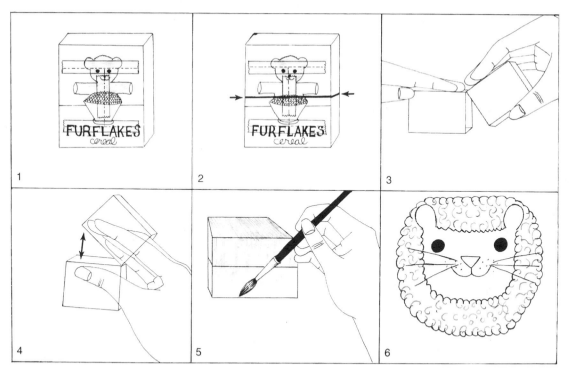

Figure 15-4 CEREAL BOX PUPPETS

Materials: small cereal box, scissors, paintbrush, paint, glue, construction paper.

1. Tape the box closed.
2. Cut the front and two sides of the box.
3. Bend the box in half.
4. Insert fingers to manipulate the two halves of the box.
5. Paint the box to cover all the lettering.
6. Add features to the box.

ment of facial features makes it possible for the puppet's mouth to open and close.

Crepe paper, cloth, yarn, or other materials can be used to add details such as hair, fur, eyebrows, and whiskers to the puppet. Construction paper or felt can be used to add a hat or other features to the puppet.

The top and bottom ends of the cereal box offer a limited surface for the desired facial features. A larger face for the puppet can be obtained by using construction paper or oak tag instead of the top and bottom ends of the box. The upper and lower jaw portions of the face are sketched on a surface so that they can be cut into two separate sections. One section should represent the upper jaw, and is glued to the top end of the box. The other represents the lower jaw, and is glued to the bottom end of the box. Features are added by using a wide variety of materials.

The cereal box puppet is operated by placing the thumb in the bottom half, and the fingers in the top half of the box. Opening and closing the fingers

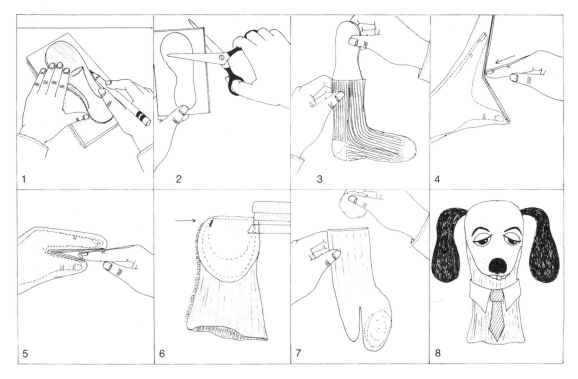

Figure 15-5   SOCK PUPPETS

Materials: sock, cardboard, cotton or old nylon stockings, scissors, stapler, felt or cloth.

1. Trace the outline shape of the sock onto a piece of cardboard.
2. Cut out the cardboard shape of the foot.
3. Put the cutout shape of the foot into the sock.
4. Put the left hand in the sock, while the right hand pushes against the bottom of the sock.
5. As the right hand is pushed in against the sock, the left hand is folded to form the mouth of the puppet.
6. Staple the sides of the mouth at both corners.
7. Stuff the sock with old stockings or cotton.
8. Add features to the puppet.

will cause the puppet's mouth to move. Some cereal boxes are a little wider than others, causing difficulty in their operation. Masking tape can be used to form loops for the fingers and thumb on the inside surface of the box. These loops will make it easier to manipulate the puppet. Two cereal box puppets can be operated by one individual.

Sock Puppets

An old cotton sock can be used to make hand puppets that actually hold a wide variety of small materials in their mouth. Sock puppets are very helpful when the teacher wants to present three-dimensional materials to the children. He can put a sock puppet on each hand; one holds the object, while the other one talks to the children.

Place a piece of cardboard or oak tag on a flat surface. A sock is then placed so that the bottom shape of the foot lies flat on the cardboard. Care should be taken to lay out the sock so that the outline of the foot can be traced with a pencil. With a pair of scissors, cut out the cardboard pattern of the foot being careful to cut on the line and make the cut smooth. Place the cardboard pattern of the foot into the sock, making sure that it fits flat on the bottom of the sock.

The mouth of the puppet is shaped by placing the left hand into the sock, with the fingers in the toe area of the sock, while the thumb is extended back into the heel area. The right hand is placed on the outside of the sock against the middle of the foot. As the right hand is pushed into the foot of the sock, the left hand should be folded closed. This pushing of the right hand and folding of the left hand forms the mouth of the puppet. The final mouth shape depends on the features of the puppet being constructed. When the desired mouth shape is obtained, staple the sides of the mouth at both corners so that the sock will keep its shape.

The puppet head is ready to shape. Cotton or old silk stockings can be used to fill the sock and form the required shape. Features can be added to the puppet by using felt for the hair, marbles for the eyes, and golf tees for the teeth. Scrap materials, such as wood, plastic beads, tinfoil, and fur can make the puppet more interesting.

Sock puppets are operated by placing the fingers in the upper jaw of the mouth and the thumb in the lower jaw. The mouth of the puppet opens and closes as the thumb and fingers are manipulated. The wrist of the hand acts as the puppet's neck.

Pinch Puppets

The basic form for a pinch puppet can be made by folding oak tag or construction paper. One of the advantages of pinch puppets is that all the basic materials are usually found in every classroom or on any playground.

To make a pinch puppet, take a 12-inch square of construction or drawing paper and fold it in half. Open the folded piece of paper and fold it in half again in the opposite direction. The 12-inch square of paper has been divided into quarters or four 6-inch squares. With the piece of paper open and flat on the desk, fold each of the four corners into the center of the 12-inch square. The folded piece should form a new 8-1/2-inch square with four folded flaps that form an X on one surface. Turn the new square over so that the folded four flaps are facing the desk top. Fold the four corners into the center of the 8-1/2-inch square. The size of the new square is 6 inches, with flaps forming an X on one side and a + on the other side. Glue the tips of the triangular flaps at the points that meet in the center of the square. After the tips are secured, apply glue to the two side edges of the square. Fold the bottom edge up to the top edge and press the two glued side edges together. A staple is inserted about 1 inch from both sides along the folded edge, but should not secure the flaps.

The base is formed by holding the folded piece of paper in the lower corners and pushing both hands toward the center. The folded paper should form an opening at the top that is shaped like the interior of a pyramid. This becomes the inside of the puppet's mouth. The bottom will form the outside

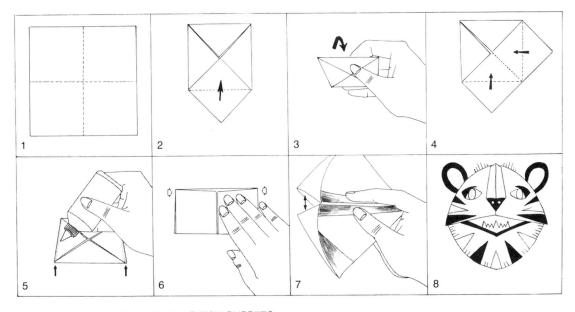

Figure 15-6   PINCH PUPPETS

Materials: construction paper, paint, scissors, paintbrush, glue.

1. Fold a piece of paper in quarters and then unfold it.
2. Fold the four corners into the center.
3. Turn the folded paper over.
4. Fold the four corners into the center.
5. Apply glue along two edges.
6. Fold half so that the top meets the bottom.
7. Insert fingers and form the puppet's mouth.
8. Add features to the puppet.

of the pyramid and four pockets. To operate the puppet, insert two fingers next to the thumb in the two top pockets and the thumb and fourth finger into the bottom two pockets. Moving the fingers and thumb up and down will cause the puppet's mouth to move.

The basic form for the pinch puppet is completed and is ready to become a character. Many different character puppets can be made from this form. The base form can become any creature by adding eyes, ears, nose, and mouth. Features can be drawn on construction paper and cut out and glued onto the base. A whole face can be drawn on construction paper and glued to the base. The mouth is more effective when it moves. The face should be planned so that the upper and lower face features can be separated when cut from the construction paper.

Some interesting results can be obtained by drawing and painting features directly on the base. The inside of the mouth can be painted and teeth cut from construction paper glued inside. Notches can be cut around the outside edges to give the puppet the appearance of fur.

Substitute Clay and Papier-mâché Puppets

Sawdust clay, salt and cornstarch, salt and flour, and papier-mâché can be used over a crumbled newspaper base to construct a hand puppet. The base construction for these various materials is identical and consists of a crumbled newspaper ball attached to a paper tube with masking tape. The essential difference is the type of material used to cover the crumbled newspaper and model the facial features.

Substitute clay and papier-mâché puppets require a great deal of time to construct, because the covering materials have to dry. They also are more difficult to construct because the substitute clay and papier-mâché needs to be modeled into the necessary shape. More skills and coordination are needed. However, the end product is much more durable than one constructed from paper bags and construction paper.

Making the Base   The base is constructed by crumbling a sheet of newspaper into a ball or oval around the top of a 5-inch paper tube. If the paper ball is not large enough, additional sheets of newspaper can be crumbled around the original shape to obtain the desired size. When the size and shape are acquired, wrap masking tape around the paper tube so that it catches the edges of the newspaper. The masking tape is then used to hold down any loose edges of newspaper. The base is completed and is ready to be covered.

Sawdust Clay Puppets   Mix together 5 cups of fine sawdust and 1/2 cup of wheat paste. After the dry sawdust and wheat paste are mixed thoroughly add a small amount of water to the mixture. The mixture is continuously stirred while adding water until the material can be rolled into a ball. A handful of sawdust can be squeezed to determine the consistency. If it drips, more sawdust and wheat paste are needed. If the mixture crumbles, add more water.

The mixture is ready to apply over the newspaper core. Take a handful of sawdust clay and place it over the newspaper core. The sawdust clay will not just stick to the newspaper. A shell of sawdust clay must be built around the newspaper. Sawdust clay should be added to the core until no newspaper is showing. Continuous wetting of the fingers prevents the sawdust clay from sticking to the hands when being applied. Wetting also makes the material more pliable.

When the newspaper core is covered, features can be added to the shape. Take a small amount of sawdust clay and roll it into a ball. The ball can be shaped into a nose. Additional balls can be made and shaped into other features. When adding features, work the material into the base surface. The new shape will not stick to the base unless it is worked into it; otherwise, it will crack in the drying process.

A bead may be formed around the bottom of the neck with sawdust clay to hold the puppet's head to the costume. When the correct shape has been obtained, the puppet's head should be placed in an upright position to dry. While the head is drying, hands for the puppet can be modeled from a ball of sawdust clay. In shaping the hands, allow a 1-inch wrist so that the costume can be attached. A bead formed from sawdust clay around the end of the wrist will assist in holding the hands to the sleeves of the costume.

When the puppet's head is dry, it can be sanded smooth with fine sandpaper. However, some characters might look better with a rough texture.

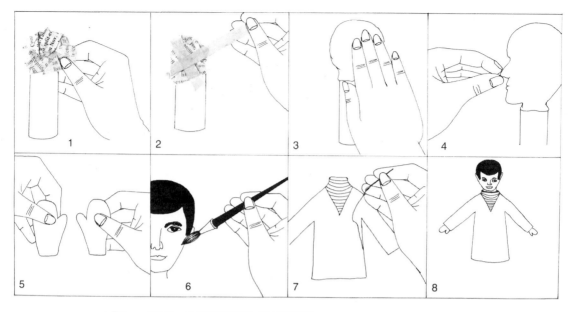

Figure 15-7 SAWDUST CLAY PUPPET
Materials: cardboard tube, newspaper, masking tape, sawdust clay mixture, paint, glue, paintbrush, cloth.
1. Crush a ball of newspaper around the tube.
2. Tape the newspaper ball to the tube.
3. Apply a coat of sawdust clay to the newspaper ball, forming the desired head shape.
4. Model features from sawdust clay and add to the basic head shape.
5. Model the hands from sawdust clay.
6. Paint the facial features and hair.
7. Make a costume for the puppet.
8. Glue the head and hands to the costume.

The puppet's head and hands are ready to be painted. A wide variety of colors can be used to obtain the effect wanted. Yarn, steel wool, angel hair, wool, straw, or wood shavings can be used to add hair to the puppet. After the head and hands have been painted, the puppet is ready for a costume.

Cornstarch-baking soda clay, salt-cornstarch clay, and salt-flour clay can all be used to cover a crumbled or crushed paper base. The crumbled paper base is covered utilizing the same techniques as for sawdust clay. Features are formed the same way. Tempera and watercolor paints can be used to add color to puppets constructed with one of these substitute clays.

Papier-mâché Puppets Many different materials can be used for the base of a papier-mâché puppet's head—a light bulb, milk carton, plastic soap container, cardboard box, or crumbled newspaper over a paper tube. By selecting the proper base, time can be saved and the desired shape and size are easier to obtain.

Take a dish pan and measuring cup and fill the dish pan with 5 cups of cool water. Slowly add 1/2 cup of wheat paste to the water, while stirring

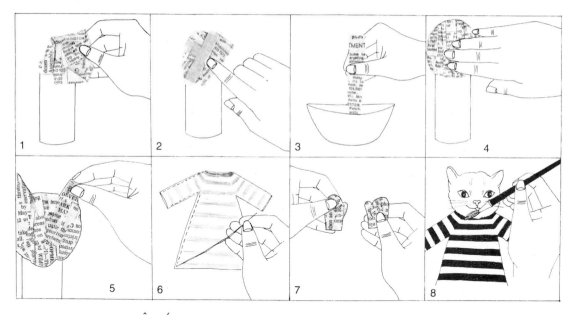

Figure 15-8   PAPIER-MÂCHÉ PUPPETS

Materials: glue, cardboard tube, masking tape, wheat paste mixture, needle and thread, paint, paintbrush, cloth, newspaper.

1. Crush newspaper into a ball around the tube.
2. Tape the newspaper to the tube.
3. Dip newspaper strips into the paste.
4. Apply the pasted strips to the crushed paper base.
5. Add features to the base shape.
6. Make a costume for the puppet.
7. Form the hands from crushed paper, covered with pasted strips of newspaper.
8. Paint the puppet's head.

the mixture to prevent it from becoming lumpy. The mixture should be stirred until there is no powder on the surface of the water.

Pick up two or three pages from a newspaper and tear them into strips that are about 3/4 inch wide. If the newspaper is torn with the grain, strips will tear evenly. Tear about fifty strips and keep them in a cardboard box for easy handling.

To prevent the paste from setting on the bottom, which occurs when the mixture is permitted to stand, stir again before using. Take a strip of newspaper and hold it between the thumb and index finger. Dip the strip into the pan of paste, making sure that it is completely covered with the mixture. As the strip is lifted from the pan, run it gently between the index and third finger to remove excess paste. Place the strips gently around the base in one direction. Before adding another strip, smooth out the edges of the pasted newspaper strips with your fingers. After the base is covered with strips in one direction, a second layer of strips running in the opposite direction can be placed over the first layer. Care should be taken to smooth out each strip as it is added to the base. Lumps or wrinkles should be smoothed while the strips are wet. Add one more layer to the base, making three layers in all. The strips for the third layer should run in the opposite direction from the second layer.

Place the base to one side to dry. Papier-mâché usually dries in twenty-four hours. It is important to keep the covered base in an upright position while drying. Flat spots will result if the wet base is placed on its side to dry. The wet base can be held in an upright position by placing it in any empty food container.

Features can be added to the basic form by using rolled, crumbled, crushed, or cut newspaper. Strips of paper can be rolled into a cylinder to form a nose, horns, or hands. Take three or four strips of newspaper of the desired width and roll them into a cylinder. The diameter of the cylinder can be changed by increasing or decreasing the number of strips.

A sheet of newspaper can be crushed or crumbled into a ball or oval to form cheeks, jaws, hands, or a nose for the puppet. The size and number of paper sheets will determine how large the feature shape will be.

Layers of newspaper or cardboard can be cut into a variety of shapes and used for ears, teeth, or fangs. Take three or four layers of newspaper or a piece of cardboard and cut out the desired shape. Masking tape, pasted strips, or string can be used to attach all the materials at appropriate places.

Features shaped with one of these three methods can be attached by using the following techniques. Use one hand to hold the shape in place while connecting it with a wet strip of newspaper. Some shapes will require two or three strips to hold them secure before layers of paper strips can be built up. Once the rough shape has been secured, additional layers can be applied to the surface to obtain the finished shape. These strips are added by running them from the head, around the rough shape and back to the head in one direction, and then in the opposite direction. When all the puppet's features have been added and the layers of paper strips are smooth, place the head to one side to dry.

A piece of heavy string can be tied to the end of the neck and the wrists and then built up with layers of paper to form a lip. This lip will be used to attach the head and arms of the puppet to the costume. The costume for a papier-mâché puppet head has drawstrings around the neck and wrist openings; when the drawstrings are pulled tight, the costume cannot slip off over the lip.

The puppet's head and hands can be smoothed with fine sandpaper, although some characters look more realistic if the texture is rough. Special colors can be used to paint the eyes, hands, mouth, cheeks, ears, and face. Use many different colors. Colors can be used to tell about the character of the puppet. If the character is happy, it can be painted a bright color, such as red or orange. If the character is mean, it can be painted green, purple, or some other dark color.

Yarn, felt, or straw can be used for hair, moustache, eyebrows, or beard. The puppet can be changed or made to look different with eyeglasses, cap, or moustache. After the head and hands are completed, the puppet is ready for a costume.

Making Clothing for the Puppet   Clothing adds to the appearance of the puppet and gives the character identity. It is also important to the manipulation of the puppet because the costume hides the puppeteer's hand and arm from the audience. The hands of the puppet are also connected to the puppet's head by the costume.

A piece of wrapping paper should be used to design a costume and to test for the appropriate size. On a piece of wrapping paper, lay out a pattern for the costume and cut it out with a pair of scissors. One of the major functions of the costume is to hide the arm and hand of the puppeteer from the audience. Although this puts some limitations on the style, some different and attractive costumes have been designed for use with this type of puppet head.

Select a piece of material (cotton, wool, or leather) that matches or will look well with the colors used to paint the features on the puppet's head. Lay out the material on a flat surface and fold it in half. Place the pattern on the material and pin it in place with straight pins. With a pair of scissors cut the material along the edge of the pattern. Remove the pattern from the material. The two pieces of material, front and back, should be exactly the same shape. The material used may have a bright and dull side. If so, put the bright sides facing each other and pin them together. With a needle and thread, sew along the edge of the material, leaving an opening for the neck and hands.

A drawstring can be added to the neck and arms of the costume. This is accomplished by turning a hem large enough to take a piece of string around the openings for the neck and hands. Turn the dress inside out so that the bright side is facing outward and the stitching is inside.

The costume may be glued rather than sewn together. The two dull sides are placed together, the glue is applied along the dull edges of the costume, and the pieces are pressed together. An opening for the puppet's neck and hands must remain. The puppet's head and hands can be glued to the costume instead of using a drawstring. Gluing is less useful than drawstrings because costumes cannot be changed.

The costume is ready for decorating. Buttons, lace, or other ornaments can be added to make the costume more attractive and interesting. Various types of clothing and accessories can be added to the puppet.

Finger Puppets

There are two basic finger puppets. The first is cut from oak tag or cardboard, while the second has a head modeled from substitute clay, paper pulp, or clay and secured to the end of a rod or stick.

Sketch a clown, elephant, or other figure on a piece of 3 X 5 inch cardboard. The details can be colored with crayons, watercolors, or tempera paints. Cut out the outline shape and at the bottom of the figure in the position of the feet, cut out two holes large enough for the second and middle fingers. If the second and middle fingers are placed through these holes, the figure can be made to kick his feet and walk.

To make an elephant puppet, cut out a hole for the elephant's trunk and glue two paper loops to the bottom of the back side of the front legs. To operate the elephant puppet, place the middle finger through the trunk hole and the second and fourth fingers in the leg loops. Then, using the thumb and little finger as the rear legs, make the elephant walk.

Sawdust clay, paper pulp, or clay can be modeled into a small head around a 3-inch rod or stick. The head should not exceed 1-1/2 inches in diameter. Pipe cleaners can be used for the arms and legs. An outfit for the puppet can be made from scrap pieces of yard goods. The puppet is tied to the operator's finger with a waist band from a piece of 6 X 1/2 inch cloth. This band should be sewed to the puppet's waist. A puppet can be tied to a finger on each hand and manipulated by moving fingers.

Paper Tube Puppets

The paper tubes used as a core in a number of everyday household products can be used to construct interesting and effective puppets. It is a good idea to have on hand a large number of different sized tubes so that some puppets can be constructed from long, thin tubes, while others are made from short, squat ones. Some individuals may even deviate from the paper tube and choose to make a cone, square, or triangle for the head of their puppet. Children should be encouraged to try different shapes and sizes as they develop their individual puppets.

Select a suitable tube for the puppet character. With a pencil and ruler, draw a straight line the length of the tube. Draw another line around the tube in the position that will represent the puppet's mouth. Cut along this line, leaving about 1/2 inch of the tube uncut on either side of the vertical line. This uncut section of the tube will be a hinge and can be reinforced with a piece of masking tape 1/2 X 1 inch. Cut two pieces of heavy string, 10 inches longer than the tube, and tie a loop, large enough for a finger, at one end of each string. Apply glue to the vertical line for about 1 inch from the top of the tube. Place the untied end of one string along the glued line and let it dry. The mouth will open and close when tension is applied to the string and released. Glue the second piece of string to the inside of the tube just above the mouth. The back and front strings will enable the operator to manipulate the opening and closing of the mouth. One string will open the mouth. The second string gives the operator greater control of the mouth's movement. The puppet is held by a wooden stick glued to the inside of the bottom of the paper tube. The puppet is manipulated by using the fingers to pull on the strings, while the stick is held with the other hand.

The base of the puppet is ready for features. Make a sketch of how the puppet is going to look. Using scrap materials, design the eyes, ears, nose, and mouth for the puppet. The puppet can have a pleasant or grouchy appearance. The ears can have a three-dimensional rather than a flat two-dimensional look.

MARIONETTES
Spool Marionettes

A marionette is a special kind of puppet with movable limbs, which are manipulated by strings, wires, or rods from above. Wooden or plastic spools strung on heavy string can be used to construct attractive marionettes.

A 2-inch Styrofoam ball is used for the head of the marionette. It can be painted with watercolor, tempera, or latex paints. Facial features can be cut from construction paper, felt, or yard goods and glued to the Styrofoam ball. Buttons, beads, and a wide variety of other three-dimensional

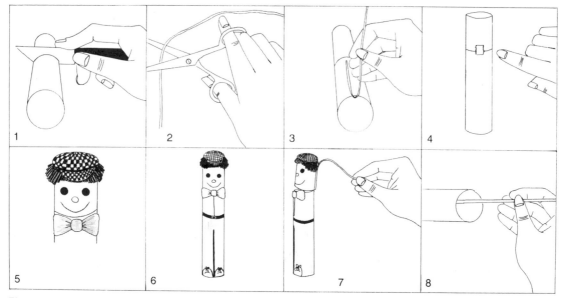

Figure 15-9 TUBE PUPPET

Materials: pencil, knife, paper tube, stick or dowel, scissors, string, masking tape, glue, construction paper, paint, paintbrushes, and scrap pieces of fabrics.

1. Cut the tube 4 inches from the top, leaving 1/2 inch connected in the back to act as a hinge.
2. Cut a piece of string 10 inches longer than the tube.
3. Glue the string to the top half of the tube.
4. Use a piece of masking tape to reinforce the hinge.
5. Paint facial features and add a hat.
6. Use felt or cloth to make clothing.
7. Pull on the end of the string to open the puppet's mouth.
8. Glue the dowel to the inside bottom of the tube.

materials can also be used. Hair, beard, or whiskers may be made from yarn, rope, or cotton and glued to the Styrofoam ball.

When the head of the marionette is completed, start painting the spools with tempera or latex paint. The color of the spools depends upon the character that the finished marionette is going to represent. Three small spools are needed for each arm and leg and two large spools for the body. The spools are ready to be threaded onto a heavy piece of string. Thread a large needle with about 15 inches of string. If a large needle is not available, a small amount of glue can be applied to the end of the string and allowed to dry. The glue will harden and stiffen the end of the string, making it easier to thread the string through the hole in the spools.

Thread the string through a 3/8-inch wooden or plastic bead and tie a knot around it to secure it to the end of the string. Thread three spools onto the string with a bead between each spool. The string should have four beads and three spools with a bead between each spool and one on each end of the three spools. Repeat this threading procedure until you have two arms and two legs for the marionette.

With the remaining string, tie the two legs tightly together and cut off one of the strings. Thread a bead onto the string that is left and set the legs to one side.

Thread another piece of 15-inch string through the two larger spools, being sure to place a bead in the middle and one at the end. Tie the end of the body string without a bead to the legs. Tie the arms to the top body string above the neck bead. Cut off the ends of the arm strings, leaving only the body string. Add another bead to this body string.

With the large needle, pull the remaining piece of body string through the center of the head of the marionette. This piece of string should be cut about 2 inches above the marionette's head.

Costume   A costume can be made from felt or cloth for the marionette. The costume can be either a dress or pants. The costume for the marionette does not require a hand opening. A pattern sketched on a piece of paper can be used in planning an outfit for the marionette.

The marionette's hands and feet can be constructed from felt or cloth. Two pieces of the desired shape for the hands or feet are cut from a piece of cloth. The edges of the material are sewn together, forming a pocket. The hands and feet should be stuffed with small stones or sand so that they flip down when manipulated by the string attached to the T control. The hands and feet are sewn to the ends of the arms and legs.

T control   The T control is constructed from two pieces of wood 10 X 3/4 X 1/4 inch and a third piece 12 X 1-1/2 X 1/2 inch. Cross the 10 and 12 inch sticks in the center and tie them tightly with a piece of heavy thread. Cross the second 10-inch stick 1 inch from the end of the 12-inch stick. The T control is ready to be attached to the marionette.

Cut a piece of black thread 16 inches long and tie it to the body string that was pulled through the head of the marionette. Tie the other end of the thread to the center of the T control. Cut two pieces of thread 23 inches long and tie one end of each piece of thread to the hands. The hand threads are tied to the two ends of the 10-inch center cross stick. Cut two pieces of thread 30 inches long. Tie one end of each piece of thread to the feet. The leg threads are tied to the two ends of the 10-inch cross stick, located 1 inch from the end of the 12-inch stick. Cut a piece of thread 23 inches long and tie it to the back of the marionette underneath the last large body spool. The other end is tied to the center of the cross stick located 1 inch from the end of the 12-inch stick.

Hold the T control in one hand and let the marionette hang down. All the strings should be straight and the legs and arms should be at their lowest point. If they are not in this position, adjust the various strings to obtain the desired lengths. When all the strings are the correct length, staple them to the stick to keep them from slipping. Cut off all loose ends of the thread.

The marionette is ready to operate. Hold the T control in one hand at the end of the 12-inch stick. Turn the stick from one side to the other to make the marionette move. Use the free hand to pull on the various strings.

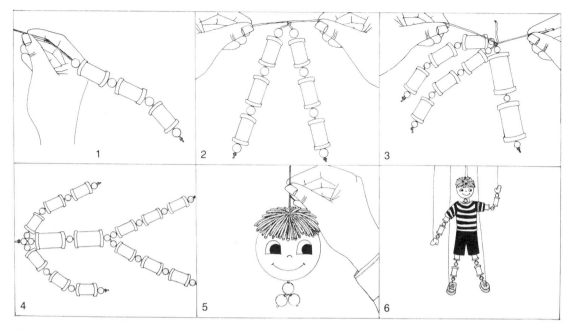

Figure 15-10   SPOOL MARIONETTE
Materials: string, Styrofoam ball, thread, scissors, needle, spools (large), spools (small), beads, cloth, wooden control sticks, glue.
1. Place three small spools and four beads on a piece of thread to form a leg.
2. Tie the legs together.
3. Tie the legs to the body (two large spools, and three beads on a piece of thread).
4. Tie the arms (three small spools and four beads) to the body.
5. Connect the head to the body.
6. Add features, clothing, and control strings to the marionette.

Two controls are usually used to manipulate a marionette, but because of the difficulty in operating two, one is sufficient with elementary school children.

Older children who have become skillful in using one control stick may decide to try handling a second stick. The second control is constructed from a piece of wood 12 X 1-1/2 X 1/2 inch. Remove the knee strings from the control stick and fasten them to the new control stick. To manipulate the T control, hold the first control in the right hand while holding the second in the left hand. When the knee control is manipulated separately, the marionette has a more natural walk.

Balsa Wood Marionettes

Balsa wood can be used to carve the body, head, arms, and legs of a marionette. The various parts of the body are connected with small screw eyes.

Balsa is a light, fibrous wood that is easy to carve and work with a knife, rasp, file, or sandpaper. It can be purchased in blocks, strips, and sticks in a wide variety of lengths, widths, and thicknesses.

Model airplane cement can be used to connect pieces of balsa together to obtain various shapes. Sanding sealer is applied to the wood surface after all shaping and sanding are completed.

The sealer will dry in about ten minutes and can be sanded and a second coat applied. The sanding sealer saves on the number of coats of paint needed to obtain a glossy finish.

Airplane dope, latex paint, or other types of paint can be used to obtain a wide variety of textures. However, airplane dope is the best material to use to obtain a high-gloss finish. It dries rapidly and comes in many rich colors.

Wooden Marionettes

A wooden marionette can be constructed from two pieces of wood 1-1/2 X 1-1/2 X 1/2 inch and 3 X 2 X 1/2 inch, a wooden dowel, nineteen small screw eyes, cloth or felt, and thread. Tools required include a coping saw, needle-nose pliers, and file.

Sketch the desired head shape on the small piece of wood and cut it out with a coping saw. On the larger block, sketch the desired body shape and cut it out. The edges should be sanded smooth. The facial detail can be painted with watercolor, tempera, or latex paints.

Cut four pieces of dowel 2-1/2 inches long for the arms and four pieces 3 inches long for the legs. The limbs and body parts are connected together with screw eyes. Two screw eyes are located at each limb or body joint. To connect the screw eyes, pry open the end of one, slip it through the other screw eye, and close it again. A single screw eye is positioned in the top of the head.

Making hands and feet and clothing and the procedures for connecting the control strings are the same as indicated above. The wooden marionette is controlled and manipulated in the same manner as the spool marionette.

Paper Bag Marionettes

Children enjoy making and playing with paper bag marionettes. They are very simple to make and can be constructed by very young children without too much difficulty. Paper bag marionettes do not require any elaborate materials, but can be constructed with those materials found in most classrooms, on organized playgrounds, or in recreational centers.

Take a medium-sized paper bag and fill about three-quarters of it with crumbled newspaper. With a piece of string, tie the open end closed. This paper bag stuffed with crumbled newspaper represents the head and body of the marionette.

The arms and legs of the marionette are constructed from strips of folded paper called "catstairs." Cut eight strips of construction paper 1/8 inch wide and 18 inches long. Glue the ends of two separate strips together so that they form a right angle. Fold the strips one over the other until the end is reached. Take two more strips and repeat the procedure for the other arm. The legs of the marionette are made in the same manner as the arms. These strips for the arms and legs are made up of a series of accordionlike folds.

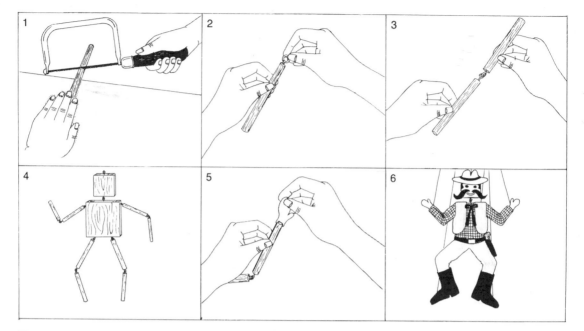

Figure 15-11 WOODEN MARIONETTE

Materials: pine block, 1/4-inch dowels, coping saw, screw eyes, string, cardboard, scrap cloth.

1. Cut the dowels to the desired length.
2. Fasten the screw eyes to the ends of the dowels.
3. Join two screw eyes together to form a leg or arm.
4. Making the head and body for the marionette.
    a. Sketch the desired head shape on a piece of wood and cut it out with a coping saw.
    b. Sketch the desired body shape on a piece of wood and cut it out with a coping saw.
    c. Assemble the head and body of the wooden marionette.

Draw two hands and two feet on a piece of construction paper or felt and cut them out. The hands and feet may be large or small. Glue the hands to the bottom of the folded arm strips. Position the arms and glue them to the paper bag. They are usually glued about 2 or 3 inches from the bottom of the bag along the side edges. Glue the feet to the folded leg strips, and then glue the legs to the bottom of the bag.

The paper bag marionette is ready for facial features. Add ears, eyes, nose, and mouth by drawing them on the bag or cutting them out of construction paper and gluing them to the face of the marionette. Yarn, rope, or string can be used to add hair to the marionette.

When the paper bag marionette is completed, strings can be added to the head, arms, and legs to provide movement. The strings are attached to a 2 X 4 inch piece of cardboard. The marionette is supported by a series of strings, and the head, arms, and legs move as the piece of cardboard is moved. Different combinations of string and cardboard can be used to obtain variations in the marionette's movement.

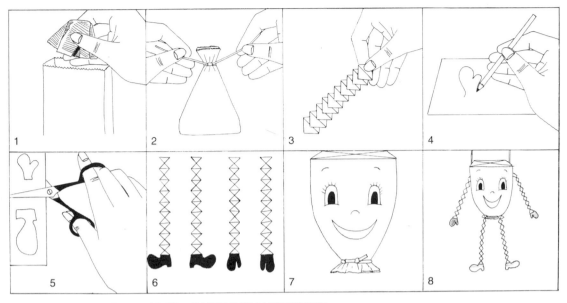

Figure 15-12 PAPER BAG MARIONETTE

Materials: small paper bag, string, scissors, pencil, 8 paper strips 18 X 5/8 inch, newspaper, glue, construction paper.

1. Stuff the bag with small pieces of newspaper.
2. Tie the top of the bag with string.
3. Make four "catstairs."
4. Draw hands and feet on a piece of construction paper.
5. Cut out hands and feet.
6. Glue hands and feet to the catstairs.
7. Add facial features to the bag.
8. Attach arms and legs to the bag.

Flip-flop People and Animals

Flip-flop people and animals are constructed from a number of different sized catstairs. A catstair is constructed by folding construction paper to form a series of stairs.

The following procedures can be used to make a catstair. Cut two strips of construction paper 1 inch wide and 6 inches long. Glue the strips at right angles. Fold the strips one over the other. As the strips are folded, the edges must be even. Continue folding until the end of the strips are reached. Glue the last flap down and the catstair is set aside to dry.

A man may be made from catstairs. The body is constructed from two strips of construction paper, 2 inches wide and 12 inches long, while the arms and legs are constructed from eight strips of construction paper 1/2 inch wide and 12 inches long. The neck strips are 1 inch wide and 4 inches long. Repeat the steps for making a catstair. When the catstairs are completed for the body, arms, legs, and neck, construct shoulder strap from a piece of construction paper 1/2 inch wide and 3 inches long. This strip is used to connect the arms to the body.

Connect the shoulder strap to the top of the body catstair by gluing it to the center of the top flap. The catstair for the neck is glued to the center

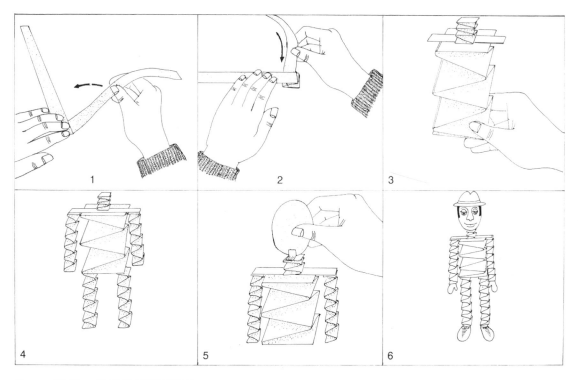

Figure 15-13   FLIP-FLOP PEOPLE

Materials: two strips of paper 12 x 2 inches (body), two strips of paper 6 x 1 inches (neck), one strip of paper 3 x 1/2 inches (shoulder strap), eight strips of paper 8 x 1/2 inches (arms and legs), construction paper, scissors, glue.

1. Glue two strips of paper together at right angles.
2. Fold one strip over the other to form a catstair.
3. Glue the shoulder strap and neck to the body.
4. Glue the arms and legs to the body.
5. Glue the head to the neck.
6. Add features to the flip-flop man.

of the top square flap directly on top of the shoulder strap. The two catstairs for the arms are glued to the shoulder straps so that they hang in a downward position. The two catstairs for the legs are glued to the square at the bottom of the body catstair. They also should hang in a downward position.

The flip-flop man is ready for a head and face. Select a piece of construction paper for the head. Facial features can be added to the head by drawing them directly on the head shape or by cutting them from construction paper or felt. When the face and head are completed, connect them to the neck of the catstair with a 1/4-inch-wide and 1-inch-long strip of construction paper. The strip is folded in half so that the strip is 1/4 X 1/2 inch. Glue one-half of this folded strip to the center of the top square of the neck catstair and the other half to the head.

On a piece of scrap paper sketch hands, paws, or mittens for the flip-flop man. Trace the hands onto a piece of construction paper or felt. The

THEATER CRAFTS

hands are folded at the wrist and the little tab is glued to the arms so that the hands will hang in the desired position.

Sketch the feet or shoes on a piece of scrap paper. When the desired size and shape are obtained trace the feet or shoes onto a piece of construction paper or felt and cut them out. They are glued to the bottom square of the legs catstair.

The flip-flop man is completed. A string or rubber band can be tied to the head to make the flip-flop man walk, hop, or lumber along. With a T control and strings to the wrists, feet, and head, the flip-flop man can be made to do interesting tricks.

PUPPET AND MARIONETTE STAGES
Cardboard Carton Stage

An inexpensive puppet or marionette stage can be constructed from an empty cardboard carton. However, this type of stage has certain limitations; it occupies a large segment of classroom space when not being utilized, and it is difficult to store because it cannot be folded. The major advantage is that it provides the teacher with a very inexpensive puppet or marionette stage.

Take a large grocery carton and cut away the top, bottom, and one long side. This will leave a folding-type screen with one long side and two short sides. Cut a window in the center of the long side for the stage opening. The puppet stage is ready to be painted and decorated. Latex paint can be used to cover the cardboard surface. Cartoons or designs make the stage attractive. Curtains for the stage as well as a backdrop curtain can be made from scrap pieces of cloth. Additional height is obtained by placing the stage on a table or desk when using it for a puppet stage.

Frame Construction Stage

A more durable and practical stage can be constructed from 1 X 1-1/2 inch strips of pine or firring in varying lengths, triangular shapes cut from hardboard or Upson board, 3/4-inch number 16 wire nails, hinges, and a material to cover the frames. The materials needed are inexpensive, and the construction method requires only a limited number of tools (crosscut saw, hammer, wooden miter box, hand drill, screw driver, and try square). This technique requires limited understanding and skill in the utilization of tools.

The first step is to determine what size puppet stage would fit the needs of a particular group. The height and width of the stage can vary according to the age of the children who are going to use it. A stage constructed from three frames 4 X 2-1/2 feet is a good size for use with children in the age group four to eight, while one 5 X 3 feet is more appropriate for older children.

Lay out the actual size of a frame on a piece of wrapping paper to assure that the frames are square and the same size. One of the 1 X 1-1/2 inch strips can be used to draw the frame onto the wrapping paper which is used to check the accuracy of the various strips.

Select a piece of wood 1 X 1-1/2 inches that is long enough for one of

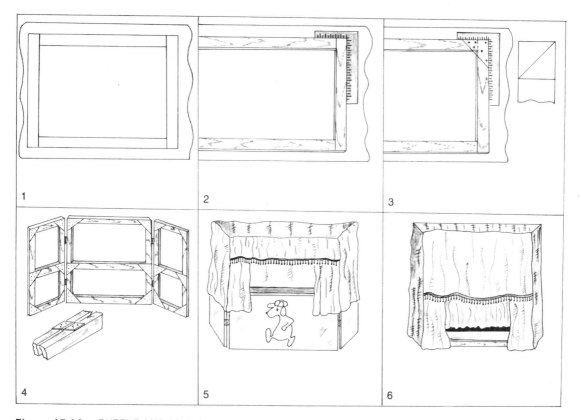

Figure 15-14 PUPPET AND MARIONETTE STAGES

Materials: 2-inch firring or strapping, 3/4-inch number 16 wire nails, 5 x 5 x 7 inch hardboard triangles, hammer, try square, fabric to cover the stage, wrapping paper.

1. Make a full-size drawing of the frame on a piece of wrapping paper.
2. Cut the wood to the correct size and lay each piece on the drawing.
3. Fasten the corners with a triangle cut from a piece of hardboard.
4. Hinge the frames together.
5. Finished puppet stage.
6. Finished marionette stage.

the required lengths. Place the piece of wood into a miter box and cut one of the ends square with a crosscut saw. From the squared end, measure the desired length and mark it. Place back into the miter box and cut this end square. If an actual-size layout for the frame was made, check the length of the piece of wood against it. Repeat this procedure until the wooden strips have been cut for all the frames.

Select a piece of Upson board or hardboard and measure and lay out a 5-inch square. Cut out the square with a handsaw, being careful not to tear the material. With a straight edge draw a diagonal line across the square from corner to corner. This will form two triangles approximately 5 X 5 X 7 inches. The triangles will be used to secure the 1 X 1-1/2 inch strips of wood into rectangular frames.

Place the four pieces of wood in position on the actual-size drawing, they should form a rectangle. With a try square, check to be sure that each corner is square. Place a triangle over the corner so that the edges are even with the outside edges of the strips of wood. The triangle is nailed in position with 3/4-inch number 16 wire nails. The nails should be placed about 3/4 inch from the edge of the triangles, and they should be staggered. Repeat this operation for all four corners of the three frames. To give the frame additional strength, place a strip of wood across the center of each frame dividing the length in half. On the center frame, this strip can be located in a position to obtain the necessary stage opening. In planning the stage, remember that puppets are manipulated from under the stage opening, while marionettes are operated from above the stage opening.

The frames are ready to be covered. They can be covered with plywood, hardboard, Upson board, cardboard or some type of fabric. If a fabric is used, triangles should be added to the other side of each corner to increase the strength of the frame. If the other materials are used, they will serve the same purpose as the triangle and will increase the strength of the frame. Fabric or cardboard can be attached to the frame with upholstery tacks, while the other materials can be held in position with 3/4-inch number 16 wire nails or wood screws.

One-inch folding screen hinges can be used to secure two of the frames together, while two-inch butt hinges can be used to secure the other frame to the center frame. Folding screen hinges are used when it is important for the frame to fold in either direction. This combination of hinges will allow the side panels of the stage to fold in against the center panel for easy storage.

The stage is completed and is ready to be painted or decorated with designs or cartoons. Latex paints are excellent for this purpose. They are much more durable than tempera paints and are very inexpensive. Brushes and containers can be cleaned with warm water and soap. Curtains for the stage can be constructed from scrap materials. A backdrop curtain for the stage is required and is usually situated half the distance from the stage opening and the rear of the stage.

An alternative marionette stage can be constructed by using a freestanding rectangular frame as the backdrop. The height and width of the frame vary according to the size of the children. It should be slightly higher than the child's waist. A scene is painted on a piece of cardboard and hung on the backdrop. The frame can be made free-standing by adding two cross pieces to represent feet at the bottom of the frame. The advantage of this type of marionette stage is that it can be used for many other purposes, such as a room divider or display board.

MASKS

Almost every culture, ancient or modern, primitive or sophisticated, has used masks for one purpose or another. When studying any culture, it is important to explore how and why masks were used. An investigation of this aspect of any culture will reveal some interesting facts about the people and their customs. In Africa, South America, and North America, various tribes used masks for many different purposes. They were used by some tribes to ward off evil spirits and by others as part of the dress for special

Figure 15-15   MASKS
1. Paper bag masks.
2. Paper plate masks.
3. Papier-mâché masks.
4. Papier-mâché head piece.

ceremonies. Masks are still used in Greece, Japan, and India as part of the costume in the traditional theater. Masks in the United States are associated with Halloween and masquerade parties.

Masks should be constructed by children with a purpose in mind. The activity should provide children with an opportunity to explore a wide variety of materials. It also should allow the children to use their imagination and be creative. However, it is just as important to utilize this experience to enrich learning in other subject areas. For example, masks can be used to depict animals, heroes, or other characters in a play. A head-piece such as those worn by our astronauts in space can be made. Young children can make masks for parties or to depict a character from their storybooks, while older children can use their imagination to study cultures of different civilizations.

Papier-mâché Face and Head Masks

Face and head masks can be modeled over a wide variety of bases with strips of newspaper, soaked in wheat paste. The head mask fits over the individual's head, covering it entirely, while the face mask covers only facial features.

Sawdust and modeling clay can be modeled into a facial form. These bases should be covered with petroleum jelly before applying the pasted newspaper strips. This coating will allow the finished paper mask to be lifted freely from the mold when dry.

Aluminum foil can be placed over an individual's face and pressed into a facial form. The pasted newspaper strips can be applied directly over the aluminum foil base. Care should be taken when covering the aluminum foil base, because it is very soft and pliable. The first three coverings of crisscrossed pasted strips should be formed without applying great pressure to the surface. The pasted strips must follow the contour of the aluminum foil base.

The head mask is formed over a crushed or crumbled newspaper ball. The ball should be large enough to allow the finished form to fit over the individual's head. When the desired size is obtained, a sheet of dry newspaper is used to cover the crumbled paper ball. Dry newspaper sheet is used so that the finished head mask can be separated from the crumbled paper ball.

When the bases for the face masks are ready to cover, tear sheets of newspaper into strips and soak them in a wheat paste—water mixture of five parts of paste to one part of water. Three layers of pasted strips are carefully applied over the base in alternating directions. It is important that the strips be fitted to the base form to obtain the desired facial shape. These layers are allowed to dry. Features can be added to the mask before any additional pasted strips are added.

If the head of a horse or duck is to be the finished product, the head mask base may require additional crumbled newspaper shapes. A ball of crumbled paper is shaped and tied or taped in place to the original crumbled paper core. This crumbled paper form becomes a permanent part of the finished head mask and is not removed. The pasted newspaper strips are applied over the crumbled paper base, first in one direction and then in the opposite direction. Three layers can be applied to the form and allowed to dry before additional features are added. The surface should be covered with two more layers of pasted newspaper strips. The third and final layer can be strips of pasted hand towel material for interesting effect.

Features for both the face and head mask can be added by utilizing the techniques described under the procedures for making papier-mâché objects.

Paper Bag Masks

A wide variety of masks can be constructed from different sized paper bags. Place the paper bag over the individual's head and mark the position of the eyes, nose, and mouth with a crayon. Remove the paper bag from the individual's head and sketch the facial features of the planned character on the face incorporating these positions. After drawing the eyes, nose, and mouth on the bag, cut them out. The face is then painted or colored and additional facial features are added. Construction paper, yarn, rope, and felt can be used to decorate the mask.

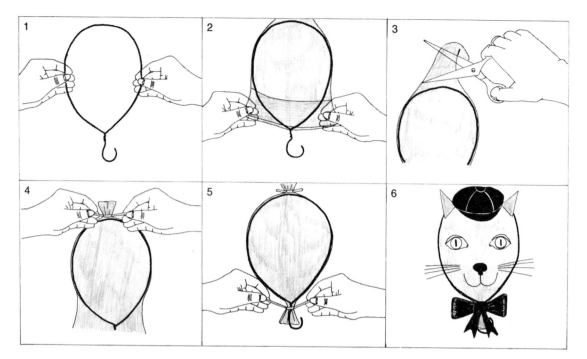

Figure 15-16   COAT HANGER MASKS

Materials: wire, coat hanger, string, old nylon stockings, scissors, glue, cloth or felt.

1. Shape the coat hanger.
2. Cover the hanger with the nylon stocking.
3. Cut off the end of the stocking.
4. Tie the end with string.
5. Pull the stocking tight and tie the opposite end.
6. Add features.

Attractive masks can be constructed for Halloween, Thanksgiving, Christmas, and Valentine's Day. They also can be used to present a play about some historical event. Sometimes the paper bag is stuffed with cotton, rags, stockings, or other material and placed on the end of a broomstick. The paper bag mask becomes an oversized stick puppet.

Coat Hanger Masks

Old coat hangers can be shaped into an oval, square, triangle, or circle to form a base for the mask. After the desired shape is obtained, cover the coat hanger by pulling a woman's mesh stocking over it. Cut the top and bottom of the stocking 2 inches longer than the coat hanger shape. Then tie the top of the stocking with a piece of string. Pull the opposite end of the stocking so that it fits tightly over the coat hanger frame and tie it with a piece of string.

The base of the coat hanger mask is completed and ready for features to be added. Draw a sketch of the face on a piece of scrap paper. Select material for the eyes, ears, nose, and mouth. The ears can be made out of coat hanger wire bent to the desired shape and covered with the mesh

THEATER CRAFTS

stocking scraps. They can also be cut from felt, yard goods, or construction paper. When the shapes for the features have been cut from suitable material, glue them to the mesh stocking surface. Straw, yarn, rope, and yard goods can be used for the hair, while cloth or oak tag can be used for a neck or collar. Many materials can be used for a hat or other features. When the mask is completed, it can be held in front of the child's face as he acts out his part in a play.

Paper Plate Masks

A very simple face mask can be constructed from a paper plate. This activity is excellent for introducing children to the craft of paper sculpture. The paper plate mask can be given a three-dimensional appearance by cutting two slits 2 inches deep and 2 or 3 inches apart on the edge of the plate. The cut slits are overlapped slightly and stapled together forming a simple chin cup which makes the mask fit the face snugly. The position for the eyes should be located and marked with a crayon. The slits should be cut for the eyes after the facial details have been sketched on the paper plates. The nose can be cut on the two sides and on the bottom so that it can be pushed out to give a three-dimensional effect. Cut construction paper and fold to form a cone, pyramid, box, or triangle for the nose. A nose may be constructed from a crumpled ball of paper. A rubber band or string is stapled to each side of the mask to hold it in place.

A scrap box with such things as raffia, yarn, shavings, steel wool, feathers, fur, cotton, or hair will be invaluable in suggesting new and different approaches to decorating or making a mask.

FLATS AND PROPS FOR SCENERY

Scenery flats and props are constructed using the same methods that were utilized to make each panel of the puppet stage. The major difference lies in the size of the frames. The scenery flats are typically much larger. The frames can be used for the sides of a house with windows and doors. The door and opening for the door are constructed with the same procedure as described for making a frame. The triangles for the door opening should be in a position not to interfere with the swinging door. The windows are also constructed similarly. The scenery flats or props are usually covered with cardboard or unbleached muslin. The unbleached muslin should be covered with glue sizing (mixture of glue and water) before it is painted.

The flats or props are connected with corner braces or corner plates. The corner braces can be used for forming the frames at right angles or bent to form other angles. The corner plates are used to join the flats side by side.

DIORAMAS

A diorama is a small scale model on any subject. It could be the operation of a lumber camp, prehistoric animals, landing on the moon, life in the ocean, or flight in space. The Smithsonian Institute and many museums make extensive use of dioramas to take the viewer into the past and future or show him some unfamiliar aspect of the present. When good design is used along with the principles of color, realistic results can occur.

The front frame of a diorama can be constructed by using the technique described for making a puppet stage. The cardboard back is curved to give the scene a more lifelike appearance. A diorama 36 inches long, 18 inches high, and 18 inches deep at the farthest point is a good size for obtaining the desired effect.

The diorama is viewed from a restricted angle, not from all sides. Thus, in planning a diorama, the exhibit is prepared from the viewer's position. The various elements of the diorama should be constructed to scale and the illusion of distance created utilizing the principles of perspective. Position, size, surface lines, overlapping, shading and shadow, density, foreshortening, and converging lines are elements used to increase the realistic appearance of the diorama scene. Fences, buildings, roads, animals, and other objects should be constructed with these elements in mind. This can be accomplished by making each successive building, animal, tree, or other object smaller as it recedes into the background. It is very effective to use bright colors and a high degree of contrast in the foreground compared with the background, to obtain the illusion of depth. Shade, shadow, and detail can also be used for this purpose.

Simplicity is the most important factor in the construction of any diorama. Too much material in a scene is confusing. Because of the cluttered appearance, it is difficult for the observer to obtain the full value of the display. A few well-constructed objects effectively placed are much more meaningful than a crowded scene in conveying a message.

Before constructing any diorama, sketch a plan of how the finished product should look. This sketch will be very helpful and is necessary if more than one individual is working on the project. Several sketches may be required to achieve what is sought. Photographs and pictures may also be used as a guide to the construction and layout of the scene for a diorama.

The final product depends upon the utilization of materials to carry out the theme. Children should be encouraged to use a great number of resource materials in the development of their diorama. Experimentation will foster a greater understanding and appreciation of the properties and characteristics of these materials for more effective use.

Miniature Dioramas

A miniature diorama can be constructed within a small cardboard box with a clear plastic cover. Measure the length and width of the bottom of the cardboard box and use these measurements to locate a greeting card with a suitable scene for the desired background. Cut the card to the correct dimensions of the bottom of the box and glue it in place. Place the box on the working surface so that the picture is in an upright position. The side against the working surface and the bottom of the picture is the base of the diorama. Measure the length and width of this surface and cut a piece of 1/4- or 1/2-inch-thick Styrofoam for the base. The thickness of the Styrofoam will depend upon the size of the box used for the diorama.

This Styrofoam base can be cut with a knife or sandpaper to obtain the desired shape. With an Exacto knife cut several slits, the length of the Styrofoam base, 1/4 inch apart. Care should be taken not to cut the slits completely through the Styrofoam base.

Select some old greeting cards and cut out people, animals, houses, trees, or any other objects that can be used in the scene planned for the diorama. Try to find figures that are the appropriate size for the objects found in the background scene. Size can be used to give the illusion of depth. Take the cutout figures and insert them into the various slits in the base. When all the cutouts are in place, put the base into the box. Check to see how the figures look in relationship to the background. Adjust any of the shapes that appear out of position. Some shapes may be deleted or new ones added to enhance the overall appearance of the scene. Place the plastic cover in position and the diorama is completed.

Peep Shows

An interesting peep show can be constructed inside a shoe box. This activity requires some imagination in the selection and use of scrap materials. It is important to experiment with materials to determine how they can be used to create various effects. Many of the techniques and materials utilized in the construction of a diorama can be used in building a peep show. Shells, sawdust, twigs, cotton, Styrofoam, clay, and pebbles are but a few of the materials that may be needed.

At one end of the box, cut a 1-inch square hole. Take the top and cut away the center section of the top, leaving a 1-inch margin on all four edges.

The inside of the box can be painted any color depending upon the scene. Wallpaper, greeting cards, or tissue paper can also be used to decorate the inside of the box. The scene is constructed on the inside bottom of the box and should be planned with consideration of the position of the viewer.

Peep shows make excellent activities for children with artistic ability. The activity also provides the child with means by which he can express his ideas regarding a topic with a three-dimensional dioramic effect.

CRAFTS FROM RECYCLED MATERIALS 16

Old bottles, tin cans, yarn, pieces of driftwood, thread, feathers, and mechanical junk provide the craftsman with an endless supply of materials to create interesting craft objects. Children delight in experimenting with scrap materials. They will use scrap materials to create model cars, trains, satellites, lunar modules, and robots. Children will also use scrap materials to make pins, flowers, and other decorative objects.

Mechanical junk is particularly suitable for constructional work. For example, the various parts from old appliances are more versatile than commercial kits and are infinitely cheaper. An environment with scrap materials is far less restrictive than one limited to commercial materials. Scrap materials provide children with an opportunity to work with sophisticated apparatus that requires a great deal of improvising on the part of the individual. These scrap materials usually stimulate ideas, while commercial materials sometimes inhibit the individual's creative expression.

Some children will have a definite model in mind and will carefully select the components needed to construct their craft object. However, many of the models will be an outgrowth of what the children see in a specific component. The following suggestions are some ideas of models and items that could be constructed from recycled materials.

MECHANICAL JUNK:
DISMANTLING AND USING AN OLD TELEVISION SET

Man's natural urge to create and to invent is stimulated by those materials found in his everyday environment. An individual's creative endeavor can be enhanced by a crafts program that makes more effective utilization of commercial and industrial waste. This section is devoted to a demonstration of how children can dismantle an old television set and use the components in a wide variety of ways in a crafts program.

The first step in dismantling a television set is to tame the tube. The cathode ray tube contains a vacuum and there is the risk of an implosion taking place if the tube is accidently struck or dropped. It is, therefore, imperative to remove the tube before allowing children to work on any television set. In some communities the local television repairman will remove the tube. If outside help is not available, the following procedure is the safest for removing the tube.

The television set may retain an electrical charge for up to two weeks after its final operation. A set which has been recently used should be stored for a few weeks before the tube is removed. Pry off the plastic snap connector fitted to the top of the tube. Then slide off the spring-held clip (the ion-trap magnet) and the wire-packed cylinder (the focusing magnet) from the neck of the tube. With a pair of side-cutting pliers, cut the high-tension cable on the side of the tube and all wires joining the chassis to the cabinet. Remove all screws and bolts used to secure the chassis to the base of the cabinet, including the control knobs.

Slide or lift out the chassis assembly from the cabinet and set on a table or working bench. Blow out any dust or dirt that may have collected on the chassis with an air hose or bellows. Remove the tube from the chassis. It is now ready to be tamed.

Taming the Tube

Wrap an old coat or blanket around the tube, leaving only the neck exposed. At the neck end of the tube there is a small extrusion or nipple which is formed when the tube is sealed. Cut off the nipple with a pair of side cutters, creating a small hole in the end of the tube. Air will rush through the hole creating a loud sound as it fills the tube (the hissing sound will be inhaled, not exhaled, air). The neck of the tube can be cut with a glass cutter, burning string, or hot wire after five or ten minutes.

Glass Cutter   Wrap a piece of masking tape around the neck of the tube to act as a guide for cutting the glass. Score a line around the neck of the tube by sliding the cutter along the edge of the masking tape. Wrap the end of the tube with an old rag and hold it with one hand, while striking the neck of the tube on the waste side of the line with the end of the cutter to crack the glass. The glass should crack along the scored edge. Smooth the edge with a fine mill file or a piece of emery cloth.

Burning String   Place a piece of masking tape around the neck of the tube at the point to be cut. Using the edge of the masking tape as a guide, score a line around the neck with a triangular file. Remove the piece of masking tape and add another piece about 1/2 inch from the scored line on the side toward the front of the picture tube. Select a piece of string long enough to be tied around the neck of the tube and dip it into a small container of kerosene. Place the string in the scored line around the neck and tie the ends. Care should be taken when tying the string that loose ends are not hitting the neck of the tube. If burning ends of the string hit the neck, they may cause it to crack unevenly. With a match, light the end of the string and allow to burn until the string falls off. Touch the hot glass with a cold metal rod along the scored line. The glass should crack, forming an even cut around the neck of the tube.

Hot Wire This technique is similar to the burning-string technique, except that a hot wire is used to heat the area around the scored line. Take a piece of resistance wire (Nichrome) and make one turn around the neck of the tube, leaving a 1/8-inch gap in the wire at the top of the tube. If the wire touches at any point, it will not form a complete circuit around the neck of the tube. Secure one end of the wire to a metal support (nail or clamp) about 1 foot from the neck of the tube. Wrap the opposite end of the resistance wire around a piece of wood. Connect the bared ends of a piece of electrical house wire to the support and to the terminal of a power source (12-volt car battery or 12-volt supply). Use another piece of electrical house wire to connect the other terminal of the power source to the metal base of a screwdriver. When the end of the screwdriver touches the free end of the resistance wire, the circuit is completed and electric current will flow, heating up the resistance wire around the neck of the tube. With one hand, pull on the piece of wood to keep the resistance wire taut, while the other hand is used to move the screwdriver along the wire toward the neck of the tube. Continue moving the screwdriver until the resistance wire glows bright red and hold in this position for ten seconds. Open the circuit by removing the screwdriver and touch the neck along the scored line with a cold metal rod. This cold rod will cause the glass to crack around the neck of the tube.

The contraption inside the neck is called the "gun" and contains a wide variety of interesting metals. The tube can be used for a bottle garden or a number of other projects, but before it is used, great care should be taken to remove the toxic chemicals on the inside of the tube. These can be washed out with water.

Dismantling the Chassis and Using the Parts
The chassis assembly is ready to be dismantled. The various parts should be placed in cardboard shoe or IBM punch-card boxes, which can be stored on shelving. The success of the mechanical junk program depends upon the method used to control the use and storage of the various television components. These television components can be used in a whole range of intriguing ways to enrich any crafts program. The following suggestions are based upon how children successfully used the various components.

Mobiles Polish the aluminum value holders and suspend them using the copper wire from the transformer.

Silhouettes Arrange the components in a design on a sheet of black paper and spray with paint, creating a silhouette design.

Collages Components can be glued to a suitable base in a wide variety of different arrangements to create an interesting collage. The various parts can be painted with acrylic paint or sprayed with enamel paints. A Styrofoam base can be used and the small components can be pressed into the surface, while with others, the wires can be bent over and stuck into the surface to hold the part in place.

Satellites Fasten two identical speakers together for the base and add wires to the base for antennas. Paint and decorate the satellite.

Trains Use transformers for the cab, and gang capacitors or large cylindrical capacitors for the boiler. Secure these to a piece of wood with glue and use other components to add the finishing touches to the train.

Robots Use the old cabinet as the base and add the components to obtain the desired effect. Flashing lights, switches, alarm bells, and push buttons can also be used to add to the appearance of the robot.

Monsters The chassis makes an excellent base for adding the various components to form the monster.

Puppet Stage An empty television cabinet makes an excellent puppet stage just by adding curtains, lights, and scenery.

Pet Cages An empty television cabinet can be used as an animal cage by adding a wire-covered frame to the back for a door. With some slight modifications, the cabinet also can be made into a vivarium for frogs, toads, and lizards.

Molds and Impressions Pour about 3/8 inch of plaster of Paris into the top of a cardboard box (candy or shoe). While the plaster of Paris is still tacky, press the various components into the surface. The complexity and variation of the components make them extremely suitable for making these impressions. Paint, stain, or dyes can be added to obtain the desired effect.

In the bottom of a container, roll out a piece of Plasticine about 1/4 inch thick. Take the various components and make a series of impressions in the Plasticine. Pour about 1/4 inch of plaster of Paris over the surface and allow to dry. The shapes of the various components will appear in relief on the front surface. Wet sand can be used instead of the Plasticine (see Sand Casting).

Collect parts from other old appliances and allow children to utilize these parts to develop crafts projects. They can use cams, pulleys, and gears to construct monsters or robots that move. Old motors can be used to construct a buffing wheel or drive a wood lathe. The example presented

Figure 16-1 DECORATING OLD BOTTLES
Materials: acrylic medium, tissue paper, glass bottle, string, paints, eggshells, glue, paintbrush.
1. Decorating the surface of a bottle with tissue paper.
2. String used to cover the surface of a bottle.
3. Painting the surface of a bottle.
4. Using eggshells to cover the surface of a bottle.

for using an old television set is merely to stimulate interest in utilizing the parts from old appliances in a crafts program.

OLD BOTTLES

Ash trays and small dishes can be made from old bottles. Take a fire brick and with a knife or chisel carve out the desired mold on the top surface. Place the bottle over the mold on the brick and insert both in the kiln. Fire the kiln at a temperature of $1750°F$. When the glass becomes pliable, the surface can be pushed into the desired shape with a wooden stick. Remove from the kiln and allow to cool.

Bottles having interesting shapes, but poor color, can be made into decanters and vases by covering the surface with fabric or string. Cut a piece of fabric for a small area of the total surface to be covered. Place the piece of fabric on a piece of wax paper and dampen with a clear acrylic medium. Brush a coat of acrylic medium over the area to be covered with the fabric.

CRAFTS FROM
RECYCLED
MATERIALS

403

Place the piece of fabric in position against the surface of the bottle and with your fingers smooth out the material. When the surface is dry enough to handle, add another piece, making sure that the edges fit together. Shapes for small areas can be obtained by placing a piece of tracing paper over the spot to be covered and rubbing the surface with a pencil. This operation should produce a clearly defined shape of the area to be covered. Pin the pattern to a piece of fabric and carefully cut it out. Fit the fabric in place, using the technique described for the first shape. When the bottle is completely covered, the seams can be outlined with paint, string, and yarn. If great care was taken in matching the shapes together, no further decoration is required. Apply four coats of clear acrylic medium to the covered surface, allowing each application to dry before adding the next coat. The acrylic medium will seal and waterproof the surface.

String-covered Bottles

Brush a 1-inch strip of clear acrylic medium on the side of the bottle at the bottom edge. Take a piece of soft cotton string and press it against the bottle. Wrap the string around the bottle, overlapping the end. Continue wrapping the string around the bottle, pushing each layer into place with a toothpick, until the total surface is covered. Add additional acrylic medium as it is needed. Finish the string covering by coating the surface with four applications of acrylic medium, allowing each coat to dry before adding the next one. The acrylic will seal and waterproof the surface. Wood-antiquing paints and stains can be used to antique the surface.

Painted Bottles

Old bottles can be sprayed a solid color and motifs painted directly on the surface. Fabric shapes can be glued to the surface to decorate the decanter or vase. A decorative stopper can be made by gluing a wooden shape to a piece of cork.

Old bottles can be decorated with melted wax. The colored wax is melted and then applied with a brush, creating the desired effect. After the wax solidifies, a design can be etched in the surface with a heated knife blade or nail.

Terrarium

A terrarium can be constructed from a wide-mouth gallon glass container. Mix 1/2 pound of plaster of Paris in a can with water until it is as thick as pancake batter. Add food coloring to obtain the effect desired. Pour the plaster into a shoe box lid. Place the bottle on its side in the wet plaster and press down very lightly. Allow to set for about an hour. The glass container is imbedded in a solid base to prevent it from rolling. The next step is to choose the kind of habitat needed for the plant or animal specimens that will be kept in the terrarium.

Commercial Bottle and Jug Cutter

Old bottles and jugs can be used to construct mugs, goblets, canisters, wind chimes, dishes, candle holders, mobiles, and glass chains. The commercial glass cutter is simple to operate and will produce a high degree of

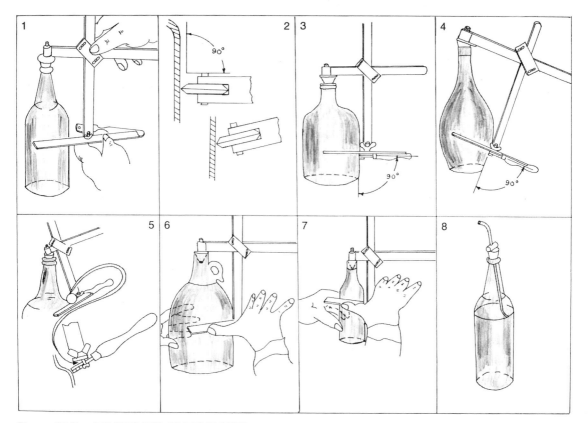

Figure 16-2 COMMERCIAL GLASS CUTTER

Materials : glass cutter, glass bottle.

1. Adjust the cutter to the shape of the bottle.
2. Glass cutter cutting edge should be at right angles to the side of the bottle.
3. Position of glass cutter for cutting straight surfaces.
4. Position of glass cutter for cutting curved surfaces.
5. Insert a small piece of material between the glass cutter and stabilizer to obtain a 90-degree angle.
6. Press hands toward each other with about 1 pound of pressure and rotate the bottle.
7. Fingers should be straight out during the cutting operation, and the cutter should make a sound similar to facial tissue being torn.
8. Insert tapper into the neck of the bottle and tap the hammer against the cut line to separate the glass.

successful cuts if used according to the instructions. Figure 16-2 illustrates the glass cutter being used.

OLD CLOTHING

Like mechanical junk, the uses of old clothing in a crafts program are endless. Young children enjoy rummaging through a box of old clothing and trying the different garments on as they role play. The clothing is used by older children for costumes in their theater crafts activities. Some children just enjoy trying on a pair of high-heel shoes or different hats.

Old clothing also provides a wide variety of materials to make stuffed animals, bean bags, hooked rugs, or braided rugs. Women's stockings or panty hose are excellent for stuffing objects, while men's socks can be used as base for a puppet.

The material from an old woolen dress can be used to construct a flannel board or for hooking rugs. The use of old clothing in a crafts program is limited only by the imagination of those individuals participating in the various activities. The biggest difficulty is storing the materials once they are collected so that they are available for use by the participants in the program.

SUGGESTED PROJECTS FROM RECYCLED MATERIALS
Empty Wire Reels
Empty wire reels that vary widely in size can be obtained free from most electric power companies. These reels make excellent workbenches, game tables, and picnic tables. They also can be used to construct playground equipment for an adventure area. A reel cut in half can be used as a teeter; reels with different diameters placed one on top of another make an excellent device for children to climb about.

Plastic Spoon Flowers
An attractive bouquet of flowers can be constructed from plastic spoons, green felt, and pipe cleaners. The spoons used can be the same or many different colors.

With a pair of scissors cut the handles off six plastic spoons. Take a large needle and heat it over a candle until it is red hot. Make two holes in each spoon with the hot needle, 1/8 inch in from the edge and above where the handle was cut off.

Take a pipe cleaner and lace it through the six spoons to form tuliplike flowers. Make as many flowers as needed to complete the desired bouquet.

Cut a piece of wire 10 inches long and insert it through the center of each flower. Attach a shank button or wooden bead to the top of the wire. Pull the wire down so that the button or bead rests in the center of the flower.

Draw patterns for a calyx, vein, and leaf on a piece of cardboard and cut them out. The leaf should be the same shape as those found on tulips. Secure the patterns to a piece of green felt with straight pins. Cut around the patterns with a pair of scissors. Three calyx shapes, two vein shapes, and two leaf shapes are needed for each flower.

Take the three calyx shapes and place one on every other spoon. Hold the felt calyxes in place by wrapping a thin piece of wire around their bases.

Take the felt vein shape and spread glue on one side. Place the pipe cleaner on the wet glue and then put the pipe cleaner and vein on top of the leaf. Press the leaf, vein, and pipe cleaner together to form a leaf for one side of the flower. Make a leaf for the other side of the flower. Two additional leaves are needed for each flower.

Wrap each wire stem with florist's tape. Start the tape at the top, covering the calyx bases and working downward. Hold two leaves at the bottom of each stem and wrap the thin wire around the base of the leaves.

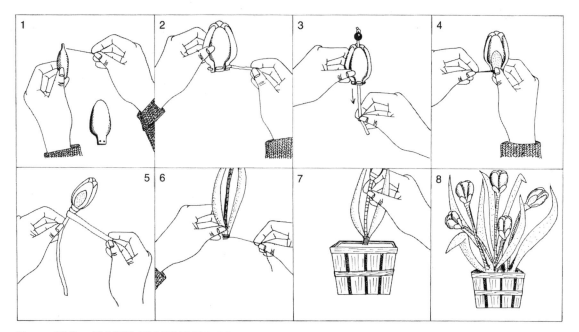

Figure 16-3 PLASTIC SPOON FLOWERS
Materials: plastic spoons, wooden beads, pipe cleaners, florist's tape, felt, basket, needle, Styrofoam.
1. Make two holes in the base of each spoon with a hot needle.
2. Lace six spoons together with a pipe cleaner.
3. Attach a wooden bead to the top of a piece of wire and pull it through the center of the flower.
4. Take three calyx shapes and place them around a plastic flower. Hold in place with a piece of wire.
5. Wrap the stem with florist's tape.
6. Wrap florist's tape around the base of each stem covering the base of the leaves.
7. Poke the stem into the Styrofoam filler.
8. Finished display of flowers.

Wrap florist's tape around the base, covering the wire that is holding the leaves and stem together.

Take a berry or fruit basket and paint it with any color paint and allow to dry. Cut a piece of Styrofoam that fits snugly inside the basket and comes within 1 inch of the top. Place the Styrofoam inside the basket. Arrange the flowers by poking each stem into the Styrofoam. Leaves and stems can be bent and twisted to make the arrangement more interesting. Cover the Styrofoam surface with small pebbles.

Container Sculpture

Children obtain a special satisfaction in transforming discarded containers into a wide variety of interesting items. Plastic, metal, cardboard, or wooden containers when combined with other miscellaneous materials lend themselves to the construction of animals, figures, airplanes, automobiles, trucks, and percussion instruments.

Figure 16-4 CONTAINER SCULPTURES
Creative sculptures constructed from egg cartons, paper cups, wooden beads, plastic soap containers, boxes of all sizes and shapes, and other miscellaneous containers.

The first step is to make a decision on the kind of sculpture desired. With the appropriate cutting tool, make any necessary cuts. Additional parts can be fastened with glue, masking tape, paper fasteners, nails, and other appropriate techniques. The finished sculpture can be painted. A few drops of liquid detergent added to tempera paint will allow the paint to adhere to waxy or plastic surfaces.

Making a Robot

Take a small box and cut two holes in the bottom for the eyes of the robot. Attach the small box to a large box with staples or masking tape. Construct the legs by taping the top edges of two large cottage cheese containers together with masking tape. Connect the legs to the large box in the proper position. The robot is finished by adding other containers and material to create facial features. See Figure 16-6.

Add lights to the robot by cutting five pieces of wire, the length depending upon the size of the robot, and removing about 1 inch of insulation from both ends of the wires. Take one piece of wire and connect it to one terminal of a 6-volt battery. Connect two wires to the other battery terminal and the other ends of these wires to the light bulb sockets. Wrap the wire directly

Figure 16-5 CARDBOARD BOX SCULPTURES
Creative sculptures constructed from boxes of all sizes and shapes, paper
tubes, and other miscellaneous materials.

around that metal part of the light bulb. Take two more wires and connect
the ends to the opposite side of the socket terminals. Solder these wires to
the metal strip on the bottom of each light bulb. The other ends of these
wires are left free.

Secure the light bulb in place in the holes made in the small box for
this purpose. The 6-volt battery should be attached to the inside surface of
the small box. Cut a hole in the neck of the robot and pull the wires through
into the large box. Make two holes in both side panels of the large box about
shoulder height. Pass the wires through to the outside. On one side there
will be two wires and on the opposite side only one. The single wire will be
the first wire connected to the battery. The two wires will be those connected to the bulbs. One bulb will light up when the bare end of this wire
touches one of the bare ends of the other wires. If two wires from the bulb
touch the first wire together, both will light simultaneously. The eyes can
be made to wink if the wires are touched separately.

Salvaging Sheet Tin and Aluminum
Sheets of tin and aluminum can be retrieved from cans and used to construct entirely new forms. Remove top and bottom of the can with a can
opener. Cut the cylinder shape along the seam with a pair of tin snips. Flat-

Figure 16-6   MAKING A ROBOT THAT LIGHTS UP
The Circuit:

To the battery terminal.
To the robot's hands.

ten the sheet by gradually bending the metal in the opposite direction from the curl. Place the sheet on a hard flat surface and rub the surface with a block of wood. Interesting designs can be cut out from the metal sheets. Aluminum sheets can also be used for metal tooling.

Egg-carton People and Creatures
All kinds of creatures and people can be constructed from egg cartons and a few other materials. Cut apart an egg carton with a pair of scissors, leaving some sections attached, while others are cut apart. Attach the different sections together to create a man, woman, or creature. Experiment with different combinations to create the desired egg-carton sculpture.

Eggshell Mosaics
Eggshells can be painted and then broken into small pieces and used to make a mosaic. Paint a number of eggshells a variety of different colors and allow to dry. Break the eggshells into a variety of different sizes, keeping the colors separated. Take a piece of cardboard and lay out an abstract design or picture. Spread glue over a small area of the cardboard and start placing the pieces of colored eggshell on the cardboard until the design is

Figure 16-7 EGG-CARTON PEOPLE AND CREATURES

Materials: Styrofoam balls, pipe cleaners, wooden beads, straight pins, egg cartons, scissors, paints, construction paper, glue.

1. Glue two sections from an egg carton together to form a body.
2. Glue the feet and hands onto the body.
3. To make a girl, cut four slits in an egg carton section. Place the cut egg carton section over an uncut one.
4. Finished egg carton man and woman.
5. Attach the egg carton sections with pipe cleaners.
6. To make an animal, use a Styrofoam ball for the head and wooden beads and pipe cleaners for other parts of the body.
7. Attach the facial features with straight pins.
8. A few sample creatures.

completed. Cover a large area with a large piece of eggshell and press it with a finger until it cracks, creating a number of smaller pieces forming a mosaic appearance. See Figure 16-8.

Painted eggshells can be used to cover a wide variety of other objects. For example, a glass bottle can be covered to create an eggshell vase.

Thread Spools

Empty thread spools of different sizes can be used to create many different items. Spools can be combined with pipe cleaners, felt, cloth, and other materials to construct people, animals, trucks, and trains.

Computer Cards

Computer cards can be used to construct a Christmas tree or wreath. Turn in the two corners at one end of an old computer card toward the center and staple the corners, forming a point. Each card forms one leaf of a tree. Cut

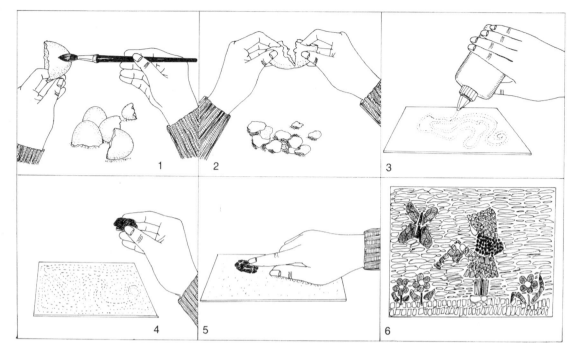

Figure 16-8   EGGSHELL MOSAICS
Materials: dry eggshells, paint, paintbrush, heavy paper or cardboard, glue.
1. Paint each eggshell a solid color.
2. Break the eggshells into large pieces.
3. Spread glue over the piece of heavy paper or cardboard.
4. Place a large piece of colored eggshell on the glued surface.
5. Press the eggshell with a finger until it cracks.
6. Continue placing the eggshells on the paper until the picture or design is completed.

out a tree shape from a piece of cardboard, and starting at the top staple the computer cards onto the surface. When the surface has been covered with computer cards, spray the surface with green paint and decorate.

The wreath is constructed by cutting a circular base from the cardboard and stapling the pointed computer cards in position to form a circle.

Foil Pie-pan Decorations
Large and small foil pie-pans can be twisted, cut, bent, and flattened into a wide variety of shapes. Staples can be used to ensure that the foil holds its shape or to attach shapes together. The finished shape is painted with tempera paint to which a little soap or gum arabic is added.

Stacking Sticks and Lids
Creative mobiles and stabiles can be constructed from a collection of plastic can lids, 1/4-inch square sticks, 1/4 X 3/8 inch flat sticks, and wooden dowels. Punch holes in the plastic with large nails or an awl and slip the sticks through the holes, supporting the lids at different angles. Coat

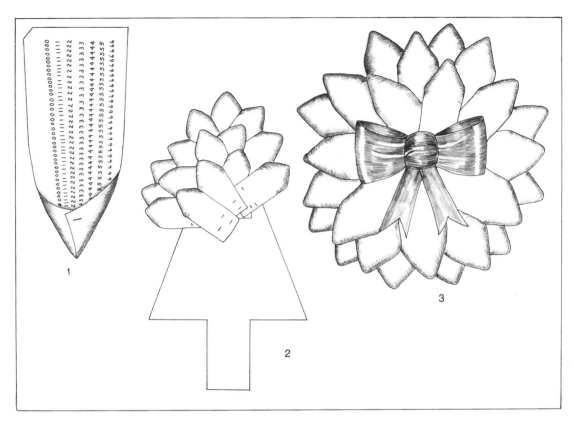

Figure 16-9   COMPUTER CARD TREE AND WREATH
Materials : computer cards, scissors, stapler, cardboard, ribbon material.
1.   Turn in the two corners of the computer card and staple them to form a point.
2.   Form a tree by stapling the computer cards to a cardboard base.
3.   Finished wreath constructed from computer cards.

hanger wire, pipe cleaners, yarn, button molds, bottle caps, and other objects can be added to the structure.

Bone Sculpture

Creative sculptures can be constructed from bones that have been boiled clean. Children will enjoy discovering the hidden objects in a pile of bones. Paint, felt, wire, yarn, and pipe cleaners can be used to define the object.

Carpet Remnants

Small and large carpet remnants can be used to construct a collage. Utility shears or tin snips can be used to cut the carpeting. Glue is used to attach buttons, yarn, feathers, pipe cleaners, and other materials to the carpeting to obtain the desired effect.

Old carpet scraps can be cut into a variety of different shapes. To print the shape, brush a heavy coating of paint on the surface or drip the paint directly on the carpet and spread it with a brush. Press the carpet shape against the surface to be imprinted. Printing on wet paper, tissue, construction paper, or burlap produces interesting effects.

Mosaics from Scavenger Materials

Gravel, pebbles, seeds, pods, grain, bottle caps, and other scrap materials can be used to construct a mosaic. Draw the design on a piece of cardboard and secure the decorative material to the surface with glue. A complex mosaic can be constructed using a combination of materials. Spray the finished mosaic with a clear plastic to protect the surface.

Xerox Webbing

A flannel board can be constructed by covering a piece of cardboard or hardboard with the old webbing from a Xerox machine. Letters and objects to use on the flannel board can be constructed from Styrofoam, felt, wool, or sandpaper.

Metal Coat Hangers

Old hangers can be bent into a wide variety of useful household items. A plate hanger is constructed by squeezing a wire hanger into a diamond shape. The corners are bent in to form a hook to hold the plate. A belt hanger is constructed by cutting the wire in the center and twisting the ends upward. A little experimentation and ingenuity will suggest dozens of other items that can be constructed from coat hangers.

Yarn Drawing

Scrap pieces of yarn can be used to enhance a simple design or drawing. On a piece of heavy cardboard, draw a design or picture. With a crayon, repeat the outline shape over and over, filling in the outline of the design or picture. These crayon lines are the guidelines for the pieces of yarn used to form the design. Apply rubber cement to a small area of the picture. Take a piece of the appropriate colored yarn and twist it around the cemented area following the crayon lines. The yarn can be placed close together or with small gaps between the strands. Continue to cement an area and apply the appropriate colored yarn until the picture is completed. Buttons, rickrack, or any other material may be used to enrich the finished picture.

Yarn Designs

Select a piece of cardboard 9 X 11 inches and place it on a working surface. With a ruler measure in 1-1/2 inches on the two 9-inch edges and mark the distance with a pencil. Cut a slit 1/4 inch deep at these two markings. Measure 1-1/2 inches on the opposite side and two 1/4-inch slits. Select two pieces of yarn of the same color about 15 inches long. Slip one piece of yarn into the top right slit and the opposite end in the bottom left slit. Tape the ends to the back with masking tape. Take the second piece of yarn and slip one end in the top left slit; insert the other end in the bottom right slit. Tape the ends to the back with masking tape.

    With a ruler, mark off three measurements on the two 11-inch edges.

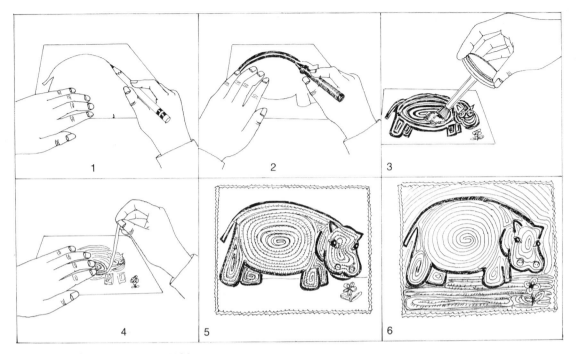

Figure 16-10 YARN DRAWINGS

Materials: cardboard, yarn, rubber cement, crayons, buttons or rickrack, pencil.

1. Sketch a design or picture on a piece of cardboard.
2. Fill in the outline of the design or picture with a crayon. Draw the lines as if they were a piece of yarn.
3. Apply rubber cement to one area of the picture or design.
4. Take a piece of yarn and twist it, following the lines drawn with the crayon.
5. Buttons, rickrack, or any other material can be used to add detail.
6. Finished yarn drawing.

The first is 2-1/2 inches from the top 9-inch edge, the second is 5-1/2 inches from the same edge, and the third measurement is 2-1/2 inches from the bottom edge. At each of these measurements, cut a slit that is 1/4 inch long. Cut three pieces of yarn 11 inches long of the same color. With one piece of yarn, connect the two side slits that are 2-1/2 inches from the top edge and tape the ends to the back surface. Connect the two 5-1/2-inch side slits with another piece of yarn and then the last two slits with the third piece of yarn. The ends of all five pieces of yarn should be taped to the back surface.

Slip a small piece of construction paper between the yarn and cardboard and with a pencil draw the outline of the area formed by the yarn. Slip the piece of construction paper out from under the yarn design and with a pair of scissors cut out the shape. Apply rubber cement to the back of the shape cut from the construction paper and cement in place on the cardboard base. Fill in all the shapes formed with the yarn with different colored construction paper by tracing each shape formed by the crossing strands of yarn and cutting it out. Each piece is then cemented in place.

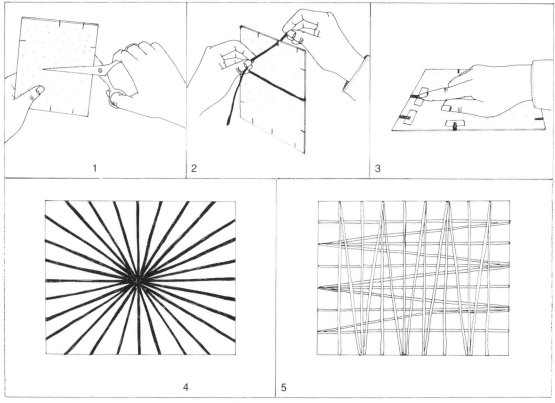

Figure 16-11   YARN DESIGNS

Materials: cardboard (9 × 11 inches), yarn (different colors), scissors, ruler, masking tape.

1. Cut a series of 1/4-inch slits along the edge of a piece of cardboard.
2. Slip the end of a piece of yarn into one of the slits.
3. Turn the piece of cardboard over and tape down the ends of the yarn.
4. Sample design made from a piece of yarn running from one slit to another on the opposite edge.
5. Sample design made by running more than one piece of yarn from a slit.

There are many techniques that may be used to alter the finished yarn design. The first is to use only one color of construction paper for the background and different colors for each piece of yarn used to form the design. The second is to locate the slits in different positions along the four edges or to increase the number of slits along the edges, creating a design with more than five strands.

Yarn Octopus

An octopus can be made with scrap pieces of yarn over an old ball. Cut sixty pieces of yarn 4 feet long and lay them out on a table. Cut two pieces of string about 6 inches long. Pick up the long strands and loop them over one arm, making sure the ends of the yarn are equal. Holding the strands in the center, lift them from the arm. Tie one piece of the 6-inch string

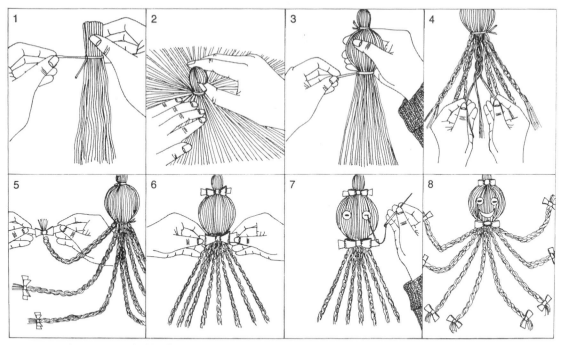

Figure 16-12 YARN OCTOPUS

Materials : balls of yarn, Styrofoam ball, buttons, scissors, 1/2 yard of ribbon, string, thread and needle, scrap yard goods, glue.

1. Make a loop with the strands of yarn and tie it with a piece of string.
2. Hold the tied loop with one hand and spread the strands of yarn.
3. Place the Styrofoam ball under the loop and cover it with the strands of yarn. Tie the ball in place.
4. Weave the strands together.
5. Tie a ribbon to the end of each leg.
6. Tie a ribbon around the yarn above and below the head.
7. Sew the buttons to the head.
8. Finished octopus.

around the loop formed by the folded strands. Hold the tied loop in one hand and place the yarn on a flat surface with the loop on top. With the left hand holding the loop, use the right hand to spread the yarn out evenly in all directions from the center. Take the ball and place it under the loop, covering the ball on all sides with the strands of yarn. Hold the ball in one hand and use the other hand to gather the strands of yarn under the ball. Tie the other 6-inch string around the strands of yarn as close to the ball as possible.

Hold the ball up, allowing the strands to hang, and divide the hanging strands of yarn into eight bunches of fifteen strands each. Tie the ends of each bunch with a piece of string. Select one of the bunches and divide it into three groups of five strands. To braid the strands, imagine that each of the three groups of yarn are labeled A, B, and C. Take strand A and place it over strand B so that it is in the center. Take strand C and cross it over strand A so that strand C is in the center. Strand B is crossed over strand C so that strand B is in the center. Then strand A is crossed over strand B so that strand A is in the center. Continue braiding by crossing the left and then the right strands to the center until the end is reached. Join the ends of the yarn with a safety pin. This is one leg of the octopus. Repeat the braiding operation until all eight legs have been joined. Finish each leg by removing the safety pin and tying a ribbon at the end of each leg. Insert the scissors in the loop above the ball and cut the yarn. Tie a ribbon around the cut ends over the string. Tie another ribbon under the head to cover up the string. Two buttons can be sewed to the head for eyes, and felt can be used to cut shapes for the mouth. The felt shapes can be sewed in place.

Yarn Dolls

Cut out a 4-inch square of cardboard and a 3-inch square of cardboard. Take the end of the yarn and place it against one edge of the 4-inch square, winding the yarn evenly around the square twenty-eight times. Cut two pieces of yarn of a different color 4 inches long. Put the two pieces of yarn side by side and slip them under the yarn wrapped around the 4-inch square of cardboard. Tie the ends of the two 4-inch pieces of yarn together tightly so that they pull the strands into a bunch along the top edge. Slip the coil of yarn off the cardboard square. With a pair of scissors, cut the end of the yarn opposite the tied end.

To make arms for the doll, wind the yarn around the 4-inch cardboard square fourteen times. Carefully remove the yarn from the square, keeping the coil together. Hold the yarn in the center and with a pair of scissors cut both ends of the coil. Tie both ends with a strand of different colored yarn about 1/4 inch from the ends.

The head for the doll is made by taking the first coil of yarn with the knot at one end and with another piece of yarn 4 inches in length tying the body 1 inch down from the top. Separate the remaining yarn forming the body. Pick up the arms and slip them up between the separated body halves until they are at shoulder height. Cut another piece of 4-inch yarn and tie it below the arms forming the waist of the doll. Trim the ends of the yarn evenly at the bottom to form the skirt. Eyes, nose, and mouth can be added to the face by using different colored yarns, sequins, or pieces of pipe cleaners. To make the yarn doll into a pin, sew a small safety pin or pinback to the back of the doll.

A smaller doll can be made by using a 3-inch square and wrapping the yarn around the surface twenty-four times instead of twenty-eight times. To make a male doll, divide the yarn below the waist into two sections to form the legs and tie them about 1/4 inch from the bottom.

String Dolls

Floppy string dolls, each dressed in a distinctive felt, leather, or cloth outfit, can be made from scrap material. Cut a piece of string or yarn 14 inches long and tie a knot at both ends. Fold the yarn in half and glue the strands together 2 inches from the folded end. This piece of string is the body of the doll. Cut another piece of yarn 7-1/2 inches long for the arms. Glue the center of this piece of yarn to the top of the body. The body and arms of the string doll are completed and are ready to be dressed in a colorful outfit.

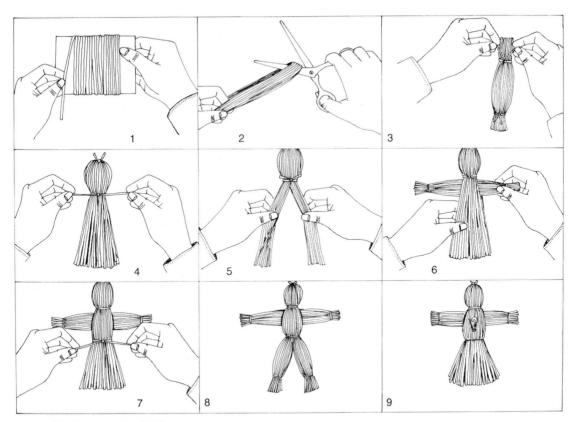

Figure 16-13 YARN DOLLS

Materials: cardboard (one piece 3 X 3 inches and one piece 4 X 4 inches), yarn (two different colors), scissors, safety pin.

1. Wrap the yarn around a piece of cardboard twenty-eight times.
2. Cut the ends of the coil of yarn.
3. Tie the ends of the yarn together.
4. Form the head for the doll.
5. Divide the remaining yarn in half.
6. Slip the arms in position.
7. Tie the arms in place.
8. Tie the ends of the yarn to form legs for the doll.
9. Sew a small safety pin to the back of the doll.

Select some scrap material to make an outfit for the doll. On a piece of paper draw a pattern for the doll's outfit. With a pair of scissors, cut out the pattern and pin it to the surface of the fabric. Cut out a front and back piece for the outfit. Apply glue to the edges of the inside surface of the fabric. Place the back surface underneath the yarn, and then place the front of the outfit over the string. Press the edges of the outfit together with body string running down the center of the outfit. The outfit or dress can also be sewed together using a running stitch.

On a piece of paper draw a pattern for the head, hands, and feet or shoes for the doll. Cut out these patterns and pin them to the appropriate fabric. Two head shapes and four hands and feet are needed to complete the doll. Apply glue to the inside surface of each head shape and then place one under and one over the string. Press the edges together, keeping the string or yarn in the center. Repeat this procedure for the other parts of the doll. Hair and facial features can be added to the head.

Junk Sculptures

Children enjoy transforming discarded blocks of wood, spark plugs, different sized containers, bottle caps, TV tubes, sticks, gears, plastic covers, and other pieces of junk into interesting sculpture. Artistic forms can be developed by joining the various pieces of junk together with glue, nails, string, and wire.

Cylindrical Faces

Use a salt carton or oatmeal box as the base of the cylindrical face. Cover the base with a piece of paper. Eyes, nose, and mouth features are made by cutting the desired shapes from a piece of paper or fabric and gluing them to the base. A hat may be made from a half carton, while the brim is made from a piece of cardboard. Hair, ears, and other facial features can be made by folding, twisting, curling, and bending paper into the appropriate forms.

Sawdust Texture Picture

Place a fine-meshed screen over a pan and sift a handful of sawdust through the mesh. Keep sifting sawdust until the right amount is obtained. Put the sifted sawdust into a container of poster paint and allow to soak. Remove the sawdust from the container and allow to dry on a piece of newspaper. More than one color will be needed to make a picture.

With a pencil, draw an outline of a picture on a piece of cardboard. Spread glue on the areas that are to be a particular color and take a handful of the sawdust and sprinkle it over the wet glue. Set aside to dry. When the glue has dried, shake the piece of cardboard to remove any loose sawdust. Apply glue to another area and cover it with sawdust. Repeat the process until all the textured areas are covered.

Hats and Masks

Old plastic gallon containers may be used to construct hats and masks. The children derive the basic shape for hat or mask from the discarded plastic container.

Select a container and cut it into the basic shape with a pair of scissors. Since the plastic is pliable, it can be bent, curled, folded, rolled, scored, and pierced to form a wide variety of shapes. A paper punch may be used to make holes, while sharp curves can be held in place with pipe cleaners, paper fasteners, or wire. Crayons, tempera, felt-tip markers, and spray paint can be used to add features and color to the finished hat or mask. Yarn, glitter, netting, feathers, tissues, and other scrap materials can be used to make the finished object more attractive.

Cardboard Tube Sculptures

Scrap wood, wooden dowels, and different sized cardboard tubes can be used to create artistic sculptures. Cut a tube into different lengths with a saw. Smooth the rough edges with sandpaper and join tube sections with varying lengths of wooden dowels by drilling a hole in the tube at the desired position. Slip the wooden dowel into the hole. Some dowels will go through only one side of the tube, while others will go through both sides of the tube. Dowels can be glued to the cardboard tubing.

Postcard Villages

Old postcards and greeting cards can be used to build an imaginative village filled with people, animals, plants, trees, flowers, and mountains. With a pair of scissors, cut out the desired objects from the postcards or greeting cards, leaving a 1/2-inch margin at the bottom. Make several cuts into the margin with a pair of scissors, forming a number of flaps. Fold one flap forward and one back, one forward and one back until each flap has been folded. Apply glue to the bottom of the flaps and glue to a cardboard base.

Bottle-cap Sculptures

Bottle caps offer a wealth of opportunities for creative art activities. The caps themselves can be arranged in all sorts of designs, pictures, collages, and other forms. Remember the little piece of cork that comes inside each cap. If enough corks are carefully removed, they can be used for a cork mosaic.

Burlap Flowers

Scrap pieces of burlap can be used to construct attractive artificial flowers. Take a piece of burlap and cut it along the lines of the thread into a 4 X 6 inch rectangle. If a large flower is desired, the size of the rectangle should be increased. Hold the piece of burlap so that the 4-inch width is at the top and bottom. Pull out and save the lengthwise burlap strands leaving a 1/2 inch border on each side. The residual strands can be used to construct flowers or as embroidery threads on another project. Apply glue along one of the 1/2-inch borders. Fold and press the unglued 1/2-inch border over against the glued surface and allow to dry.

Take a piece of number 20 wire and insert the end into the glued edge of the burlap until it extends 1 inch beyond the burlap surface. Bend the end of the wire down and over against the burlap surface. Roll the glued edge of the burlap from the wire insert, being careful to keep the wire tightly secured to the center of the coil. Take a piece of florist's tape and wrap it around the glued edge of the flower, wrapping the tape around the burlap and down the entire length of the piece of wire. The burlap is ready to be formed. Gently open the strands of burlap to obtain the desired appearance. When the appropriate figure is formed, attach a pompon or small ball of cotton to the center of the flower with glue.

Leaves are made from green cloth or paper. Fold a piece of cloth or paper in half. Sketch a leaf shape on the top surface of the material. Cut out this shape. When the material is separated, there should be two leaves.

Take a piece of number 20 wire and twist it into the form and size of the cutout leaf. Apply glue to the edge of the wire that forms the basic leaf shape. Place the piece of wire against one of the cutout leaf shapes. Apply

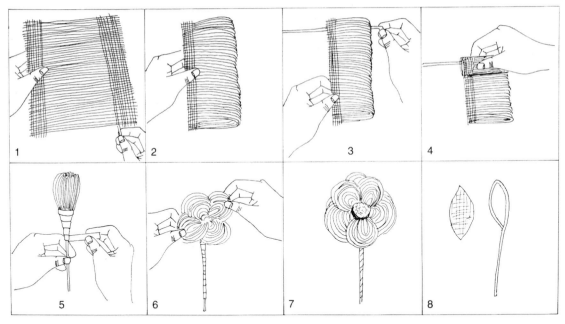

Figure 16-14   BURLAP FLOWERS

Materials : burlap, florist's tape, wire, pompon, green cloth, glue.

1. Pull out strands lengthwise, leaving 1/2-inch margin on each edge.
2. Fold in half lengthwise and glue.
3. Push the wire through the burlap and bend it over.
4. Roll the burlap around the wire.
5. Wrap the florist's tape around the bottom of the flower.
6. Separate the burlap to form the flower.
7. Glue the pompon to the center of the flower.
8. Bend the wire to the form of a leaf shape.

glue to the top edge of the wire. Place the second piece of material on top of the piece of wire. This will form a leaf with a wire armature.

Cut this piece of wire about 2 inches from the stem of the flower and attach it to the stem of the flower with florist's tape. Bend or twist the armature to obtain a leaf with a realistic appearance. More than one leaf can be made for each flower. Finished flowers can be arranged into a bouquet or centerpiece.

Flower Centers   Two different types of centers can be used when making burlap flowers. The first type of flower center is constructed by knotting the ends of burlap threads. Take three or four burlap threads and knot one end together. Make up seven or eight of these bundles. Place these knotted strands together into one bundle and secure the unknotted ends by wrapping them with a piece of wire or thread.

The second type of center is derived by forming a number of loops with burlap threads. Cut a burlap thread about 1 inch long and fold it in half. Make between fifteen and twenty of these loops. Bundle the loops together and secure the unlooped end by wrapping it with a piece of thin wire or thread.

Flowers from Burlap Strands   Take ten to twelve burlap strands and place them on the working surface. The size of the flower is determined by the number of burlap strands used. Fold these strands into loops and place four or more of these loops evenly around the flower center. These loops can be overlapped to obtain the desired shape.

Take a piece of number 20 wire and apply a small amount of glue to the end. Insert the glued end of the wire into the base of the flower. The glue will help hold the wire in place. To tie off the base of the flower, wrap a piece of thin wire or thread very tightly around the strands and stem of the flower. Crepe paper or florist's tape can be used to cover the base of the flower and stem wire. If crepe paper is used, the end can be secured with a drop of glue.

Egg-carton Buds

It may be helpful before constructing a rose to study its different stages of development. Should the rose have a tight bud, slightly blown bud, half-opened bud (almost tulip-shaped) or a fully blown one? How do rose petals grow? Are they small near the center and larger toward the outer edge? The answers to these questions are important if the flower is to have a realistic appearance. The following techniques can be used to construct roses in different stages of growth.

Rose Bud A   Take an egg box that is used for jumbo eggs and note that this box has five pointed projections down the center. These projections can be used to construct a tight rose bud.

Look at Figure 16-15 (rose bud A). With a pencil, draw a series of dotted lines around each pointed projection as shown in steps A and B. Cut along the dotted line with a pair of scissors to obtain the shape in step C. Fold the points along the dotted lines in toward the center so that the points form a flat surface. This flat surface illustrated by step D becomes the base of bud A and is glued to the center of the rose petals.

Rose Bud B   Cut two petals from an egg carton using the shape shown in Figure 16-15 (rose bud B step A) as a pattern. Fold the cutout petals lengthwise along the dotted line and pinch the tip into a point. The two petals are interlocked, forming a shape like that shown in steps B and C.

Rose Bud C   Cut out a petal from an egg carton using the shape shown in Figure 16-15 (rose bud C) as a pattern. The base, indicated by points w, x, y, and z, is cut out. Form the bud by rolling the petal into a cylinder and wrapping a piece of thread or wire around the base to hold the shape (see rose bud C). The base of the bud is flat and is glued to the center of the cup formed by the petals.

Forming the Rose   After selecting and constructing a rose bud, finish the rose with petals. Cut out two petals using the pattern for petals shown in Figure 16-15. Apply a small amount of glue to the slits in the base of the petal. Place the bud between the petals as shown in Figure 16-15 (steps for assembling a rose) and allow to dry.

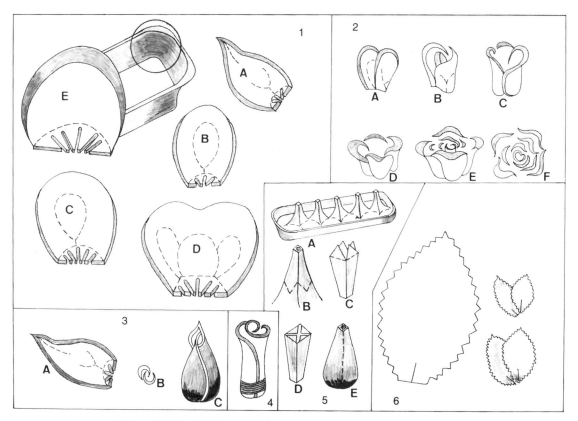

Figure 16-15 EGG-CARTON FLOWERS
  1. Different size rose petal patterns.
  2. Steps for assembling a rose.
  3. Rose bud A.
  4. Rose bud B.
  5. Rose bud C.
  6. Rose leaves.

Cut out three petals using the pattern for petal C shown in Figure 16-15. With these three petals, form a cup as shown in Figure 16-15 (steps for assembling a rose) and glue together. Apply a drop of glue to the center of the previously made section of the rose and place it in the center of the cup formed by the three petals. The size of the rose can be increased by using petals D and E in Figure 16-15 as patterns.

Rose Leaves Rose leaves are made from waffle design packing paper salvaged from a carton of new dishes or other packages. Draw the outline of the leaf on the piece of paper using the leaf pattern in Figure 16-15. With a pair of scissors, cut out the leaf. Leaves can be formed by pleating the bottom edge.

BIBLIOGRAPHY

Aldrich, Dot, and Genevieve Aldrich. *Creating with Cattails, Cones, and Pods.* Great Neck, New York: Hearthside Press, Inc., 1971.

Alkema, Chester J. *Complete Crayon Book*: *In Color*. New York: Sterling Publishing Company, Inc., 1970.

Almeida, Oscar. *Metalworking.* Rev. ed. South Holland, Ill.: Goodheart-Wilcox Company, Inc., 1968.

Alton, W. G. *More Woodworking Projects.* New York: Taplinger Publishing, Inc., 1969.

Anderson, Edwin P. *Home Workshop and Tool Handy Book.* Indianapolis, Ind.: Theodore Audel, 1964.

Anderson, Harriette. *Kiln-fired Glass.* Philadelphia: Chilton Book Company, 1970.

Anderson, Mildred. *Original Creations with Papier Mâché.* New York: Sterling Publishing Company, Inc., 1967.

Arnold, James. *Shell Book of Country Crafts.* New York: Hastings House Publishing, Inc., 1972.

Babcock, Robert, and Carl Gerbracht. *Elementary School Industrial Arts.* New York: Bruce Publishing Company, 1969.

Baker, Muriel L. *Handbook of American Crewel Embroidery.* Rutland, Vt.: Charles E. Tuttle Company, Inc., 1966.

Baxter, William T. *Jewelry, Gem Cutting and Metalcraft.* 3d ed. New York: McGraw-Hill Book Company, 1950.

Beitler, Ethel J. *Create with Yarn.* Scranton, Pa.: Intex Educational Publishers, 1964.

Benbow, Mary, et al. *Traditional and Topical and How to Make Them.* Boston: Plays, Inc., 1970.

Bernstein, Marion H. *Off-Loom Weaving.* New York: Sterling Publishing Company, 1971.

Blumenau, Libi. *Creative Design in Wall Hangings.* New York: Crown Publishers, Inc., 1967.

Borglund, Erland, and Jacob Flauensgaard. *Working in Plastic, Bone, Amber, and Horn.* New York: Van Nostrand Reinhold Company, 1970.

Boyd, Gardner T. *Metalworking.* Rev. ed. South Holland, Ill.: Goodheart-Wilcox Company, Inc., 1968.

Brooke, W. E., and K. Barkly. *Design Your Own Craftwork.* Levittown, New York: Transatlantic Arts, Inc., 1970.

Butler, Anne, *Embroidery for School Children.* Newton Center, Mass.: Charles T. Branford Company, Inc., 1970.

Butler, Anne, and David Green. *Pattern and Embroidery.* Newton Center, Mass.: Charles T. Branford Company, Inc., 1970.

Butler, Winifred. *Complete Book of Needlework and Embroidery.* New York: G. Putnam's Sons, Inc., 1967.

Capua, Sarajean. *Jewelry Anyone Can Make.* Hollywood, Fla.: Dukane Press, Inc., 1971.

Cartnell, Ronald. *Wood Sculpture.* New York: Taplinger Publishing, Inc., 1970.

Choate, Sharr. *Creative Gold and Silversmithing: Jewelry, Decorative Metalcraft.* New York: Crown Publishers, Inc., 1970.

Clark, Geoffrey, et al. *Technique of Enameling.* New York: Van Nostrand Reinhold Company, 1967.

Cole, Jeanne, and Joyce Hundley. *Decorative Painting, Folk Art Style.* New York: Doubleday and Company, Inc., 1971.

Collingwood, Peter. *Techniques of Rug Weaving.* New York: Watson-Guptill Publications, Inc., 1969.

Cutler, Katherine N. *Creative Shellcraft.* New York: Lothrop, Lee & Shepard Co., 1971.

Davenport, Elsie G. *Your Handweaving.* Pacific Grove, Cal.: Craft & Hobby Books Service Select Books, 1970.

DiValentin, Louis, and Maria DiValentin. *Practical Encyclopedia of Crafts.* New York: Sterling Publishing Company, Inc., 1971.

Dreesman, Cecile. *Embroidery.* New York: The Macmillan Company, Inc., 1969.

Dutton, Ninette. *Beautiful Art of Enameling.* New York: Arc Books, 1968.

Dutton, M. E. *Student's Guide to Model Making.* Elmsford, New York: Pergamon Press, Inc., 1970.

Edwards, H. Wayne. *Karton Kuties.* San Antonio, Tex.: Naylor Company, 1971.

Egge, Ruth S. *How to Make Something from Nothing.* New York: Coward-McCann & Geoghegan, Inc., 1968.

Feirer, John L. *Advanced Woodworking and Furniture Making.* Rev. ed.: Perria, Ill.: Charles A. Bennett Company, Inc., 1971.

Fleming, Gerry. *Scrap Craft for Youth Groups.* New York: John Day Company, Inc., 1969.

Fraser, B. Kay. *Tole Painting.* New York: Sterling Publishing Company, Inc., 1971.

Fressard, M. J. *Creating with Burlap.* New York: Sterling Publishing Company, Inc., 1970.

Gaszner, George. *Working with Plastics.* New York: Drake Publishers, 1971.

Glass, F. J. *Metal Craft.* Kentfield, Calif.: Newton J. Gregg Publisher, 1971.

Grando, Michael D. *Jewelry: Form and Techniques.* New York: Van Nostrand Reinhold, 1970.

Graumont, Roaul, and Elmer Wesstrom (eds.). *Square-Knot Handi-Craft Guide.* Westminster, Md., Random House, Inc., 1971.

Gruber, Elmar. *Metal and Wire Sculpture.* New York. Sterling Publishing Company, Inc., 1969

Guild, Vera P. *Creative Use of Stitches.* Rev. ed. Worcester, Mass: Davis Publications, Inc., 1969.

Gustavson, Ragner, and Ollie Olson. *Creating in Wood with the Lathe.* New York: Van Nostrand Reinhold Company, 1968.

Hanauer, Elsie. *Art of Whittling and Woodcarving.* Cranbury, N.J.: A. S. Barnes and Company, 1970.

_____. *Creating with Leather.* Cranbury, N. J.: A. S. Barnes and Company, 1970.

Hand, Jackson. *How to Do Your Own Wood Finishing.* New York: Drake Publishers, 1971.

Harp, Sybil C. (ed.). *Creative Crafts Sampler.* Ramsey, N.J.: Model Craftsman Publications Corp., 1971.

Hawkins, Leslie V. *Art Metal and Enameling.* Peoria, Ill.: Charles A. Bennett Company, 1967.

Hays, M. Vincent. *Artistry in Wood.* New York: Drake Publishers, 1971.

Hayward, Charles H. *Making Toys in Wood.* New York: Drake Publishers, 1971.

_____. *Woodwork Joints.* New York: Drake Publishers, 1970.

Hein, Gisela. *Basic Stitches of Embroidery.* New York: Van Nostrand Reinhold Company, 1971

Hofman, Armin. *Graphic Design Manual.* New York: Van Nostrand Reinhold Company, 1965.

Horn, George F. *Crayon.* Worcester, Mass.: David Publications, Inc., 1969.

Iido, Miyuki, and Tomoko Iido. *Art of Handmade Flowers*. Palo Alto, Cal.: Kodansha International/ USA, Ltd., 1971.

Johnson, Pauline. *Creative Bookbinding*. Rev. ed. Seattle, Wash.: University of Washington Press, 1965.

Kampmann, Lothar. *Creating with Clay*. New York: Van Nostrand Reinhold Company, 1971.

Kroncke, Grete. *Weaving with Cane and Reed*. New York: Van Nostrand Reinhold Company, 1968.

LaCroix, Grethe. *Beads Plus Macrame: Applying Knotting Technique to Beadcraft*. New York: Sterling Publishing Company, Inc., 1971.

Landon, M. T., and S. B. Swan. *American Crewel Work*. New York: The Macmillan Company, Inc., 1970.

Lang, N. M. *Egg Decorating*. New York: Bruce Books, 1971.

Laskin, J. *Arts and Crafts Activities Desk Book*. Englewood Cliffs, N.J.: Prentice-Hall, Inc., 1971.

Laury, Jean R. *Appliqué Stitching*. New York: Van Nostrand Reinhold Company, 1966.

Lidstone, John. *Building with Balsa Wood*. New York: Van Nostrand Reinhold Company, 1965.

Lobley, Priscilla. *Flower Making for Beginners*. New York: Taplinger Publishing Company, Inc., 1971.

Lord, Louis. *Collage and Construction in School—Preschool and Junior High*. Rev. ed. Worcester, Mass.: Davis Publications, Inc., 1971.

Maloney, Joan. *Creative Crafts*. New York: Drake Publishers, 1971.

Maryon, Herbert. *Metalwork and Enameling*. 4th ed. New York: Dover Publications, Inc., 1971.

Martens, Charles R. *Technology of Paints, Varnishes, and Lacquers*. New York: Van Nostrand Reinhold Company, 1970.

Masters, Rachel. *Modern Patchwork*. New York: Doubleday and Company, 1971.

Mathews, John. *Creative Light Woodcarving*. New York: St. Martin's Press Inc., 1971.

Mattil, Edward L. *Meaning in Crafts*. Englewood Cliffs, N.J.: Prentice-Hall, Inc., 1971.

McArthur, Jeanette. *Creative Crayon Technique*. Hollywood, Fla.: Dukane Press, Inc., 1971.

McIllhaney, Sterling. *Art As Design: Design As Art*. New York: Van Nostrand Reinhold Company, 1970.

Meilach, Dona. *Contemporary Leather*. Chicago: Henry Regnery Company, 1971.

Mell, Howard, and Eric Fisher. *Modelling. Building and Carving*. New York: Drake Publishers, 1971.

Newsome, Arden. *Spoolcraft*. New York: Lothrop, Lee and Shepard Co., 1970.

Palmer, Dennis. *Introducing Pattern: Its Development and Application*. New York: Watson-Gumptill Publications, 1970.

_____. *Introducing Enameling*. New York: Watson-Gumptill Publications, 1970.

Parish, Peggy. *Sheet Magic: Games, Toys & Gifts from Old Sheets*. New York: The Macmillan Company, Inc., 1971.

Perry, Kenneth F., and Clarence T. Baab. *Binding of Books*. Rev. ed. New York: McKnight & McKnight Publishing Company, 1967.

Plunkrose, Henry (ed.). *The Book of Crafts*. Chicago: Henry Regnery Company, 1971.

Rainey, Sarita R. *Weaving without a Loom*. Worcester, Mass.: Davis Publications, Inc., 1966.

Regensteiner, Elsa. *Art of Weaving*. New York: Van Nostrand Reinhold Company, 1970.

Robbins, I. *Elementary Teacher's Arts & Crafts Ideas for Every Month of the Year*. Englewood Cliffs, N.J.: Prentice-Hall, Inc., 1970.

Rothenberg, Polly. *Metal Enameling*. New York: Crown Publishing Inc., 1969.

Schaffer, Florence M. *ABC of Driftwood & Dried Flower Designs*. Great Neck, New York: Hearthside Press, Inc., 1971.

Schilt, Stephen, and Doona J. Weir. *Enamel without Heat*. New York: Sterling Publishing Company, Inc., 1971.

Schuler, Frederick W., and Lilli Schuler. *Glassforming: Glassmaking for the Craftsman*. Philadelphia: Chilton Book Co., 1970.

Seeler, Margaret E. *Art of Enameling*. New York: Van Nostrand Reinhold Company, 1969.

Seyd, Mary. *Designing with String*. New York: Watson-Gumptill Publications, 1968.

Shea, John G. *Woodworking for Everybody*. 4th rev. ed. New York: Van Nostrand Reinhold Company, 1969.

Tidball, Harriet. *Weaving Inkle Bands*. Pacific Grove, Calif.: Craft & Hobby Book Service Select Books, 1952.

Tovey, John. *Weaves and Pattern Drafting.* New York: Van Nostrand Reinhold Company, 1969.

Van Rensselaer, Eleanor. *Decorating with Seed Mosaics, Chipped Glass & Plant Material.* New York: Van Nostrand Reinhold Company, 1960.

Villiard, Paul. *First Book of Leather Working.* New York: Abelard-Schuman, Ltd., 1971.

Wasley, Ruth, and Edith Harris. *Bead Design.* New York: Crown Publishing, Inc., 1970.

Waterer, John W. *Leather Craftsmanship.* New York: Praeger Publishers, 1968.

Wilcox, Donald. *Modern Leather Design.* New York: Ballantine Books, Inc., 1971.

_____. *Technique of Ryn Knotting.* New York: Van Nostrand Reinhold Company, 1971.

_____. *New Design in Ceramics.* New York: Van Nostrand Reinhold Company, 1970.

Winslow, Amy, and Harriet Turner. *Index to Handicraft, Modelmaking & Workshop Projects.* Westwood, Mass.: F. W. Faxan Company Co., Inc., 1965.

Wood, Paul W. *Stained Glass Crafting.* Rev. ed. New York: Sterling Publishing Company, Inc., 1971.

Wright, Dorothy. *Baskets & Basketry.* Newton Center, Mass.: Charles T. Branford Company, 1959.

Wright, Kenneth. *Woodworking.* New York: Emerson Books, Inc., 1970.

Zarbock, Barbara. *Complete Book of Rug Hooking.* 2d ed. New York: Van Nostrand Reinhold Company, 1969.

Zechlin, Ruth. *Complete Book of Handicrafts.* Rev. ed. Newton Center, Mass.: Charles T. Branford Company, 1968.

Zimelli, Umberto, and G. Vergerio. *Decorative Ironwork.* New York: International Publications Service, 1969.

Zimmerman, Fred W. *Leathercraft.* South Holland, Ill.: Goodheart-Wilcox Company, Inc., 1969.

APPENDIX

SOURCES OF SUPPLY

This section offers information concerning the places where a variety of materials may be obtained for almost any type of arts and crafts activity. While it is impossible to offer an exhaustive listing of firms which supply items for use within an arts and crafts program, this suggested guide should serve to illustrate available sources. Use of the classified section of the telephone directory will provide listings and information about products within any given locality.

The following firms may be contacted for specialized craft supplies or for comprehensive lines of craft materials:

American Art Clay Company (Clay products)
    4717 West 16th Street
    Indianapolis, Ind.
American Crayon Company (Textile paint and clay products)
    1706 Hayes Avenue
    Sandusky, Ohio
American Handicraft Company, Inc. (Reed, raffia, and batik supplies)
    45 South Harrison Street
    East Orange, N.J.

Art-Craft Industries (Cotton net and threads)
    34 Brattle Street
    Cambridge, Mass.
Arts & Crafts Materials Corp. (General crafts supplies)
    321 Park Avenue
    Baltimore, Md. 21201
L.L. Bean (Firkins, wooden buckets)
    Freeport, Maine
Binney and Smith, Inc. (Clay products)
    380 Madison Avenue
    New York, N.Y. 10017
L. H. Butcher Company (Clay products)
    3628 East Olympic Boulevard
    Los Angeles, Calif.
California Ink Company (Fabric printing ink and thinner)
    545 Sansome Street
    San Francisco, Calif.
Contessa Yarn Company (Weaving materials)
    P.O. Box # 336
    3-5 Bailey Avenue
    Ridgefield, Conn.
The Craftint Manufacturing Company (Lac)
    1615 Collamer Avenue
    Cleveland, Ohio
Drakenfield Ceramic Supply Company (Ceramics products)
    45 Park Place
    New York, N.Y. 10007
E. I. du Pont de Nemours & Company (Dyes)
    7 South Dearborn Street
    Chicago, Ill.
Favour Ruhl Company (Looms)
    435 South Wabash Avenue
    Chicago, Ill.
Frederick J. Fawcett, Inc. (Looms)
    129 South Street
    Department A-2
    Boston, Mass
Gordon's (Jewelry materials)
    P.O. Box # 4073
    Long Beach, Calif
G-H Specialty Company (Wood products)
    3408 North Holton Street
    Milwaukee, Wis.
Grieger's Inc. (Jewelry materials)
    1633 East Walnut Street
    Pasadena, Calif.
Gypsy Dyes, Inc. (Dyes)
    414 South Wabash Avenue
    Chicago, Ill.
W. A. Hall (Looms)
    250 Devonshire Street
    Boston, Mass.
The Handicrafters (Looms)
    Waupun, Wis.
Thomas Hodgson & Sons, Inc. (Yarns)
    Concord, N. H.

Home Yarns Corporation (Weaving materials)
    42 Lexington Avenue
    Department A
    New York, N.Y.
Hook-Art Guild (Rug-making supplies)
    P.O. Box # 57
    Cumberland Mills, Maine
Itasca Weavers (Cotton cloth)
    Itasca, Tex.
Kelbar Sales, Inc. (Canvas and jute products)
    P.O. Box # 1685
    Grand Central Station
    New York, N.Y. 10017
Lady Stuart (Hooking frames)
    P.O. Box # 467
    Geneva, Ill.
Leclerc Looms, (Looms)
    L'Isletville, Quebec, Canada
Leisurecrafts (Jewelry materials)
    941 East Second Street
    Los Angeles, Calif.
Lily Mills (Yarn products)
    Hand Weaving Department C
    Shelby, N. C.
Walter H. Loeber (Looms)
    1231 North Third Street
    Milwaukee, Wis.
Norwood Loom Company (Looms)
    Baldwin, Mich.
Osborn Brothers (Leather materials)
    223 West Jackson Boulevard
    Chicago, Ill.
Paternayan Brothers, Inc. (Rug-making materials)
    10 West 33rd Street
    New York, N.Y.
S&S Arts and Crafts (General craft supplies)
    Colchester, Conn.
Sto-Rex Crafts (Enamels)
    Western Manufacturing Company, Inc.
    149 Ninth Street
    San Francisco, Calif.
Waldcraft Company (Dyes for batik)
    257 North Tacoma Avenue
    Indianapolis, Ind.
Western Ceramics Supply Company (Ceramic supplies)
    1601 Howard Street
    San Francisco, Calif.

B APPENDIX

PERIODICALS ON SPECIFIC CRAFTS

American Art Journal
　　Kennedy Galleries
　　20 East 56th Street
　　New York, N.Y. 10022
American Artist
　　American Artist
　　2160 Patterson Street
　　Cincinnati, Ohio 45215
Art in America
　　Art in America
　　115 Tenth Street
　　Des Moines, Iowa 50301
Better Homes and Gardens
　　Better Homes and Gardens
　　1716 Locust Street
　　Des Moines, Iowa 50303
Canadian Author and Bookmen
　　Canadian Authors Association
　　10907-62 Avenue
　　Edmonton, Alberta 62, Canada

Ceramics Monthly
     Ceramics Monthly
     P.O. Box # 4548
     Columbus, Ohio 43212
Design
     Design Magazine
     1100 Waterway Boulevard
     Indianapolis, Ind. 46202
Everyday Art Quarterly
     Walker Art Center
     Minneapolis, Minn.
Hobbies
     Lightner Publishing Corporation
     1006 S. Michigan Avenue
     Chicago, Ill. 60605
Industrial Arts and Vocational Education
     Bruce Publishing Company
     400 North Broadway
     Milwaukee, Wis.
Junior Arts and Activities
     Jones Publishing Company
     542 N. Dearborn Parkway
     Chicago, Ill.
Metal Finishing
     Metals and Plastics Publications, Inc.
     99 Kinderkamack Road
     Westwood, N.J. 07675
National Sculpture Review
     National Sculpture Society
     280 East 51st Street
     New York, N.Y. 10022
School Arts
     School Arts
     Printers Building
     Worcester, Mass. 01608
Woman's Day
     19 West 44th Street
     New York, N.Y. 10036

APPENDIX

FILMS, SLIDES, AND FILMSTRIPS ON ARTS AND CRAFTS

Alchemy of Fire. Color, 15 minutes, sound. (Enameling)
    Quebec Government House
    The Film Officer
    Rockerfeller Center
    17 West 50th Street
    New York, N.Y. 10020
Art of Gift Wrapping. Color, 21 minutes, sound. (Gift wrapping)
    Modern Talking Picture Service
    1212 Avenue of the Americas
    New York, N.Y. 10036
Arts and Crafts. Color, 16 minutes, sound. (General crafts)
    Austrian National Tourist Office
    Midwest Office
    Room 1401
    332 South Michigan Avenue
    Chicago, Ill. 60604
Belgian Crystal and Cut Glass of Val St. Lambert. (Fine glass making)
    Association Films, Incorporated
    600 Madison Avenue
    New York, N.Y. 10022

Ceramic Art of Japan. Color, 18 minutes, sound. (Ceramics)
    Consulate General of Japan
    % Associated Films, Inc.
    600 Madison Avenue
    New York, N.Y. 10022
Chucalissa Indian Crafts. Color, 40 minutes, sound. (Indian crafts)
    Consulate General of Canada
    Film requests must be made at the office which serves a specific section of the United States.
Crafts of My Province. Black and white, 20 minutes, sound. (Pottery, jewelry, and weaving)
    Consulate General of Canada
Craftsman Young and Old. Black and white, 10 minutes, sound. (Various craft activities)
    Counsulate General of Canada
Craftsmanship in Clay Series. Color. (Clay manipulation and crafts)
    University of Indiana
    Audio-Visual Center
    Bloomington, Ind.
Creative People. Black and white, 7 minutes, sound. (Wood sculpture)
    Consulate General of Canada
Eskimo Artist Kenojuak. Color, 20 minutes, sound. (Stone prints)
    Consulate General of Canada
Flaming the Kiln. Color, 15 minutes, sound. (Ceramics)
    Consulate General of Canada
From Yarn to Cloth. Color, 15 minutes, sound. (Hand weaving)
    Quebec Government House
Ikebana: The Art of Flower Arrangement. Color, 20 minutes, sound. (Flower settings)
    Consulate General of Japan
Irons in the Fire. Black and white, 10 minutes, sound. (Iron forging)
    Consulate General of Canada
Lace and Metal. Color, 14 minutes, sound. (Iron working)
    Quebec Government House
The Little Glass Ball. Color, 18 minutes, sound. (Glass blowing)
    Corning Museum of Glass
    Curator of Education
    Corning Glass Center
    Corning, N.Y. 14830
Loon's Necklace. Color, 10 minutes, sound. (Masks and carvings)
    Consulate General of Canada
Man the Creator. Black and white, 13 minutes, sound. (Pottery)
    Information Service of India
    Film Section
    3 East 64th Street
    New York, N.Y. 10021
Mosaic Experiments. Color, 20 minutes, sound. (Mosaic techniques)
    Corning Museum of Glass
New Designs for an Old Craft. Color, 14-1/2 minutes, sound. (Cabinetmaking)
    Consulate General of Canada
Origami—The Folding Paper of Japan. Color, 16 minutes, sound. (Paper manipulation)
    Consulate General of Japan
Rugs and Murals. Black and white, 15 minutes, sound. (Rug and tapestry making)
    Quebec Government House
Scandinavian Arts and Crafts. Color, 11 minutes, sound. (General crafts)
    Corning Museum of Glass
Simple Molds. Black and white, 10 minutes, sound. (Ceramic molds)
    Corning Museum of Glass
Story of Peter and the Potter. Color, 27 minutes, sound. (Pottery making)
    Consulate General of Canada
World of Mosaic. Color, 27 minutes, sound. (Mosaic production)
    Corning Museum of Glass

All the following films may be obtained from the University of Connecticut, Audio Visual Center, Storrs, Conn. 06268:

Art and Motion. Color, 14 minutes, sound.
Basic Sewing Skills. Color, 12 minutes, sound.
Brush Technique. Color, 10 minutes, sound.
Color. Color, 6 minutes, sound.
Color Keying in Art and Living. Color, 10 minutes, sound.
Crayon. Color, 15 minutes, sound.
Design into Space. Color, 10 minutes, sound.
Design with Paper. Color, 10 minutes, sound.
How to Make a Puppet. Black and white, 12 minutes, sound.
How to Make and Use a Diorama. Color, 20 minutes, sound.
Industrial Arts: Joining and Gluing. Black and white, 14 minutes, sound.
Industrial Arts: Knowing Woods and Their Uses. Black and white, 14 minutes, sound.
Industrial Arts: Measuring and Squaring. Black and white, 10 minutes, sound.
Industrial Arts: Planes. Black and white, 10 minutes, sound.
Industrial Arts: Using Nails and Screws. Black and white, 10 minutes, sound.
Industrial Arts: Wood Finishing. Black and white, 13 minutes, sound.
Lettering Instructional Materials. Black and white, 23 minutes, sound.
Light and Dark. Color, 6 minutes, sound.
Rag Tapestry. Color, 20 minutes, sound.

The following filmstrips may also be obtained from the same source:

Ceramic Art through the Ages. Arts and Crafts Series. 60 frames, color, grades 7 through 12.
We Work with Clay. Art in Our Classroom Series. 49 frames, color, Kindergarten through grade 3.

INDEX